D1685282

Czech (& Central European)
Yearbook of Arbitration®

Czech (& Central European) Yearbook of Arbitration®

Volume XII

2022

Jurisdiction of Arbitral Tribunals

Editors

Alexander J. Bělohlávek
Professor
at the VŠB TU
in Ostrava
Czech Republic

Naděžda Rozehnalová
Professor
at the Masaryk University
in Brno
Czech Republic

Questions About This Publication

www.czechyearbook.org; www.lexlata.pro; editor@lexlata.pro

LEX LATA

COPYRIGHT © 2022

By Lex Lata B.V.

All rights reserved. No part of this publication
may be reproduced in any form or by any electronic
or mechanical means including information storage
and retrieval systems without permission
in writing from the publisher.

Printed in the EU.
ISBN/EAN: 978-90-829824-7-3
ISSN: 2157-9490

Lex Lata B.V.
Mauritskade 45-B
2514 HG – THE HAGUE
The Netherlands

The title *Czech (& Central European) Yearbook of Arbitration*®
as well as the logo appearing on the cover are protected by EU
trademark law.

Typeset by Lex Lata B.V.

Advisory Board

Anton Baier
Vienna, Austria

Silvy Chernev
Sofia, Bulgaria

Bohuslav Klein
Prague, Czech Republic

Hon. Rajko Knez
Ljubljana, Slovenia

Andrzej Kubas
*Warsaw and Krakow,
Poland*

Piotr Nowaczyk
Warsaw, Poland

Stanislaw Soltysiński
Warsaw, Poland

Jozef Suchoža
Košice, Slovakia

Vladimír Týč
Brno, Czech Republic

Evangelos Vassilakakis
Thessaloniki, Greece

Editorial Board

Alena Bányaiová
Prague, Czech Republic

Radu Bogdan Bobei
Bucharest, Romania

Viorel Mihai Ciobanu
Bucharest, Romania

Marcin Czepelak
Krakow, Poland

Filip Černý
Prague, Czech Republic

Ian I. Funk
Minsk, Belarus

Marek Furtek
Warsaw, Poland

Aldo Frignani
Torino, Italy

Wolfgang Hahnkamper
Vienna, Austria

Vít Horáček
Prague, Czech Republic

Miluše Hrnčiříková
*Olomouc,
Czech Republic*

Lászlo Kecskes
Budapest, Hungary

Vladimir Khvalei
Moscow, Russia

Martin Magál
Bratislava, Slovakia

Ricardo Ma. P. G.
Ongkiko
*Makati City,
Philippines*

Niek Peters
*Amsterdam,
Netherlands*

Asko Pohla
Talinn, Estonia

Roman Prekop
Bratislava, Slovakia

Květoslav Růžička
*Pilsen/Prague,
Czech Republic*

Matthias Scherer
Geneva, Switzerland

Thomas Schultz
Geneva, Switzerland

Jiří Valdhans
Brno, Czech Republic

Kamil Zawicki
*Warsaw and Krakow,
Poland*

Address for communication & manuscripts

Czech (& Central European) Yearbook of Arbitration®

Jana Zajíce 32, Praha 7, 170 00, Czech Republic

editor@lexlata.pro

Editorial support:

Jan Šamlot, Dr.TF. Lenka Němečková,
Dipl. Ing. Karel Nohava, Anna Dušková

Impressum

Institutions Participating in the CYArb® Project

Academic Institutions

University of West Bohemia in Pilsen, Czech Republic
Faculty of Law, Department of International Law
& Department of Constitutional Law
Západočeská univerzita v Plzni, Právnická fakulta
Katedra mezinárodního práva & Katedra ústavního práva

Masaryk University in Brno, Czech Republic
Faculty of Law, Department of International and European Law
Masarykova univerzita v Brně, Právnická fakulta
Katedra mezinárodního a evropského práva

Pavol Jozef Šafárik University in Košice, Slovakia
Faculty of Law, Department of Commercial Law and Business Law
Právnická fakulta UPJŠ, Košice, Slovensko
Katedra obchodného a hospodárskeho práva

VŠB – TU Ostrava, Czech Republic
Faculty of Economics, Department of Law
VŠB – TU Ostrava, Ekonomická fakulta Katedra práva

Institute of State and Law of the Academy of Sciences of the Czech Republic, v.v.i.
Ústav státu a práva Akademie věd ČR, v.v.i.

Institute of State and Law, Slovak Academy of Sciences, Slovakia
Ústav štátu a práva Bratislava, Slovenská akadémia vied, Slovensko

Non-academic Institutions Participating in the CYArb® Project

International Arbitral Centre of the Austrian Federal Economic Chamber
Wiener Internationaler Schiedsgericht (VIAC), Vienna

Court of International Commercial Arbitration attached to the Chamber of Commerce and Industry of Romania
Curtea de Arbitraj Comercial Internaţional de pe lângă Camera de Comerţ şi Industrie a României, Bucharest

Arbitration Court attached to the Hungarian Chamber of Commerce and Industry
A Magyar Kereskedelmi és Iparkamara mellett szervezett Választottbíróság, Budapest

Arbitration Court attached to the Economic Chamber of the Czech Republic and Agricultural Chamber of the Czech Republic
Rozhodčí soud při Hospodářské komoře České republiky a Agrární komoře České republiky, Prague

International Arbitration Court of the Czech Commodity Exchange, Prague, Czech Republic
Mezinárodní rozhodčí soud při Českomoravské komoditní burze (Prague, Czech Republic)

ICC National Committee Czech Republic
ICC Národní výbor Česká republika

The Court of Arbitration at the Polish Chamber of Commerce in Warsaw
Sąd Arbitrażowy przy Krajowej Izbie Gospodarczej w Warszawie

Proofreading and translation support provided by:
SPĚVÁČEK překladatelská agentura s.r.o., Prague, Czech Republic and Pamela Lewis, USA.

Contents

CASE LAW

Czech Republic

Poland

NEWS & REPORTS

BIBLIOGRAPHY, CURRENT EVENTS, IMPORTANT WEB SITES

All contributions in this book are subject to academic review.

Neither the editorial board nor the publisher collects any fees or other performance for publishing contributions from the authors and distances itself from such practices. Authors do not receive any royalty or other remuneration for their contributions.

List of Abbreviations

AA	The Arbitration Act
ADR	Alternative dispute resolution
AIAC	The Asia International Arbitration Centre
APC	The Arbitrazh Procedural Code of the Russian Federation
ArbAct	Act of the Czech Republic No. 216/1994 Coll., on Arbitration and the Enforcement of Arbitral Awards
BIT	Bilateral investment treaty
CAC	Czech Arbitration Court
CCP	Code of Civil Procedure
CEE	Central and Eastern Europe
DAB	Dispute adjudication board
DPO	Data protection officer
ECJ	The European Court of Justice
ECT	The Energy Charter Treaty
EO	Austrian regulation on enforcement (Exekutionsordnung - Gesetz vom 27. Mai 1896, über das Exekutions- und Sicherungsverfahren)
EU	European Union
FIDIC	The International Federation of Consulting Engineers
HKIAC	The Hong Kong International Arbitration Centre
IAA	The International Arbitration Act
ICC	The International Chamber of Commerce
ICCA	International Council for Commercial Arbitration
ICC Arbitration Rules	Rules of Arbitration of the International Chamber of Commerce, in force as from 1 January 2021
ICSID	The International Centre for Settlement of Investment Disputes
ILA	International Law Association
IPRG	Swiss Federal Act on Private International Law (Bundesgesetz über das Internationale Privatrecht)
LCIA	London Court of International Arbitration

LFI	The Russian Federation's Law on Foreign Investment
NAFTA	The North American Free Trade Agreement
New York Convention	The Convention on the Recognition and Enforcement of Foreign Arbitral Awards (New York, 1958)
OFAC's	The U.S. Department of the Treasury's Office of Foreign Assets Control
OGH	Austrian Supreme court (Oberster Gerichtshof)
OLG	Higher Regional Court, Vienna (Oberlandesgericht)
PILA	(Swiss) Private International Law Act
PRIAC	Prague International Arbitration Court
PRIAC Rules	The PRIAC Board completed work on the new Rules of Arbitration
SCC	Arbitration Institute of the Stockholm Chamber of Commerce
SDN-list	The list of Specially Designated Nationals
SEE	South Eastern Europe
SIAC	The Singapore International Arbitration Centre
TAI	Thai Arbitration Institute
TFEU	The Treaty on the Functioning of the European Union
TPF	third party funding
The Washington Convention	The Convention on the Settlement of Investment Disputes between States and Nationals of Other States
UNCITRAL	The United Nations Commission on International Trade Law
UNCITRAL (Arbitration) Rules	UNCITRAL Arbitration Rules, as amended in 2013
UNCITRAL Model Law	The UNCITRAL Model Law on International Commercial Arbitration (1985), with amendments as adopted in 2006
US	The United States
USD	U.S. dollar
USMCA	The United States-Mexico-Canada Agreement
VIAC	Vienna International Arbitral Centre

VMR	The Vienna Mediation Rules
VMRI	The Vienna Investment Mediation Rules
VR	Vienna Rules of Arbitration
VRI	Vienna Investment Arbitration Rules
ZPO	Zivilprozessordnung

Articles

Maciej Durbas | Agata Ziobroń |
Maciej Truszkiewicz

Supplying 'the Original Version of the Arbitration Agreement' Under Article IV of the New York Convention when No Such Document Exists

Key words:
arbitration agreement |
New York Convention on the
recognition and enforcement
of foreign arbitral awards |
recognition or enforcement
of foreign arbitral awards
| requirements | standard
of proof

Czech (& Central European) Yearbook of Arbitration®

Abstract | *This article discusses the practical problem of the recognition and enforcement of foreign arbitral awards based on the provisions of the New York Convention in situations in which the parties have not entered into an arbitration agreement in writing. The Convention was signed in 1958 and, for obvious reasons, only takes the standards prevailing in arbitration at the time into account. Consequently, the Convention explicitly only provides for cases in which the arbitration agreement meets the formal requirements of Article II. It also requires the applicant to supply the original agreement to recognise or enforce the arbitral award (Article IV(1)(b)). The text of the Convention, therefore, does not take into account the growing tendency to relax the formal requirements of arbitration agreements, including allowing arbitration clauses to be concluded implicitly, e.g., by waiving the objection to the jurisdiction of an arbitral tribunal or extended to non-signatories. This article attempts to answer whether, in all those situations, the recognition of*

Maciej Durbas is an attorney at law and of counsel at Kubas Kos Gałkowski law firm. As a practitioner, he specialises in court and arbitration proceedings, international commercial law, and private international law. He is also a scholar in arbitration law. He defended his doctorate on the jurisdiction of arbitral tribunals with honours at the Jagiellonian University of Kraków. He has been coaching the Jagiellonian University team in the Willem C. Vis Moot international commercial arbitration competition for many years.
E-mail: maciej.durbas@kkg.pl

Agata Ziobroń is an attorney-at-law and a senior associate at Kubas Kos Gałkowski law firm. She cooperates with the team handling complex proceedings in the field of civil law and broadly defined commercial law, including company law. She provides comprehensive advice to business entities at the pre-litigation stage, prepares litigation strategies, and

| 3

an award under the Convention is possible and concludes that the award is recognisable and enforceable if the applicant can demonstrate the jurisdiction of the arbitral tribunal by any evidentiary means.

represents parties in court and arbitration proceedings. E-mail: agata.ziobron@ kkg.pl

Maciej Truszkiewicz is an attorney-at-law and a senior associate at Kubas Kos Gałkowski law firm. He specialises in litigation as well as corporate and civil law. He cooperates with a team that specialises in business law with a specific focus on construction disputes and infrastructure projects. E-mail: maciej. truszkiewicz@kkg.pl

| | |

I. Introduction[1]

1.01. One of the most important tendencies in international arbitration is the increasing liberalization of the formal requirements for arbitration agreements.[2] This also corresponds with the process of recognition of less and less formalized ways of giving consent to arbitration and fits into the debate between consensualism and formalism that has been going on for years.[3] In the context of the requirements of the New York Convention,[4] this debate focuses on Article II (formal requirements of the arbitration agreement) and Article V (grounds for refusal of recognition/enforcement). In our view, Article IV(1)(b) is at least equally important. According to the said provision, 'the party applying for recognition and enforcement shall, at the time of the application, supply [...] [t]he original agreement referred to in article II or a duly certified copy thereof'.

1.02. Under a literal interpretation of Article IV, if a party cannot supply the 'original arbitration agreement',[5] a party cannot

---

[1] The authors would like to thank Tadeusz Zbiegień for his invaluable support in preparing and reviewing this paper.

[2] JULIAN D. M. LEW & LOUKAS A. MISTELIS & STEFAN KRÖLL, COMPARATIVE INTERNATIONAL COMMERCIAL ARBITRATION, Kluwer Law International (2003), et. 697; Albert J. van den Berg, *When is an Arbitration Agreement in Writing Valid under Article II(2) of the New York Convention of 1958?*, in PIETER SANDERS, EEN HONDERDJARIGE VERNIEUWER, Boom Juridische Uitgevers (2012), et. 325 – 331; ALBERT J. VAN DEN BERG, HYPOTHETICAL DRAFT CONVENTION ON THE INTERNATIONAL ENFORCEMENT OF ARBITRATION AGREEMENTS AND AWARDS EXPLANATORY NOTE (2009), available at: https://www.newyorkconvention.org/draft+convention (accessed on 17 August 2021), et. 17 - 18; Piotr Wiliński, *Should the Miami Draft be given a second chance? The New York Convention 2.0*, 34 SPAIN ARBITRATION REVIEW, Wolters Kluwer España (2019), et. 85 – 86.

[3] EMMANUEL GAILLARD & JOHN SAVAGE, FOUCHARD GAILLARD GOLDMAN ON INTERNATIONAL COMMERCIAL ARBITRATION, Kluwer Law International (1999), et. 361, paragraph 591.

[4] United Nations Convention on the Recognition and Enforcement of Foreign Arbitral Awards (New York, 10 June 1958).

[5] In this paper we will only discuss the cases in which a party cannot supply 'a duly certified copy of the arbitration agreement'. Furthermore, this paper does not deal with situations in which the original (e.g., a written) arbitration agreement exists, but the petitioner does not possess it. Cf e.g., a case in which the

successfully enforce an arbitral award. This interpretation could effectively lead to the inability to seek the enforcement of the arbitral awards that were based on the jurisdiction of the tribunal established in a non-traditional manner. Non-traditional manner as used here means cases in which there is no 'classic' arbitration agreement between the parties as prescribed by Article II of the New York Convention. This might be the case, for example, if the jurisdiction has been established through the waiver of jurisdictional objections or extended to non-signatories.[6]

1.03.   This creates a paradox – the arbitration agreement (or rather the jurisdiction of the tribunal) exists, but at the same time, cannot be proven for the purpose of enforcement. On the one hand, the arbitral tribunal that rendered the award was competent to hear the case (e.g., because the respondent failed to object to its jurisdiction on time or at all). On the other hand, the literal application of Article IV of the New York Convention would lead to the inability to successfully enforce or recognise the award for the lack of the original of the agreement in such cases. Consequently, a party opposing the enforcement could invoke that the requirements from Article IV of the New York Convention are not met.[7] Such an approach, if adopted, would jeopardize all the effects of interpreting the formal requirements of Article II of the New York Convention broadly.

1.04.   To resolve the said paradox, it is necessary to analyse several minor issues directly affecting the final answer. First, what is the nature of Article IV(1)(b) requirements (section 2) and the approach of domestic legal orders to the requirements of Article IV(1)(b), especially in the context of countries with the most liberal approach to the form of arbitration agreements (section 3)? Second, what is their relation to formal and substantive requirements (section 4)? Third, what is the standard of proof under the said provision (section 5)? Finally, how can the

---

Polish Supreme Court refused a request for document production pertaining to the arbitration agreement in enforcement proceedings as the opposing party claimed it did not enter into such an agreement and the petitioner did not even make its existence probable. See Polish Supreme Court Case No. III CK 510/03, judgement, 3 November 2004.

[6]   On the assumption that the issue of non-signatories should be evaluated from the perspective of the validity of the arbitration agreement, rather than entirely autonomously, see GARY BORN, INTERNATIONAL COMMERCIAL ARBITRATION, Third Edition, Kluwer Law International, 2021, et. 1605 – 1606; STAVROS BREKOULAKIS, THIRD PARTIES IN INTERNATIONAL COMMERCIAL ARBITRATION, Oxford University Press (2010), et. 189; Philipp Habegger, *Extension of Arbitration Agreements to Non-signatories and Requirements of Form*, 22(2) ASA BULLETIN 390 (2004), et. 398.

[7]   STEFAN KRÖLL & LOUKAS A. MISTELIS & PILAR PERALES VISCASILLAS & VIKKI ROGERS (eds.), LIBER AMICORUM ERIC BERGSTERN. INTERNATIONAL ARBITRATION AND INTERNATIONAL COMMERCIAL LAW: SYNERGY, CONVERGENCE AND EVOLUTION, Alphen aan den Rijn (2011), s. 321.

said conclusions be applied to non-traditional arbitration agreements (section 6)?

II. The Nature of the Requirements under Article IV(1)(b) of the New York Convention

1.05.   There are two approaches to the requirements established in Article IV(1)(b) of the New York Convention.[8] The first view follows the viewpoint that the requirements of the Article are restrictive and may not be lowered by the national laws. The second view is that these requirements are just a maximum above which no national law may exceed.[9]

1.06.   This second view is the correct one. Procedures for enforcing arbitral awards are left to the states, which are free to reduce the burden of requirements imposed on the parties seeking enforcement.[10] The Convention is based on a 'pro-enforcement' bias.[11] Therefore, the formal requirements specified by the Convention should be interpreted in a way that allows facilitating to the greatest extent possible the recognition / enforcement.

1.07.   Moreover, many of the significant arbitral jurisdictions have already taken advantage of this possibility.[12] This approach resonates with the worldwide criticism of the formal requirements of the Convention.[13]

1.08.   The first conclusion is that Article IV(1)(b) of the New York Convention standard is a maximum one and can be reduced by national laws. The said provision (understood as providing only a maximum level of procedural requirements) does not come into play if the state law prescribes for a lower level of such requirements.

---

[8]   GARY BORN, INTERNATIONAL COMMERCIAL ARBITRATION, Third Edition, Kluwer Law International (2021), et. 3706 n. 55.

[9]   United Nations General Assembly, *Report of the United Nations Commission on International Trade Law on the work of its thirty-ninth session* (19 June – 7 July 2006), available at: https://undocs.org/en/A/61/17(SUPP) (accessed on 17 August 2021), et. 28 – 29; United Nations General Assembly, *Settlement of commercial disputes: Form of arbitration agreement, Note by the Secretariat* (19 June – 7 July 2006), available at: https://undocs.org/en/A/CN.9/606 (accessed on 17 August 2021); et. 7; United Nations General Assembly, *Report of Working Group II (Arbitration) on the work of its forty-fourth session* (23 – 27 January 2006), available at: https://undocs.org/en/A/CN.9/592 (accessed on 17 August 2021), et. 16 – 17.

[10]   Maxi Scherer, *Article III*, in NEW YORK CONVENTION – COMMENTARY, Beck Hart Nomos (Reinmar Wolff ed., 2012), no. 2, et. 194.

[11]   ALBERT J. VAN DEN BERG, THE NEW YORK ARBITRATION CONVENTION OF 1958: TOWARDS A UNIFORM JUDICIAL INTERPRETATION, Boston: Kluwer Law and Taxation (1981), et. 151.

[12]   In the context of formal requirements see for example: Luca Beffa, *Enforcement of "Default Awards"*, 31(4) ASA BULLETIN 756 (2013), et. 772 n. 79.

[13]   Pieter Sanders, *A Twenty Years' Review of the Convention on the Recognition and Enforcement of Foreign Arbitral Awards*, 13(2) THE INTERNATIONAL LAWYER 269 (1979), et. 277 – 286. See also Emmanuel Gaillard, *The Urgency of Not Revising the New York Convention*, in ICCA CONGRESS SERIES NUMBER 14, Dublin, Kluwer Law International (A. J. Van Den Berg ed., 2009), et. 689 – 696.

Supplying 'the Original Version of the Arbitration Agreement' Under Article IV...

Czech (& Central European) Yearbook of Arbitration®

III. The Requirement to Supply the Original of the Arbitration Agreement under National Laws

1.09. One must therefore examine whether Article IV(1)(b) of the New York Convention standard is indeed reduced by national laws. We identified five legislative approaches in this regard. At the same time, there is a growing number of jurisdictions where traditional formal requirements for international arbitration agreements have been loosened or waived.[14]

1.10. First, some jurisdictions maintained both the similar standard of formal requirements from Article II of the New York Convention and the requirement to supply the original of the arbitration agreement from Article IV(1)(b) of the New York Convention. This is the case, e.g., with the Polish law. One must note, however, that this does not change the fact that the Article IV(1)(b) requirement can be interpreted in a relaxed way, as will be discussed below or that there are scholarly propositions to change this state of law.[15]

1.11. Second, some jurisdictions maintained a similar standard of formal requirements from Article II of the New York Convention, but relaxed the requirement to supply the original of the arbitration agreement from Article IV(1)(b) of the New York Convention. The Austrian Code of Civil Procedure requires submitting an arbitration agreement only when requested by the court. Section 1064 of the German Code of Civil procedure does not require submitting the arbitration agreement at all.

1.12. Third, some of these jurisdictions both dropped or relaxed the requirement for the arbitration agreement to be in writing and dropped the requirement to provide the arbitration agreement. Such is the case in Belgium (Articles 1681 and 1720(4) of the CCP, respectively) or Sweden (Section 56 Arbitration Act). The Hypothetical Draft Convention on the International

---

[14]   E.g., France (Article 1507 CCP), Belgium, Scotland, England and Wales (Section 5 Arbitration Act), Sweden, Norway, Singapore (Section 2A International Arbitration Act), Hong Kong (Section 19 Arbitration Ordinance) or New Zealand (Schedule 1 Section 7 Arbitration Act).
[15]   Marcin Asłanowicz, *Commentary to Art. 1213 paragraph 3*, in SĄD POLUBOWNY (ARBITRAŻOWY). KOMENTARZ. DO CZĘŚCI PIĄTEJ KODEKSU POSTĘPOWANIA CYWILNEGO [COURT OF ARBITRATION. COMMENTARY TO PART FIFTH OF THE CODE OF CIVIL PROCEDURE], C.H. Beck (2017); Tomasz Strumiłło, *Commentary to Art. 1213, paragraph 3*, in KODEKS POSTĘPOWANIA CYWILNEGO. TOM II. KOMENTARZ. ART. 730-1217 [CODE OF CIVIL PROCEDURE. VOL. II. COMMENTARY. ART. 730-1217], C.H. Beck, (J. Jankowski ed. 2019).

Enforcement of Arbitration Agreements and Awards (the Miami Draft) also envisages such an approach.[16]

1.13. Fourth, some jurisdictions dropped or relaxed the requirement for the arbitration agreement to be in writing but maintained the requirement to provide the arbitration agreement.[17] Such is the case in France (Article 1443 and 1515 of the CCP), Scotland (Section 4 and Section 21.1(b) of the Arbitration Act 2010), and Hong Kong (Section 19 and Section 88(b) of the Arbitration Ordinance).

1.14. Fifth, there is a group of countries that adopted a more nuanced approach. The Norwegian arbitration law loosened formal requirements of arbitration agreements. It does not go as far as the Swedish law with its complete elimination of the requirement to produce an arbitration agreement. Still, in Chapter 10 Article 45 of the Arbitration Act, it creates a requirement that: '[d]ocumentary proof for the existence of an agreement or other basis for arbitration may be demanded'. So, first, it limits the requirement to evidentiary matters only; second, in Austrian and German style, it makes it subject to the court's request; third, it does not require 'the original' of the arbitration agreement but merely documentary proof of its existence.

1.15. Finally, New Zealand requires the production of the arbitration agreement only if it was recorded in writing (Schedule 1 Section 35 Arbitration Code).

1.16. The second conclusion of this article is that the formal requirements of the arbitration agreement stemming from a given legal system are irrelevant to solve the paradox as the requirement to supply the original of the arbitration agreement is also present in those systems that relaxed formal requirements under Article II of the New York Convention.

1.17. The third conclusion is that the paradox from Article IV of the New York Convention does not occur in those legal systems that resigned from the requirement to supply the motion for recognition or enforcement with 'the original of the arbitration agreement'. It is also resolved by state laws that do not automatically require the supplying of the original of the arbitration agreement or that allow other evidence in this regard.

---

[16] ALBERT J. VAN DEN BERG, HYPOTHETICAL DRAFT CONVENTION ON THE INTERNATIONAL ENFORCEMENT OF ARBITRATION AGREEMENTS AND AWARDS EXPLANATORY NOTE (2009), available at: https://www.newyorkconvention.org/draft+convention (accessed on 17 August 2021), et. 17 - 18.

[17] With respect to France: Michael Wietzorek, *The Form of the International Arbitration Agreement under the 2011 French Arbitration Law*, KLUWER ARBITRATION BLOG (7 April 2011), available at: http://arbitrationblog.kluwerarbitration.com/2011/04/07/the-form-of-the-international-arbitration-agreement-under-the-2011-french-arbitration-law/ (accessed on 17 August 2021).

Czech (& Central European) Yearbook of Arbitration®

IV.   The Relationship between Article IV(1) (b) and Articles II and V of the New York Convention

1.18.   If the state law did not relax the Article IV(1)(b) requirements, it is necessary to determine the relationship that exists between this provision and Articles II and V of the New York Convention. Two main approaches can be distinguished. We refused a third approach at the outset, under which Article IV(1)(b) is *lex imperfecta*, that is a provision providing no sanction if the rule specified therein is not fulfilled. It would, in our view, not be correct to interpret certain provisions of the Convention as they had not existed.

1.19.   The first approach to Article IV would be to impose a formal and substantive validity examination already at the preliminary stage while analysing the motion on formal grounds. This approach identifies the concept of an arbitration agreement in Article IV with the concept of a valid (Article V(1)(a)) written arbitration agreement (Article II). It reads those requirements 'as a whole'.[18]

1.20.   However, adopting this approach would deny the basic premise of the New York Convention by shifting the burden of proof to the party seeking enforcement from the objecting party.[19] Additionally, as rightfully noted by D. Otto and A. van den Berg, authors of the leading commentaries to the New York Convention, one must distinguish between the requirement to 'supply' under Article IV and the requirement to 'furnish proof' under Article V.[20] In this sense, the party objecting to the recognition or enforcement has to prove that there is no arbitration agreement or it is defective.[21] There is no such obligation on the part of the party seeking enforcement.

1.21.   The second approach does not assume that the question of validity is examined at the stage when Article IV of the New York Convention applies, i.e., while analysing the motion on formal grounds, but later, when the opposing party objects to

---

[18]   See US Court of Appeals for the 3rd Circuit, *China Minmetals Materials Import and Export Co., Ltd.* v. *Chi Mei Corporation*, Appellant, 334 F.3d 274 (3d Cir. 2003), judgement, 26 June 2003.
[19]   GARY BORN, INTERNATIONAL COMMERCIAL ARBITRATION, Third Edition, Kluwer Law International (2021), et. 3712.
[20]   Dirk Otto, *Article IV*, in RECOGNITION AND ENFORCEMENT OF FOREIGN ARBITRAL AWARDS: A GLOBAL COMMENTARY ON THE NEW YORK CONVENTION, Kluwer Law International (Herbert Kronke, Patricia Nacimiento et al. eds., 2010), et. 167 – 168; ALBERT J. VAN DEN BERG, THE NEW YORK ARBITRATION CONVENTION OF 1958: TOWARDS A UNIFORM JUDICIAL INTERPRETATION, Boston: Kluwer Law and Taxation (1981), et. 250.
[21]   STEFAN KRÖLL & LOUKAS A. MISTELIS & PILAR PERALES VISCASILLAS & VIKKI ROGERS (eds.), LIBER AMICORUM ERIC BERGSTERN. INTERNATIONAL ARBITRATION AND INTERNATIONAL COMMERCIAL LAW: SYNERGY, CONVERGENCE AND EVOLUTION, Alphen aan den Rijn (2011), s. 329.

the recognition/enforcement.[22] In this view, the Article IV(1)(b) requirement is merely a preliminary obligation to demonstrate the existence of an arbitration agreement.[23] This approach is based on three premises: (i) Article IV is a provision that merely establishes evidentiary requirements designed to 'set in motion' the enforcement procedure,[24] (ii) it sets an independent standard for evaluating procedural requirements,[25] (iii) it refers to supplying the 'original' of the arbitration agreement, but it does not specify the form of this original. Some authors go even further and argue that Article IV establishes the presumption of the existence of an arbitration agreement.[26] Consequently, for instance, under Article IV of the New York Convention, it is not necessary to show the authority of the parties to enter into the arbitration agreement. This is solely an issue under Article V raised on objection by the opposing party.[27]

1.22.   As the rules governing the procedural requirements are, in most part, based on Article II,[28] any form allowed under the New York Convention is appropriate from the perspective of Article IV. Therefore, Article IV must be seen in the light of Article II and

---

[22]   ICCA, ICCA'S GUIDE TO THE INTERPRETATION OF THE 1958 NEW YORK CONVENTION: A HANDBOOK FOR JUDGES (2011), et. 75.

[23]   Albert J. van den Berg, New York Convention of 1958: Refusals of Enforcement, 18(2) ICC INTERNATIONAL COURT OF ARBITRATION BULLETIN 1 (2007), et. 34; England and Wales Court of Appeal, Yukos Oil Co v. Dardana Ltd, [2002] 1 All ER (Comm) 819, judgement, 18 April 2002.

[24]   Beata Gessel-Kalinowska vel Kalisz, Admissibility of Electronic Awards in the UNCITRAL Model Law Jurisdiction: Polish Law Example, 38(2) JOURNAL OF INTERNATIONAL ARBITRATION, Kluwer Law International 147 (2021), et. 155 – 156.

[25]   GARY BORN, INTERNATIONAL COMMERCIAL ARBITRATION, Third Edition, Kluwer Law International (2021), et. 3709; UNCITRAL Secretariat Guide on the Convention on the Recognition of Foreign Arbitral Awards (New York, 1958) (2016), et. 114 – 115 paragraph 65; ICCA, ICCA'S GUIDE TO THE INTERPRETATION OF THE 1958 NEW YORK CONVENTION: A HANDBOOK FOR JUDGES (2011), et. 75; Maxi Scherer, Article IV, in NEW YORK CONVENTION – COMMENTARY, Beck Hart Nomos (Reinmar Wolff ed., 2012), et. 218 – 219. See England and Wales Court of Appeal, Yukos Oil Co v. Dardana Ltd, [2002] 1 All ER (Comm) 819, judgement, 18 April 2002.

[26]   Albert J. van den Berg, New York Convention of 1958: Refusals of Enforcement, 18(2) ICC INTERNATIONAL COURT OF ARBITRATION BULLETIN 1 (2007), et. 34; Stefan Kröll, The Arbitration Agreement in Enforcement Proceedings of Foreign Awards. Burden of Proof and the Legal Relevance of the Tribunal's Decision, in LIBER AMICORUM ERIC BERGSTERN. INTERNATIONAL ARBITRATION AND INTERNATIONAL COMMERCIAL LAW: SYNERGY, CONVERGENCE AND EVOLUTION, ALPHEN AAN DEN RIJN (S. Kröll, L. A. Mistelis, P. Perales Viscasillas, V. Rogers eds., 2011), et. 324.

[27]   Dirk Otto, Article IV, in RECOGNITION AND ENFORCEMENT OF FOREIGN ARBITRAL AWARDS: A GLOBAL COMMENTARY ON THE NEW YORK CONVENTION, Kluwer Law International (Herbert Kronke, Patricia Nacimiento et al. eds., 2010), et. 166.

[28]   UNCITRAL Secretariat Guide on the Convention on the Recognition of Foreign Arbitral Awards (New York, 1958) (2016), et. 114 – 115 paragraph 67; Dirk Otto, Article IV, in RECOGNITION AND ENFORCEMENT OF FOREIGN ARBITRAL AWARDS: A GLOBAL COMMENTARY ON THE NEW YORK CONVENTION, Kluwer Law International (Herbert Kronke, Patricia Nacimiento et al. eds., 2010), et. 160 – 161. Stacie I. Strong, What Constitutes an "Agreement in Writing" in International Commercial Arbitration? Conflicts Between the New York Convention and the Federal Arbitration Act, 48(1) STANFORD JOURNAL OF INTERNATIONAL LAW 47 (2012), et. 56. For similar reasoning see: US Court of Appeals for the 11th Circuit, Czarina, L.L.C. v. W.F. Poe Syndicate, 358 F.3d 1286, judgement, 4 February 2004, and Supreme Court of Spain, Glencore Grain Limited (United Kingdom) v. Sociedad Ibérica de Molturación, S.A. (Spain), judgement, 14 January 2003, in: ALBERT J. VAN DEN BERG (ed.), YEARBOOK COMMERCIAL ARBITRATION, Volume XXX (2005), et. 605 - 609.

thus cannot undermine the rationale of the Convention's formal requirements.[29] Consequently, as the Convention allows for arbitration agreements to be contained in a signed document,[30] a document referring to standard business terms,[31] in an e-mail exchange,[32] the presentation of these signed documents or a print-out of these e-mails would suffice from the perspective of Article IV(1)(b) requirements. Therefore, the rules of interpretation of Article II will affect the evidence that must be provided under Article IV.[33] In a nutshell, as correctly noted by an English court, it is sufficient for the applicant to supply: 'valid documentation, containing an arbitration clause, by reference to which the arbitrators have accepted that the parties had agreed on arbitration or in which the arbitrators have accepted that an agreement to arbitrate was recorded with the parties' authority.'[34]

1.23.   The fourth conclusion of our analysis is that the courts should analyze the requirements from Article IV(1)(b) only from the procedural side. The courts should not *sua sponte* examine the prerequisites of the formal validity of the arbitration agreement under Article II or grounds for refusal of recognition or enforcement under Article V of the New York Convention at the stage when they assess whether the applicant supplied its motion with 'the original of the arbitration agreement'. However, Article II of the New York Convention governs the acceptable form of entering into the arbitration agreement. Thus it also determines the form of the 'original of the arbitration agreement' that needs to be supplied under Article IV(1)(b) of the Convention.

V.   Standard of Proof under Article IV.

1.24.   Even taking the view that Article IV is only of a procedural or evidence nature does not solve the paradox described at the outset. Procedural or not, this requirement needs to be satisfied.

---

[29]   Polish Supreme Court Case No. V CSK 323/11, judgement, 13 September 2012.
[30]   Polish Supreme Court Case No. I CKN 240/00, judgement, 29 August 2000.
[31]   Polish Supreme Court Case No. III CSK 406/16, judgement, 28 November 2018; Polish Court of Appeals for Katowice Case No. V AGo 11/17, judgment 26 April 2018; Polish Court of Appeals for Katowice Case No. V AGo 11/18, judgment 4 September 2017.
[32]   Polish Supreme Court Case No. V CSK 323/11, judgement, 13 September 2012; Polish Supreme Court Case No. V CSK 672/13, judgement, 23 January 2015; Polish Supreme Court Case No. III CSK 406/16, judgement, 28 November 2018.
[33]   UNCITRAL Recommendation regarding the interpretation of Article II, paragraph 2, and Article VII, paragraph 1, of the Convention on the Recognition and Enforcement of Foreign Arbitral Awards, done in New York, 10 June 1958 (2006); ICCA, ICCA'S GUIDE TO THE INTERPRETATION OF THE 1958 NEW YORK CONVENTION: A HANDBOOK FOR JUDGES (2011), et. 42 – 50.
[34]   England and Wales Court of Appeal, *Yukos Oil Co v. Dardana Ltd*, [2002] 1 All ER (Comm) 819, judgement, 18 April 2002.

1.25. The most widely accepted approach to Article IV is that it only creates a requirement of a *prima facie* arbitration agreement.[35] Such is the approach in Singapore. Section 30(1)(b) of the Singapore International Arbitration Act requires the person seeking enforcement to produce 'the original arbitration agreement under which the award purports to have been made, or a duly certified copy thereof' to the court. Section 30(2) clarifies, however, that such a document shall be treated merely 'as *prima facie* evidence of the matters to which it relates'.

1.26. But there can be no *prima facie* agreement if there is no agreement at all (e.g., when a non-signatory was a party to the proceedings). From that perspective, the *prima facie* standard does not help. With no parties to the arbitration agreement identified (or with a non-existent party identified) in the evidence provided, courts have rejected enforcement.[36] However, it is worth noting that the case law in question dates back almost 25 years. Since then, arbitration law has developed theories of extending the effectiveness to non-signatories.[37]

1.27. Therefore, one needs to analyse other approaches. These approaches need to be examined while considering that Article IV of the New York Convention shall be interpreted following the pro-enforcement bias of the Convention.[38] Consequently, evidentiary formalities cannot overshadow the principles of the New York Convention and the fact that Article IV is only a procedural regulation.[39]

1.28. The Polish Supreme Court underlined that in the event the arbitration agreement is concluded via e-mail, there is no 'original' thereof within the meaning of Article IV(1)(b) of the

---

[35] GARY BORN, INTERNATIONAL COMMERCIAL ARBITRATION, Third Edition, Kluwer Law International (2021), et. 3711; Dirk Otto, *Article IV*, in RECOGNITION AND ENFORCEMENT OF FOREIGN ARBITRAL AWARDS: A GLOBAL COMMENTARY ON THE NEW YORK CONVENTION, Kluwer Law International (Herbert Kronke, Patricia Nacimiento et al. eds., 2010), et. 167 – 168; UNCITRAL Secretariat Guide on the Convention on the Recognition of Foreign Arbitral Awards (New York, 1958) (2016), et. 114 – 115, paragraph 65; ALBERT J. VAN DEN BERG, THE NEW YORK CONVENTION OF 1958: AN OVERVIEW, ICCA Website (2003), et. 13.
LEW, supra note 2, at 704.

[36] See for example Moscow District Court, *Sokofl Star Shipping Co. Inc. v. GPVO Technopromexport* (decided 1997) quoted in Dirk Otto, *Article IV*, in RECOGNITION AND ENFORCEMENT OF FOREIGN ARBITRAL AWARDS: A GLOBAL COMMENTARY ON THE NEW YORK CONVENTION, Kluwer Law International (Herbert Kronke, Patricia Nacimiento et al. eds., 2010), et. 164, 187.

[37] See point 5.4 below.

[38] Albert J. van den Berg, *New York Convention of 1958: Refusals of Enforcement*, 18(2) ICC INTERNATIONAL COURT OF ARBITRATION BULLETIN 1 (2007), et. 2, 32-34.

[39] Martin Frederik Gusy, *The Validity of an Arbitration Agreement Under the New York Convention – Remarks on the Order of OLG Schleswig, March 30, 2000 (16 SchH 5/99)*, 19(4) JOURNAL OF INTERNATIONAL ARBITRATION, Kluwer Law International 363 (2002), et. 368.

Convention; in such a case supplying the court with written confirmation of the agreement is sufficient.[40]

1.29. It has also been held that it is sufficient to show by any means provided by law that parties consented to arbitration (e.g., transcription of the hearing) – thus making the question of being 'in writing' effectively a secondary issue.[41]

1.30. Even if only an arbitration agreement with one party's signature was provided, but the other party's agreement is possible to interpret from other documents, it should be deemed satisfying the requirements of Article IV. Whether such arbitration is valid would depend on the applicable law in question, and the wording of Article II of the New York Convention is restrictive in that respect.[42] The burden of proof then shifts to the party opposing enforcement, and it will be free to present its case under Article V(1)(a).[43]

1.31. Not always satisfying requirements from Article IV(1)(b) using 'documents upon which the tribunal based its jurisdiction,' as advocated by S. Kröll who tackled the discussed paradox as well, based on English case law,[44] would be sufficient or possible to solve the paradox discussed. This would not be possible if the tribunal has not referred to any documents. Such a reference and even the reference to the basis of the tribunal's jurisdiction is not required in all cases, e.g., by Article 31 of the Model Law determining the content of the award. Also, the lack of the original arbitration agreement may become a point at issue only at the enforcement stage.

1.32. Therefore, the fifth conclusion of our analysis is that authorities allow for the existence of an arbitration agreement to be proven under Article IV(1)(b) of the New York Convention by any means permitted by law, not just by providing the arbitration agreement in writing itself.

---

[40] Polish Supreme Court Case No. V CSK 323/11, judgement, 13 September 2012.
[41] Dirk Otto, *Article IV*, in RECOGNITION AND ENFORCEMENT OF FOREIGN ARBITRAL AWARDS: A GLOBAL COMMENTARY ON THE NEW YORK CONVENTION, Kluwer Law International (Herbert Kronke, Patricia Nacimiento et al. eds., 2010), et. 171.
[42] ICCA, ICCA'S GUIDE TO THE INTERPRETATION OF THE 1958 NEW YORK CONVENTION: A HANDBOOK FOR JUDGES (2011), et. 49; Dirk Otto, *Article IV*, in RECOGNITION AND ENFORCEMENT OF FOREIGN ARBITRAL AWARDS: A GLOBAL COMMENTARY ON THE NEW YORK CONVENTION, Kluwer Law International (Herbert Kronke, Patricia Nacimiento et al. eds., 2010), et. 161.
[43] Maxi Scherer, *Article IV*, in NEW YORK CONVENTION – COMMENTARY, Beck Hart Nomos (Reinmar Wolff ed., 2012), no. 2, et. 216.
[44] STEFAN KRÖLL & LOUKAS A. MISTELIS & PILAR PERALES VISCASILLAS & VIKKI ROGERS (eds.), LIBER AMICORUM ERIC BERGSTERN. INTERNATIONAL ARBITRATION AND INTERNATIONAL COMMERCIAL LAW: SYNERGY, CONVERGENCE AND EVOLUTION, Alphen aan den Rijn (2011), et. 331.

VI. Fulfillment of Requirements in the Cases of a Non-traditional Arbitration Agreement

1.33. The above considerations can now be transferred to the problem of non-traditional arbitration agreements.

VI.1. Waiver of Jurisdictional Objections

1.34. The legal principle prohibiting self-contradictory behaviour forms a part of the New York Convention.[45] This principle is also widely recognised in both common and civil law jurisdictions.[46] The consequence of this is the recognition of arbitration agreements concluded by failure to object. This is also the method of consent recognised by Option 1 of Article 7 of the UNCITRAL Model Law.

1.35. There are older judgments that take a restrictive approach to evidence of such agreements.[47] But this approach has changed. It is now recognised, for example, that even the delivery of correspondence in which the other party recognised the jurisdiction is sufficient to satisfy the requirements of Article IV(1)(b) of the New York Convention if the other party has not raised jurisdictional objections.[48] It would also be entirely reasonable in such a case to resign from this requirement altogether[49] or to allow the applicant to prove the arbitral jurisdiction in another way. Moreover, the Polish Supreme Court supported the view that a party that has entered an arbitration without objecting to the tribunal's jurisdiction (e.g., on the grounds of the ineffectiveness of the arbitration clause) waives its right to object in postarbitral proceedings. The essence of the New York Convention is that the parties are required to act in accordance with the principles of good faith

---

[45] Martin Frederik Gusy, *The Validity of an Arbitration Agreement Under the New York Convention – Remarks on the Order of OLG Schleswig, March 30, 2000 (16 SchH 5/99)*, 19(4) JOURNAL OF INTERNATIONAL ARBITRATION, Kluwer Law International 363 (2002), et. 371 – 372.

[46] Celle Court of Appeals Germany, OLG Celle, OLGR Celle 2007, 664, judgement, 31 May 2007; US Court of Appeals for the 4th Circuit, *International Paper Co. v. Schwabedissen Maschinen & Anlagen GmbH*, 206 F.3d 411, judgement, 14 March 2000; England and Wales Court of Appeal, *Yukos Oil Co v. Dardana Ltd*, [2002] 1 All ER (Comm) 819, judgement, 18 April 2002.

[47] For example, see: Netherlands Court of Appeal of The Hague, *James Allen Ltd. v. Marea Producten B.B*, judgement, 17 February 1984, in PIETER SANDERS (ed.), YEARBOOK COMMERCIAL ARBITRATION, Volume X-1985, Kluwer, Netherlands (1985).

[48] See, for example Brazil Superior Court of Justice, *L'Aiglon SA v. Textil União*, SEC 856, judgement, 18 May 2005.

[49] Celle Court of Appeals Germany, OLG Celle, OLGR Celle 2007, 664, judgement, 31 May 2007; Spain Supreme Court *Shaanxi Provincial Medical Health Products I/E Corp. v. Olpesa, SA*, ATS 599/2003, judgement, 21 January 2003. For an overview of the ways in which the New York Convention has been interpreted in Eastern European countries, including the issue of formal validity, see in particular: Christoph Liebscher, *Application of the New York Convention in Austria and Eastern Europe*, 25(6) JOURNAL OF INTERNATIONAL ARBITRATION, Kluwer Law International 771 (2008).

and morality, and therefore prohibited from acting contrary to those principles. This interpretation makes it impossible to act disloyally towards the co-parties and the arbitral tribunal, causing unnecessary costs and wasting time. There is no fear that a party's procedural rights will be restricted, as it decides on the agreement autonomously.[50] This approach is, in our view, a correct one.

1.36. In another case, the Polish Supreme Court further clarified that the applicant's failure to submit the agreement referred to in Article IV(1)(b) of the New York Convention does not preclude the possibility of granting the application if the existence of a foreign arbitration clause is undisputed.[51] This is in line with the approach present in many jurisdictions under which courts should exempt the applicant from supplying the arbitration agreement in case 'its existence, wording, and authenticity are undisputed'.[52] However, the Polish Supreme Court found that if the defendant objects to the jurisdiction, the requirements from Article IV(1)(b) of the Convention are not relaxed. Such requirements should be interpreted strictly, and statements made by both parties must be made in writing.[53]

1.37. Whether signing of the terms of reference can be treated as an arbitration agreement remains an open question.[54] It seems, in our view, that the sole signing of the terms is insufficient to establish proof under Article IV of the New York Convention. On the one hand, if a party does not raise a procedural objection, signs the terms of reference, and enters into a dispute on merits, one may, in certain circumstances, find that this party waived its objection. On the other hand, where one party has already raised a jurisdictional objection, the mere signing of the terms of reference would not automatically 'overwrite' that objection.

VI.2. Oral and Tacit Arbitration Agreements

1.38. As shown above, oral arbitration agreements are permitted under certain legal systems, or at least these systems relaxed the Article IV(1)(b) requirement. At the same time, some legal systems (e.g., France, Scotland, and Hong Kong) decided to maintain the said requirement despite relaxing the formal

---

[50] Polish Supreme Court Case No. V CSK 323/11, judgement, 13 September 2012.
[51] Polish Supreme Court Case No. V CSK 672/13, judgement, 23 January 2015.
[52] Maxi Scherer, *Article IV*, in NEW YORK CONVENTION – COMMENTARY, Beck Hart Nomos (Reinmar Wolff ed., 2012), no. 27-29, et. 224-226 and caselaw cited therein.
[53] Polish Supreme Court Case No. III CSK 81/17, decision, 4 April 2019.
[54] JULIAN D. M. LEW & LOUKAS A. MISTELIS & STEFAN KRÖLL, COMPARATIVE INTERNATIONAL COMMERCIAL ARBITRATION, Kluwer Law International (2003), et. 532.

requirements of the arbitration agreement, therefore deepening the described paradox.

1.39. Irrespective of the formal requirements of the arbitration agreement, the solution would be to either dispose of the Article IV(1)(b) requirement when there is no written arbitration agreement (as is the case, e.g., in New Zealand) or interpret the requirement as to allow any other evidence to show the tribunal's jurisdiction in a given case. In the case of oral arbitration agreements, a transcript of the consent expressed by the parties orally suffices.[55]

1.40. As to the tacit arbitration agreements in some cases, even an arbitration agreement with only one party's signature was recognised.[56] Nevertheless, additional evidence would be required to show the consent of the other party.

1.41. However, a Polish court found that if the applicant believes that the presented documents constitute an arbitration agreement in writing, the court should not request supplementation of the motion on formal grounds (by supplying the original of the agreement), but hear the case and establish, at a later stage, whether indeed the documents submitted meet the requirements of Article II of the Convention.[57] This approach is beneficial and allows the case to proceed at the substantive stage (where the court applies Articles II and V of the Convention) when there is no traditional arbitration agreement.

1.42. Polish case law further underlines that the requirements to present the original of the arbitration agreement are of 'a double, formal and substantive nature'. Consequently, if the requirement of Article IV(1)(b) is not met, the motion should be rejected on formal grounds. If it is not and the court initiates the case and only later discovers the lack of the agreement, it denies the motion on substantive grounds.[58]

VI.3. Extension Over Non-Signatories

1.43. Parties may also face challenges in supplying the original of the arbitration agreement concluded in the event of the extension of the scope of the arbitration agreements. Such challenges will, however, not occur in those systems that do not directly

---

[55] Beeatrice Castellane, *The New French Law on International Arbitration*, 28(4) JOURNAL OF INTERNATIONAL ARBITRATION, Kluwer Law International 371, 374 (2011).
[56] Swiss Federal Tribunal, *Compagnie de Navigation et Transports SA v. MSC Mediterranean Shipping Company SA*, DFT 121 III 38, judgement, 16 January 1995; United States Court of Appeals for 3rd Circuit, *Standard Bent Glass Corp. v. Glassrobots OY* [Fin.] 333 F.3D 440, judgement, 20 June 2003.
[57] Kraków Court of Appeal Case No. I ACo 53/16; decision of 28 October 2017.
[58] Polish Supreme Court Case No. III CK 510/03, judgement, 3 November 2004; Polish Supreme Court Case No. I CSK 186/12, judgment, 23 January 2013; Polish Supreme Court Case No. V CSK 257/15, judgment, 25 May 2016..

apply the requirements for the arbitration agreement to the question of extension, as is the case under Swiss law in certain circumstances.[59] In such a situation, it is sufficient to provide the initial agreement itself. Indeed, the problem of non-signatories, if anything, exists primarily under Article V(1)(a).[60] International authorities seem to support this view.[61]

1.44. Nevertheless, there is still a second view, which does not allow to separate the issue of extension from the issue of the arbitration agreement itself. Courts have required plaintiffs to provide the initial arbitration agreement together with the documents justifying the changes of the parties to the agreement.[62] The Polish Supreme Court has required these documents to be in the form appropriate for concluding the arbitration agreement itself.[63]

1.45. It is also questionable whether the requirements of Article IV can be satisfied by solely relying on the arbitral tribunal's findings. S. Kröll argued that one needs to give at least 'the benefit of the doubt' to the tribunal's decision on jurisdiction, which means, as we assume, that in cases where the tribunal explicitly confirmed its jurisdiction, the standard of Article IV(1)(b) needs to be reduced.[64] However, this would make the Article IV(1)(b) requirement redundant in all such cases. We excluded such a *'per non est'* reading of this provision at the outset. A US court found, in turn, that '[t]he requirement to submit the [...] arbitration agreement cannot be overcome by any findings of an arbitration tribunal that such agreement

---

[59] Swiss Federal Tribunal, *X. S.A.L., Y. S.A.L. A.v. Z. Sàrl*, DFR 129 III 727, judgement, 16 October 2003. Elliott Geisinger, *Implementing the New York Convention in Switzerland*, 25(6) JOURNAL OF INTERNATIONAL ARBITRATION, Kluwer Law International 691 (2008), et. 695 – 696.

[60] STAVROS BREKOULAKIS, THIRD PARTIES IN INTERNATIONAL COMMERCIAL ARBITRATION, Oxford University Press (2010), et. 189.

[61] Martin Frederik Gusy, *The Validity of an Arbitration Agreement Under the New York Convention – Remarks on the Order of OLG Schleswig, March 30, 2000 (16 SchH 5/99)*, 19(4) JOURNAL OF INTERNATIONAL ARBITRATION, Kluwer Law International 363 (2002), et. 367.

[62] Dirk Otto, *Article IV*, in RECOGNITION AND ENFORCEMENT OF FOREIGN ARBITRAL AWARDS: A GLOBAL COMMENTARY ON THE NEW YORK CONVENTION, Kluwer Law International (Herbert Kronke, Patricia Nacimiento et al. eds., 2010), et. 173 - 174. See also Canada Court of Appeal of Manitoba, *Sheldon Proctor v. Leon Schellenberg*, AI02-30-05317, judgement, 11 December 2002 and Polish Supreme Court, C. III. 778/34, judgement, 8 February 1935 where many years before the New York Convention was signed it was held that the signature of the legal predecessor must be regarded as equivalent to the signature of the plaintiff themselves as assignee.

[63] Polish Supreme Court Case No. V CSK 257/15, judgment, 25 May 2016.

[64] STEFAN KRÖLL & LOUKAS A. MISTELIS & PILAR PERALES VISCASILLAS & VIKKI ROGERS (eds.), LIBER AMICORUM ERIC BERGSTERN. INTERNATIONAL ARBITRATION AND INTERNATIONAL COMMERCIAL LAW: SYNERGY, CONVERGENCE AND EVOLUTION, Alphen aan den Rijn (2011), s. 331-334.

existed'.[65] This approach was followed in other jurisdictions.[66] The latter approach seems to be more appropriate.

1.46. The above examples lead us to our sixth and final conclusion. The applicant should be able to prove the existence of an arbitration agreement under Article (IV)(1)(b) of the New York Convention by any means permitted by law, not just by providing the arbitration agreement itself. This should also be the case where the applicable law allows the arbitration to take place despite no written arbitration agreement (in a 'classic' form) between the parties (e.g., through the waiver of a procedural objection or by extension to non-signatories). In such a case the first, procedural phase of the enforcement proceedings can be continued even if the applicant has not submitted the arbitration agreement at all.[67]

VII. Conclusions

1.47. The findings of our analysis can be summarized as follows.

1.48. Article IV(1)(b) of the New York Convention provides for a maximum standard and can be reduced by national laws. The said provision (understood as providing only a maximum level of procedural requirements) does not apply if the state law prescribes for a lower level of such requirements.

1.49. The formal requirements of the arbitration agreement stemming from given legal systems are irrelevant to solve the paradox. The requirement to supply the original of the arbitration agreement is also present in those systems that relaxed formal requirements under Article II of the New York Convention.

1.50. The paradox from Article IV of the New York Convention is also resolved by state laws that do not automatically require supplying the original of the arbitration agreement or that allow other evidence in this regard. Therefore, the requirement to provide the original of an arbitration agreement is a principle

---

[65] See for example: United States Court of Appeals for 11th Circuit, *Czarina L.L.C. v. W.F. Poe Syndicate*, 358 F.3d 1286, judgement, 4th February 2004.
[66] Maxi Scherer, *Article IV*, in NEW YORK CONVENTION – COMMENTARY, Beck Hart Nomos (Reinmar Wolff ed., 2012), no. 23, et. 223-224.
[67] STEFAN KRÖLL & LOUKAS A. MISTELIS & PILAR PERALES VISCASILLAS & VIKKI ROGERS (eds.), LIBER AMICORUM ERIC BERGSTERN. INTERNATIONAL ARBITRATION AND INTERNATIONAL COMMERCIAL LAW: SYNERGY, CONVERGENCE AND EVOLUTION, Alphen aan den Rijn (2011), s. 331.

with exceptions permitted in particular circumstances or where it is possible under domestic law.[68]

1.51. The requirements from Article IV(1)(b) should be analysed by the courts, if at all, only from the procedural side. The courts should not *sua sponte* examine the prerequisites of the formal validity of the arbitration agreement under Article II or grounds for refusal of the recognition or enforcement under Article V of the New York Convention at the stage when they assess whether the applicant supplied its motion with 'the original of the arbitration agreement'.

1.52. However, Article II of the New York Convention governs the acceptable form of entering into the arbitration agreement. Thus it also determines the form of the 'original of the arbitration agreement' that needs to be supplied under Article IV(1)(b) of the Convention.

1.53. Finally, and in our view, the most important, the existence of an arbitration agreement under Article (IV)(1)(b) of the New York Convention and the jurisdiction of an arbitral tribunal (where the applicable law allows the arbitration to take place despite no arbitration agreement between the parties) can be demonstrated by any means, not just by providing the arbitration agreement itself. In such cases, the 'original of the arbitration agreement' should be understood as 'proof for the tribunal's jurisdiction'. Such language is also better for Article IV(1)(b) of the New York Convention and can be proposed *de lege ferenda* as a change in the wording of this provision.

1.54. Having said that, we need to clarify that the proposed interpretation of Article IV(1)(b) of the New York Convention would only allow the first obstacle to the recognition / enforcement to be removed by kickstarting the proceedings in cases where the jurisdiction of the tribunal was established in a non-traditional manner. Whether the enforcement court agrees with the arguments proposed by the opposing party on the basis of Article V (in particular (1)(a) and (c)), would be decided in the second, substantive stage of the proceedings, which was not discussed in this paper.

Czech (& Central European) Yearbook of Arbitration®

Summaries

FRA [*La question de la production de « l'original de la convention d'arbitrage » selon l'article IV de la Convention de New York en l'absence d'un tel document*]
Le présent article réfléchit sur le problème pratique de la reconnaissance et de l'exécution de sentences arbitrales étrangères en vertu de la Convention de New York dans une situation où les parties n'ont pas conclu de convention d'arbitrage écrite. Il est évident que la Convention, signée en 1958, ne reflète que les normes qui s'appliquaient à la procédure arbitrale au moment de son adoption. Ainsi, elle ne prévoit explicitement que les cas où la convention d'arbitrage remplit les conditions de forme énoncées dans son article II. Par ailleurs, la Convention de New York exige de la partie qui demande la reconnaissance et l'exécution d'une sentence arbitrale qu'elle produise, afin que sa demande soit accueillie, l'original de la convention d'arbitrage (article IV, paragraphe 1, point b)). La teneur de la Convention de New York fait ainsi abstraction de la tendance croissante à l'assouplissement des conditions de forme de la convention d'arbitrage, y compris la conclusion implicite des clauses compromissoires, par exemple en renonçant à la possibilité de contester la compétence du tribunal arbitral, ou en étendant les effets de la convention d'arbitrage aux personnes qui ne sont pas signataires de la clause compromissoire. L'article tente de répondre à la question de savoir si la reconnaissance de la sentence arbitrale en vertu de la Convention de New York est possible dans toutes ces situations. Les auteurs concluent que la sentence arbitrale peut être reconnue et exécutée dès lors que la partie qui demande sa reconnaissance et son exécution a la faculté d'établir la compétence du tribunal arbitral par tout moyen.

CZE [*Předložení „prvopisu rozhodčí smlouvy" ve smyslu článku IV Newyorské úmluvy, když takový dokument neexistuje*]
Článek pojednává o praktickém problému uznání a výkonu cizích rozhodčích nálezů na základě ustanovení Newyorské úmluvy v situacích, kdy strany neuzavřely rozhodčí smlouvu v písemné formě. Úmluva byla podepsána v roce 1958 a ze zjevných důvodů zohledňuje pouze ty standardy, které se v rozhodčím řízení uplatňovaly v době jejího přijetí. Úmluva tak výslovně upravuje pouze případy, kdy rozhodčí smlouva splňuje formální požadavky článku II. Dále Newyorská úmluva rovněž vyžaduje, aby strana, která žádá o uznání a výkon, předložila za účelem uznání a výkonu rozhodčího nálezu prvopis rozhodčí

smlouvy (čl. IV odst. 1 písm. b)). Dikce Newyorské úmluvy tudíž nezohledňuje sílící tendence rozvolňování formálních požadavků na rozhodčí smlouvy, včetně implicitního uzavírání rozhodčích doložek, a to například vzdáním se námitek proti pravomoci rozhodčího soudu nebo rozšířením účinků rozhodčí smlouvy na osoby, které rozhodčí doložku nepodepsaly. Tento článek se pokouší odpovědět na otázku, zda je ve všech těchto situacích uznání rozhodčího nálezu dle Newyorské úmluvy možné, a dochází k závěru, že rozhodčí nález je uznatelný a vykonatelný, pokud může strana, která o uznání a výkon žádá, prokázat pravomoc rozhodčího soudu jakýmikoli důkazními prostředky.

| | |

POL [*Wymóg przedłożenia 'oryginału pisemnej umowy arbitrażowej" zgodnie z Artykułem IV Konwencji Nowojorskiej a brak umowy arbitrażowej w takiej formie. Próba rozwiązania paradoksu*]
Konwencja Nowojorska została zawarta w 1958 r. i z oczywistych przyczyn uwzględnia jedynie ówczesne standardy występujące w arbitrażu. Z tego względu Konwencja przewiduje wyłącznie przypadek zawarcia umowy arbitrażowej w formie pisemnej, podczas gdy w ostatnich latach dochodzi do rozluźniania wymogów formalnych zapisu na sąd polubowny. Artykuł stanowi próbę odpowiedzi na pytanie, czy w oparciu o postanowienia Konwencji możliwe jest spełnienie wymogów formalnych wniosku o uznanie lub stwierdzenie wykonalności wyroku sądu arbitrażowego w sytuacji, gdy wnioskodawca nie jest w stanie przedłożyć „oryginału umowy o arbitraż", gdyż takowy nie istnieje. Zdaniem autorów orzeczenie podlega uznaniu i wykonaniu, jeżeli wnioskodawca może wykazać istnienie właściwości sądu polubownego za pomocą jakichkolwiek środków dowodowych.

DEU [*Die Vorlage der „Urschrift der Schiedsvereinbarung" im Sinn von Artikel IV des New Yorker Übereinkommens, dort, wo ein solches Dokument nicht existiert*]
Das New Yorker Übereinkommen wurde im Jahre 1958 abgeschlossen; aus begreiflichen Gründen berücksichtigt es lediglich die schiedsgerichtlichen Gepflogenheiten zum Zeitpunkt des Abschlusses dieses 'Bereinkommens. Deshalb regelt das New Yorker Abkommen den Fall des Abschlusses einerer Schiedsvereinbarung lediglich in schriftlicher Form. In jüngerer Zeit beobachten wir allerdings eine gewisse Lockerung der formalen Anforderungen, die an die Schiedsvereinbarung gestellt

werden. Der vorliegende Artikel unternimmt den Versuch der Beantwortung der Frage, ob auf der Grundlage der Bestimmungen des New Yorker Übereinkommens die formalen Anforderungen im Zusammenhang mit dem Antrag auf Anerkennung oder die Erklärung der Vollstreckung eines Schiedsspruchs auch dort erfüllt sind, wo die antragstellende Partei außer Stande ist, die „Urschrift der Schiedsvereinbarung" vorzulegen – weil eine solche Urschrift gar nicht besteht. Nach Auffassung der Autoren ist der Schiedsspruch auch in einem solchen Fall anzuerkennen und vollstreckbar, soweit die Partei, die die Anerkennung und Vollstreckung begehrt, die Zuständigkeit des Schiedsgerichts mit irgendwelchen Beweismitteln belegen kann.

RUS [*Представление «подлинника арбитражного соглашения» согласно статье IV Нью-Йоркской конвенции в случае отсутствия данного документа*]
Нью-Йоркская конвенция была заключена в 1958 году, и в ней по понятным причинам предусмотрены только те стандарты, которые применялись в арбитраже на момент ее принятия. Следовательно, Нью-Йоркской конвенцией регулируется заключение арбитражного соглашения исключительно в письменной форме. Однако в последнее время произошло некоторое ослабление формальных требований к арбитражному соглашению. В данной статье предпринимается попытка ответить на вопрос о том, позволяют ли положения Нью-Йоркской конвенции выполнить формальные требования в связи с требованием о признании или заявлением о приведении в исполнение арбитражного решения в случаях, когда сторона, добивающаяся признания и приведения в исполнение, не может представить «подлинник арбитражного соглашения», т. к. такого подлинника не существует. По мнению авторов, даже в таком случае арбитражное решение должно быть признано и подлежит приведению в исполнение, если сторона, ходатайствующая о признании и приведении в исполнение, способна подтвердить компетенцию арбитражного суда любыми средствами доказывания.

ESP [*Presentación del „original del acuerdo de arbitraje" en virtud del artículo IV de la Convención de Nueva York en situaciones en las que no exista tal documento*]
La Convención de Nueva York se celebró en 1958 y, por razones obvias, solo refleja las normas aplicadas al arbitraje en el momento de su adopción. Por lo tanto, la Convención de Nueva

York solo prevé las situaciones en las que el acuerdo de arbitraje se haya celebrado en formato escrito. Sin embargo, recientemente se ha producido cierta relajación de los requisitos formales del acuerdo de arbitraje. Este artículo intenta responder a la pregunta sobre la posibilidad de cumplir con los requisitos formales establecidos por la Convención de Nueva York a la hora de presentar una solicitud de reconocimiento o declaración de ejecutabilidad de un laudo arbitral en una situación en la que la parte solicitante no pueda presentar „el original del acuerdo de arbitraje" dada su inexistencia. Según la opinión de los autores, el laudo arbitral también es reconocible y ejecutable en tal caso si la parte que solicita el reconocimiento y la ejecución puede probar la competencia del tribunal de arbitraje mediante cualquier prueba.

| | |

Bibliography:

Marcin Asłanowicz, *Commentary to Art. 1213 paragraph 3*, in SĄD POLUBOWNY (ARBITRAŻOWY). KOMENTARZ DO CZĘŚCI PIĄTEJ KODEKSU POSTĘPOWANIA CYWILNEGO [COURT OF ARBITRATION. COMMENTARY TO PART FIFTH OF THE CODE OF CIVIL PROCEDURE], C.H. Beck (2017).

Luca Beffa, *Enforcement of "Default Awards"*, 31(4) ASA BULLETIN 756 (2013).

ALBERT J. VAN DEN BERG, HYPOTHETICAL DRAFT CONVENTION ON THE INTERNATIONAL ENFORCEMENT OF ARBITRATION AGREEMENTS AND AWARDS EXPLANATORY NOTE (2009), available at: https://www.newyorkconvention.org/draft+convention (accessed on 17 August 2021).

Albert J. van den Berg, *New York Convention of 1958: Refusals of Enforcement*, 18(2) ICC INTERNATIONAL COURT OF ARBITRATION BULLETIN 1 (2007).

ALBERT J. VAN DEN BERG, THE NEW YORK CONVENTION OF 1958: AN OVERVIEW, ICCA Website (2003).

ALBERT J. VAN DEN BERG, THE NEW YORK ARBITRATION CONVENTION OF 1958: TOWARDS A UNIFORM JUDICIAL INTERPRETATION, Boston: Kluwer Law and Taxation (1981).

Albert J. van den Berg, *When is an Arbitration Agreement in Writing Valid under Article II(2) of the New York Convention of 1958?*, in PIETER

Czech (& Central European) Yearbook of Arbitration®

SANDERS, EEN HONDERDJARIGE VERNIEUWER, Boom Juridische Uitgevers (2012).

ALBERT J. VAN DEN BERG (ed.), YEARBOOK COMMERCIAL ARBITRATION, Volume XXX (2005).

GARY BORN, INTERNATIONAL COMMERCIAL ARBITRATION, Third Edition, Kluwer Law International (2021).

STAVROS BREKOULAKIS, THIRD PARTIES IN INTERNATIONAL COMMERCIAL ARBITRATION, Oxford University Press (2010).

Beeatrice Castellane, *The New French Law on International Arbitration*, 28(4) JOURNAL OF INTERNATIONAL ARBITRATION, Kluwer Law International 371 (2011).

Emmanuel Gaillard, *The Urgency of Not Revising the New York Convention*, in ICCA CONGRESS SERIES NUMBER 14, Dublin, Kluwer Law International (A. J. Van Den Berg ed., 2009).

EMMANUEL GAILLARD & JOHN SAVAGE, FOUCHARD GAILLARD GOLDMAN ON INTERNATIONAL COMMERCIAL ARBITRATION, Kluwer Law International (1999).

Elliott Geisinger, *Implementing the New York Convention in Switzerland*, 25(6) JOURNAL OF INTERNATIONAL ARBITRATION, Kluwer Law International (2008).

Beata Gessel-Kalinowska vel Kalisz, *Admissibility of Electronic Awards in the UNCITRAL Model Law Jurisdiction: Polish Law Example*, 38(2) JOURNAL OF INTERNATIONAL ARBITRATION, Kluwer Law International 147 (2021).

Martin Frederik Gusy, *The Validity of an Arbitration Agreement Under the New York Convention – Remarks on the Order of OLG Schleswig, March 30, 2000 (16 SchH 5/99)*, 19(4) JOURNAL OF INTERNATIONAL ARBITRATION, Kluwer Law International 363 (2002).

Philipp Habegger, *Extension of Arbitration Agreements to Non-signatories and Requirements of Form*, 22(2) ASA BULLETIN 390 (2004).

ICCA, ICCA'S GUIDE TO THE INTERPRETATION OF THE 1958 NEW YORK CONVENTION: A HANDBOOK FOR JUDGES (2011).

STEFAN KRÖLL & LOUKAS A. MISTELIS & PILAR PERALES VISCASILLAS & VIKKI ROGERS (eds.), LIBER AMICORUM ERIC BERGSTERN. INTERNATIONAL ARBITRATION AND INTERNATIONAL COMMERCIAL LAW: SYNERGY, CONVERGENCE AND EVOLUTION, Alphen aan den Rijn (2011).

Stefan Kröll, *The Arbitration Agreement in Enforcement Proceedings of Foreign Awards. Burden of Proof and the Legal Relevance of the Tribunal's Decision*, in LIBER AMICORUM ERIC BERGSTERN. INTERNATIONAL ARBITRATION AND INTERNATIONAL COMMERCIAL LAW: SYNERGY, CONVERGENCE AND EVOLUTION, ALPHEN AAN DEN RIJN (S. Kröll, L. A. Mistelis, P. Perales Viscasillas, V. Rogers eds., 2011).

JULIAN D. M. LEW & LOUKAS A. MISTELIS & STEFAN KRÖLL, COMPARATIVE INTERNATIONAL COMMERCIAL ARBITRATION, Kluwer Law International (2003).

Christoph Liebscher, *Application of the New York Convention in Austria and Eastern Europe*, 25(6) JOURNAL OF INTERNATIONAL ARBITRATION, Kluwer Law International 771 (2008).

Gunnar Nerdrum, *Norway*, in INTERNATIONAL ARBITRATION COURT DECISIONS (Stephen Bond, Frédéric Bachand eds., 3rd ed. 2011).

Dirk Otto, *Article IV*, in RECOGNITION AND ENFORCEMENT OF FOREIGN ARBITRAL AWARDS: A GLOBAL COMMENTARY ON THE NEW YORK CONVENTION, Kluwer Law International (Herbert Kronke, Patricia Nacimiento et al. eds., 2010).

PIETER SANDERS (ed.), YEARBOOK COMMERCIAL ARBITRATION, Volume X-1985, Kluwer, Netherlands (1985).

Pieter Sanders, *A Twenty Years' Review of the Convention on the Recognition and Enforcement of Foreign Arbitral Awards*, 13(2) THE INTERNATIONAL LAWYER 269 (1979).

Maxi Scherer, *Article III*, in NEW YORK CONVENTION – COMMENTARY, Beck Hart Nomos (Reinmar Wolff ed., 2012).

Maxi Scherer, *Article IV*, in NEW YORK CONVENTION – COMMENTARY, Beck Hart Nomos (Reinmar Wolff ed., 2012).

Stacie I. Strong, *What Constitutes an "Agreement in Writing" in International Commercial Arbitration? Conflicts Between the New York Convention and the Federal Arbitration Act*, 48(1) STANFORD JOURNAL OF INTERNATIONAL LAW 47 (2012).

Tomasz Strumiłło, *Commentary to Art. 1213, paragraph 3*, in KODEKS POSTĘPOWANIA CYWILNEGO. TOM II. KOMENTARZ. ART. 730-1217 [CODE OF CIVIL PROCEDURE. VOL. II. COMMENTARY. ART. 730-1217], C.H. Beck, (J. Jankowski ed. 2019).

UNCITRAL Secretariat Guide on the Convention on the Recognition of Foreign Arbitral Awards (New York, 1958) (2016).

UNCITRAL Recommendation regarding the interpretation of Article II, paragraph 2, and Article VII, paragraph 1, of the Convention on the Recognition and Enforcement of Foreign Arbitral Awards, done in New York, 10 June 1958 (2006).

United Nations General Assembly, *Report of the United Nations Commission on International Trade Law on the work of its thirty-ninth session* (19 June – 7 July 2006), available at: https://undocs.org/en/ A/61/17(SUPP) (accessed on 17 August 2021).

United Nations General Assembly, *Report of Working Group II (Arbitration) on the work of its forty-fourth session* (23 – 27 January 2006), available at: https://undocs.org/en/A/CN.9/592 (accessed on 17 August 2021).

United Nations General Assembly, *Settlement of commercial disputes: Form of arbitration agreement, Note by the Secretariat* (19 June – 7 July 2006), available at: https://undocs.org/en/A/CN.9/606 (accessed on 17 August 2021).

Michael Wietzorek, *The Form of the International Arbitration Agreement under the 2011 French Arbitration Law*, KLUWER ARBITRATION BLOG (7 April 2011), available at: http://arbitrationblog.kluwerarbitration. com/2011/04/07/the-form-of-the-international-arbitration-agreement-under-the-2011-french-arbitration-law/ (accessed on 17 August 2021).

Piotr Wiliński, *Should the Miami Draft be given a second chance? The New York Convention 2.0*, 34 SPAIN ARBITRATION REVIEW, Wolters Kluwer España (2019).

Vasily N. Anurov

Domestic Law and Jurisdiction of Arbitral Tribunals in International Investment Disputes

Key words:
domestic law | international law | international investment arbitration | jurisdiction of Arbitral Tribunals | rule of law | foreign investor | host State

Vasily N. Anurov has a PhD in Law. At the current time he is an associate professor, Arbitrator of the Vilnius Court of Commercial Arbitration, Arbitration Centre at the Russian Union of Industrialists and Entrepreneurs. He also holds an LL.M with distinction from Dundee, Scotland.
E-mail: vasily.anurov@googlemail.com

Abstract | *The role of domestic law in establishment of jurisdiction of Arbitral Tribunals is underestimated in arbitration and court practice. International arbitrators are used to apply more familiar sources of law, particularly, principles and rules on international law rather than ascertain the content of domestic law. Such attitude endangers a perspective of international investment arbitration in many host States as they are losing trust in arbitration and searching for a substitute to settle international investment disputes. These negative consequences will be examined in the example of the YUKOS case and the Achmea issue. These examples were intended to pay more attention to the above said problems and encourage arbitrators to increase the role of domestic law in considering particular cases.*

| | |

Czech (& Central European) Yearbook of Arbitration®

I. Introduction

2.01. International investment arbitration is intended to fulfill one of the main functions in protecting investments made by foreign corporations and persons into the host State's economy. Following the traditional view on arbitration, the contending parties need to achieve a consent to bring their dispute before an Arbitral Tribunal. There is no doubt that foreign investors are willing to use the above said mechanism of dispute resolution as arbitration is associated with a neutral forum composed of unbiased and independent arbitrators who feel free from any influence carried out by State authorities. The situation is more complicated in relation to the host State's consent. Even though investments usually trigger capital flow, involvement of additional production and labor resources, that positively affect any economy, the host State may be exposed to claims submitted by foreign investors when they consider that the host State violated the relevant treaty. By expressing its consent to arbitration, the host State automatically derogates its sovereignty by excluding jurisdiction of the State courts. In this case domestic law remains the most important remedy for the host State to protect its interest in the arbitration proceedings. Unfortunately, the role of domestic law is 'under-appreciated' as noted by author Jarrod Hepburn noted in his book, DOMESTIC LAW IN INTERNATIONAL INVESTMENT ARBITRATION.[1]

2.02. Having an independent status, arbitrators seem to not demonstrate a great willingness to ascertain the content of domestic law in most of the cases. They prefer to directly invoke principles and rules of international law using their power of discretion and to ban judicial review of awards set out in many legal orders. This article will analyze, first the interaction between domestic and international law and then deal with the role of the former in establishment of jurisdiction of Arbitral Tribunals. The most disputable issues will be illustrated with examples from recent cases in arbitration and court practice in the European Union (EU).

II. Interaction Between Domestic and International Law

2.03. Domestic law seems to be the most familiar legal instrument to be applied by Arbitral Tribunals for settlement of cross-border

---

[1] JARROD HEPBURN, DOMESTIC LAW IN INTERNATIONAL INVESTMENT ARBITRATION, Oxford (2017), et. 103.

commercial disputes. The starting point of any legal analysis is establishment of the applicable law which will govern the relevant relationship between the contending parties and deal with all arguments submitted by them during the arbitration proceedings. This algorithm also keeps its effectiveness in settlement of international investment disputes even though the respondent in each proceeding is not a private party but a host state. The Arbitral Tribunal still needs to have a source of law if its mandate is based on a conservative model of arbitration, i.e., the arbitrators doesn't act as *amiable compositeurs* or decide *ex aequo et bono*, but should stick to strict application of legal rules. Article 42(1) of the Convention on the Settlement of Investment Disputes between States and Nationals of Other States on 18 March 1965 (The Washington Convention) follows the above said model by adoption of two rules. The first one allows the parties to designate the law as applicable to the dispute. The second rule addresses the situation when the parties failed to reach such an agreement. In this case, 'the Tribunal shall apply the law of the Contracting State party to the dispute (including its rules on the conflict of laws) and such rules of international law as may be applicable.' In an attempt to comprehend the meaning of the wording cited above and find out the mutual intent of the Contracting States there have been many disagreements. As one of the founders of the Washington Convention, Aron Broches noted in his special course reading in the Hague Academy of International Law that was devoted to interpretation of the Washington Convention, the initial idea of an opportunity to invoke domestic and international law had been strongly opposed by delegates of the developing countries and therefore corrected to achieve a compromise.[2] It serves no purpose to second-guess this decision, but it is important to try to access its ramifications in arbitration practice.

2.04.   The first proposal how to define an applicable law in the absence of the relevant agreement between the parties comes from the *ad hoc* Committee in the *Klockner* case.[3] Having considered the law of the host State and 'such principles as may be applicable', this Committee attributed to international law

---

[2]   Aron Broches, *The Convention on the Settlement of Investment Disputes between States and Nationals of Other States*, 136 HAGUE ACADEMY OF INTERNATIONAL LAW COLLECTED COURSES ('*RECUEIL DES COURS*') 390 (1972).

[3]   *Klockner Industrie-Anlagen GmbH and others v. United Republic of Cameroon*, ICSID case № ARB/81/2 (*Klockner v. Cameroon*). Complementary and corrective function of international law was confirmed by later cases, *inter alia*: *Amco Asia Corporation, P.T. Amco, Pan American Development Limited v. Republic of Indonesia*, ICSID case № ARB/81/1 (*Amco v. Indonesia*), *Liberian Eastern Timber Corporation v. Republic of Liberia*, ICSID case № ARB/83/2 (*LETCO v. Liberia*) and *AGIP S.p.A. v. People's Republic of the Congo*, ICSID case № ARB/77/1 (*AGIP v. Congo*).

only as a complementary and corrective function. Although this interpretation endowed the foreign investor with a right to revise a lacuna or inconsistency of domestic law, the later had an advantage over international law whose role was boiled down to a subsidiary legal source. Emmanuel Galliard and Yas Banifatemi strongly objected to such approach referring to the history of the Washington Convention and its *travaux preparatoires*.[4] There is no express wording neither in the text of the Washington Convention nor in the Report of the Executive Directors on the Washington Convention or any other documents prepared during Legal Committee Meetings that trigger application of international law subject to existence of lacuna in the domestic law or detection of an inconsistency. The problem remains unsolved. Even the *ad hoc* Committee in the *Wena* case didn't shed enough light on this obscure area.[5] It recognized two equal systems of law in governing international investment disputes but didn't create any guidelines in which one case should prevail over the other.[6]

2.05. When the *ad hoc* Committee in the *Klockner* case mentioned principles, it must be remembered that these are not rules of law. Further it specified its position when it stated that 'arbitrators may have recourse to the "principles of international law" only after having inquired into and established the content of the law of the State party to the dispute (which cannot be reduced to one principle, even a basic one) and after having applied the relevant rules of the State's law'.[7] Although one may argue that the definition of 'principles of law' includes rules of law or reflects the most general and fundamental rules, it needs to make some reservations, supporting the difference between the two definitions in question.

2.06. Adoption of traditional legal sources in international law (treaties, customs) mostly depends on convergence of wills, expressed by States in international conferences or their

---

[4]   Emmanuel E. Gaillard & Yas Banifatemi, *The Meaning of "and" in Article 42 (1), Second Sentence, of the Washington Convention: The Role of International Law in the ICSID Choice of Law Process*, 18(2) ICSID REVIEW: FOREIGN INVESTMENT LAW JOURNAL 382 (2003).
[5]   *Wena Hotels Limited* v. *Arab Republic of Egypt*, ICSID case № ARB/98/4 (*Wena* v. *Egypt*).
[6]   The *ad hoc* Committee interpreted Article 42(1) of the Washington Convention in the following way: 'What is clear that the sense and meaning of the negotiations leading to the second sentence of Article 42 (1) allowed for both legal orders to have a role. The law of the host State can indeed be applied in conjunction with international law if this is justified. So too international law can be applied by itself if the appropriate rule is found in this other ambit' (*Wena* v. *Egypt*, Decision on the Application by the Arab Republic of Egypt for Annulment of the Arbitral Award dated 8 December 2000 in the above matter, 5 February 2002 (*Wena* v. *Egypt* (Decision on Annulment), paragraph 40 available at: https://www.italaw.com/sites/default/files/case-documents/ita0903.pdf (accessed on 15 August 2021).
[7]   *Klockner* v. *Cameroon*, Ad hoc Committee Decision, 3 May 1985 (*Klockner* v. *Cameroon* (Decision on Annulment)), paragraph 122 available at: https://www.italaw.com/sites/default/files/case-documents/italaw11161.pdf (accessed on 15 August 2021).

reaction on challenges caused by escalation of relationships with other States. Such an agreement is hardly achieved in the relevant negotiations due to opposite and sometimes contradicting interests pursued by States. Therefore, the Contracting Parties managed to fix only a general approach to address disputable issues in hope that this approach will be later clarified by the Parties' subsequent behavior and practice regarding implementation of the agreed terms. Apparently, this general approach or principle cannot be qualified as a fully-fledged rule of law that is supposed to provide a sufficient legal regulation of the relationship arising between the parties in the future. Thus, international law has less opportunities to give its sources a normative character in comparison with domestic law and settle disputes without broadening the discretion power of arbitral tribunals. W. Reisman has interpreted Article 42(1) of the Washington Convention based on the restrictive role of international law which is supposed to be applied in case of inconsistency of domestic law with non-derogatory norms or rules of *jus cogens*[8] (in Russian doctrine these norms are called principles). Scholars from the opposite camp, including Galliard and Banifatemi, argue that international law is a 'body of substantive rules' and may fulfill the independent function to govern 'a particular issue presented to an ICSID tribunal.'[9]

2.07.   Adherence to the conservative perception of law requires one to find out the appropriate rule, which is capable of dealing with disputable issues not in an abstract manner but take into account all details contained in each case. To do so arbitrators need to follow, at least in their mind, some consistency in analysis of the relevant legal sources. It is not a hierarchy of two systems of law: national and international law, which was rejected by Broches,[10] but a mere attempt to put thoughts in order and structure the subject-matter of the examination.[11] Any favor granted by Arbitral Tribunals to one of the legal sources, being under analysis entails creation of a new hierarchy. For instance, in the *APPL* case the Arbitral Tribunal recognized the BIT as a primary source, general international law and the host State

---

[8]   Michael W. Reisman, *The Regime for Lacunae in the ICSID Choice of Law Provision and the Question of Its Threshold*, 15(2) ICSID REVIEW: FOREIGN INVESTMENT LAW JOURNAL 375 (2000).

[9]   Gaillard, Banifatemi, supra note 4, at 397, 403.

[10]   A. Broches made a special note in his comments to Article 42(1) that 'the order in which the two systems of law are mentioned, national law first and international law second, does not denote their hierarchical order.' (Broches, supra note 2, at 390).

[11]   This consequence of analysis is clearly fixed in the following A. Broches' comments: 'The Tribunal will first look at the law of the host State and that law will in the first instance be applied to the merits of the dispute. Then the result will be tested against international law. That process will not involve the confirmation or denial of the validity of the host State's law, but may result in not applying it where that law, or action taken under that law, violates international law.' (Broches, supra note 2, at 392).

law as a supplementary source. Such hierarchy is substantiated by tacit and mutual agreement achieved by the parties in their submissions or inferred from the relevant BIT.[12]

2.08. The turning point in interpretation of Article 42(1) happened when the Arbitral Tribunal in the *CMS* case declared 'a more pragmatic and less doctrinaire approach', excluding any preference or consequence in application of international and domestic law.[13] In accordance with this approach there will no longer be any limits on arbitrators' freedom to establish an applicable law: choice-of-law mechanism and motivation to implement strict rule of law without any substitutes, such as sources of so-called 'soft law' comprising private codifications, guidelines, recommendations and draft of articles to be incorporated into future treaties. Ironically, the argument made by Galliard and Banifatemi against the 'Klockner-Amco doctrine' may be used against this pragmatic approach as it was rejected in the preparation of the Washington Convention in favor of application of international and domestic law cumulatively rather than as alternatives.[14] However, it is worth noting that domestic law is not mentioned in the following treaties at all: North American Free Trade Agreement on 17 December 1992 (NAFTA) replaced by United States-Mexico-Canada Agreement on 30 November 2018 (USMCA) and Energy Charter Treaty on 17 December 1994 (ECT). These treaties directly give a preference to applicable rules of international law, including them as well in settlement of international investment disputes.[15]

2.09. Besides a high level of abstraction that occurs in most of the principles and rules of international law, Arbitral Tribunals face other challenges restricting their power of discretion. The first group of limits relates to a fixed choice-of-law mechanism set out in the relevant treaty. This mechanism is

---

[12] *Asian Agricultural Products Limited* v. *Democratic Socialist Republic of Sri Lanka*, ICSID case № ARB/87/3, Final Award, 27 June 1990 (*AAPL* v. *Sri Lanka* (Award)), paragraphs 20-22 available at: https://www.italaw.com/sites/default/files/case-documents/ita1034.pdf (accessed on 15 August 2021). The key role of BIT is supported in later cases: *MTD Chile S.A., MTD Equity Sdn. Bhd.* v. *Republic of Chile*, ICSID case № ARB/01/7, Award, 25 May 2004 (*MTD* v. *Chile* (Award), available at: https://www.italaw.com/sites/default/files/case-documents/ita0544.pdf (accessed on 15 August 2021); *ADC Affiliate Limited and ADC & ADMC Management Limited* v. *The Republic of Hungary*, ICSID case № ARB/03/16, Award of the Tribunal, 2 October 2006 (*ADC* v. *Hungary* (Award), paragraphs 290-292 available at: https://www.italaw.com/sites/default/files/case-documents/ita0006.pdf (accessed on 15 August 2021).

[13] *CMS Gas Transmission Company* v. *The Republic of Argentina*, ICSID case № ARB/01/8, Award, 12 May 2005 (*CMS* v. *Argentina* (Award)), paragraph 116 available at: https://www.italaw.com/sites/default/files/case-documents/ita0184.pdf (accessed on 15 August 2021). Also see: *Sempra Energy International* v. *Argentine Republic*, ICSID case № ARB/02/16, Award, 28 September 2007 (*Sempra* v. *Argentina* (Award)), paragraphs 236, 240, available at: https://www.italaw.com/sites/default/files/case-documents/ita0770.pdf (accessed on 15 August 2021).

[14] ANTONIO R. PARRA, THE HISTORY OF ICSID, Oxford (2012), et. 306.

[15] See Article 1131(1) of NAFTA; Article 14.D.9(1) of USMCA and Article 26(6) of ECT.

incorporated in Article 42(1) of the Washington Convention. However, arbitrators may muster their efforts in examining of international law and neglect similar research of domestic law. Due to the binding effect of the award and obligations of each Contracting State to recognize and enforce the pecuniary obligations imposed by that award, as it is prescribed by Article 54(1) of the Washington Convention, local courts have no right to interfere or somehow influence an arbitrators' decision in relation to the applicable law. The second group of limits may be demonstrated by the example of arbitration proceedings conducted based on the ECT and UNCITRAL Arbitration Rules in edition of 1976 and 2010 (UNCITRAL Rules). In this case arbitrators are not tied to apply domestic law, that is not mentioned in the relevant Article 26(6) of the ECT. However, they should consider that the award will be checked by a local court for compliance with requirements enumerated in the New-York Convention on the Recognition and Enforcement of Foreign Arbitral Awards on 10 June 1958. Although the award cannot be reviewed on merits by the local court, the latter may have a different view on interpretation of international law and refer to local public policy as a ground for refusal to recognize and enforce the award. Therefore, both groups of limits require Arbitral Tribunals to draw special attention to domestic law in settlement of international investment disputes.

III. The Role of Domestic Law in the Establishment of Jurisdiction of Arbitral Tribunals

2.10. There is no doubt that Article 42(1) of the Washington Convention is devoted to the choice of substantive law governing the merits of the dispute. This Article does not address jurisdiction of the ICSID Tribunal and gives no guidelines which law should be applied to solve such issues. We can see the same situation in other treaties, including the ECT. Therefore, Arbitral Tribunals are entitled to use a broad power of discretion to establish a consent to arbitration expressed by the host State in the relevant terms of treaties and considered as a standing offer in accordance with the arbitration without the privity approach proposed by Jan Paulsson.[16] He asserted that based on the well-known principle of competence-competence,

---

[16] Jan Paulsson, *Arbitration Without Privity*, 10(2) ICSID REVIEW, FOREIGN INVESTMENT LAW JOURNAL 256 (1995). Also see: CHRISTOPH H. SCHREUER, CONSENT TO ARBITRATION, The Oxford Handbook of International Investment Law, Oxford (P. Muchlinski, F. Ortino and C. Shreuer eds., 2008), et. 836.

arbitrators do not care whether the consent to arbitration is recognized by official authorities or courts of the host State. As Gus Van Harten noted, Arbitral Tribunals' propensity to broad interpretation of treaties, frequently in favor of investors may be explained by arbitrators' strong motivation 'to expand the system's appeal to potential claimants and, in turn, their own prospects for future appointment'.[17] Apparently, it is not acceptable for host States that are losing their trust in arbitration and trying to replace it by international courts to be established for settlement of international investment disputes. One of the key reasons to do so is a natural desire to be judged by a predictable and understandable attitude for interpretation and implementation of rules of law. Unfortunately, neither international law nor discretion of arbitrators can provide that. The only source capable to meet with Contracting States' requirements is domestic law or Union of States law which has a special court capable to secure uniform interpretation of such law, for instance EU law. Further consider its effectiveness in two of the most notorious events in recent arbitration practice: the *YUKOS* case and the *Achmea* issue.

2.11. The jurisdiction of the Arbitral Tribunal in the *YUKOS* case could not be considered without application of the Russian law to access whether the provisional application of the ECT is consistent with the Russian Constitution, laws or regulations. As the Russian Federation only signed the ECT but did not ratify it and even notified the ECT Depository of its intention not to become a party to the ECT, provisional application of the ECT in the Russian Federation envisaged in Article 45 of the ECT remained the sole basis for the Arbitral Tribunal's jurisdiction. Several forums took the opposite views on this subject and the issue is still not finalized pending a decision of the Supreme Court of Netherlands. First, the Arbitral Tribunal concluded that the ECT, including its dispute resolution provision set out in Article 26 of the ECT is inconsistent with Russian law and dismissed the objections to the jurisdiction raised by the Russian Federation. To make this decision the arbitrators examined the Russian Federation's Law on Foreign Investment in the 1991 and 1999 editions (LFI 1991 and LFI 1999 correspondingly), Civil Code of the Russian Federation and even the ECT Explanatory Note to the Duma (lower chamber of the Russian Parliament). This directly stipulated that the ECT 'is consistent with the provisions of the existing law on foreign investment and does

---

[17] GUS VAN HARTEN, INVESTMENT TREATY ARBITRATION AND PUBLIC LAW, Oxford (2007), et. vii.

not require the acknowledgement of any concessions or the adoption of any amendment to the abovementioned Law.'[18] This wording was reviewed by the Hague District Court and its interpretation produced an opposite result in comparison with the Arbitral Tribunal's finding. The Court elucidated that the opinion of the Russian government cannot be ascribed to the legislative power and the fact that the ECT was never ratified refuted a presumption that the above said opinion prevailed in Russian law. Also, the ECT Explanatory Note did not address provisional application of Article 26 of the ECT which is contrary to Russian law.[19]

2.12. The third round of the debate on the provisional application of the ECT occurred in the Court of Appeal of the Hague. It did not agree with the view taken by the lower court (the Hague District Court) and quashed the latter's judgment. The Court of Appeal clarified the subject of the analysis by locating any grounds or support in sources of Russian law, including LFI 1991, LFI 1999, the ECT Explanatory Note and explanatory notes to other BITs referred by the Russian Federation for conclusion that international investment arbitration is inconsistent with Russian law. The Court of Appeal found no grounds or support to this position and directly noted that it cannot be deduced from the Russian law.[20]

2.13. The *YUKOS* case demonstrates the significant role of domestic law in solving of one of the essential issues of jurisdiction – the host State's consent to arbitration. Both courts (the Hague District Court and Court of Appeal of the Hague) made a thorough and independent analysis of Russian law to check the correctness of the decision on jurisdiction made by the Arbitral Tribunal. The scope of examination covers so many acts of the Russian legislation, articles of the Russian scholars and witness statements of the prominent experts in Russian law,

---

[18] *Hulley* v. *The Russian Federation*, Interim Award on Jurisdiction and Admissibility, 30 November 2009 (*Hulley* v. *Russia* (Award on Jurisdiction), paragraph 367 available at: https://www.italaw.com/sites/default/files/case-documents/ita0411.pdf (accessed on 15 August 2021); *Yukos* v. *The Russian Federation*, Interim Award on Jurisdiction and Admissibility, 30 November 2009 (*Yukos* v. *Russia* (Award on Jurisdiction), paragraph 367 available at: https://www.italaw.com/sites/default/files/case-documents/ita0910.pdf (accessed on 15 August 2021); *Veteran* v. *The Russian Federation*, Interim Award on Jurisdiction and Admissibility, 30 November 2009 (*Veteran* v. *Russia* (Award on Jurisdiction), paragraph 367 available at: https://www.italaw.com/sites/default/files/case-documents/ita0891.pdf (accessed on 15 August 2021).

[19] *De Russische Federetie t. Yukos Universal Limited*, № C/09/477162/HA ZA 15-2; *De Russische Federetie t. Hulley Enterprises Limited*, № C/09/481619/HA ZA 15-112, Rechbank Den Haag, Vonnis, 20.04.2016 (*De Russische Federetie t. HVY* (Vonnis)), paragraph 5.60 available at: https://www.italaw.com/sites/default/files/case-documents/italaw7255.pdf (accessed on 15 August 2021).

[20] *De Russische Federetie t. Yukos Universal Limited*, № C/09/477162/HA ZA 15-2; *De Russische Federetie t. Hulley Enterprises Limited*, № C/09/481619/HA ZA 15-112, Gerechshof Den Haag, Arrest, 18.02.2020 (*De Russische Federetie t. HVY* (Arrest)), paragraphs 4.7.56.-4.7.57 available at: https://www.italaw.com/sites/default/files/case-documents/italaw10079.pdf (accessed on 15 August 2021).

that designates the provision of the ECT on dispute resolution as a rule of law rather than the usual offer addressed to potential investors. To understand the meaning of such rules of law it needs to go beyond the arbitrators' discretion, their skills to interpret treaty provisions and delve into details of the host State law including all its legal sources: legislation, court practice and doctrine.

2.14. The *Achmea* issue was raised by several EU States in the arbitration proceedings to convince the Arbitral Tribunals that settlement of intra-EU investment disputes in arbitration is inconsistent with the EU law. The first attack against international investment arbitration was carried out by the European Court of Justice (ECJ) on 6 March 2018. Actually, the ECJ proclaimed that the EU law, particularly Article 267 (preliminary rulings procedure) and Article 344 (settlement of disputes concerning the interpretation and application of the EU treaties) of the Treaty on the Functioning of the European Union on 13 December 2007 (TFEU), precludes an investor from one of the EU States to initiate arbitration proceedings against the other EU State if the latter is alleged to violate a BIT concluded between these two EU States. As an arbitral tribunal does not belong to the EU judicial system there is a great concern that certain values of the EU legal order may be exposed by the award: principles of mutual trust, sincere cooperation and uniform interpretation of the EU.[21] However, arbitrators prefer to apply only Article 26 of the ECT as a sole legal source relating to issues of jurisdiction. The EU law and ECJ judgment on the *Achmea* issue mentioned above are not to be considered since they do not constitute general principles of international law.[22] Even Article 344 of the TFEU which must have derogated from Article 26 of the ECT in part due to *lex posterior* effect, cannot restrict the power of discretion used by the arbitrators to continue arbitration proceedings.[23] They merely state that there

---

[21] *Slowakische Republik* v. *Achmea BV*, Court (Grand Chamber), case № C-284/16, Judgment, 6 March 2018 (*Slovakia* v. *Achmea* (Judgment)), paragraph 57-58 available at: https://www.italaw.com/sites/default/files/case-documents/italaw9548_0.pdf (accessed on 15 August 2021).
[22] *Vattenfall AB, Vattenfall GmbH, Vattenfall Europe Nuclear Energy GmbH, Kernkraftwerk Krummel GmbH & Co. oHG, Kernkraftwerk Brunsbuttel GmbH & Co. oHG* v. *Federal Republic of Germany*, ICSID case № ARB/12/12, Decision on the Achmea Issue, 31 August 2018 (*Vattenfall* v. *Germany* (Decision on the Achmea Issue), paragraphs 129, 133, 166-167 available at: https://www.italaw.com/sites/default/files/case-documents/italaw9916.pdf (accessed on 15 August 2021). Also see: *Eskosol S.p.A. in liquidazione* v. *Italian Republic*, ICSID case № ARB/15/50, Decision on Italy's Request for Immediate Termination and Italy's Jurisdictional Objection Based on Inapplicability of the Energy Charter Treaty to Intra-EU Disputes, 7 May 2019 (*Eskosol* v. *Italy* (Decision on Inapplicability of ECT to Intra-EU Disputes), paragraph 121 available at: https://www.italaw.com/sites/default/files/case-documents/italaw10512.pdf (accessed on 15 August 2021).
[23] Bukhard Hess, *The Fate of Investment Dispute Resolution after the Achmea Decision of the European Court of Justice*, 3 MAX PLANK INSTITUTE LUXEMBURG FOR PROCEDURAL LAW RESEARCH PAPER SERIAS 16 (2018).

is no identity of subject matter between the EU law, including TFEU and the ECT or the relevant BIT – a precondition for application of Article 30 of the Vienna Convention on the Law of Treaties on 23 May 1969, giving a priority for a successive treaty.[24]

2.15. The similar formalistic approach is demonstrated by Arbitral Tribunals in not recognizing the next attempt made by the EU States to express their negative attitude to international investment arbitration – adoption of the Declaration of the Governments of the Member States on the legal consequences of the judgment of the Court of Justice in *Achmea* and on investment protection in the European Union on 15 January 2019 signed by 22 EU States (Declaration 2019).[25] The binding effect of this Declaration was denied by the Arbitral Tribunal in *Addiko* case because of lack of identity between the original intent of the Contracting parties (Austria and Croatia) during BIT negotiations and their new shared understanding enshrined in the Declaration 2019.[26] We can hope that the Agreement for the termination of bilateral treaties between the Member states of the European Union on 29 May 2020 will put an end to the uncertain regime of intra-EU disputes.

IV. Conclusion

2.16. In the *YUKOS* case and cases concerning the *Achmea* issue the host States desperately tried to challenge jurisdiction of the Arbitral Tribunals invalidating the provisions on dispute resolution set out in the relevant treaties. The host States invoked all admissible remedies to show their disinclination to settle the investment dispute in arbitration, but the arbitrators were not

---

[24] *Eastern Sugar B.V.* v. *Czech Republic*, SCC case № 008/2004, Partial Award, 27 March 2007 (*Eastern Sugar* v. *Czech Republic* (Award), paragraphs 159-160 available at: https://www.italaw.com/sites/default/files/case-documents/ita0259_0.pdf (accessed on 15 August 2021); *Jan Oostergetel and Theodora Laurentius* v. *Slovak Republic*, UNCITRAL case, Decision on Jurisdiction, 30 April 2010 (*Oostergetel* v. *Slovak Republic*, Decision on Jurisdiction)), paragraphs 74-75 available at: https://www.italaw.com/sites/default/files/case-documents/ita1073_0.pdf (accessed on 15 August 2021); *EURAM* v. *Slovak Republic*, Award on Jurisdiction, 22 October 2012 (*EURAM* v. *Slovak Republic* (Award on Jurisdiction)), paragraphs 184-185 available at: https://www.italaw.com/sites/default/files/case-documents/italaw4226.pdf (accessed on 15 August 2021); *Electrabel S.A.* v. *The Republic of Hungary*, ICSID case № ARB/07/19, Decision on Jurisdiction, Applicable Law and Liability, 30 November 2012 (*Electrabel* v. *Hungary* (Decision on Jurisdiction)), paragraph 4.176 available at: https://www.italaw.com/sites/default/files/case-documents/italaw1071clean.pdf (accessed on 15 August 2021); *Eskosol* v. *Italy* (Decision on Inapplicability of ECT to Intra-EU Disputes), paragraphs 146-147; *Vattenfall* v. *Germany* (Decision on the Achmea Issue), paragraph 214.
[25] There are two more Declarations signed by other EU States: Declaration of 5 Member States on the enforcement of the *Achmea* Judgment on 16 January 2019 and Declaration of Hungary on the Legal consequences of the *Achmea* Judgment on 16 January 2019.
[26] *Addiko Bank AG and Addiko Bank d.d.* v. *Republic of Croatia*, ICASID case № ARB/17/37, Decision on Croatia's Jurisdictional Objection Related to the Alleged Incompatibility of the BIT with the EU Acquis, 12 June 2020 (*Addiko* v. *Croatia* (Decision on Inapplicability of BIT with EU Acquis), paragraph 289 available at: https://www.italaw.com/sites/default/files/case-documents/italaw11546.pdf (accessed on 15 August 2021). | **37**

persuaded by such efforts. The tactic victories achieved by the investors in particular cases led to a loss of trust in arbitration as a fair mechanism for settlement of disputes and enhanced a search for its substitute – international courts. Probably investment arbitration will soon leave the international stage and the emergence of new treaties and cases at the beginning of this century, which was compared with the 'baby boom' will be transferred to a stampede of the host States from the arbitration area.

2.17. The reasons for such a negative scenario lie on the surface as they derive from the history of investment arbitration, particularly the history of the Washington Convention. The great concern expressed by developing countries that comprise a majority of host States was to have sufficient legal guaranties to protect their interest in arbitration proceedings. One of these guaranties was the application of domestic law. Unfortunately, most of Arbitral Tribunals neglect this concern and prefer to concentrate their attention at international law rather than finding out an appropriate and detailed answer in domestic law. This is true in relation to the merits of the dispute as well as jurisdiction of the Arbitral Tribunal. A host State deserves the right to be judged by the rules of law belonging to its own legal order and only if these rules contradict with international law, should the latter be considered.

| | |

Summaries

DEU [*Das nationale Recht und die Gerichtsbarkeit von Schiedsgerichten in internationalen Investitions-streitigkeiten*]

Die Rolle des innerstaatlichen Rechts betreffend die Gerichtsbarkeit von Schiedsgerichten wird in der schiedsgerichtlichen und gerichtlichen Praxis vernachlässigt. Internationale Schiedsrichter sind es gewöhnt, bekanntere Rechtsquellen anzuwenden – insbesondere die Grundsätze und Regeln des internationalen Rechts – anstelle den Inhalt des jeweiligen nationalen Rechts in Erfahrung zu bringen. Dieser Ansatz verheißt in einer Reihe von Gastländern nichts Gutes für die Aussichten des internationalen kommerziellen Schiedsverfahrens, denn diese Länder verlieren damit ihr Vertrauen in das Schiedsverfahren und suchen nach alternativen Beilegungswegen für internationale Investitionsstreitigkeiten. Der Autor bewertet diese nachteiligen

Folgen am Beispiel der YUKOS-Entscheidung und des Problems Achmea. Diese Beispiele sollten die o.g. Probleme in den Brennpunkt des Interesses rücken und Schiedsrichter anregen, dafür zu sorgen, dass dem nationalen Recht künftig bei der Verhandlung nnd Entscheidung von konkreten Rechtssachen eine größere Rolle eingeräumt wird.

CZE   [***Vnitrostátní právo a pravomoc rozhodčích soudů v mezinárodních sporech z investic***]
Úloha vnitrostátního práva ohledně pravomoci rozhodčích soudů se v rozhodčí a soudní praxi podceňuje. Mezinárodní rozhodci jsou zvyklí aplikovat známější prameny práva, zejména zásady a pravidla mezinárodního práva, spíše než zjišťovat obsah práva vnitrostátního. Tento přístup ohrožuje perspektivu mezinárodní obchodní arbitráže v řadě hostitelských zemí, neboť tyto země přestávají rozhodčímu řízení důvěřovat a hledají náhradní řešení mezinárodních sporů z investic. Tyto negativní důsledky autor posuzuje na příkladu rozhodnutí ve věci YUKOS a problému Achmea. Tyto příklady měly za cíl zviditelnit výše uvedené problémy a pobídnout rozhodce k tomu, aby zajistili, že při projednávání konkrétních věcí bude vnitrostátní právo hrát větší roli.

| | |

POL   [***Prawo krajowe i kompetencje sądów arbitrażowych w międzynarodowych sporach inwestycyjnych***]
Głównym celem artykułu jest podkreślenie kluczowej roli prawa krajowego w zakresie kompetencji sądów arbitrażowych w odniesieniu do międzynarodowych sporów inwestycyjnych. Analiza prawna składa się z dwóch części: pierwsza część została poświęcona wzajemnym relacjom między prawem krajowym i międzynarodowym, w drugiej części omówiono rolę prawa krajowego w odniesieniu do kompetencji sądów arbitrażowych. Autor pokazuje najbardziej kontrowersyjne problemy w drugiej części na przykładzie orzeczenia w sprawie YUKOS i problemu Achmea – dwóch istotnych sporów w ostatnim czasie, które prawdopodobnie wpłyną na rozwój międzynarodowego arbitrażu inwestycyjnego w Unii Europejskiej.

FRA   [***Le droit national et la compétence des tribunaux arbitraux dans les litiges internationaux relatifs aux investissements***]
Le principal objectif du présent article est de souligner le rôle que joue le droit national en ce qui concerne la compétence des

tribunaux arbitraux dans les litiges internationaux relatifs aux investissements. L'analyse juridique présentée se fait en deux temps : tout d'abord, l'auteur examine les relations qui existent entre les droits national et international, puis il réfléchit sur le rôle du droit national par rapport à la compétence des tribunaux arbitraux. Dans cette deuxième catégorie, l'auteur illustre les cas les plus controversés : la décision rendue dans l'affaire YUKOS et l'affaire Achmea, deux importants litiges récents, qui sont susceptibles d'influencer l'avenir de l'arbitrage international d'investissement dans l'Union européenne.

RUS   [*Национальное право и компетенция арбитражных судов в международных инвестиционных спорах*]
Главная цель настоящей статьи заключается в том, чтобы подчеркнуть ключевую роль национального права в установлении юрисдикции арбитражных трибуналов, рассматривающих международные инвестиционные споры. Правовое исследование состоит из двух частей: первая часть – взаимодействие между национальным и международным правом и вторая – роль национального права в установлении юрисдикции арбитражных трибуналов. Автор иллюстрирует наиболее спорные вопросы второй части на примере дела YUKOS и вопроса Achmea – двух значительных недавних событий, которые вероятно окажут влияние на развитие международного инвестиционного арбитража в Европейском союзе.

ESP   [*Derecho nacional y competencia de los tribunales de arbitraje en los litigios de inversión internacionales*]
El objetivo principal de este artículo es destacar el papel clave de la legislación nacional en lo que respecta a la competencia de los tribunales de arbitraje en materia de los litigios de inversión internacionales. El análisis jurídico consta de dos partes: en la primera se indaga sobre la interrelación entre el derecho nacional y el derecho internacional, mientras que la segunda parte da cuenta del papel del derecho nacional con respecto a la competencia de los tribunales de arbitraje. El autor presenta las cuestiones más controvertidas expuestas en la segunda parte y las demuestra con el ejemplo de los laudos relativos al caso YUKOS y Achmea, dos importantes litigios recientes que muy probablemente influirán en la evolución del arbitraje de inversiones internacional en la Unión Europea.

| | |

Czech (& Central European) Yearbook of Arbitration®

Bibliography:

Aron Broches, *The Convention on the Settlement of Investment Disputes between States and Nationals of Other States*, 136 HAGUE ACADEMY OF INTERNATIONAL LAW COLLECTED COURSES ('*RECUEIL DES COURS*') 390 (1972).

Emmanuel E. Gaillard & Yas Banifatemi, *The Meaning of "and" in Article 42 (1), Second Sentence, of the Washington Convention: The Role of International Law in the ICSID Choice of Law Process*, 18(2) ICSID REVIEW: FOREIGN INVESTMENT LAW JOURNAL 382 (2003).

GUS VAN HARTEN, INVESTMENT TREATY ARBITRATION AND PUBLIC LAW, Oxford (2007).

JARROD HEPBURN, DOMESTIC LAW IN INTERNATIONAL INVESTMENT ARBITRATION, Oxford (2017).

Bukhard Hess, *The Fate of Investment Dispute Resolution after the Achmea Decision of the European Court of Justice*, 3 MAX PLANK INSTITUTE LUXEMBURG FOR PROCEDURAL LAW RESEARCH PAPER SERIAS 16 (2018).

ANTONIO R. PARRA, THE HISTORY OF ICSID, Oxford (2012).

Jan Paulsson, *Arbitration Without Privity*, 10(2) ICSID REVIEW, FOREIGN INVESTMENT LAW JOURNAL 256 (1995).

Michael W. Reisman, *The Regime for Lacunae in the ICSID Choice of Law Provision and the Question of Its Threshold*, 15(2) ICSID REVIEW: FOREIGN INVESTMENT LAW JOURNAL 375 (2000).

CHRISTOPH H. SCHREUER, CONSENT TO ARBITRATION, The Oxford Handbook of International Investment Law, Oxford (P. Muchlinski, F. Ortino and C. Shreuer eds., 2008).

Silvia Petruzzino

The Enforcement of Arbitral Interim Measures in the Framework of International Commercial Arbitration

Key words:
Interim measures | enforcement | arbitral tribunals | national courts | international commercial arbitration | arbitral proceedings | interim award | injunction | New York Convention | 2006 UNCITRAL Model Law

Czech (& Central European) Yearbook of Arbitration®

Abstract | *This article analyses the function, importance and development of the arbitral interim measures in the framework of international commercial arbitration. More particularly, the text examines the key issues to be considered for ensuring the effectiveness of arbitral interim measures. In this context, the crucial point is the enforcing system of such provisional reliefs and the relevant legal evolution. Due to the norms set forth under the 2006 UNCITRAL Model Law and to the consistent alignment of most national jurisdictions, it is undeniably within the wide power, respectively, of arbitral tribunals to order interim measures and national courts to enforce such measures. However, the force of these injunctions depend on: i) the legal instruments available in each jurisdiction system where the injunctive interim measures are likely to be enforced in the case of noncompliance with the arbitral order by the enjoined party and ii) the existence of the arbitral interim provision requested in the potential place of enforcement. In that respect this paper, after having outlined the difference between the civil law and the common law jurisdictions with reference to the powers of the national courts if a party does not observe the arbitral injunction, focuses on the recent case law. From the analysis of such jurisprudence, it appears that arbitral interim measures are likely to be gaining ground by most jurisdictions in terms of their enforcement. However, some exceptions to this general trend still exist.*

Silvia Petruzzino is the founding member of the Petruzzino Law Firm, a law firm which specializes in corporate commercial and technical law for Swiss and foreign clients, based in Lugano, Switzerland. She is a member of the Ticino Bar Association, the Swiss Bar Association and the Swiss Arbitration Association. Silvia Petruzzino focuses on commercial and corporate matters, transnational litigation and arbitration.
E-mail: sp@ petruzzinolawfirm.com

| | |

I. Introduction

3.01. The scope of the interim measures is to protect the parties' rights before or during the arbitral proceedings in order to prevent certain circumstances from occurring prior or during the arbitration that may affect a successful award.[1] However, when a party of an international commercial arbitration needs an interim measure, there are several key issues to be considered such as the kind of interim orders to be issued, the competent body which grants those reliefs, the seat of the arbitral proceeding, the enforcing countries and the interaction/ cooperation between the arbitral tribunals and the national courts to ensure the effectiveness of an interim provision.

3.02. Accordingly, it is crucial to trace the current international practices to comprehend the enforcing system of interim measures issued by arbitral tribunals and how to secure the applicant's rights if the enjoined party does not spontaneously abide by the arbitral interim order.

II. The Legal Framework and Its Evolution of Arbitral Interim Measures

3.03. Any interim, partial or interlocutory award is likely to represent an interim measure. The interlocutory award may cover matters arising during the arbitral proceedings that require an interim decision prior to the phase of issuing the final award. Therefore, an interim decision does not finally set the parties' claims on the merits, but its function is to provide a temporary or provisional decision on an issue.

3.04. A provisional order may be appropriate, for instance, to demand payment on a provisional basis, to safeguard the interest of one party, the subject matter of the proceedings or the evidence.[2] Obviously, the final award can integrally modify or cancel the interim measure granted by the partial award.

3.05. The temporary nature is, therefore, the main characteristic of an interim measure. Accordingly, a partial award that imposes an

---

[1] For instance a lack of assests of the losing party inevitable frustrates the rights of the winning party.

[2] A comprehensive definition of interim measures granted by the arbitral tribunal is contained in the 2010 Uncitral Arbitration Rules as follows:

An interim measure is any temporary measure by which, at any time, prior to the issuance of the award by which the dispute is finally decided, the arbitral tribunal orders to a party, for example and without limitation, to:

Maintain or restore the status quo pending determination of the dispute;

Take action that would prevent, or refrain from taking action that is likely to cause, (i) current or imminent harm or (ii) prejudice to the arbitral process itself;

Provide a means of preserving assets out of which a subsequent award may be satisfied; or Preserve evidence that may be relevant and material to the resolution of the dispute (Article 26 of 2010 Uncitral Arbitration Rules).

interim order seems to be not enforceable under the New York Convention,[3] which only deals with the awards that achieve the status of finality.[4] However, according to the case law,[5] albeit the New York Convention is silent about the enforceability and finality of arbitral interim orders, such interim provisions become final and enforceable when they are in the form of final award to be pronounced by the tribunal.

3.06. The power of arbitrators to issue interim measures depends, from one side, on the rules applicable to the arbitral proceedings, and from the other side, on the law of the national court of competent jurisdiction, e.g. the place of the *exequatur* of the arbitral injunction.

3.07. Certainly, the rules of international arbitration adopted by the major arbitral institutions permit the arbitrators to grant interim measures.[6] However, despite the fact that since 1998 the interim measures have become increasingly important,[7] national law has frequently denied arbitrators the power to order interim measures.[8]

3.08. A decisive innovation in interim measure enforcement has occurred thanks to the new Article 17 of UNCITRAL Model Law of International Commercial Arbitration as amended in 2006,[9] which contains extensive provisions on interim measures.

---

[3]   The New York Convention of 15 June 1958 on the Recognition and Enforcement of Foreign Arbitral Awards, available at: http://www.uncitral.org/uncitral/en/uncitral texts/arbitration/NYConvention.html (accessed on 06 September 2021).

[4]   The lack of enforceability of the interim measures under the New York Convention has been debated for several years by the scholars and by the drafters of the UNCITRAL 1976 Arbitration Rules. The latter fashioned the provisions of the UNCITRAL 1976 Arbitration Rules in a such manner that the arbitrators' interim measures might conceivably benefit from the enforcement system of the New York Convention. They did this by authorizing arbitral tribunals not only to 'take any interim measures it deems necessary', but to do so possibly 'in the form of an interim award' and by further providing that an arbitral tribunal usually 'shall be entitled to make interim, interlocutory, or partial awards' in addition to 'final award'. By underlying that interim measures might be issued in the form of award, the drafters seemed to aim at their possible enforcement under the New York Convention. Albeit the New York Convention does not describe enforceable award in any way that expressly excludes interim awards, Article III of such convention requires that 'each Contracting State shall recognize arbitral awards as binding and enforce them'. However, the majority of jurisdictions exclude the enforceability of an interim measure under the New York Convention. To such regard see James E. Castello & Rami Chahine, *Enforcement of interim measures*, GLOBAL ARBITRATION REVIEW (08 June 2021), available at: https://globalarbitrationreview.com/guide/the-guide-challenging-and-enforcing-arbitration-awards/2nd-edition/article/enforcement-of-interim-measures (accessed on 06 September 2021). For a further analysis on this topic see Jan K. Schäfer, *Enforcement of Interim Measures*, in VIII CONGRESSO DO CENTRO DE ARBITRAGEM COMERCIAL, CENTRO DE ARBITRAGEM COMERCIAL (2015), et. 77 ff.

[5]   See paragraph IV.

[6]   See also the arbitration rules adopted by ICC, Uncitral, LCIA, AAA, Swiss Arbitration Centre.

[7]   On the evolution of the legal framework for the enforcement of the interim measures issued by the arbitrators see James E. Castello & Rami Chahine, *supra* note 4.

[8]   For instance, Switzerland, Italy, Austria, Spain, Germany, Greece and Austria that barred arbitrators from issuing interim measures, which were thus only available from national courts. See GARY B. BORN, INTERNATIONAL COMMERCIAL ARBITRATION, New York: Wolters Kluwer (2009), et. 1949 - 1950.

[9]   See Article 17 of UNCITRAL Model Law of International Commercial Arbitration as amended in 2006, available at: https://uncitral.un.org/sites/uncitral.un.org/files/media-documents/uncitral/en/19-09955_e_ebook.pdf (accessed on 06 September 2021). On UNCITRAL arbitration see THOMAS H. WEBSTAR, | 45

Notably, subsections 17H and 17I establishes an explicit right and mechanism to enforce arbitral interim measures in the national courts of any relevant jurisdiction. Paragraph 17H requires that an arbitral interim measure, 'shall be recognized as binding and (...) enforced upon application to the competent court, irrespective of the country in which it was issued', subject to certain limited grounds for non-enforcement set forth in paragraph 17I.

3.09. The Article 17 of the 2006 UNCITRAL Model Law, also, contains several provisions concerning the temporary nature of interim measures and the relevant power of revision granted to the arbitrators, confirming that a tribunal that has issued an interim measure may at any time 'modify, suspend or terminate' such measure. Thereby, the tribunals can require any party that has obtained an interim measure 'promptly to disclose any material change in the circumstances on the basis of which the measure was requested or grounded'. Likewise, a party that has obtained court enforcement of such a measure 'shall promptly inform the court of any termination, suspension, or modification of that interim measure'.

3.10. Another provision that extends the enforcement of the interim measure permits the tribunals that confronts an interim measure 'incompatible with the powers conferred upon' to 'reformulate the interim measure to the extent necessary to adapt it to its own powers and procedures for the purposes of enforcing that (...) measure'.

3.11. At last, any court that enforces an interim measure 'shall not, in making that determination, undertake a review of the substance of the interim measure'.

3.12. From the analysis of the above provisions as introduced by the 2006 UNCITRAL Model Law, it is immediately noted that such provisions are addressed to arbitral tribunals rather than State courts: this approach adopted by the drafters of the 2006 UNCITRAL Model Law is an indication about which interim measures tribunals are entitled to issue and when and how they can do so. Therefore, the scope is 'to reassure courts that were asked to enforce arbitral interim measures that these measures were issued pursuant to a tribunal's clear authority, and (...) to encourage national legislatures to enact a Model Law that required courts to enforce such measures'.[10]

3.13. Indeed, even though the requests of interim measures constantly increase, arbitral tribunals may be hesitant about issuing interim

HANDBOOK OF UNCITRAL ARBITRATION, London: Sweet & Maxwell (2015).
[10] For further remarks see James E. Castello & Rami Chahine, *supra* note 4.

measures due to the uncertain enforceability, a key point for the effectiveness of the measure and, as a result, decide not to issue such measures. Therefore, the parties seek interim measures from national courts instead of arbitrators in situation where the latter would be fully entitled to issue an interim measure. It causes unnecessary costs and delay (e.g., because of the need to translate documents into the language of the court and the need to present evidence and arguments to the judge)[11] and may compromise the effectiveness of the entire arbitral proceedings.

3.14. The new Article 17 of the 2006 UNCITRAL Model Law allows the arbitral tribunal to be more confident in issuing interim measures. The provisions contained in Article 17 of Model Law (2006) are almost identical to Article 26 of the latest version of the UNCITRAL Arbitration Rules (2010).

3.15. The huge value of the UNCITRAL provisions on the interim measures is the full recognition of the importance of such initiatives during the arbitration and their enforceability, without which the success of the whole arbitral proceedings would be jeopardized. Accordingly, most jurisdictions have now adopted national law based on the UNCITRAL Model Law.[12] As a result, almost all jurisdictions now permit the issuance of interim measures to arbitral tribunal instead of national courts. More particular, in Europe the restriction now persists only in Italy, whereas Switzerland, Germany and Austria permit the arbitrator to issue interim measures.[13]

III.   Nuts and Bolts on the Enforcement of Arbitral Interim Measures

3.16. Even though the arbitral interim measures have a temporary nature like all protective injunctions, once ordered, they are final and binding for the parties of the arbitral proceedings. Hence, the enjoined party must comply with those arbitral provisions.

3.17. As analysed in the previous Paragraph, according to the requirements set forth under the UNCITRAL Model Law and to the consequent aligning of most national jurisdictions, the

---

[11]   See Secretary General, *Possible Uniform Rules on Certain Issues Concerning Settlement of Commercial Disputes: Conciliation, Interim Measures of Protection, Written Form for Arbitration Agreement*, United Nations Digital Library, UN Doc. A/CN.9/WG.II/WP.108 24, 24 (2000), available at: https://digitallibrary.un.org/record/407425 (accessed on 06 September 2021).

[12]   Available at: https://uncitral.un.org/en/texts/arbitration/modellaw/commercial_arbitration/status (accessed on 06 September 2021). As rightly stated by an eminent author 'the constitutional character of the Convention contemplated that Contracting States' legislation would need to change, to give full effect to the Convention, and that States' views of non-arbitrability and public policy would evolve over time; there is no reason that the term 'award' should not include reasoned, signed decisions by arbitrators on requests for provisional measures when Contracting States have (almost universally) recognized the authority of arbitrators to grant such relief' (GARY B. BORN, *supra* note 8, at 2515).

[13]   *Ibid.*, at 1949, 1950.

arbitral tribunals have wide authority to order interim measures and the national courts are entitled to enforce arbitral interim measures. In any case, the effectiveness of the enforcement of arbitral interim measures depends upon the national law of the country in which the measure shall be enforced. In this context, prior to requesting to the national court, the enforcement of an interim relief issued by the arbitrators, the parties should ascertain if the form of the relief sought can be effectively enforced by the national court.

3.18. It is noted that the parties are open to retain the national courts for enforcing a measure issued by the arbitral tribunal, however, in the framework of the international commercial arbitration, where the parties have different nationalities from the seat of arbitration, usually they do not address to the court of the seat of arbitration due to the lack of territorial competence.

3.19. Another sensible point to be considered by the party who seeks interim relief is that the *lex arbitri* may limit the arbitral tribunal's jurisdiction to issue an interim measure.

3.20. Given all the above, it is now essential to analyse some practical aspects, including the kind of interim measures the applicant is seeking, and the enforcement phase of interim orders issued in the context of international commercial arbitration.

3.21. As previously set out, the party requesting an interim measure from an arbitral tribunal, should consider the kind of measure and in which jurisdiction it is likely to be enforced if the other party does not voluntarily comply.[14] The most common interim measure is an injunction to one party to do or refrain from doing something. Consequently, the effectiveness of these reliefs depends on the legal instruments available in each jurisdiction system in order to compel a party to comply with the injunction or to sanction the party's noncompliance. In that respect, the civil law and the common law jurisdictions are different with reference to the powers of the national courts if a party does not comply with the arbitral order.[15]

3.22. Some civil law jurisdictions permit the payment of a fine for each day the failing party does not abide by the judgment,[16] however such power is mainly granted to the judge to secure

---

[14] To such end see MICHAEL E. SCHNEIDER & JOACHIM KNOLL, PERFORMANCE AS A REMEDY: NON-MONETARY RELIEF IN INTERNATIONAL ARBITRATION: ASA SPECIAL SERIES NO. 30, New York: Juris Publishing (2011).

[15] For an in-depth analysis on this topic see Carlo Vittorio Giabardo, *'Disobeying Courts' Orders – A Comparative Analysis of the Civil Contempt of Court Doctrine and of the Image of the Common Law Judge,'* 10(1) JOURNAL OF CIVIL LAW STUDIES 35 (2018), available at: https://digitalcommons.law.lsu.edu/jcls/vol10/iss1/5 (accessed on 06 September 2021).

[16] For instance, in France a judge can order an *astreinte* (see Article L-131-1 of the French Code of Civil Enforcement Procedures). Italian, German, Luxembourg and Belgian laws also provide similar fines.

the enforcement of its decision. Consequently, it is dubious if a national court is entitled to impose a fine to ensure the enforcement of an interim relief ordered by an arbitral tribunal. It may be different where the national court issues its provisional relief which reflects the order of the arbitral tribunal: in this case the enforcement of the arbitral measure occurs indirectly.[17] If the national court is powerless to order a fine for non-compliance, the sole remedy of the beneficiary of the measure seems to be to claim extra damages from the tribunal against the party that refuses to comply with the injunction or any other non-monetary relief. It is questionable if this claim for further damages should be submitted to the arbitral tribunal that issued the relief or before the court where this order was enforced and not respected.[18]

3.23. Conversely, in some common law systems, the judges are entitled to hold the unwilling party in contempt for failing to comply with the court's decision enforcing the arbitral interim measure.[19] For instance, a petitioner came before the Southern District Court of New York seeking confirmation and enforcement of an interim arbitral award that ordered the respondent to post security or to refrain from transferring assets abroad. The District Court subsequently held the defendant in civil contempt, imposing daily accruing civil fines and issuing a civil commitment order.[20]

3.24. In the light of above, it is essential to verify, from time to time, the coercive tools available in the jurisdictions where the injunctive interim measures are likely to be enforced in case of failure to comply with the arbitral relief by the enjoined party. As rightly noted,[21] a self-contained pecuniary sanction may avoid the need to come before a national court if the enjoined party does not comply. It could be very useful, especially considering that usually the interim measures are urgently ordered.

3.25. Likewise, the parties seeking arbitral interim measures should consider if the arbitral measures requested exist in the potential place of enforcement. To this end, it may occur that an arbitral

---

[17] For instance it occurs in Switzerland where the Swiss court orders the interim measures through a self-standing ruling subject to the enforcement under the Swiss procedural law, therefore the measure is *de facto* issued by the Swiss court. On this topic see PHILIPPE BÄRTSCH & DOROTHEE SCHRAMM, ARBITRATION LAW OF SWITZERLAND: PRACTICE & PROCEDURE, New York: JurisNet LLC (2014), et. 66.

[18] On this matter see James E. Castello & Rami Chahine, *supra* note 4, at 13.

[19] See Carlo Vittori Giabardo, *supra* note 15, at 38.

[20] See the decision and order granting petitioner's application for confirmation and enforcement of the interim arbitral award of the United States District Court for the Southern District of New York, *CE International Resources Holdings LLC* v. *SA Minerals Ltd. Partnership* (2013), available at: https://jusmundi. com/en/document/decision/en-ce-international-resources-holdings-llc-v-s-a-minerals-ltd-partnership-tantalum-technology-inc-and-yeap-soon-sit-decision-and-order-granting-petitioners-application-for-confirmation-and-enforcement-of-the-interim-arbitral-award-of-the-united-states-district-court-for-the-southern-district-of-new-york-monday-10th-december-2012 (accessed on 06 September 2021).

[21] See James E. Castello & Rami Chahine, *supra* note 4, at 14.

interim measure is not allowed in the enforcing country for public policy reasons.[22] Indeed, some jurisdictions deem that disproportionate damages are contrary to their international public policy and reject interim reliefs that provide severe sanctions in case of non-compliance.[23]

IV. The Case Law's Trend on the Enforceability of Arbitral Interim Measures

3.26.   Whereas substantial differences exist across jurisdictions, as resulting from the analysis of the relevant case law there are different approaches for the enforcement of arbitral interim measures issued in the framework of the international commercial arbitration. However, as noted above, in the light of the wide power of the arbitrators to issue interim measures of protection, the current trend is the broader pro-enforcement stance of arbitral interim orders by most jurisdictions.

3.27.   In some jurisdictions[24] national courts can issue interim measure only prior to the constitution of the arbitral tribunal. Thereby, once the arbitral tribunal has been established, national courts should refrain from granting interim reliefs. In accordance with such method, the Brazilian Superior Court of Justice upholds that the national courts can intervene in controversies subject to arbitration only in provisional and exceptional cases as when the arbitral tribunal is not already existing. Once the arbitral tribunal is formed, the interim measure issued by the national court is subject to the arbitrators' ratification and if this decision is not ratified by the arbitral tribunal, the whole arbitral proceedings will be rendered ineffective.[25] Such ruling confirms the pro-arbitration attitude of the Brazilian Courts

---

[22]   For instance an anti-suit injunction issued by an arbitral court in Paris was contrary to the enjoined Egyptian party's constitutional rights and, thereby, thus the Egyptian *ordre public*. See Ibrahim Shehata, *Are Arbitral Anti-Suit Injunctions Enforceable before Egyptina Courts?*, KLUWER ARBITRATION BLOG (23 January 2019), available at: http://arbitrationblog.kluwerarbitration.com/2019/01/23/are-arbitral-anti-suit-injunctions-enforceable-before-egyptian-courts/ (accessed on 06 September 2021).

[23]   Some jurisdictions forbid judicial penalties if they would lead to an undue enrichment of the creditor. See Alexis Mourre, *Judicial Penalties and Specific Performance in International Arbitration*, in LAURENT LEVY, FILIP DE LY, INTEREST, AUXILIARY AND ALTERNATIVE REMEDIES IN INTERNATIONAL ARBITRATION, Alphen aan den Rijn: Kluwer Law International (2008), et. 69.

[24]   For instance Brazil and France.

[25]   See the case *Itarumã Participações S.A. v. Participações em Complexos Bioenergéticos S.A. – PCBIOS*, Resp No. 1,297,974-RJ, (2012), available at: http://arbitrationblog.kluwerarbitration. com/2012/10/26/brazilian-court-clarifies-jurisdiction-for-interim-measures/?print=print (accessed on 06 September 2021).

and guarantees the exclusive jurisdiction of a duly appointed arbitral tribunal with respect to the grant of interim measures.

3.28. Another case law recognizes the primary jurisdiction of the arbitral tribunal, once constituted. In this context, the national courts can issue interim measures also after the formation of the arbitral tribunal, where the forcing powers of the courts are necessary for enforcing arbitral interim measures sought in the matter at hand. In light of the party autonomy's principle, the national courts cannot replace the arbitrators in ordering interim measures. In this respect, in the case *Cetelem SA v. Roust Holdings Limited*, the English Court of Appeal, according to Section 44 of the English Arbitration Act 1996 that empowered the courts to decide a request of interim measures only under very following strict conditions,[26] emphasises that the interferences between the arbitral proceedings as the dispute resolution chosen by the parties and the legislations of the national courts must be kept to the minimum.[27]

3.29. Equally, the Singapore Courts corroborate the prevalent position of the arbitral tribunals in comparison to national judges in ordering interim relief. For instance, the Court of Appeal of Singapore provides that, even though the national court has a jurisdiction to issue interim measures just as well as the arbitrators, the national court will refrain to prevaricate the arbitral tribunal's powers in ordering interim relief and, in this respect, will issue interim measures only for helping and supporting the arbitration.[28]

3.30. The Singapore Courts will affirm the finality of awards ordering interim relief and their enforceability under the Singapore Arbitration Act.[29] In this case, the interim relief is quite unusual,

---

[26] That is the following: i) those measures are urgently in order to secure the assets or crucial evidence, ii) the tribunal so permits or if there is an agreement in writing from other parties, iii) the tribunal lacks the power to act efficiently or effectively. See Section 44 of the Arbitration Act 1996, available at: https://www.legislation.gov.uk/ukpga/1996/23/section/44 (accessed on 06 September 2021). It is noted that under sections 41 and 42 of the Arbitration Act 1996, where the place of arbitral proceedings in England, interim measures ordered by arbitrators are enforceable as peremptory orders by the tribunal e.g. orders unappealable and unchallengeable.

[27] See the decision of the England and Wales Court of Appeal issued on 24 May 2005, *Cetelem SA v. Roust Holdings Limited*, available at: https://www.casemine.com/judgement/uk/5a8ff71160d03e7f57ea70a4 (accessed on 06 September 2021). For a comment on this decision see Chris Newmark & Thomas Yates, *Striking a Balance for Court Intervention in Arbitration Disputes: The Decision in Cetelem S.A. v. Roust Holdings Limited*, TRANSNATIONAL DISPUTE MANAGEMENT (2005), available at: www.transnational-dispute-management.com (accessed on 06 September 2021).

[28] See the decision of the Singapore Court of Appeal issued on 26 February 2008, *NNC International AB v. Alliance Concrete Singapore Pte Ltd.*, available at: https://www.supremecourt.gov.sg/docs/default-source/module-document/judgement/2008-sgca-5.pdf (accessed on 06 September 2021).

[29] See the decision of the Singapore Court of Appeal issued on 27 May 2015, *PT Perusahaan Gas Negara (Persero TBK) v. CRW Joint Operation (2015) SGCA 30*, available at: https://www.supremecourt.gov.sg/docs/default-source/module-document/judgement/2015-sgca-30.pdf (accessed on 06 September 2021). See the comment of Kevin Elbert, *On The Nomenclature And Characterization Of Arbitral Awards: PT. Perusahaan Gas Negara (Persero) TBK v. CRW Joint Operation [2015] 4 SLR 364*, SINGAPORE LAW

namely an arbitral order that compels one party to abide by a prior decision by the dispute adjudication board (DAB), set up under the 1999 FIDIC Red Book which imposes on the party the obligation to pay a sum of money to the other party.

3.31. Likewise, the Indian Courts recently upheld the arbitral proceedings in ordering interim measures. In this context, the Indian Courts adopted a pro-enforcement stance with a stringent adherence to the principle of non-interference with arbitral awards.[30] In particular, the Delhi High Court validated an emergency arbitrator order, highlighting that a refusal to enforce such arbitral determination would render the whole emergency proceeding worthless. The key point of the court's decision was the parties' bond to the terms of their arbitral agreement, namely the parties should be bound by the outcome of the proceeding when they choose arbitral rules that recognize an emergency arbitrator as an arbitrator and provide the possibility of emergency arbitration. The arbitral rules chosen are incorporated by reference as part of the parties' arbitration agreement and, as a result, were valid and enforceable.[31]

3.32. Equally, the U.S. Court of Appeals confirmed that an arbitral tribunal decision that imposes, as an interim provision, for the plaintiff to turn over certain tax documents to the defendant is final and enforceable. In the same vein of the decisions mentioned above, the national judge pointed out that if the party seeking interim relief must wait to enforce an urgent matter until all the other issues are arbitrated to finality, the arbitral interim decision is a meaningless waste of time.[32] This decision

---

BLOG (06 April 2016), available at: https://www.singaporelawblog.sg/blog/article/155 (accessed on 06 September 2021). See also Eugene Tan & Rupert Coldwell, *Another (Unsuccessful) Challenge to the Finality of Interim Arbitral Awards in Singapore and Enforcing DAB Decisions on International Projects under FIDIC*, KLUWER ARBITRATION BLOG (15 June 2015), available at: http://arbitrationblog.kluwerarbitration.com/2015/06/15/another-unsuccessful-challenge-to-the-finality-of-interim-arbitral-awards-in-singapore-and-enforcing-dab-decisions-on-international-projects-under-fidic/ (accessed on 06 September 2019).

[30] See the comment of D. Malik & M. Sabharwal, *Pro-enforcement regime for foreign arbitral awards: Is India really headed towards it?*, available at: https://www.ibanet.org/article/7CC3CF19-09D7-474C-A2CE-8B8227CD92DE (accessed on 06 September 2021).

[31] See the decision of the Delhi High Court issued on 18 March 2021, *Amazon.com NV Investment Holdings LLC* v. *Future Coupons Private Limited & Ors*, available at: https://indiankanoon.org/doc/194413351/ (accessed on 06 September 2021), that enforced a SIAC emergency arbitrator's award in a SIAC arbitration seated in India as an order of the Indian courts under the Indian Arbitration and Conciliation Act 1996. This decision underlines the efficacy of emergency arbitrator proceedings in obtaining urgent interim relief and the need for careful selection of an appropriate seat of arbitration to ensure that the emergency arbitrator's award is swiftly enforced. For a comprehensive comment on this judgement see Sherina Petit & Katie Chung & Kenneth Tan, *Picking battles and battlefield: Are emergency arbitrator awards enforceable a tor outside the arbitral seat?* (April 2021), available at: https://www.nortonrosefulbright.com/en/knowledge/publications/73ee2271/picking-battles-and-battlefields (accessed on 06 September 2021).

[32] See the decision of the U.S. Court of Appeals, Seventh Circuit issued on 14 May 2000, *Publicis Communications and Publicis S.A.* v. *True North Communications*, available at: https://www.casemine.com/judgement/us/59147e80add7b04934451755 (accessed on 06 September 2021). In this case the plaintiff abided by the arbitral measure and resisted the relevant enforcement on the basis that such order could

represents a precedence for the U.S. Courts to follow when dealing with the issue of enforceability of interim provisions issued as emergency arbitral relief.[33]

3.33. Another interesting decision, issued by a U.S. Federal District Court, substantiates the pro-arbitration enforceability of interim orders, providing that 'an award of temporary equitable relief (...) was separable from the merits of the arbitration' and, consequently, was capable of immediate recognition and enforcement.[34] Thereby the U.S. judges confirmed the interim award, stating that 'the styling of an award as 'interim' does not insulate it from review if it finally determines a severable issue in the case'. The judges stated that '[i]n the context of arbitration, the public policy favouring the enforcement of arbitration agreements and the confirmation of arbitral awards trumps' any countervailing concerns. It, finally, deserves to be noted this decision confirmed the injunctive aspect of the interim award on the grounds of the arbitration rules implemented by the International Dispute Resolution Procedures. Based on these provisions, the arbitrators are expressly entitled to grant injunctive measures 'for the protection or conservation of property'. Accordingly, by adopting the above procedures, the parties agreed that the arbitrator had the power to award interim security.[35]

---

not be enforced under the New York Convention because it was not an award. The U.S. Court of Appeals provided that 'finality was the touchstone for the enforceability of any arbitral decision, regardless of how it may be designated and that the content of the decision – not the its nomenclature – determines finality'.

[33] Other U.S. decisions consistent with the *Publicis Communications* case are, *inter alia*, the following: *Toyo Tire Holdings of Americas Inc.* v. *Continental Tire North America*, issued on 17 June 2010, available at: https://caselaw.findlaw.com/us-9th-circuit/1528114.html (accessed on 06 September 2021), *Yahoo! Inc.* v. *Microsoft Corp.*, issued on 21 October 2013, available at: https://cases.justia.com/federal/district-courts/new-york/nysdce/1:2013cv07237/418671/26/0.pdf?ts=1411562499 (accessed on 06 September 2021), *Chinmax Medical Systems, Inc.* v. *Alere San Diego, Inc.*, issued on 08 December 2010, available at: https://www.courtlistener.com/docket/5996785/chinmax-medical-systems-inc-v-alere-san-diego-inc/, *Pre-Paid Legal Services, Inc.* v. *Kidd*, issued on 26 October 2011, available at: https://cases.justia.com/federal/district-courts/oklahoma/okedce/6:2011cv00357/20780/28/0.pdf?ts=1411567074 (accessed on 06 September 2021).

[34] See the decision of the U.S. district court for the Southern district of New York, *CE International Resources Holdings LLC* v. *S.A. Minerals Ltd. et al.*, issued on 10 December 2012, available at: https://jusmundi.com/en/document/decision/en-ce-international-resources-holdings-llc-v-s-a-minerals-ltd-partnership-tantalum-technology-inc-and-yeap-soon-sit-decision-and-order-granting-petitioners-application-for-confirmation-and-enforcement-of-the-interim-arbitral-award-of-the-united-states-district-court-for-the-southern-district-of-new-york-monday-10th-december-2012 (accessed on 06 September 2021).

[35] In this dispute the sole arbitrator, seated in New York, issued an award ordering the posting of prejudgment security or, in default of that, enjoining the respondent from transferring any assets, wherever located. The defendant rebutted that the kind of interim measure ordered by the arbitrator was not available under the law of the seat of arbitration and, consequently, the arbitrator exceeded his powers, breaching public policy. The national court admitted that the relief granted was not available from the New York laws, however it has not adjudged that the arbitrator exceeded his powers. The court relied upon the parties' agreement to settle their claims under the International Centre for Dispute Resolution arbitration rules of the America Arbitration Association that expressly permitted the arbitrator to take all the necessary interim measures "*including injunctive relief and measures for the protection or conservation of property*". The court excluded that "[n]othing about enforcing an order rendered in accordance with the procedures to which the parties agreed offends either New York law or New York public policy".

3.34. Following the same approach, another example of pro-enforcement regime for provisional relief was expressed by the Supreme Court of Ukraine.[36]

3.35. Similarly, the Egyptian Court enforced an interim order issued by a foreign tribunal.[37] In particular, the Cairo Court of Appeal recognized an interim order granted by an ICC arbitral tribunal placed in Paris arising from a claim under a contract for the supply of ship-to shore gantry cranes. That order stayed the liquidation bonds valued at more than USD 18 million. The Egyptian Court affirms that the mandatory conditions that must be respected for enforcing the award (which included a translation into Arabic and a deposit with the court) do not apply to interim measures and consequently, a simple application of the interested party is enough to obtain the recognition and enforcement of such arbitral provision. According to the pro-enforcement stance, the Egyptian Court declared that the enforcement of arbitral interim orders was in accordance with the scope of the New York Convention, e.g. to favour the enforcement of arbitral award, to ensure harmony among jurisdictions and predictability in the framework of international commercial affairs and dispute resolution.

3.36. It must finally be highlighted that this Egyptian decision refers to the UNCITRAL Model Law (2006) that, as said above,[38] is aligned with the facilitation and support of the enforcement of arbitral interim orders.

3.37. Notwithstanding the ever-increasing favour for the enforcement of arbitral interim measures by the national courts, some jurisdictions keep opposing the trend.

---

[36] See the decision of the Supreme Court of Ukraine issued on 24 February 2016, *JKX Oil & Gas plc, Poltava Gas B.V. and Poltava Petroleum JV* v. *Ukraine*, available at: https://www.italaw.com/sites/default/files/case-documents/italaw7391.pdf (accessed on 06 September 2021). The case concerns an interim provision granted by the Stockholm Chamber of Commerce arbitral tribunal in the context of an investor-state proceedings. Such measure has been issued in the form of an award enjoining the state from collecting royalties on gas production form the investor at a higher rate that one previously in place. Pursuant to the investor's position, the emergency award is full enforceable in Ukraine because such provision is rendered in the form of an award and, accordingly, it is enforceable under the New York Convention. The Ukrainian Supreme Court annulled the Court of Appeal's decision, affirming that solely on the bases listed in Article V of the New York Convention it is allowable to reject the recognition and enforcement of an arbitral award. The Ukrainian Court of Appeal had not contemplated these bases in rebutting the decision rendered by the judge of first instance.

[37] See the decision of the Cairo Court of Appeal, Chamber 7, issued on 09 May 2018, *Doosan Heavy Industries and Construction* v. *Damietta International Port Company SAE and Kuwait Gulf Link Ports International*, No. 44/134JY, available (only in Arabic language) at: https://jusmundi.com/en/document/pdf/decision/ar-doosan-heavy-industries-construction-co-ltd-v-damietta-international-port-company-s-a-e-and-kuwait-gulf-link-ports-international-decision-of-the-cairo-court-of-appeal-wednesday-9th-may-2018 (accessed on 06 September 2021). A comment of this decision is available at: https://globalarbitrationreview.com/provisional-measures/cairo-court-fills-interim-measures-void-in-egyptian-law (accessed on 06 September 2021).

[38] See paragraph II above.

3.38.   For instance, the Russian Supreme Court affirmed that final arbitral awards relating to the examination of the case on the merits and rendered at the end of the arbitral proceedings are eligible for enforcement in the Russian Federation.[39] The Russian judge expressly refers to Article V(1)(e) of the New York Convention and, on these grounds, considers the New York Convention not applicable to interlocutory awards, including decisions of arbitrators on procedural matters.[40]

3.39.   Likewise, the Chilean Supreme Court set aside the enforcement of an arbitral interim order concerning assets situated in Chile.[41]

3.40.   Finally, the Korean Arbitration Act, notwithstanding that it has incorporated the 2006 UNCITRAL Model Law and, accordingly, adopted recent developments in international arbitration practice to the efficiency of arbitration proceedings,[42] limits the *exequatur* of arbitral interim injunctions to those ordered by tribunals placed in Korea and consistent with Korean law.

V.   Conclusions

3.41.   As highlighted in this article, the main goal of interim measures is to safeguard the parties' rights before or during the arbitration or to prevent frustration of the final award. Even though in most jurisdiction arbitral tribunals and national courts are generally both competent bodies to grant interim relief - unless proscriptions contained in the rules of the arbitral proceedings and/or in the national laws - it has not always been in the past (and also now in certain jurisdictions) automatic the enforcement of interim measures by the State courts. Indeed, as said before, national law frequently denied arbitrators the power to order interim measures. A decisive change in trend occurred thanks to the Article 17 of the 2006 UNCITRAL Model Law that

---

[39]   See the decision of the Highest Arbitrazh Court of the Russian Federation, issued on 05 October 2010, *Living Consulting Group AB (Sweden)* v. *OOO Sokotel (Russia)*, No. 6547/10, available at: https://arbitrationlaw.com/sites/default/files/free_pdfs/living_consulting_group_ab_sweden_v_ooo_sokotel_russia_no_6547-10.pdf (accessed on 06 September 2021). The case concerns an arbitral proceeding at the Stockholm Chamber of Commerce (SCC) seated in Stockholm (Sweden). The arbitral tribunal issued a separate award ordering the Russian company Sokotel to reimburse the Swedish company Living Consulting Group the portion of the advance on arbitration costs paid by the Swedish party in place of the Russian party, the latter having refused to pay its share. The Arbitrazh Court of Saint-Petersburg and the Leningrad Region enforced the separate award. The Federal Arbitrazh Court for the North-Western District confirmed the first instance ruling. By contrast, the Presidium of the RF Highest Arbitrazh Court set aside the decisions of the lower courts, refused to recognize and enforce the SCC partial award and ceased the corresponding court proceedings.

[40]   Notably collection of arbitration costs, determination of jurisdiction, or security measures.

[41]   See the decision of the Chilean Supreme Court issued on 10 May 2010, *Western Technology Services International Inc. (Westech)* v. *a Chilean company, Cauchos Industriales SA (Cainsa)*, No. 5468/2009, described in UNCITRAL's Case Law, A/CN.9/SER.C/ABSTRACTS/111, at 5, available at: https://www.uncitral.org/clout/clout/data/chl/clout_case_1090_leg-2862.html (accessed on 06 September 2021).

[42]   See the Korean Arbitration Act, last version amended in 2016, available at: https://elaw.klri.re.kr/kor_service/lawView.do?hseq=38889&lang=ENG (accessed on 06 September 2021).

'opened' a more effective enforcing of arbitral interim orders by national courts. The power of arbitral tribunal to effectively grant interim orders that are successfully enforced by the state courts is a noticeable point to increase the effectiveness of the entire arbitral proceedings.

3.42. The current trend is a wider pro-enforcement approach of arbitral interim orders by most jurisdictions and accordingly, by pro-arbitration friendly states.

3.43. As stated above, the mechanism for the enforcement of arbitral interim measures depends upon the national law of the country in which the measure shall be enforced. It is fundamental to require interim provisions that can be successfully enforced. Therefore, the arbitral tribunals should evaluate and grant interim orders maximising their potential enforceability.

| | |

Summaries

DEU [*Die Vollstreckung einstweiliger Verfügungen, die von Schiedsrichtern in internationalen Handelsschiedsverfahren erlassen wurden*]
Der Artikel analysiert die Funktion, Bedeutung und Entwicklung von einstweiligen Verfügungen im Kontext internationaler Handelsschiedsverfahren. Konkret widmet sich der Beitrag Schlüsselfragen, die berücksichtigt sein wollen, um die Effektivität einstweiliger Verfügungen sicherzustellen. In diesem Kontext liegt der Schwerpunkt des Problemkreises auf dem System für die Vollstreckung dieser einstweiligen Korrekturmaßnahmen und der einschlägigen rechtlichen Entwicklung. Betrachtet man die im UNCITRAL 2006-Mustergesetz verankerten Normen und den konsequenten Abgleich der meisten nationalen Rechtsordnungen, so kann kein Zweifel daran bestehen, dass der Erlass von einstweiligen Verfügungen zum breiten Spektrum der Zuständigkeit von Schiedsgerichten gehört, und deren Vollstreckung sodann zur Zuständigkeit der ordentlichen (nationalen) Gerichte. Die Reichweite solcher Verfügungen hängt allerdings von folgenden Aspekten ab: (i) Über welche Rechtsinstrumente verfügt der Staat, in dem es mit einer gewissen Wahrscheinlichkeit zur Vollstreckung der einstweiligen Verfügung kommt, wenn die verpflichtete Partei die ihr in der schiedsrichterlichen Entscheidung auferlegten Pflichten nicht erfüllt? Und (ii): bestehen am potenziellen Vollstreckungsort Bestimmungen über einstweilige Verfügungen, die von

Schiedsrichtern erlassen wurden? Hier zieht die Autorin die allerneueste Rechtssprechung heran, um den Unterschied zwischen Rechtsordnungen des kontinentalen Rechts und Common Law-Rechtsordnungen zu beleuchten, wenn es um Fälle geht, in denen ein Verfahrensbeteiligter die schiedsrichterlich ergangene einstweilige Verfügung missachtet. Diese Analyse der Rechtssprechung zeigt, dass schiedsrichterliche einstweilige Verfügungen sich in einer Reihe von Rechtsordnungen bereits eine gewisse Stellung erkämpft haben, wenn es um deren Vollstreckbarkeit geht. Dennoch gibt es noch immer Ausnahmen von diesem allgemeinen Trend.

CZE   *[Výkon předběžných opatření vydaných rozhodci v mezinárodní obchodní arbitráži]*
Tento článek analyzuje funkci, důležitost a vývoj předběžných opatření v rámci mezinárodní obchodní arbitráže. Příspěvek se konkrétně věnuje klíčovým otázkám, které je nutno zohlednit, tak aby byla zajištěna efektivita předběžných opatření. V tomto kontextu je těžištěm předmětné problematiky systém výkonu těchto prozatímních prostředků nápravy a příslušný právní vývoj. Vzhledem k normám obsaženým ve Vzorovém zákoně UNCITRAL 2006 a důslednému sladování většiny vnitrostátních právních řádů je nepochybné, že součástí široké pravomoci rozhodčích soudů je předběžná opatření nařizovat a součástí pravomoci vnitrostátních soudů je tato opatření vykonávat. Síla těchto opatření však závisí na: i) právních nástrojích, které má k dispozici právní řád státu, v němž k výkonu předběžného opatření s určitou pravděpodobností dojde v případě nesplnění povinnosti stanovené v rozhodnutí rozhodců ze strany povinného, a ii) existenci úpravy o předběžných opatřeních vydávaných rozhodci v potenciálním místě výkonu. V tomto ohledu se autorčin příspěvek po nastínění rozdílu mezi právními řády kontinentálního práva a právními řády common law, s odkazem na pravomoci vnitrostátních soudů v případech, kdy účastník řízení nesplní předběžné opatření vydané rozhodci, zaměřuje na nejnovější judikaturu. Z analýzy judikatury vyplývá, že předběžná opatření vydávaná rozhodci již patrně začínají získávat určité postavení v řadě jurisdikcí co do možností jejich výkonu. Určité výjimky z tohoto obecného trendu však stále existují.

Czech (& Central European) Yearbook of Arbitration®

| | |

POL [*Wykonywanie środków tymczasowych wydanych przez arbitrów w międzynarodowym arbitrażu handlowym*]
Artykuł omawia funkcję, wagę i rozwój środków tymczasowych wydawanych przez arbitrów w ramach międzynarodowego arbitrażu handlowego z uwzględnieniem systemu wykonywania tych odwoławczych środków tymczasowych i odnośnego rozwoju prawa.

Bez względu na aktualne szerokie kompetencje trybunałów arbitrażowych w zakresie zarządzania środków tymczasowych i sądów krajowych w zakresie ich wykonywania, moc wspomnianych środków zależy od: i) instrumentów prawnych dostępnych w porządku prawnym kraju, w którym najprawdopodobniej dany środek tymczasowy zostanie wykonany w razie niezaspokojenia przez stronę zobowiązaną obowiązku przewidzianego w orzeczeniu arbitrażowym oraz ii) istnienia regulacji w przedmiocie środków tymczasowych wydawanych przez arbitrów w potencjalnym miejscu ich wykonywania.

FRA [*L'exécution des mesures provisoires ordonnées par les arbitres dans les arbitrages commerciaux internationaux*]
Le présent article examine la fonction, l'importance et l'évolution des mesures provisoires ordonnées par les arbitres dans les arbitrages commerciaux internationaux, en tenant compte du système d'exécution de ces remèdes provisoires, ainsi que de l'évolution législative dans ce domaine.

Nonobstant la large compétence des tribunaux arbitraux pour ordonner des mesures provisoires et celle des tribunaux nationaux pour les exécuter, la force de ces mesures dépend : i) des instruments juridiques disponibles dans le système juridique de l'État où l'exécution de la mesure provisoire est susceptible de se réaliser si la personne concernée ne se conforme pas à l'obligation imposée par la sentence arbitrale, et ii) de l'existence, dans le lieu d'exécution potentielle, de règles applicables aux mesures provisoires.

RUS [*Приведение в исполнение обеспечительных мер, принятых арбитрами в международном коммерческом арбитраже*]
В данной статье рассматриваются функции, важность и развитие обеспечительных мер, принимаемых арбитрами в международном коммерческом арбитраже, в частности, с учетом системы приведения в исполнение этих

обеспечительных средств защиты и соответствующего развития законодательства.

Несмотря на существующую широкую компетенцию арбитражных судов применительно к принятию обеспечительных мер и национальных судов к их исполнению, сила таких мер зависит от: (i) правовых инструментов, которыми располагает законодательство государства, в котором, вероятно, будут применяться обеспечительные меры в случае невыполнения обязанным лицом обязанностей, установленных арбитражным решением; и (ii) наличия регулирования обеспечительных мер, принимаемых арбитрами, в потенциальном месте исполнения.

ESP [*Ejecución de las medidas cautelares dictadas por los árbitros en el arbitraje comercial internacional*]
Este artículo analiza la función, la importancia y la evolución de las medidas cautelares dictadas por los árbitros *en el contexto del arbitraje comercial internacional, teniendo en cuenta el sistema de ejecución de estas medidas y la evolución del derecho pertinente.*

A pesar de la amplia competencia de los tribunales de arbitraje para dictar medidas cautelares y de los tribunales nacionales para ejecutarlas, la fuerza de dichas medidas depende de: i) los instrumentos legales del ordenamiento jurídico del Estado donde se llevará a cabo la ejecución de la medida cautelar en cuestión, dictada por el incumplimiento de las obligaciones impuestas por un laudo arbitral; y ii) la existencia de normas que establezcan un marco legal de las medidas cautelares dictadas por los árbitros *en el lugar de su eventual ejecución.*

| | |

Bibliography:

PHILIPPE BÄRTSCH & DOROTHEE SCHRAMM, ARBITRATION LAW OF SWITZERLAND: PRACTICE & PROCEDURE, New York: JurisNet LLC (2014).

GARY B. BORN, INTERNATIONAL COMMERCIAL ARBITRATION, New York: Wolters Kluwer (2009).

James E. Castello & Rami Chahine, *Enforcement of interim measures*, GLOBAL ARBITRATION REVIEW (08 June 2021), available at: https://globalarbitrationreview.com/guide/the-guide-challenging-and-

Czech (& Central European) Yearbook of Arbitration®

enforcing-arbitration-awards/2nd-edition/article/enforcement-of-interim-measures.

Kevin Elbert, *On The Nomenclature And Characterization Of Arbitral Awards: PT. Perusahaan Gas Negara (Persero) TBK v. CRW Joint Operation [2015] 4 SLR 364*, SINGAPORE LAW BLOG (06 April 2016), available at: https://www.singaporelawblog.sg/blog/article/155.

Carlo Vittorio Giabardo, *'Disobeying Courts' Orders – A Comparative Analysis of the Civil Contempt of Court Doctrine and of the Image of the Common Law Judge'*, 10(1) JOURNAL OF CIVIL LAW STUDIES 35 (2018).

Secretary General, *Possible Uniform Rules on Certain Issues Concerning Settlement of Commercial Disputes: Conciliation, Interim Measures of Protection, Written Form for Arbitration Agreement*, United Nations Digital Library, UN Doc. A/CN.9/WG.II/WP.108 24, 24 (2000), available at: https://digitallibrary.un.org/record/407425.

Alexis Mourre, *Judicial Penalties and Specific Performance in International Arbitration*, in LAURENT LEVY, FILIP DE LY, INTEREST, AUXILIARY AND ALTERNATIVE REMEDIES IN INTERNATIONAL ARBITRATION, Alphen aan den Rijn: Kluwer Law International (2008).

Chris Newmark & Thomas Yates, *Striking a Balance for Court Intervention in Arbitration Disputes: The Decision in Cetelem S.A. v. Roust Holdings Limited*, TRANSNATIONAL DISPUTE MANAGEMENT (2005).

Sherina Petit & Katie Chung & Kenneth Tan, *Picking battles and battlefield: Are emergency arbitrator awards enforceable a tor outside the arbitral seat?* (April 2021), available at: https://www.nortonrosefulbright.com/en/knowledge/publications/73ee2271/picking-battles-and-battlefields.

Eugene Tan & Rupert Coldwell, *Another (Unsuccessful) Challenge to the Finality of Interim Arbitral Awards in Singapore and Enforcing DAB Decisions on International Projects under FIDIC*, KLUWER ARBITRATION BLOG (15 June 2015), available at: http://arbitrationblog.kluwerarbitration.com/2015/06/15/another-unsuccessful-challenge-to-the-finality-of-interim-arbitral-awards-in-singapore-and-enforcing-dab-decisions-on-international-projects-under-fidic/.

Ibrahim Shehata, *Are Arbitral Anti-Suit Injunctions Enforceable before Egyptina Courts?*, KLUWER ARBITRATION BLOG (23 January 2019), available at http://arbitrationblog.kluwerarbitration.com/2019/01/23/are-arbitral-anti-suit-injunctions-enforceable-before-egyptian-courts/.

Jan K. Schäfer, *Enforcement of Interim Measures,* in VIII CONGRESSO DO CENTRO DE ARBITRAGEM COMERCIAL, CENTRO DE ARBITRAGEM COMERCIAL (2015).

MICHAEL E. SCHNEIDER & JOACHIM KNOLL, PERFORMANCE AS A REMEDY: NON-MONETARY RELIEF IN INTERNATIONAL ARBITRATION: ASA SPECIAL SERIES NO. 30, New York: Juris Publishing (2011).

THOMAS H. WEBSTAR, HANDBOOK OF UNCITRAL ARBITRATION, London: Sweet & Maxwell (2015).

Czech (& Central European) Yearbook of Arbitration®

Tereza Profeldová

Does Undisputed Jurisdiction of Arbitral Tribunal Also Provide Parties with Effective Control Mechanism from Side of Courts?

Key words:
Domestic and Foreign
Arbitral Proceedings |
Lex Arbitri | Arbitration
agreement | Seat of the
Arbitral proceedings |
Judicial Assistance of the
State Courts | Control
Functions of the State Courts
| New York Convention |
UNCITRAL Model law |
Jurisdiction of the State
Courts | Arbitral Award |
Recognition and Enforcement
of Arbitral Awards | Interim
Measures

Abstract | The jurisdiction of the courts is not something one usually thinks of when it comes to the conclusion of an arbitration agreement. Despite doctrines advocating for a transnational or anational approach to international arbitration, arbitral proceedings are being conducted under the national lex arbitri. In some ways, they are reliant on the courts, especially with regard to judicial assistance and the performance of the controlling functions that the state retains over arbitration. Unlike the jurisdiction of the Arbitral Tribunal, which is the direct result of the Parties' autonomy, the jurisdiction exercised by courts is determined by the law of the particular state and cannot be influenced by the Parties. Contrary to the general belief, the involvement of courts may prove to be quite complicated.
The national lex arbitri usually reserves the full jurisdiction of the courts only for proceedings that are considered domestic in the relevant state. When it comes to foreign proceedings, the scope of jurisdiction of the courts varies significantly. In some cases, the Parties to such proceedings or the Arbitral Tribunal have no access to the courts of another state at all. What makes the situation even more complex is the fact that the seat of arbitration as the decisive (but not exclusive) connecting factor needs to be seen as an "artificial" legal concept. It does not have to have any real connection to the Parties or the subject of arbitration, which makes the need for intervention by the courts of another state (that has an actual

Mgr. Tereza Profeldová,
attorney-at-Law,
successfully completed
the master's programme
for Law and Legal Science
at the Faculty of Law of
Charles University in
Prague. Currently studying
for Ph.D. at the Faculty of
Law, University of West
Bohemia in Pilsen, with
a Ph.D. thesis entitled:
Doctrinal Approach
to Independence of
Arbitrators.
Arbitrator on List of
Arbitrators administered
by the Arbitration Court
attached to the Czech
Chamber of Commerce
and the Agricultural
Chamber of the Czech
Republic.
E-mail: tereza.profeldova@
ablegal.cz

Czech (& Central European) Yearbook of Arbitration®

connection to the proceedings) more likely.
There are different ways in which the choice made by the Parties with regard to the seat of arbitration influences the way in which judicial assistance of the courts may be sought. When determining the seat of arbitration, the Parties should take into account several key issues in order to ensure that the arbitral proceedings won´t be jeopardised due to a lack of judicial assistance.

| | |

I. Introduction

4.01. While there are undoubtedly many different reasons for the Parties to an international commercial contract to choose arbitration[1] over litigation as a dispute resolution mechanism, one such motivation to enter into an arbitration agreement may be to avoid the jurisdiction of state courts, especially of those having general jurisdiction over the opposing party.[2] At the same time, the conclusion of an arbitration agreement does not mean the absolute exclusion of possible intervention by state courts. Under national arbitration laws, state courts are often entrusted with the task of providing judicial assistance with regard to procedural steps falling outside the powers of the Arbitral Tribunal.

4.02. The national *lex arbitri* usually reflects the contractual nature of the arbitration agreement, which means that an arbitration agreement is only binding on the Parties. This effectively prevents the Arbitral Tribunal from compelling third persons to appear before the Arbitral Tribunal and to give evidence, to submit documents or to otherwise provide information relevant to the merits of the case.[3] Apart from that, the state courts play an important role when it comes to interim and conservatory measures, as well as preliminary orders. While some national arbitration laws, especially those that are based on the UNCITRAL Model Law on International Commercial

---

[1]   From a commercial perspective, international arbitration is perceived as providing a neutral, expedient and expert dispute resolution process, largely subject to the parties´ control, in a single, centralized forum, with internationally enforceable dispute resolution agreements and decisions. See GARY B. BORN, INTERNATIONAL COMMERCIAL ARBITRATION, VOL. I, Austin: Wolters Kluwer (2009), et. 71.

[2]   FRANK-BERND WEIGAND, ANTJE BAUMAN, PRACTITIONER'S HANDBOOK ON INTERNATIONAL COMMERCIAL ARBITRATION, Oxford: Oxford University Press, (2nd ed. 2009), et. 33.

[3]   PHILIPPE FOUCHARD, EMMANUEL GAILLARD, JOHN SAVAGE, BERTHOLD GOLDMAN, FOUCHARD GALLARD GOLDMAN ON INTERNATIONAL COMMERCIAL ARBITRATION, The Hague: Kluwer Law International (1999), et. 414.

Arbitration[4] (hereinafter the Model Law), provide the Arbitral Tribunal with the powers to grant interim measures, etc.,[5] other national arbitration laws leave the authority to grant interim measures exclusively with the state courts.[6]

4.03. Another example of state court intervention is the appointment of arbitrator(s) in the event it is not possible to constitute the Arbitral Tribunal in any other way, i.e. if a party fails to choose an arbitrator. Admittedly, the need for the court's assistance in this respect is usually limited to *ad hoc* arbitration. In the majority of cases, the procedural rules applied in proceedings before arbitration institutions (both international and domestic) contain provisions under which an arbitrator can be appointed by the arbitration court.

4.04. However, probably the most important task entrusted to the state courts is the authority to review the arbitral award, should a Party apply for it to be set aside. This is not to be seen as interference with the jurisdiction of the Arbitral Tribunal, but rather as a way to ensure that the arbitral award complies with the basic requirements and procedural principles of fair trial that are needed so that the state can declare it enforceable

---

[4] As adopted by the United Nations Commission on International Trade Law on 21 June 1985, and as amended by the United Nations Commission on International Trade Law on 07 July 2006, available at: https://uncitral.un.org/sites/uncitral.un.org/files/media-documents/uncitral/en/19-09955_e_ebook. pdf (accessed on 22 March 2022). The Arbitral Tribunal is granted substantial authority in this respect in Articles 17 through 17G. Whereas the original version of the Model Law from 1985 already provided for the possibility of interim measures being ordered by the Arbitral Tribunal, the 2006 revision of the Model Law significantly broadened the scope of authority of the Arbitral Tribunal in this respect. Nevertheless, even in those cases where the Arbitral Tribunal is authorized to order certain interim and other measures, the state courts may intervene when the person against whom such decision was rendered refuses to comply with it and to perform the respective obligation imposed on said person. Article 17H together with Article 17I of the Model law stipulate conditions for the recognition and enforcement of the interim measure issued by the Arbitral Tribunal. The following Article 17J foresees the possibility of the interim measures being ordered by the state courts. In other words, it is widely accepted that even if the national arbitration law provides the Arbitral Tribunal with the authority to order interim measures, it may be in the interests of the Parties and the effectiveness of the interim measure ordered for the respective decision to be rendered by a state court.

[5] See also (i) Austria - see section 593 of the Austrian Civil Procedure Code - Gesetz vom 01 August 1895, über das gerichtliche Verfahren in bürgerlichen Rechtsstreitigkeiten (Zivilprozessordnung – ZPO). StF: RGBl. Nr. 113/1895, available at: https://www.ris.bka.gv.at/GeltendeFassung.wxe?Abfrage=Bundes normen&Gesetzesnummer=10001699 (accessed on 22 March 2022), (ii) Germany – see Section 1041 of the German Civil Procedure Code - Zivilprozessordnung in der Fassung der Bekanntmachung vom 05 Dezember 2005 (BGBl. I S. 3202; 2006 I S. 431; 2007 I S. 1781), die zuletzt durch Artikel 3 des Gesetzes vom 05 Oktober 2021 (BGBl. I S. 4607) geändert worden ist, available at: https://www.gesetze-im-internet. de/zpo/BJNR005330950.html (accessed on 22 March 2022), (iii) Ukraine – see Art. 17 of the Ukrainian Act on International Commercial Arbitration - Закон України Про міжнародний комерційний арбітраж, available at: https://zakon.rada.gov.ua/laws/show/4002-12#Text (accessed on 22 March 2022), (iv) Sections 38 and 39 of the UK Arbitration Act 1996 applicable in England, Wales and Northern Ireland, available at https://www.legislation.gov.uk/ukpga/1996/23/contents (accessed on 22 March 2022) or (v) Section 25 of the Swedish Arbitration Act - Lag (1999:116) om skiljeförfarande, available at: https://sccinstitute.com/media/408923/skiljeforfarandelagen_1mars2019_swedish.pdf (accessed on 22 March 2022).

[6] A typical example of this approach, which is nowadays not often seen, is the Czech arbitration law – See section 20 of Act No. 216/1994 Coll., on Arbitral Proceedings and on the Enforcement of Arbitral Awards.

(guarantee its enforceability) in exactly the same manner as judgements of the state courts.

4.05. Whereas the jurisdiction of the Arbitral Tribunal constitutes a necessary precondition for the arbitral proceedings to be held, judicial assistance, together with the exercise of the control functions of the state courts, is to be seen as equally important. Since the scope of the authority of the state court varies significantly based on the content of the national arbitration law, the connection between the jurisdiction of the Arbitral Tribunal and the role of the state courts may play a role when the Parties draft their arbitration agreement. As will be demonstrated below, the Parties to an arbitration agreement cannot automatically assume that a valid arbitration agreement is going to provide them with the possibility to make full use of judicial assistance and the control functions of the state courts.

II.   Significance of Seat of Arbitration

4.06. As already stated above, the scope of intervention by the state courts does not fall within the principle of the autonomy of the parties, but it is instead governed by the applicable national arbitration law (lex arbitri). Under the localization theory (seat theory), arbitral proceedings are governed by the *lex loci arbitri* (the arbitration law at the seat of the respective arbitral proceedings). From this perspective, the seat of the arbitral proceedings represents a territorial connection between the proceedings and the arbitration law of the place where the proceedings are formally (legally) localized.[7]

4.07. It follows that the seat (or as it is sometimes referred to, the "place") of the arbitral proceedings is a legal concept, rather than an actual (geographical) one.[8] Usually, the seat of the arbitral proceedings is the place where the award is deemed to be made.[9] Based on the above, the choice of the seat of the arbitral proceedings is crucial. The stipulation of the seat of the arbitral proceedings does not constitute a *condicio sine qua non* for the valid conclusion of the arbitration agreement. Nevertheless, the increasing number of arbitral proceedings in which the seat of arbitration was directly agreed by the Parties is considered to

---

[7]   ALEXANDER J. BĚLOHLÁVEK, ARBITRATION LAW OF CZECH REPUBLIC: PRACTICE AND PROCEDURE, New York: JurisNet LLC (2013), et. 832-833.

[8]   See also the place where the hearing is held, evidence is taken or the deliberations of the Arbitral Tribunal take place.

[9]   MICHAEL W. BÜHLER, THOMAS H. WEBSTER, HANDBOOK OF ICC ARBITRATION: COMMENTARY AND MATERIALS, London: Sweet & Maxwell (2nd ed. 2008), et. 209.

be positive.[10] It provides additional protection of the Parties' interests.

4.08.   In the absence of the Parties' choice of the seat of the Arbitral Proceedings, it is usually the Arbitral Tribunal[11] or the relevant arbitral institution[12] that makes the ultimate decision on the seat of the arbitral proceedings. In accordance with the Model Law,[13] the national arbitration law usually stipulates that when determining the seat of the arbitral proceedings, regard should be given to the circumstances of the case, including the convenience of the Parties. While it is understandable that, because of the individual circumstances of the case and often different interests of the Parties, there are no specific criteria based on which the seat of the arbitral proceedings is to be chosen, with only a general reference to the suitability of the place that should be determined as the seat of the arbitral proceedings, it may lead to results not anticipated and intended by the Parties.

4.09.   Some authors try to list specific criteria, such as the logistical convenience of the Parties, the language and the applicable law of the contract, political neutrality, the likelihood of excessive intervention by the state courts, anticipated costs of the proceedings at a certain venue and the legal framework ensuring the enforceability of the arbitral award.[14] Nevertheless, it is to be noted that these criteria have very little connection with the actual purpose of the seat of the arbitral proceedings and do not reflect its significance for the Parties. As has been stated above, the importance of the seat of the arbitral proceedings lies in the fact that it connects the arbitral proceedings with a particular law that governs the procedure - to the extent that this does not fall within the autonomy of the Parties and/or within the

---

[10]   W. LAURENCE CRAIG, WILLIAM W. PARK, JAN PAULSSON, INTERNATIONAL CHAMBER OF COMMERCE ARBITRATION, New York: Oceana Publications, Inc. (3rd ed. 2000), et. 185-186. For the increase in the number of arbitration agreements containing a valid choice of the seat of the arbitration, compare also PHILIPPE FOUCHARD, EMMANUEL GAILLARD, JOHN SAVAGE, BERTHOLD GOLDMAN, FOUCHARD GALLARD GOLDMAN ON INTERNATIONAL COMMERCIAL ARBITRATION, The Hague: Kluwer Law International (1999), et. 675.

[11]   Section 17 of Czech Act No. 216/1994 Coll., on Arbitral Proceedings and on the Enforcement of Arbitral Awards, Section 1043 of the German Civil Procedure Code, Section 595 of the Austrian Civil Procedure Code, Article 20 of the Ukrainian Act on International Commercial Arbitration, Section 3(c) of the UK Arbitration Act 1996 applicable in England, Wales and Northern Ireland (however, Section 3(b) of the said legislation specifically refers to the possibility that the seat of the arbitral proceedings be designated by the arbitral institution before which the proceedings are being held), Section 22 of the Swedish Arbitration Act.

[12]   Article 18(1) of the ICC Rules of Arbitration available at: https://iccwbo.org/dispute-resolution-services/arbitration/rules-of-arbitration/#article_18 (accessed on 22 March 2022), Article 25(1) of the Arbitration Rules of the Arbitration Institute of the Stockholm Chamber of Commerce ("SCC"), available at: https://sccinstitute.com/media/1407444/arbitrationrules_eng_2020.pdf (accessed on 22 March 2022).

[13]   See Article 20(1).

[14]   W. LAURENCE CRAIG, WILLIAM W. PARK, JAN PAULSSON, INTERNATIONAL CHAMBER OF COMMERCE ARBITRATION, New York: Oceana Publications, Inc. (3rd ed. 2000), et. 186.

Czech (& Central European) Yearbook of Arbitration®

autonomy of the Arbitral Tribunal to decide on the conduct of the arbitral proceedings.

4.10.   The Parties' choice of the seat of the arbitral proceedings usually has little to do with the subject of the proceedings. The substantive law governing the contract is independent from the law of the state where the arbitral proceedings are seated. The same can be said about the language. As far as the practicalities, including the potential costs, are concerned, it needs to be reiterated that procedural acts do not necessarily need to be carried out at the seat of arbitration. Similarly, there is little to no connection between the seat of arbitration and the place where it shall be enforced. Since the New York Convention[15] is considered be one of the most successful international treaties and provides an effective mechanism for the enforcement of arbitral awards throughout the world, there is no need for the Parties to insist on a venue where the award is likely going to be enforced to be designated as the seat of the arbitral proceedings.[16]

4.11.   Moreover, the interests of the Parties with regard to intervention by state courts may differ. It would not be correct to automatically assume that by consenting to arbitration, a Party has also expressed an interest in minimising the influence of the state courts. One can easily imagine that a Party may want to enjoy the advantages that are usually ascribed to international arbitration, but at the same time requests assurances of possible (strong) legal remedies, should the arbitral proceedings not be conducted in accordance with the procedural principles of fair trial, etc.

4.12.   Given the potential individual and possible different interests of the Parties that are not and cannot be known to the person deciding on the seat of arbitration, it somehow seems to be understandable that reference is usually made to general criteria with which the Arbitral Tribunal or arbitral institution can work. However, the limits of this way of designating the seat of the arbitral proceedings are undeniable. Therefore, it is highly advisable for the Parties to decide on the seat of the

---

[15]   Convention on the Recognition and Enforcement of Foreign Arbitral Awards adopted by the United Nations Conference on International Commercial Arbitration held between 20 May – 10 June 1958 in New York, available at: https://uncitral.un.org/sites/uncitral.un.org/files/media-documents/uncitral/en/new-york-convention-e.pdf (accessed on 22 March 2022).

[16]   Setting aside the fact that the Parties´ interests may differ here and therefore a conclusion according to which such venue would be suitable for the Parties is unlikely. Under the principle of the fair and equal treatment of the Parties, it would breach the duties of the Arbitral Tribunal (arbitral institution) to determine the seat of the arbitral proceedings based on the interests of one Party only. Secondly, it may often be unclear at the stage of the determination of the seat of the arbitral proceedings, in which state could the arbitral award be enforced.

arbitral proceedings themselves, while thoroughly examining the implications of their choice under the relevant *lex arbitri.*

4.13. The relevance of the Parties' choice is even greater in a situation in which the seat of the arbitral proceedings would be determined by default in the absence of the Parties' will under the applicable procedural rules. They provide little to no space for consideration and choose the seat of the arbitral proceedings directly.[17] It is exactly such default designation of the seat of the arbitral proceedings that may lead to unexpected results that can even harm the Parties' legitimate interests.

III. Seat of Arbitral proceedings and Influence Thereof on Jurisdiction of State Courts to Exercise Judicial Assistance and Control Functions Towards Arbitration

4.14. Such problematics often tend to be diminished to the notion that a direct consequence of the Parties' choice of the seat of the arbitral proceedings is the selection of the state courts responsible for assistance in any aspects of the arbitral proceedings, including the setting aside of the arbitral award.[18]

4.15. While the above is correct in the majority of instances, it needs to be reiterated that the jurisdiction of the state courts can only be determined by the national legislature or by the international treaty that establishes the jurisdiction of the national courts of a certain state in specific circumstances.[19] What this means in practice is that the Parties to arbitral proceedings cannot establish the jurisdiction of the state courts where the seat of the arbitral proceedings is situated, should the national arbitration law stipulate different/additional criteria for the determination of jurisdiction. This is why the Parties should pay extra attention to how the *lex arbitri* defines the jurisdiction of the state courts

---

[17] See also Article 25(1) of the VIAC (Vienna International Arbitral Centre) Rules of Arbitration and Mediation according to which absent any agreement by the Parties, the place of arbitration shall be Vienna – available at: https://www.viac.eu/en/arbitration/content/vienna-rules-2021-online (accessed on 22 March 2022). Similarly, Article 16.2 of the LCIA (London Court of International Arbitration) Arbitration Rules stipulates that in default of any agreement by the Parties, the seat of the arbitration shall be London (England), unless and until the Arbitral Tribunal orders, in view of the circumstances, that another arbitral seat is more appropriate – available at: https://www.lcia.org/Dispute_Resolution_Services/lcia-arbitration-rules-2020.aspx (accessed on 22 March 2022).

[18] GARY B. BORN, INTERNATIONAL COMMERCIAL ARBITRATION, VOL. I, Austin: Wolters Kluwer (2009), et. 176 or MICHAEL W. BÜHLER, THOMAS H. WEBSTER, HANDBOOK OF ICC ARBITRATION: COMMENTARY AND MATERIALS, London: Sweet & Maxwell (2nd ed. 2008), et. 208-209.

[19] As will be elaborated on further, a typical example is the New York Convention stipulating the jurisdiction of state courts with regard to the enforcement of certain arbitral awards.

and whether they will be able to revert to the state courts, if need be.

4.16. Moreover, the content of the national arbitration law is only one of the things that needs to be considered. As will be demonstrated, the consequences of the choice of the seat of the arbitral proceedings may also differ based on additional circumstances, such as the existence of an international element in the legal relationship that is the subject of the arbitral proceedings,[20] or the possibility to establish (based on additional facts) the jurisdiction of the state court of another state than the one on the territory of which the seat of the arbitral proceedings is situated. The approach of the individual states may differ. The most common approaches are the following.

III.1. Jurisdiction of State Courts Based on Existence of Seat of Arbitral Proceedings

4.17. An example of national arbitration law based strictly on territorial principle is the German Civil Procedure Code.[21] The jurisdiction of German state courts is, however, not limited to domestic arbitral proceedings, i.e. proceedings that have their seat on the territory of Germany. Paragraphs 2 through 4 of Section 1025 of the German Civil Procedure Code determine the international jurisdiction of German state courts. The reason for this provision is the protection of the legitimate interests of the persons concerned.[22] The clear and unambiguous determination of the seat of the arbitral proceedings is therefore recommended not only because of the need for legal certainty with regard to the *lex arbitri* governing the proceedings, but also as a way to exclude any doubts as to the jurisdiction of state courts.[23]

4.18. Paragraph 2 stipulates general jurisdiction without the need for a specific connection to Germany. The Parties are free to revert to the German state courts regardless of the place of arbitral

---

[20] The lack of which led in the past even to the rejection of jurisdiction by the courts of the state of the seat of the arbitral proceedings.

[21] Section 1025(1) thereof provides that the provisions governing arbitration are to be applied where the seat of the arbitral proceedings in the sense as defined by Section 1043(1) of the German Civil Procedure Code is located in Germany. The last mentioned provision simply confirms the principle of Party autonomy, when it comes to the determination of the seat of the arbitral proceedings, and establishes the powers of the Arbitral Tribunal to determine the seat of the arbitral proceedings in the absence of the Parties choice. The provision is clearly influenced by Article 1(2) of the Model Law, according to which it shall apply (with the exemption of certain measures concerning the judicial assistance of the state courts) only if the only the seat of arbitration is in the territory of said state.

[22] INGO SAENGER, ZIVILPROZESSORDNUNG – HANDKOMMENTAR, Beden-Baden: Nomos Verlagsgesellschaft (2nd ed. 2007), et. 1949.

[23] JENS-PETER LACHMANN, HANDBUCH FÜR DIE SCHIEDSGERICHTSPRAXIS, Köln: Verlag Dr. Otto Schmidt (3rd ed. 2008), et. 263.

proceedings[24] or any other circumstances. Undisputedly, the German legislature clearly acknowledges that the state courts exercise powers that need to be performed regardless of the foreign character of the arbitral proceedings in question. At the same time, such international jurisdiction is limited to the minimum of indispensable tasks that are essential to the effective conduct of arbitral proceedings and the protection of the Parties' legitimate rights and interests.

4.19. Under Section 1032 of the German Civil Procedure Code, the German state courts are obliged to refer the Parties to arbitration, should an actin be brought before the state court that concerns a dispute falling within the scope of an arbitration agreement concluded between the Parties.[25]

4.20. Furthermore, the state courts are authorized to rule on a petition that a provisional measure or one serving to provide security be taken with regard to the subject matter of the dispute being dealt with in the arbitration proceedings.[26] From the Parties' perspective, this provision is a practical one that will commonly be used. Finally, the state courts are authorized to provide support by taking evidence or by taking any other actions reserved for judges that the Arbitral Tribunal is not in a position to take.[27]

4.21. Apart from the general international jurisdiction described above, the scope of competence of the state courts is broadened as long as the following conditions are met: (i) the seat of the arbitral proceedings has not yet been determined, and (ii) either of the Parties has its registered seat or habitual place of residence in Germany.[28] Under these circumstances, the state courts are authorized to provide judicial assistance and perform

---

[24] Including a situation in which the seat of the arbitral proceedings has not been determined yet, since such situation also amounts to the seat of arbitral proceedings not being in Germany.

[25] To provide the state courts with the power to do so as part of Section 1025(2) of the German Civil Procedure Code seems unnecessary, because a similar duty stems for the courts from Article II(3) of the New York Convention. The priority of international is undisputed – see THOMAS RAUSCHER, PETER WAX, JOACHIM WENZEL, MÜNCHENER KOMMENTAR ZUR ZIVILPROZESSORDNUNG (ZPO) §§ 946 – 1086, München: C. H. Beck (3rd ed. 2008), et. 87. At the same time, Section 1025(2) of the German Civil Procedure Code refers to the whole Section 1032 thereof. Regardless of the (actual or envisioned) seat of the arbitral proceedings, the German state courts are also authorized to determine the admissibility or inadmissibility of arbitration proceedings (in other words, the existence and validity of the arbitration agreement). A compelling argument can be made that this is a typical task that should only be performed with regard to domestic proceedings. It is likely that the general international jurisdiction has been established in order to enable the declaration of the inadmissibility of arbitral proceedings in cases where the jurisdiction of the German state courts to hear the case would otherwise be given. Since the pending action according to Section 1032(2) of the German Civil Procedure Code does not hinder the Arbitral Tribunal from initiating and continuing the arbitral proceedings, the danger of misuse of this provision is relatively small, but still, to include this provision in Section 1025(2) of the German Civil Procedure Code seems somehow misplaced.

[26] Section 1033 of the German Civil Procedure Code.

[27] Section 1050 of the German Civil Procedure Code.

[28] Section 1025(3) of the German Civil Procedure Code.

tasks in connection with the appointment of arbitrators[29] and to decide in certain cases when a challenge against an arbitrator is raised.[30]

4.22. While such rule is not specifically mentioned in the German *lex arbitri*, a conclusion has been made that the Parties may enjoy the benefits of the jurisdiction of the German state courts if they enter into a respective agreement on jurisdiction (prorogation agreement), or instead if they agree on the application of German procedural law.[31]

III.2. Switzerland

4.23. The applicability of the *lex arbitri* and thus the jurisdiction of state courts is also governed by the territorial principle in Switzerland.[32] The distinction between national and international arbitral proceedings, together with the fact that either of them is governed by a different set of rules, results in a separate scope of jurisdiction depending on whether the proceedings are deemed to be national or international.

4.24. The revisions of arbitration law brought a more precise[33] definition of international proceedings. According to Article 176(1) IPRG, the proceedings are considered international, if at the time that the arbitration agreement was concluded, at least one of the parties thereto did not have its domicile, its habitual residence or its seat in Switzerland.[34]

4.25. The constellation at the time of the commencement of the arbitral proceedings is not relevant. The definition specifically refers to the parties to the arbitration agreement, whereas it is possible that the list of the parties taking part in the proceedings

---

[29]   Sections 1034 and 1035 of the German Civil Procedure Code.

[30]   Sections 1037 and 1038 of the German Civil Procedure Code.

[31]   ADOLF BAUMBACH, WOLFGANG LAUTERBACH, JAN ALBERS, PETER HARTMANN, ZIVILPROZESSORDNUNG: MIT FAMGB, GVG UND ANDEREN NEBENGESETZEN, München: C.H. Beck (72nd ed. 2014), et. 2610.

[32]   See Article 353(1) of the Swiss Civil Procedure Code, available at: https://www.fedlex.admin.ch/eli/cc/2010/262/en (accessed on 23 March 2022), with regard to domestic arbitral proceedings, and Article 176(1) of the Swiss Federal Act on Private International Law (IPRG), available at: https://www.fedlex.admin.ch/eli/cc/1988/1776_1776_1776/en (accessed on 23 March 2022), with regard to foreign arbitral proceedings.

[33]   This seems to be a more accurate description of the changes, despite the fact that they are presented as something almost completely new (see also Vanessa Alarcon Duvanel, Updated PILA: Switzerland revamps arbitration law, available at: http://arbitrationblog.practicallaw.com/updated-pila-switzerland-revamps-arbitration-law/ (accessed on 23 March 2022)).

[34]   Formerly, it was required that at the time of the conclusion of the arbitration agreement, at least one of the parties had neither its domicile nor its habitual residence in Switzerland. This led to discussions whether the parties to the arbitration agreement or future parties conducting the proceedings are meant. The ambiguity of the wording led to legal uncertainty on the part of the persons involved. One of the main reasons for the change was the effort to strengthen the foreseeability of the application of the relevant rules (see also the explanatory note to the amendment to PILA, available at: https://www.fedlex.admin.ch/eli/fga/2018/2548/de (accessed on 23 March 2022)).

will slightly differ.[35] As a result, proceedings that are (due to the change of the parties' legal status and other circumstances) conducted as purely domestic, without any international element, may be classed as international under the Swiss IPRG due to the situation having been different at the moment of the conclusion of the arbitration agreement.

4.26.   As far as the access to judicial assistance provided by the state courts is concerned, there are no substantial effects for the Parties. Since the international proceedings are still classed as domestic due to the seat of the arbitral proceedings being in Switzerland, there is no doubt that Parties to international arbitration have sufficient access to the state courts in case of a need for judicial assistance.[36] Even before the 2020 amendment to the IPRG that strengthened the jurisdiction of the state courts, they were able to step in where the Arbitral Tribunal did not possess sufficient power to take certain procedural steps. The changes just deepened the authority of the state courts in this respect.

4.27.   They can be called upon when it comes to the constitution of the Arbitral Tribunal,[37] when the arbitrator is challenged and a Party requests his/her removal,[38] the state courts are able to order interim or conservatory measures and may assist with the enforcement thereof, should the Party against whom such measure were ordered not comply with it.[39] Apart from that, the state courts may assist with the taking of evidence, should it become necessary due to the Arbitral Tribunal not being able to conduct the full taking of evidence itself.[40] Finally, in order to make sure that the Parties and the arbitral Tribunal will be supported by the state courts in any way possible, Article 185 IPRG stipulates that if any further assistance by a state court

---

[35]   The question of the extent to which arbitration agreement can be binding on third persons (i.e. other than their signatories) is a longstanding issue in international arbitration. This question arises especially with regard to legal concepts such as the piercing of the corporate veil, estoppel (in the United States, equitable estoppel and intertwined estoppel are used by the state courts in order to determine the personal scope of the arbitration agreement) and naturally legal succession.

[36]   It can be concluded that the major differences lay in the procedural side of the proceedings. The rules governing international proceedings provide for more party autonomy and a less restrictive approach. The main differences can be found when it comes to the review of the arbitral award. In addition to the grounds based on which an arbitral award can be challenged in both national and international proceedings, Section 393(e)(f) of the Swiss Civil Procedure Code allows for a limited substantive review of an award rendered in national proceedings. A Party can argue that the award is arbitrary in its result, because it is based on findings that are obviously contrary to the facts as stated in the case files or because it constitutes an obvious violation of law or equity. The award can further be found defective if the right to the reimbursement of costs of the proceedings as granted by the Arbitral Tribunal is obviously excessive.

[37]   Article 179 IPRG.

[38]   Articles 180a and 180b IPRG.

[39]   Article 183 IPRG.

[40]   Article 184 IPRG.

is required, the court at the seat of the arbitral tribunal has jurisdiction.

4.28. What was missing up until the 2020 amendment to the IPRG was any rule governing the relationship of the state courts towards arbitral proceedings having their seat outside Switzerland. Being in force since 01 January 2021, the new Article 185a IPRG enables Arbitral Tribunals conducting proceedings with their seat abroad, as well as the Parties thereto, to request that the state court having territorial jurisdiction over the place where evidence is to be taken participate and assist. Similarly, the state courts are called upon to enforce interim or conservatory measure ordered in foreign arbitral proceedings.

4.29. When describing the changes to the IPRG, it is emphasized that the new Article 185a IPRG does not expressly codify the jurisdiction of the state courts that has already been recognised and actually exercised. There is no doubt that the possibility to petition Swiss state courts for assistance by an Arbitral Tribunal or the Parties to foreign arbitral proceedings only exists as of 01 January 2021.[41] Until the new law came into effect, the Swiss state courts could not take any procedural steps concerning foreign arbitral proceedings.[42]

III.3. Austria

4.30. Austria is an interesting example of a state that makes a clear doctrinal distinction between the seat of the arbitral proceedings and the place of the rendering of the arbitral award. The revised *lex arbitri* is (similarly to Germany) based on the Model law.[43] Originally, the Austrian doctrine also linked the identification of the award as domestic or foreign to the seat of the arbitral proceedings.[44]

4.31. The law preceding the current regulation divided foreign and domestic arbitral awards based on the place where the arbitral

---

[41] Vanessa Alarcon Duvanel, Updated PILA: Switzerland revamps arbitration law, available at: http://arbitrationblog.practicallaw.com/updated-pila-switzerland-revamps-arbitration-law/ (accessed on 23 March 2022).

[42] Dominik Elmiger, Switzerland's revised international arbitration law from a litigation perspective, available at: https://www.ibanet.org/article/664E1D2C-A795-468F-94EC-78C4CD695889 (accessed on 23 March 2022). The same is implied in: Simon Gabriel, Axel Buhr, Johannes Landbrecht, Andreas Schregenberger, *International Arbitration – Switzerland, Law & Practice*, CHAMBERS, GLOBAL PRACTICE GUIDES (2021), available at: https://www.gabriel-arbitration.ch/en/arbitration-in-switzerland (accessed on 23 March 2022).

[43] See Section 577 of the Austrian Civil Procedure Code, which contains a general rule that links the application of this legal regulation to the set of arbitration on the territory of Austria.

[44] See also the decision of the Austrian Supreme Court (OGH – der Oberste Gerichtshof) from 30 September 1930, Ref. No. 4 Ob 321/30, published under ZBl 1930/360, in which the conclusion was reached that the place where the arbitral tribunal had its seat determines whether the arbitral award is foreign, provided that the parties were aware of that place and concurred (see STEFAN RIEGLER, ALEXANDER PETSCHE, ALICE FREMUTH-WOLF, MARTIN PLATTE, CHRISTOPH LIEBSCHER, ARBITRATION

award was rendered.[45] The rule was, however, interpreted so as to stipulate that the place of the rendering of the arbitral award cannot merely be factual and accidental, but needs to correspond with the expressed or at least logically inferable will of the Parties at the moment of the conclusion of the arbitral agreement. Should this not be the case, the place of the actual hearing of the case determined either by agreement of the Parties or in accordance with the applicable procedural rules takes precedence.[46]

4.32. The result of the identification of an arbitral award as foreign resulted in the absence of any recourse against it that would be available against so-called domestic awards.[47] The courts were probably aware that, under certain circumstances, the jurisdiction of the Austrian courts could have been established in spite of the otherwise relevant criteria if the case were heard on the territory of Austria.[48] Such approach can be seen as a result of the fact that different states can define the jurisdiction of the state courts with regard to arbitration in a different

LAW OF AUSTRIA: PRACTICE AND PROCEDURE, New York: Juris Publishing, Inc. (2007), et. 460), or the decision of the Austrian Supreme Court from 13 September 1935, Ref. No. 1 Ob 694/35, which further explains that the seat is only decisive for the determination of the character of the arbitral award in case the Parties anticipated such arbitration seat at the time of the conclusion of the arbitration agreement. Further to such problematics, see RUDOLF STOHANSL, MANZ GROßE, AUSGABE DER ÖSTERREICHISCHEN GESETZE, 6. Band: Jurisdiktionsnorm und Zivilprozeßordnung, Wien: Manzsche Verlags und Universitätsbuchhandlung (15th ed. 2002), et. 1611. It is seen that the concept of the seat of the arbitral proceedings as described in these decisions is in some ways different from its purely fictional (artificial) nature as we know it today. It was clearly anticipated – apart from the fact that the seat of the arbitral proceedings corresponds with the Parties´ will – that such place has some actual relevance to the proceedings. For example, the latter decision refers to the place where the arbitral tribunal hears the case. At the same time, it would be wrong to draw a conclusion of a completely different concept of the seat of the arbitral proceedings. More likely, the different characterization is a result and reflection of the lack of technology that nowadays allows the seat of the arbitral proceedings to be detached from the place where the actual procedural measures are being carried out. In fact, the procedural rules governing proceedings before the major arbitral institutions provide for the possibility of so-called online proceedings.

[45] Section 79 of the Austrian regulation on enforcement (Gesetz vom 27. Mai 1896, über das Exekutions- und Sicherungsverfahren (Exekutionsordnung – EO). StF: RGBl. Nr. 79/1896, available at: https://www.ris.bka.gv.at/GeltendeFassung.wxe?Abfrage=Bundesnormen&Gesetzesnummer=10001700 (accessed on 23 March 2022). It is to be noted that the aforementioned provision does not constitute *lex specialis* concerning arbitral proceedings, or rather the definition of a foreign arbitral award. It is a general provision dealing with the conditions for the recognition and enforcement of acts and decisions rendered outside the territory of Austria. Since the Austrian law did not contain an individual provision that would only be applicable in arbitration (see PETER ANGST, KOMMENTAR ZUR EXEKUTIONSORDNUNG, Wien: Manzsche Verlags und Universitätsbuchhandlung (2000), et. 529). Thus, it is questionable whether one can really speak of a doctrinal change or whether the reference to the place of the rendering of the arbitral award simply stems from the wording of the provision in question. The fact that the latter is the case is supported by the references to the respective case law, which is exactly the same case law from the 1930's quoted above and which works with the concept of the seat of the arbitral proceedings, even if with a different definition.

[46] HANS W. FASCHING, ANDREAS KONECNY, KOMMENTAR ZU DEN ZIVILPROZESSGESETZEN, BAND IV/2, Wien: Manzsche Verlags und Universitätsbuchhandlung (2nd ed. 2007), et. 784.

[47] Section 595 of the Austrian Civil Procedure Code in the wording before the 2006 arbitration law reform.

[48] HANS W. FASCHING, ANDREAS KONECNY, KOMMENTAR ZU DEN ZIVILPROZESSGESETZEN, BAND IV/2, Wien: Manzsche Verlags und Universitätsbuchhandlung (2nd ed. 2007), et. 784, and the decision of the Higher Regional Court, Vienna (OLG - Oberlandesgericht – Wien) from 21 February 1985, Ref. No. 2 R 30/85 (published under EvBl 1985/120) mentioned therein.

manner, which may result in a situation in which, from a strictly formal point of view, neither state will accept the jurisdiction of its courts. The problem is that unless the *lex arbitri* expressly provides for the jurisdiction of state courts with regard to proceedings that do not (from the point of view of the criteria stipulated by the *lex arbitri*) result in the rendering of a domestic arbitral award, the Parties to foreign proceedings or Arbitral Tribunal with its seat outside Austria do not have access to the Austrian state courts.

4.33. Nevertheless, the jurisdiction of the state courts was established by the case law only and with regard to the recourse against an arbitral award. The problematics are, however, more complicated, and as has been explained above, judicial assistance is provided in many other ways. Due to the lack of any express provision, it was up to the individual decision of the state courts that would have to determine on a case-by-case basis whether they are competent to provide the judicial assistance needed. This lessens the legal certainty for the Parties to the arbitral proceedings and may create practical problems concerning the conduct of the arbitral proceedings.

4.34. As stated above, the current legislation adopted the approach taken by the Model Law and follows the criteria of the seat of the arbitral proceedings. What is more important from the perspective of this paper is that the Austrian legislature is well aware of the issues that may arise if the *lex arbitri* applies exclusively to proceedings with their seat in Austria. The state courts are – among others – provided with the jurisdiction[49] to order interim or conservatory measures,[50] to enforce such measures ordered by the Arbitral Tribunal,[51] to provide general judicial assistance pursuant to Section 602 of the Austrian Civil Procedure Code, and to decide on the existence or non-existence of an arbitral award, if the Party requesting such determination proves it has legal interest in such decision.[52]

4.35. As far as assistance with the constitution of the Arbitral Tribunal in the event of a failure to appoint an arbitrator is concerned, the Austrian state courts have jurisdiction to perform tasks entrusted thereto in connection therewith, even before the determination of the seat of the arbitral proceedings, in case one of the Parties has its seat, actual or habitual residence in Austria. This might be especially important because, should none of the

---

[49] Section 577(2) of the Austrian Civil Procedure Code.
[50] Section 585 of the Austrian Civil Procedure Code.
[51] Section 593(3)-(6) of the Austrian Civil Procedure Code.
[52] The Austrian state courts are authorized to decide on such declaratory relief under Section 612 of the Austrian Civil Procedure Code if the person making the application shows legal interest in the declaration.

state courts of the state having some connection to the arbitral proceedings and the parties thereto assume jurisdiction, it might be impossible to constitute the Arbitral Tribunal at all. Such result would be contrary to the Parties' will to exclude the jurisdiction of the state courts and resolve their disputes in arbitration.[53]

4.36. While the current legislation effectively ensures that the Parties can make full use of the judicial assistance provided by the state courts, the former *lex arbitri* left the question open as to whether it can be applied and the jurisdiction of the Austrian courts is to be established even if the seat of the arbitral proceedings is outside Austria.[54] While it could not be excluded that, when taking into consideration the overall circumstances of the case and the connection to Austria, the state court would provide judicial assistance with regard to foreign arbitral proceedings in individual cases, there was no guarantee for the Parties that they would be able to rely on the Austrian state courts.

III.4. Czech Republic

4.37. The Czech Republic serves as an example of a state that has its arbitration law based on the criterion of the place of the rendering of an arbitral award. Such place is usually identical to the seat of the arbitral proceedings, but Czech Act No. 216/1994 Coll. and Act No. 91/2012 Coll., on Private International Law,[55] do not contain any specific (expressed) presumption to this effect.[56]

4.38. In theory, this may lead to a situation in which the Parties situate the seat of the arbitral proceedings abroad (outside the Czech Republic), but at the same time agree that the arbitral award should be situated on the territory of the Czech Republic. At first glance, this constellation seems to benefit the Parties' interests and could provide for the jurisdiction of the state courts of both

---

[53]   A similar solution was chosen by the Swedish legislature. According to Section 46, the Swedish Arbitration Act shall apply to arbitral proceedings seated in Sweden only, regardless of the otherwise international character of the proceedings. The Act further contains detailed regulation of international matters. Section 50 stipulates that provisions of Section 26 in connection with Section 44 regarding the taking of evidence during the arbitral proceedings in Sweden shall be applied in arbitral proceedings seated abroad, if the proceedings are based upon an arbitration agreement and, pursuant to Swedish law, the issues referred to the arbitrators may be resolved through arbitration (i.e. so-called objective arbitrability pursuant to Swedish law is given). Contrary to the Austrian law, which generally provides for the jurisdiction of the Austrian state courts when it comes to providing judicial assistance with regard to foreign arbitral proceedings, the Swedish Arbitration Act establishes such jurisdiction exclusively with regard to the specific case of the taking of evidence. It follows that in all other cases not specifically mentioned by the Swedish Arbitration Act, Swedish state courts are able to decline judicial assistance due to their lack of jurisdiction.
[54]   Supposing the conditions for the jurisdiction of the Austrian state courts would otherwise be met.
[55]   This law provides specific rules concerning the conduct of international arbitration.
[56]   ALEXANDER J. BĚLOHLÁVEK, ARBITRATION LAW OF CZECH REPUBLIC: PRACTICE AND PROCEDURE, New York: JurisNet LLC (2013), et. 861.

the state of the seat of the arbitral proceedings, as well as of the Czech state courts, based on the fact that the arbitral award is or shall be rendered there.

4.39. Looking at the issue more closely, the (potential) concurrent jurisdiction of the state courts of multiple states can in practice ultimately have the opposite effect, with the courts of both states declining jurisdiction, arguing that the Parties can revert to the courts of the other state, which are more suitable to provide judicial assistance with regard to the arbitral proceedings. Thus, the Parties may, in the worst case, end up without any judicial assistance, or they would have to make a compelling argument proving that the refusal to assume jurisdiction would result in *denegatio iustitiae*.

4.40. There is also the opposite possibility, i.e. that the Parties agree on the seat of the arbitral proceedings being situated in the Czech Republic, but at the same time express their joint will that the arbitral award be rendered abroad. The Czech courts are likely to decline jurisdiction due to the fact that that the arbitral award will be considered foreign, whereas the foreign state courts will argue[57] that the seat of the arbitral proceedings is in the Czech Republic and therefore they also lack jurisdiction.

4.41. The Czech state courts have repeatedly refused to extend their jurisdiction when it comes to proceedings that are considered foreign under Czech Act No. 216/1994 Coll.[58] The acceptance of jurisdiction was even refused in a situation in which all aspects of the arbitral proceedings pointed to the Czech Republic, and the only foreign element that was ascertained consisted of the Parties' choice of the seat of the arbitral proceedings (which was identical with the formal place of the rendering of the arbitral award). Apart from that, the proceedings were held between two Czech persons under Czech law. All procedural steps, such as the taking of evidence, oral hearing, etc., were conducted on the territory of the Czech Republic.

4.42. Despite all of the above, the Czech Supreme Court insisted on the strict adherence to the criteria for the establishment of the jurisdiction of the Czech courts stipulated by Czech arbitration law. It is correct that the aforementioned decisions specifically concerned the jurisdiction to hear a motion for the setting aside of the arbitral award. Considering the argumentation of the Supreme Court, a justifiable conclusion can be made that a

---

[57] Supposing their *lex arbitri* distinguishes between domestic and foreign proceedings based on the seat of the arbitral proceedings.

[58] See resolution of the Czech Supreme Court, Ref. No. 23 Cdo 1034/2012 from 30 September 2013, and judgment of the same court, Ref. No. 23 Cdo 2542/2011 from 27 November 2013.

Czech (& Central European) Yearbook of Arbitration®

similar decision would be reached as far as other acts of judicial assistance are concerned.

4.43. This does not exclude the possibility that the Czech state courts would assume jurisdiction in an individual case, possibly if the Party to the arbitral proceedings would otherwise be deprived of any possibility to defend their rights and legitimate interests. The undisputed point is that there is no legal ground based on which the Parties to arbitral proceedings taking place outside the Czech Republic would be able to revert to the Czech courts, if need be. This doctrinal stance taken and approved both in the case law as well as by academics highlights problems that the Parties may encounter if they only concentrate on ensuring that the jurisdiction of the Arbitral Tribunal is undisputed, while forgetting to consider whether the structure of their arbitration agreement provides for sufficient access to state courts.

IV. Relationship between State Courts and Foreign Arbitral Proceedings

IV.1. General Remarks

4.44. The aforementioned examples of national *lex arbitri* all show that unless the legislature specifically establishes the jurisdiction of the state courts when it comes to foreign proceedings, the state courts are not authorized to act on any corresponding request. The jurisdiction of state courts may be acknowledged in individual cases. This does not guarantee sufficient protection of the rights and legitimate interests of the Parties.

4.45. The access to state courts is even more important considering the development in the understanding of the relevance and meaning of the seat of the arbitral proceedings, especially in the international context. Whereas in the past, it was implied that the seat of the arbitral proceedings has some actual relevance to the merits of the case (the Parties' underlying legal relationship). The doctrine went so far as to suggest that in the absence of the Parties' choice of governing substantive law, the Parties' will was that their legal relationship be governed by the respective substantive law of the state in which the proceedings are to be legally situated.

4.46. Technological advances enabled the further detachment of the seat of the arbitral proceedings from the subject of the dispute and the Parties. The Parties are now able, without any practical difficulties or additional costs, to choose a seat of the arbitral proceedings based solely on the content of the respective *lex arbitri*, with the proceedings in their entirety being conducted elsewhere. Whether this possibility for a completely artificial seat of arbitral proceedings is something to aim for is up to a completely different discussion.

4.47. With regard to the subject of this article, this means that the need to conduct the taking of evidence or to take other procedural steps and to order or enforce interim or conservatory measures is now greater than ever, and that the state courts of the state where the seat of the arbitral proceedings is situated are often not in a position to provide the necessary legal assistance. This, on the other hand, significantly influences and even endangers the result of the arbitral proceedings.

4.48. As paradoxical as it may sound, it may result in the Parties' reluctance to rely on an arbitration-friendly venue and to draft their arbitration agreement in accordance with their choices concerning the conduct of the proceedings. To *quasi force* the Parties to only consider venues with some actual relevance to the subject of the dispute would contradict the primary principles governing international arbitration and undermine the Parties' autonomy.

4.49. It is recognised on an international level that the state courts may need to intervene with regard to arbitral proceedings that don't have their seat within the jurisdiction of the state courts.

IV.2. UNCITRAL Model Law

4.50. The 2006 revision of the Model Law is based on the principle that the national arbitration law should only apply if the seat of the arbitral proceedings is in the territory of the respective state. The territorial criterion governing most of the provisions of the Model Law was adopted for the sake of certainty and in view of the fact that the Model Law grants the Parties wide freedom in shaping the rules of conduct of the arbitral proceedings, so there is little need for the Parties to seek elements of a foreign (arbitration) law to be applied.

4.51. It is exactly the principle of party autonomy that is of considerable practical importance in respect of the provisions of the *lex arbitri*, which entrust the state courts at the seat of the arbitral proceedings with functions of supervision and assistance to arbitration.[59]

4.52. The drafters of the amendment to the Model Law were aware that despite the territorial approach being considered sufficient,

---

[59] United Nations Commission on International Trade law: UNCITRAL Model Law on International Commercial Arbitration 1985. With amendments as adopted in 2006 – et. 26-27, available at: https://uncitral.un.org/sites/uncitral.un.org/files/media-documents/uncitral/en/19-09955_e_ebook.pdf (accessed on 23 March 2022).

some forms of judicial assistance might be necessary and justifiable when it comes to foreign proceedings. Thus, the revised Article 1(2) of the Model Law contains important exceptions to that principle, to the effect that certain provisions thereof apply, irrespective of whether the seat of the arbitral proceedings is in a state that based its *lex arbitri* on the Model Law or elsewhere.[60]

4.53. Apart from the provisions concerning the recognition and enforcement of arbitral awards,[61] the provisions establish the jurisdiction of the state courts with regard to the recognition of the arbitration agreement and the duty of the state courts to refer the Parties to arbitration if a claim falling within the scope of the arbitration agreement is brought before a state court, and the possibility to order interim measures despite the existence of an arbitration agreement.[62] Finally, the newly added Articles 17H, 17I and 17J establish the jurisdiction of the state courts when it comes to ordering, recognising and enforcing interim measures.

4.54. In practice, it is not sufficient for the Model Law to include the establishment of the jurisdiction of the state courts with regard to foreign arbitral proceedings. In fact, unless the applicable *lex arbitri* of the state where the arbitral proceedings are seated specifically prohibits the Parties and/or the Arbitral Tribunal to seek the assistance of the state courts, it is irrelevant whether it contains provision(-s) that would provide for the jurisdiction of the state courts with regard to foreign arbitral proceedings. The national *lex arbitri* does not and cannot have any effect on the

---

[60] United Nations Commission on International Trade law: UNCITRAL Model Law on International Commercial Arbitration 1985. With amendments as adopted in 2006 – et. 27, available at: https://uncitral.un.org/sites/uncitral.un.org/files/media-documents/uncitral/en/19-09955_e_ebook.pdf (accessed on 23 March 2022).

[61] Articles 35 and 36 of the Model Law. These provisions do not differentiate between the enforcement of domestic and foreign awards (they apply to arbitral awards "irrespective of the country in which it was made"), which is also a reason why the jurisdiction of the state courts with regard to foreign arbitral awards needed to be established. As far as domestic arbitral awards are concerned, the grounds for setting such award aside as stipulated in Article 34 of the Model Law basically correspond with the grounds for the refusal of the recognition and enforcement of the arbitral award. The Model Law reflect that some states, such as Germany, don't automatically consider domestic arbitral awards to have the binding effects of a final judgment rendered by state courts, and insist on specific enforcement proceedings before a Party can rely on the award. What is interesting is that the Model Law herewith establishes equal treatment of domestic and foreign arbitral awards. So far, the national *lex arbitri* usually provided additional grounds for the setting aside of domestic arbitral awards. The Model Law does not differentiate in this respect, and even domestic awards can only be subject to limited review by the state courts, which allows for the refusal of enforcement of the arbitral award only if it shows major deficiencies.

[62] Articles 8 and 9 of the Model Law. The latter is clearly a reflection of the fact that the 2006 amendment to the Model Law opened the possibility for the state courts to order interim measures concerning foreign arbitral proceedings.

jurisdiction of foreign courts. Any other interpretation would be contrary to the principle of state sovereignty.

4.55. What determines whether a Party or Arbitral Tribunal may seek judicial assistance outside the state where the arbitral proceedings are seated is not the *lex loci arbitri*, but rather the *lex arbitri* of the state whose courts should be called upon to provide judicial assistance. It is something that the Parties should take into consideration when deciding on the seat of the arbitral proceedings. They would be well advised to review not only the *lex arbitri* that they intend to govern their proceedings, but also the *lex arbitri* of the state in which evidence or other procedural steps (including the ordering of interim measures) could potentially be taken.

IV.3. New York Convention

4.56. The primary criterion for the classification of an arbitral award as domestic or foreign used by the New York Convention is not the one generally used when determining the governing *lex arbitri*, i.e. the seat of the arbitral proceedings. Instead, according to Article I(1), the Convention shall apply to the recognition and enforcement of arbitral awards made in the territory of a state other than the state where the recognition and enforcement of the awards are sought. The provision is generally interpreted as identifying the place of the rendering of the award with the seat of the arbitral proceedings. It would, however, be wrong to suggest that an award is always made there and that these terms are identical. The qualification would have to be made individually based on the rules in force in the state where recognition and enforcement are being sight.

4.57. It is acknowledged that such narrow interpretation does not fully cover all situations that may occur in practice, since the distinction between domestic and foreign arbitral award may vary based on the national *lex arbitri*, which can use different criteria.

4.58. The scope of the Convention was therefore broadened and also encompasses arbitral awards rendered on the territory of a state where recognition and enforcement is sought, but is not considered domestic by the respective *lex arbitri*.[63] This effectively excludes the possibility that an arbitral award would not gain (because of the relevant *lex arbitri*) the effects of a domestic arbitral award, but at the same time would not be

---

[63] Yet again, the Convention does not provide any definition of a non-domestic arbitral award, and it is left up to the national legislature to stipulate which (if any) arbitral awards rendered on its territory are to be deemed foreign.

classified as foreign, and thus enforceable under the New York Convention.

4.59. The definition of a non-domestic award does not necessarily need to be included in the general provisions of the *lex arbitri*, but can form part of the regulation that (should this be a standard procedure for international treaties) implements the Convention in the national legal system.[64] There are several instances under which a state would consider an award to be non-domestic:

- an arbitral award made under the national *lex arbitri* of another state;
- an arbitral award rendered as a result of arbitral proceedings involving an international element; and
- an arbitral award that could be called anational.[65]

4.60. While it has been suggested that the first situation can only arise in case the *lex loci arbitri*[66] allows the Parties to agree to submit the proceedings to other arbitration law than the one in force in the state where the seat of the arbitral proceedings is situated,[67] it is only one of the possibilities. Moreover, the statement only holds true if we accept the assumption that the place of the rendering of the arbitral award always corresponds with the seat of the arbitral proceedings. As already explained, while it is so in the majority of cases, it is not a definite rule that always applies.

4.61. Such situation may further occur if the Parties deliberately agree on a place of the rendering of the arbitral award different than the seat of the arbitral proceedings. Since the award would be rendered on the territory of said state, the primary condition stimulated by Article I(1) of the Convention is not fulfilled. As a result, a Party would not be able to seek recognition and enforcement in said state, because the award was rendered there. This state would at the same time not consider the award to be domestic, as the seat of the arbitral proceedings lies in

---

[64] See INTERNATIONAL COUNCIL FOR COMMERCIAL ARBITRATION, ICCA'S GUIDE TO THE INTERPRETATION OF THE 1958 NEW YORK CONVENTION: A HANDBOOK FOR JUDGES, et. 22, available at: https://icac.org.ua/wp-content/uploads/ICCAs-Guide-to-the-Interpretation-of-the-1958-New-York-Convention-A-Handbook-for-Judges-2.pdf (accessed on 23 March 2022).

[65] INTERNATIONAL COUNCIL FOR COMMERCIAL ARBITRATION, ICCA'S GUIDE TO THE INTERPRETATION OF THE 1958 NEW YORK CONVENTION: A HANDBOOK FOR JUDGES, et. 22, available at: https://icac.org.ua/wp-content/uploads/ICCAs-Guide-to-the-Interpretation-of-the-1958-New-York-Convention-A-Handbook-for-Judges-2.pdf (accessed on 23 March 2022).

[66] Which incidentally is the *lex arbitri* of the state where the recognition and enforcement of the arbitral award is being sought.

[67] INTERNATIONAL COUNCIL FOR COMMERCIAL ARBITRATION, ICCA'S GUIDE TO THE INTERPRETATION OF THE 1958 NEW YORK CONVENTION: A HANDBOOK FOR JUDGES, et. 22, available at: https://icac.org.ua/wp-content/uploads/ICCAs-Guide-to-the-Interpretation-of-the-1958-New-York-Convention-A-Handbook-for-Judges-2.pdf (accessed on 23 March 2022).

another state and the proceedings were subjected to another *lex arbitri*.

4.62. The second example refers to the doctrine under which an arbitral award is only considered domestic if the proceedings did not have any connection to any other state. The United States follows this approach, and the United States Federal Arbitration Act (Title 9, Chapter 2) contains a provision to this effect.[68]

4.63. The national legislature is free to follow such doctrine. The Parties should nevertheless be careful when deciding on the seat of the arbitral proceedings in a state whose *lex arbitri* only sees proceedings without any international element as domestic. On one hand, the applicability of the Convention in this situation enables the recognition and enforcement of arbitral awards that were rendered on the territory of a particular state, but are not recognised there because of the international nature of the proceedings. It is up to the Parties to ascertain whether the enforcement regime set by the Convention is sufficient for them. They need to be prepared that, apart from the refusal of recognition and enforcement based solely on the grounds foreseen by the Convection,[69] there is no recourse against the award.

4.64. The state courts of the United States long took the view that an arbitral award made in the United States, under American law, falls within the purview of the Convention – and is thus governed by Chapter 2 of the Federal Arbitration Act – when one of the parties to the arbitration is domiciled or has its principal place of business outside the United States.[70] The Parties cannot make use of the remedies against an award otherwise available under Title 9, Chapter 1 of the United States Federal Arbitration Act.

4.65. As a general notion, the prevailing view is that the Convention can apply to arbitral awards that are the result of proceedings detached from any national arbitration law and conducted only based on transnational rules and general principles of arbitration

---

[68] See Section 202, pursuant to which an agreement or award arising out of a legal relationship, whether contractual or not, which is considered as commercial and which is entirely between citizens of the United States, shall be deemed not to fall under the Convention, unless that relationship involves property located abroad, envisages performance or enforcement abroad, or has some other reasonable relation with one or more foreign states. Á contrario, in order for the Convention to be applied, an international element as described above needs to be present.

[69] Article V of the Convention.

[70] See also US No. 276, *Industrial Risk Insurers v. Barnard & Burk Group, Inc., Barnard and Burk Engineers and Constructors, Inc. v. M.A.N.* Gutehoffnungshütte GmbH, United States Court of Appeals, Eleventh Circuit, 94-2982; 94-2530, 22 May 1998, available at: https://www.kluwerarbitration.com/document/IPN17923 (accessed on 23 March 2022), or US No. 969, *Grupo Unidos por el Canal, S.A., et al. v. Autoridad del Canal de Panama*, United States District Court, Southern District of Florida, Civil Action No. 17-23996-Civ-Scola, 20 June 2018 and 13 November 2018, available at: https://www.kluwerarbitration.com/document/KLI-KA-ICCA-YB-XLIV-219-n (accessed on 23 March 2022).

law.[71] It cannot be excluded that especially state courts exercising their jurisdiction in civil law countries might be tempted not to accept arbitral proceedings not linked to any legal system at all.[72] An arbitral award rendered in such proceedings would be subject to enforcement. On the other hand, it is at least imaginable that the state in which the proceedings were conducted and arbitral award rendered would not see the award as domestic, since it was not rendered under its *lex arbitri*.

IV.4. Problems That May Arise in Connection with Choice of Seat of Arbitral Proceedings

4.66. Problems for the Parties may arise even if their choice of the seat of the arbitral proceedings is unambiguous. First and foremost, there is the question of the possibility of the so-called subjective internalization of an otherwise purely domestic dispute. Some authors argue that it is not possible to move the jurisdiction over a purely domestic dispute abroad by agreeing on a foreign forum. This is usually rejected based on the fact that the Parties cannot exclude the control functions of otherwise competent state courts, which would constitute the evasion of the arbitration law that should govern the proceedings.

4.67. This argument would be acceptable when it comes to litigation before the state courts. Considering the autonomy of the Parties, including their legitimate interest in minimising the intervention of the state courts, to limit the Parties' choice of the seat of the arbitral proceedings would undermine the primary principles governing arbitration. The Parties' extensive freedom to submit a dispute to the legal regime they consider appropriate is widely recognised.[73]

4.68. Apart from the doctrinal argument, even those who reject the concept of subjective internalization accept that, from a practical point of view, it is impossible to prevent the Parties from entering into an arbitration agreement that would place

---

[71] INTERNATIONAL COUNCIL FOR COMMERCIAL ARBITRATION, ICCA'S GUIDE TO THE INTERPRETATION OF THE 1958 NEW YORK CONVENTION: A HANDBOOK FOR JUDGES, et. 23, available at: https://icac.org.ua/wp-content/uploads/ICCAs-Guide-to-the-Interpretation-of-the-1958-New-York-Convention-A-Handbook-for-Judges-2.pdf (accessed on 23 March 2022).

[72] This may in theory even lead to the refusal to recognize and enforce the award due to the breach of the *ordre public*.

[73] For example, arbitration is considered international under the Model Law (Article 1(3)(b)(i)) if the seat of arbitral proceedings as determined in, or pursuant to, the arbitration agreement lies (is situated) outside the state in which the Parties have their places of business.

Czech (& Central European) Yearbook of Arbitration®

the arbitral proceedings outside the state in which all elements of the Parties' legal relationship are situated.[74]

4.69. This does not prevent some state courts from rejecting jurisdiction if they consider the connection to the state in which they exercise jurisdiction to be too week.[75]

V. Conclusion

4.70. As has been demonstrated, the conclusion of a valid arbitration agreement that establishes the jurisdiction of the Arbitral Tribunal does not guarantee the successful conduct of arbitral proceedings. Since the arbitrators exercise their jurisdiction as private persons based on the free will of the Parties, they do not possess any powers towards third persons.

4.71. The outcome of the arbitral proceedings may therefore depend on the judicial assistance provided by the state courts. Similarly important is their ability to exercise control functions. While the conclusion of an arbitration agreement is usually seen as a manifestation of the Parties' will to exclude the jurisdiction of the state courts, it remains undisputed that in order for the arbitral awards to gain the effects of a final court judgment, the state needs to retain at least some degree of control over the conduct of arbitral proceedings within its territory.

4.72. Unlike the jurisdiction of state courts, the location of arbitral proceedings is not strictly determined by the law. The determination of the seat of the arbitral proceedings - which influences the arbitration law governing the proceedings - forms a facet of the autonomy of the Parties. Due to technological advancements, the proceedings are more than ever situated in a state that the Parties consider arbitration-friendly or otherwise suitable, but that has no real connection to the Parties or the subject of the dispute. This may result in a need to take evidence or order, recognise and enforce interim measures in various jurisdictions outside the state of the seat of the arbitral proceedings.

4.73. What is often forgotten is the fact that the seat of the arbitral proceedings, together with additional circumstances, play a decisive role when it comes to the jurisdiction of the state courts. Many national arbitration laws now establish jurisdiction not only with regard to domestic arbitral proceedings, but also

---

[74] NADĚŽDA ROZEHNALOVÁ, ROZHODČÍ ŘÍZENÍ V MEZINÁRODNÍM A VNITROSTÁTNÍM STYKU, Praha: ASPI/Wolters Kluwer (3rd ed. 2013), et. 65.
[75] See also the decision of the Court of Appeal in Paris (Cour d´appel de Paris) in *SA Compagnie Commerciale André* v. *SA Tradigrain France* or the decision of the Svea Court of Appeal in *Titan Corporation* v. *Alcatel CITISA* as referenced in ALEXANDER J. BĚLOHLÁVEK, ARBITRATION LAW OF CZECH REPUBLIC: PRACTICE AND PROCEDURE, New York: JurisNet LLC (2013), et. 852.

establish the powers of the state courts to provide judicial assistance to arbitral proceedings seated in another state. However, this is not always the case, and the Parties cannot take for granted that they will have free access to the courts of any state with any connection to the subject-matter. The unavailability of judicial assistance by the state courts can significantly influence the outcome of the arbitral proceedings, and as such affect the rights of the Parties.

4.74.   Furthermore, the use of different criteria in various national arbitration laws when it comes to the distinction between domestic and foreign arbitral proceedings impacts the jurisdiction of the state courts as well.

4.75.   The content of the *lex loci arbitri* should therefore not be the only criterion for the Parties to consider when they decide on the seat of the arbitral proceedings. It is advisable for the Parties to take into account the consequences of their choice for the possibility of the state courts to provide judicial assistance or to take other necessary measures, including the performance of control functions towards arbitral proceedings.

| | |

Summaries

FRA   [*La compétence incontestable des arbitres offre-t-elle aux parties un mécanisme de contrôle efficace de la part des juridictions nationales ?*]

La compétence des juridictions nationales n'est pas un facteur que l'on prendrait systématiquement en compte lors de la conclusion d'une convention d'arbitrage. Nonobstant les théories doctrinales prônant des approches transnationales ou non-nationales de l'arbitrage international, ce dernier est mené sur la base des règles nationales de la loi du tribunal arbitral. Dans le même temps, il s'appuie dans une certaine mesure sur les juridictions nationales, notamment en ce qui concerne leur fonction auxiliaire et l'exercice du contrôle de l'arbitrage, qui reste une prérogative de l'État.

Contrairement à la compétence de l'arbitre, qui résulte directement de la volonté des parties, la compétence de la juridiction est fondée sur la loi de l'État concerné et ne peut être influencée par les parties. Cependant, et en dépit de l'opinion générale, l'intervention des juridictions peut s'avérer complexe.

Les règles nationales de la loi du tribunal arbitral prévoient généralement une pleine compétence des juridictions en matière *d'arbitrage pour les procédures arbitrales considérées comme nationales dans l'État concerné. Lorsqu'il s'agit d'une procédure arbitrale étrangère, l'étendue de la compétence des juridictions varie considérablement. Dans certains cas, ni les parties à la procédure arbitrale ni les arbitres n'ont accès aux juridictions d'un autre État. Cette situation est encore compliquée par le fait que le lieu d'arbitrage, critère de rattachement décisif (mais pas exclusif) doit être considéré comme un concept juridique « artificiel ». En effet, le lieu de l'arbitrage peut être dépourvu de tout lien réel avec les parties ou l'objet de l'arbitrage, ce qui rend plus probable la nécessité d'une intervention des juridictions d'un autre État, qui a un lien de fait avec l'arbitrage.*

Il existe plusieurs facteurs qui influent sur la possibilité des parties ayant choisi le lieu du tribunal arbitral de demander aux juridictions l'exercice de leur fonction auxiliaire. Les parties devraient ainsi tenir compte de plusieurs circonstances essentielles lorsqu'elles déterminent le lieu du tribunal arbitral, afin de ne pas compromettre le déroulement de la procédure arbitrale par l'absence de la fonction auxiliaire des juridictions.

CZE   *[**Poskytuje nezpochybnitelná pravomoc rozhodců stranám efektivní kontrolní mechanismus ze strany soudů?**]*

Pravomoc soudů není něčím, na co by člověk obvykle myslel v souvislosti s uzavíráním rozhodčí smlouvy. I přes doktrinální přístupy obhajující transnacionální či anacionální přístup k mezinárodnímu rozhodčímu řízení, koná se rozhodčí řízení na základě národní úpravy lex arbitri. V určitých směrech se spoléhá na soudy, zvláště pokud jde o jejich pomocné funkce a výkon kontroly, kterou si stát nad rozhodčím řízení ponechává.

Oproti pravomoci rozhodců, která je přímým výsledkem svobodné vůle stran, pravomoc soudů vymezují právní předpisy tohoto kterého státu bez možnosti jejího ovlivnění stranami. V rozporu s obvyklým přesvědčením se však může angažovanost soudů ukázat jako komplikovaná.

Národní úprava lex arbitri obvykle vyhrazuje plnou pravomoc soudů ve vztahu k rozhodčímu řízení pro rozhodčí řízení, která jsou v daném státě považována za domácí. Co se týče cizího rozhodčího řízení, rozsah pravomoci soudů se značně liší. V některých případech nemají strany rozhodčího řízení ani rozhodci vůbec žádný přístup k soudům jiného státu. Co činí celou situaci ještě komplexnější, je skutečnost, že na místo rozhodčího řízení, jako rozhodující (ale nikoli výhradní) kolizní určovatel, je nezbytné pohlížet jako na „umělý" právní koncept. Místo rozhodčího řízení nemusí mít žádnou reálnou spojitost se stranami nebo předmětem rozhodčího řízení, v důsledku čehož je potřeba intervence ze strany soudů jiného státu (který má k rozhodčímu řízení faktický vztah) pravděpodobnější.

Existuje více faktorů, jejichž prostřednictvím stranami učiněná volba místa rozhodčího řízení ovlivňuje možnosti dožadovat se výkonu pomocných funkcí ze strany soudů. Strany by tedy při určení místa rozhodčího řízení měly zohlednit několik klíčových okolností tak, aby průběh rozhodčího řízení nebyl ohrožen v důsledku absence pomocných funkcí soudů.

| | |

POL [*Czy niepodważalne kompetencje arbitrów jest dla stron efektywnym mechanizmem kontrolnym ze strony sądów krajowych?*]

Miejsce postępowania arbitrażowego jako podstawowe kryterium rozróżniające dla postępowania arbitrażowego krajowego i zagranicznego nie tylko określa właściwe lex arbitri, ale również wpływa na zakres kompetencji sądów w odniesieniu do postępowania arbitrażowego. Pojawia się coraz więcej przypadków, kiedy sądy innego kraju zmuszone są tu do interwencji (wykonywania funkcji pomocniczych). Relacje między sądami i zagranicznym postępowaniem arbitrażowym bywają niełatwe. Różnice w krajowych przepisach lex arbitri oznaczają, że nie istnieje tutaj żadna uniwersalna zasada. Dlatego tak ważne jest, by strony w postępowaniu arbitrażowym miały świadomość problemów praktycznych, z którymi mogą się spotkać oraz tego, jak wybrane przez nie miejsce postępowania arbitrażowego wpływa na kompetencje sądów.

DEU [*Verschafft die unzweifelhaft gegebene Zuständigkeit der Schiedsrichter den am Rechtsstreit beteiligten Parteien einen wirksamen Mechanismus für die gerichtliche Kontrolle?*]

Der Ort des Schiedsverfahrens – als das primäre Kriterium für die Unterscheidung zwischen inländischen und ausländischen Schiedsverfahren – bestimmt nicht nur das anzuwendende lex arbitri, sondern beeinflusst auch die Reichweite der Kompetenz der Gerichte in Bezug auf das Schiedsverfahren. In einer wachsenden Anzahl von Fällen entsteht der Bedarf an einer Intervention (in Form der Ausübung von Hilfsfunktionen) auch seitens der Gerichte eines Drittstaates. Die Beziehung zwischen den Gerichten und dem ausländischen Schiedsverfahren ist nicht immer einfach. Die zwischen den nationalen Ausgestaltungen des Schiedsrechts bestehenden Differenzen bedeuten außerdem, dass es keine einheitliche Regel für das lex arbitri gibt. Von daher

00

ist es wichtig, dass sich die am Schiedsparteien die praktischen Probleme bewusst werden, mit denen sie möglicherweise zu kämpfen haben werden, und sich des Einflusses bewusst sind, den ihre Wahl des Schiedsorts auf die Kompetenzen der Gerichte hat.

RUS [*Предоставляет ли сторонам несомненная компетенция арбитров эффективный механизм контроля со стороны судов?*]

Как первичный критерий разграничения между внутренним и иностранным арбитражем место проведения арбитража не только определяет применимое lex arbitri, но и влияет на объем компетенций судов в отношении арбитража. С возрастающим количеством дел возникает необходимость вмешательства (выполнения вспомогательных функций) судов другого государства. Отношения между судами и иностранным арбитражем не всегда просты. Различия между национальными нормаами lex arbitri также означают, что для них не существует единого правила. В этой связи важно, чтобы стороны арбитража осознавали практические проблемы, с которыми они могут столкнуться, а также влияние выбранного ими места проведения арбитража на компетенцию судов.

ESP [*¿Proporciona la jurisdicción incuestionable de los árbitros a las partes litigantes un mecanismo de control efectivo por parte de los tribunales nacionales?*]

El lugar del arbitraje como criterio principal para distinguir entre el arbitraje nacional y el extranjero no solo determina la lex arbitri aplicable, sino que también influye en el alcance de la jurisdicción de los tribunales en relación con el arbitraje. En una número creciente de casos, se hace necesaria la intervención (el ejercicio de funciones auxiliares) de los tribunales de otro Estado. La relación entre los tribunales nacionales y el arbitraje extranjero no siempre es sencilla. Además, las diferencias entre los regímenes nacionales de lex arbitri hacen que no exista una norma uniforme para ellos. Por lo tanto, es importante que las partes litigantes del arbitraje sean conscientes de los problemas prácticos a los que se pueden enfrentar, así como del impacto de la elección del lugar del arbitraje en el alcance de la jurisdicción de los tribunales.

| | |

Bibliography:

PETER ANGST, KOMMENTAR ZUR EXEKUTIONSORDNUNG, Wien: Manzsche Verlags und Universitätsbuchhandlung (2000).

ADOLF BAUMBACH, WOLFGANG LAUTERBACH, JAN ALBERS, PETER HARTMANN, ZIVILPROZESSORDNUNG: MIT FAMGB, GVG UND ANDEREN NEBENGESETZEN, München: C.H. Beck (72nd ed. 2014).

ALEXANDER J. BĚLOHLÁVEK, ARBITRATION LAW OF CZECH REPUBLIC: PRACTICE AND PROCEDURE, New York: JurisNet LLC (2013).

GARY B. BORN, INTERNATIONAL COMMERCIAL ARBITRATION, VOL. I, Austin: Wolters Kluwer (2009).

MICHAEL W. BÜHLER, THOMAS H. WEBSTER, HANDBOOK OF ICC ARBITRATION: COMMENTARY AND MATERIALS, London: Sweet & Maxwell (2nd ed. 2008).

W. LAURENCE CRAIG, WILLIAM W. PARK, JAN PAULSSON, INTERNATIONAL CHAMBER OF COMMERCE ARBITRATION, New York: Oceana Publications, Inc. (3rd ed. 2000).

HANS W. FASCHING, ANDREAS KONECNY, KOMMENTAR ZU DEN ZIVILPROZESSGESETZEN, BAND IV/2, Wien: Manzsche Verlags und Universitätsbuchhandlung (2nd ed. 2007).

PHILIPPE FOUCHARD, EMMANUEL GAILLARD, JOHN SAVAGE, BERTHOLD GOLDMAN, FOUCHARD GALLARD GOLDMAN ON INTERNATIONAL COMMERCIAL ARBITRATION, The Hague: Kluwer Law International (1999).

Simon Gabriel, Axel Buhr, Johannes Landbrecht, Andreas Schregenberger, International Arbitration – Switzerland, Law & Practice, CHAMBERS, GLOBAL PRACTICE GUIDES (2021).

International Council for Commercial Arbitration, ICCA'S Guide to the Interpretation of the 1958 New York Convention: A Handbook for judges.

JENS-PETER LACHMANN, HANDBUCH FÜR DIE SCHIEDSGERICHTSPRAXIS, Köln: Verlag Dr. Otto Schmidt (3rd ed. 2008).

THOMAS RAUSCHER, PETER WAX, JOACHIM WENZEL, MÜNCHENER KOMMENTAR ZUR ZIVILPROZESSORDNUNG (ZPO) §§ 946 – 1086, München: C. H. Beck (3rd ed. 2008).

STEFAN RIEGLER, ALEXANDER PETSCHE, ALICE FREMUTH-WOLF, MARTIN PLATTE, CHRISTOPH LIEBSCHER, ARBITRATION LAW OF AUSTRIA: PRACTICE AND PROCEDURE, New York: Juris Publishing, Inc. (2007).

NADĚŽDA ROZEHNALOVÁ, ROZHODČÍ ŘÍZENÍ V MEZINÁRODNÍM A VNITROSTÁTNÍM STYKU, Praha: ASPI/ Wolters Kluwer (3rd ed. 2013).

INGO SAENGER, ZIVILPROZESSORDNUNG – HANDKOMMENTAR, Beden-Baden: Nomos Verlagsgesellschaft (2nd ed. 2007).

RUDOLF STOHANSL, MANZ GROßE, AUSGABE DER ÖSTERREICHISCHEN GESETZE, 6. Band: Jurisdiktionsnorm und Zivilprozeßordnung, Wien: Manzsche Verlags und Universitätsbuchhandlung (15th ed. 2002).

FRANK-BERND WEIGAND, ANTJE BAUMAN, PRACTITIONER'S HANDBOOK ON INTERNATIONAL COMMERCIAL ARBITRATION, Oxford: Oxford University Press, (2nd ed. 2009).

Andreas Respondek | Tasha Lim

Jurisdiction of Arbitral Tribunals, Kompetenz-Kompetenz and Doctrine of Separability in Selected Countries of Southeast Asia: Status, Development and Global Comparison

Key words:
jurisdiction of arbitral tribunals | arbitral jurisdiction | Kompetenz-Kompetenz | arbitrator | arbitral tribunal | arbitrability | Singapore | Hong-Kong | Malaysia | Southeast Asia

Czech (& Central European) Yearbook of Arbitration®

Abstract | *Issues pertaining to arbitral jurisdiction are often raised by disgruntled parties with the hope of having an arbitral award set aside. This article seeks to explore the principle of the determination, power and authority of the arbitral tribunal to decide a dispute. In general, the arbitral tribunal derives its powers from the arbitration agreement, the procedural rules, the applicable national law and any implied powers. The trite doctrine of Kompetenz-Kompetenz assigns the power to arbitrators to determine whether they do, or do not, have jurisdiction to determine all (or part) of the matters referred to arbitration. However, this will be subject to final review by the relevant supervisory court. In this article, the discussion on arbitral jurisdiction will be focused on three main arbitration seats in Asia, being Singapore, Hong Kong and Malaysia. All of these countries have adopted the New York Convention 1958 as well as the UNCITRAL Model Law on International Commercial Arbitration. These two frameworks remain the main standards that are applied by the aforementioned countries to determine when an arbitral tribunal is considered to possess jurisdiction.*

Dr Andreas Respondek established the firm RESPONDEK & FAN in Singapore in 1998 and its counterpart in Bangkok in 2000. He focuses on international commercial law, international contracts, M&A and international arbitration. After more than 20 years in international arbitration in Asia and beyond, Dr Respondek has acted as arbitrator or counsel in more than 80 major international proceedings in institutional (including expedited proceedings) and ad hoc arbitrations under the auspices of the ICC, SIAC, HKIAC, Swiss Rules, TAI and UNCITRAL Arbitration Rules. He is also the editor and co-author of the Asia Arbitration Guide, which is the standard reference book with the broadest geographical Asian coverage on international arbitration in Asia. E-mail: respondek@rflegal. com

Ms Tasha Lim was admitted as a Barrister-At-Law (Inner Temple) of England and Wales in 2016 and was subsequently

| | |

I. Introduction

5.01. Arbitration is generally known as 'a process by which parties consensually submit a dispute to a non-governmental decision-maker, selected by or for the parties, to render a binding decision resolving a dispute in accordance with neutral adjudication procedures affording the parties an opportunity to be heard.'[1] Despite being hit by the pandemic in 2020, various arbitral institutions are having record-breaking caseloads, with some indicating that they have seen the greatest number of cases that they have had in years. The fact that most arbitration institutions were able to move quickly to virtual hearings reinforces the notion that arbitration is a resilient and reliable avenue for commercial dispute resolution, particularly in cross-border transactions. The most popular seats selected in international arbitration are London, Singapore, Hong Kong, Paris and Geneva.

admitted as an Advocate and Solicitor of the High Court of Malaya in 2018. She currently assists Dr Respondek on various international arbitration proceedings and contributes to the publication of arbitration-related articles, available at: https://www.rf-arbitration.com/publications/insights (accessed on 02 January 2022), and advises international corporate investors in their day-to-day needs for legal advice in Singapore and beyond. E-mail: tashalim@rflegal.com

5.02. Singapore has seen years of steady growth in arbitration, and has positioned itself as one of the leading arbitration hubs. As of 2021, Singapore is the most popular seat in Asia for arbitration, and the second most popular worldwide.[2] The caseload of the leading arbitral institution in Singapore, the Singapore International Arbitration Centre (the "SIAC"), has remained strong, with more than 1,000 case filings in 2020, which is more than double the annual caseload of the past few years, and it is the first time that the SIAC's caseload has crossed the 1,000-case threshold.

5.03. Another major seat for arbitration in Asia is Hong Kong. The main arbitration institution of the Hong Kong International Arbitration Centre (the "HKIAC") has been identified as the third most preferred arbitral institution in the 2021 Queen Mary Survey on International Arbitration.[3] The latest HKIAC case statistics show that 318 arbitration cases were submitted

---

[1] GARY B. BORN, INTERNATIONAL COMMERCIAL ARBITRATION, The Netherlands: Kluwer Law International (2009), et. 217.
[2] 2021 International Arbitration Survey, Queen Mary University of London.
[3] 2021 International Arbitration Survey, Queen Mary University of London.

to the HKIAC in 2020, of which 99.4% of the arbitrations were seated in Hong Kong.

5.04. Meanwhile, statistics from the Asia International Arbitration Centre (the "AIAC"), the leading arbitration institution in Malaysia, also record a significant increase in arbitration cases since 2011, with a yearly increase in cases referred between 2012 and 2014, peaking with 226 cases registered in July 2014. In recent years, the number of new cases referred to the AIAC seems to have levelled out.

5.05. One of the important issues that invariably arise in arbitral proceedings is in relation to the tribunal's jurisdiction. Parties who intend to avoid the proceedings or set aside the arbitral award often assert that the tribunal does not have the necessary jurisdiction. In this article, we will examine this topic, starting with an outline of the legislative framework for arbitration in each of these countries, how jurisdiction is conferred upon the tribunal, and what approach the national courts take when dealing with such a dispute. For the purpose of this article, our focus will lie on the three main arbitration centres in Asia, namely Singapore, Hong Kong and Malaysia.

II.   Legislative Framework

5.06. All three countries – Singapore, Hong Kong and Malaysia – have incorporated the UNCITRAL Model Law on International Commercial Arbitration (the "Model Law") in their national laws, and are signatories to the Convention on the Recognition and Enforcement of Foreign Arbitral Awards 1958 (the "New York Convention"). Additionally, they have in place local legislation to govern arbitral proceedings, which will be discussed below.

II.1.   Singapore

5.07. The two main statutes governing arbitration proceedings in Singapore are:
   • The International Arbitration Act (the "IAA"), which gives effect to the Model Law and the New York Convention and applies to international arbitration;
   • The Arbitration Act (the "AA"), which applies to domestic arbitration.

5.08. Singapore has adopted this dual regime approach, as it was cognizant that parties should be given the full freedom to choose whether they prefer a regime that involves more, or less, curial supervision by opting into or out of either the AA or the IAA. The divide between domestic and international arbitration determines the level of the court's involvement. For international arbitration, the court's intervention will be limited to specific instances expressly provided by the IAA; it does not have any residual discretion or power to grant any form of relief that is not expressly provided for under the IAA. In contrast, for domestic arbitration, the intervention is more extensive, in that a party may appeal to the court with respect to questions of law, subject to certain conditions being met.

5.09. In addition, subject to minor modifications, Singapore has adopted the Model Law without the 2006 amendments. It is also a signatory to the New York Convention, which came into force in Singapore on 19 November 1986.

II.2. Hong Kong

5.10. Hong Kong is known to have a modern legal framework in the form of the Hong Kong Arbitration Ordinance, which applies to all arbitrations seated in Hong Kong, and is based on the most recent version of the UNCITRAL Model Law, with its amendments adopted in 2006.

5.11. The previous Arbitration Ordinance had separate regimes for domestic and international arbitration. The new Arbitration Ordinance unifies the domestic and international regimes and applies many articles in the Model Law to both domestic and international arbitration. Furthermore, under the provisions of the current Arbitration Ordinance, parties are able to opt into certain provisions from the former domestic regime, such as the ability to appeal against an arbitral award with respect to a question of law or challenge the arbitral award on the grounds of serious irregularity, as set out in Schedule 2 thereof.

5.12. Hong Kong is also party to the New York Convention by virtue of China's accession to it on 22 January 1987.

II.3. Malaysia

5.13. The principal legislation that applies to arbitration in Malaysia is the Arbitration Act, which governs both domestic and international arbitration. Malaysia's Arbitration Act is closely modelled on the UNCITRAL Model Law. In fact, since March 2006, when the Arbitration Act came into force, there have been three rounds of amendments to the Arbitration Act, with the most recent being in May 2018, to bring the Arbitration Act in line with the Model Law with amendments adopted in 2006. This is consistent with efforts of the Malaysian government to establish Malaysia as a global hub for arbitration and other ADR proceedings.

5.14. Malaysia is a signatory to the New York Convention, which came into force on 03 February 1986 in Malaysia.

III.   Definition of "Jurisdiction"

5.15. In the context of arbitration, the term 'jurisdiction' typically refers to the 'power' or 'authority' of the arbitral tribunal to decide a dispute. In other words, 'jurisdiction' defines and determines the power and authority of arbitrators to hear and decide a case, and pertains to the competence of a tribunal to adjudicate a particular case.[4]

5.16. Arbitrators generally have authority over only those parties who have agreed to arbitrate and those disputes that fall within the terms of the parties' written arbitration agreement. The term "jurisdiction" is often intertwined with arbitrability or admissibility – *i.e.* whether the claim is capable of being examined by the arbitrators. Technically, jurisdiction refers to the arbitral authority over persons, whereas arbitrability should refer to whether the subject matter of the parties' dispute is within the scope of the arbitration agreement.

5.17. When parties assert that the arbitrator/tribunal lacks authority over the parties or the subject matter, the question naturally arises as to whether arbitration is the proper forum to decide that issue. Before deciding on an admissibility challenge, the arbitrators should first be satisfied that they have jurisdiction to determine the admissibility issue.

IV.   Excluded Jurisdiction

5.18. While parties have almost complete autonomy in determining the type of matters that may be included in arbitration, not all matters are arbitrable. It is generally considered settled that issues that may contain public interest elements may not be arbitrable, for example, citizenship or the legitimacy of marriage, grants of statutory licences, the validity of the registration of trademarks or patents, the winding-up of companies, the bankruptcy of debtors, regulatory legislation relating to anti-trust, trade practices, consumer protection, environmental protection and planning.

5.19. Be that as it may, public policy is not defined in the Model Law. This may be due to the fact that the concept of fundamental

---

4   ZACHARY DOUGLAS, THE INTERNATIONAL LAW OF INVESTMENT CLAIMS, Cambridge: Cambridge University Press (2009), et. 293.

public policy can be subjective, as every country defines for itself the content of public policy. In addition, the content of fundamental public policy can change over time within a single country. To shed some light on what amounts to public policy, some commentators elucidate that public policy refers to considerations that are directed "not at doing justice as between the parties to the immediate dispute before the court, but, rather, at furthering the interests of the community as a whole".[5]

5.20. Meanwhile, a clearer position on the sphere of arbitration can be extrapolated from the Model Law's description of the term 'commercial'. It states that the term 'commercial' is to be given a broad interpretation so as to cover matters arising from all relationships of a commercial nature, whether or not contractual. Relationships of a commercial nature include, but are not limited to, the following transactions: any trade transaction for the supply or exchange of goods or services, distribution agreement, commercial representation or agency, factoring, leasing, construction of works, consulting, engineering, licensing, investment, financing, banking, insurance, exploitation agreement or concession, joint venture and other forms of industrial or business co-operation, and carriage of goods or passengers by air, sea, rail or road.[6]

5.21. Based on the foregoing, it is important for the arbitrators to determine whether the disputes arising between the parties fall within the substantive scope of the arbitration agreement, subject to any specific or different approach under the pertinent applicable laws. Otherwise, an award made in excess of the tribunal's jurisdiction may be set aside by the local courts, as both the New York Convention and the Model Law provide that a state may refuse to enforce an arbitral award if it is contrary to the public policy of that state. However, in practice, it is observed that the common law jurisdictions have adopted a restrictive approach in interpreting public policy as a bar to the enforcement of arbitral awards.

IV.1. Singapore

5.22. Section 11(1) of the International Arbitration Act provides that all disputes are arbitrable unless it is contrary to public policy.[7] Essentially, disputes are not arbitrable if they have public interest elements, or where third parties have an interest in the outcome

---

[5] Ross Grantham, Darryn Jensen, *The Proper Role of Policy in Private Law Adjudication*, UNIVERSITY OF TORONTO LAW JOURNAL 191 (2018).
[6] Model Law Article 1(1).
[7] The International Arbitration Act Section 11(1).

of the proceedings. It follows that if the subject matter of the arbitration agreement is contrary to public policy, the matter is not arbitrable and any award made may be set aside. On the other hand, the fact that an arbitral tribunal does not have the power to issue the relief sought does not make the dispute non-arbitrable.[8]

5.23. Meanwhile, there is no specific reference in the domestic Arbitration Act that addresses the issue of public policy and subject matter arbitrability. However, the High Court[9] took the view that the concept of arbitrability applicable to international arbitration under the International Arbitration Act ought to be taken into consideration when considering applications under the Arbitration Act.

5.24. Thus far, only a very limited list of dispute subject matters has been recognised as being against public policy to arbitrate,[10] which are issues in relation to:
- Citizenship;
- Legitimacy of marriage;
- Grants of statutory licences;
- Winding-up of companies;
- Bankruptcy;
- Administration of estates.

5.25. Further, in 2019, the International Arbitration Act was amended to clarify that disputes concerning intellectual property rights are arbitrable.[11]

IV.2. Hong Kong

5.26. In Hong Kong, there is also no prescribed list of claims that are not arbitrable, although the courts took into consideration English authorities that cited the categories below as being non-arbitrable:
- Criminal cases;
- Consumer claims;
- Winding up/bankruptcy claims;
- Actions *in rem* against ships;
- Competition and antitrust disputes;
- Family law matters;
- Labour or employment grievances;

---

[8]   *Tomolugen Holdings* v. *Silica Investors Ltd* [2015], SGCA 57.
[9]   In the case of *Petroprod Ltd (in official liquidation in the Cayman Islands and in compulsory liquidation in Singapore)* v. *Larsen Oil and Gas Pte Ltd* [2010], 4 SLR 501.
[10]   *Larsen Oil and Gas Pte* v. *Petroprod Ltd* [2011], SGCA 21.
[11]   The International Arbitration Act Section 26B.

- Matters reserved for resolution by state agencies and tribunals (e.g. taxation, immigration and national welfare entitlements).

5.27. Further, on 1 January 2018, Part 11A of the Arbitration Ordinance came into effect confirming that disputes relating to intellectual property rights are arbitrable. On the other hand, the question of whether or not a winding up order should be made may be arbitrable depending upon the grounds on which the winding up order is sought.[12]

IV.3. Malaysia

5.28. Similarly, in Malaysia, any dispute that the parties have agreed to submit to arbitration under an arbitration agreement can be determined by arbitration, unless the arbitration agreement is contrary to public policy, or the subject matter is not capable of settlement by arbitration under the laws of Malaysia.[13]

5.29. The types of disputes that are generally considered not arbitrable include:

- Matrimonial disputes and family law matters (divorce, child custody, judicial separation, guardianship, grant of probate, and letters of administration);
- Disputes relating to criminal offences (including bribery and corruption);
- Winding-up and bankruptcy matters;
- Competition laws.

5.30. The Malaysian apex court, following the Singapore Court of Appeal's decision in *PT Asuransi Jasa Indonesia (Persero) v. Dexia Bank,* held that *the concept of public policy ought to be read narrowly and more restrictively*[14] by stating that:

"... the general consensus of judicial and expert opinion is that public policy under the Act encompasses a narrow scope. In our view, it should only operate in instances where the upholding of an arbitral award would 'shock the conscience' ... or is 'clearly injurious to the public good or... wholly offensive to the ordinary reasonable and fully informed member of the public'... or where it violates the forum's most basic notion of morality and justice."

---

[12] *Re Southwest Pacific Bauxite (HK) Ltd* [2018], 2 HKLRD 449; *Dayang (HK) Marine Shipping Co Ltd* v. *Asia Master Logistics Ltd* [2020], HKCFI 311.
[13] Arbitration Act Section 4(1).
[14] In the case of *Jan De Nul (Malaysia) Sdn Bhd & Anor v. Vincent Tan Chee Yioun & Anor* [2018], 1 LNS 1613.

V. How Jurisdiction Is Conferred on Arbitral Tribunals

5.31. Firstly, for an arbitrator to have jurisdiction, there must be a binding agreement to arbitrate, the arbitrator must have been validly appointed and the dispute must be one that the parties had agreed to arbitrate. The arbitral tribunals have a range of powers deriving from:

- the arbitration agreement;
- the procedural rules;
- the applicable national law;
- implied powers.

5.32. Evidently, as arbitration focuses on the parties' autonomy, arbitrators derive their powers from an agreement between contracting parties, which is usually set out in the arbitration agreement, a separate document or any rules to which the parties refer in the arbitration agreement. The parties may by agreement confer on the arbitrator any power that they deem appropriate, to the extent that they do not contradict to the mandatory provisions of the applicable law of the arbitration. In addition, the chosen rules of arbitral institutions normally spell out these powers and are generally more comprehensive in scope than those granted by local statutes.

5.33. Most institutional rules include powers such as ordering discovery or interrogatories; ordering an inspection or viewing; allowing amendments or time extensions within which to file or serve pleadings; determining the language, place and time of the arbitration and/or granting an adjournment; adjournment; limiting witnesses; granting or refusing the re-opening of the hearing; using the arbitrator's own knowledge; making an award in different currencies; correcting clerical errors; extending the ambit of the arbitration proceedings; granting or refusing legal representation; or allowing documents to be filed beyond the deadline.

5.34. The other source of the arbitrators' powers is the law of the place of arbitration, which is usually spelled out in the statutes applicable to arbitration proceedings. Such statutory powers are conferred on arbitrators to assist them in the conduct of arbitration proceedings. Usually, they are empowered under the laws to correct any clerical mistake or error in an award arising from any accidental slip or omission, to award costs, to order security for costs, to order the discovery of documents and interrogatories, to enforce any obligation of confidentiality, to order the giving of evidence by affidavit, and so forth.

5.35. In addition to express powers, arbitrators increasingly exercise powers not expressly conferred by express legislation. These powers are usually referred to as "implied" or "inherent". Arbitrators may consider some powers necessary to carry out their duties not to have not been spelled out in the parties' agreement or in the law. This frequently occurs, because parties rarely exhaustively enumerate all of the arbitrators' powers in the arbitration agreement, and arbitration laws grant arbitrators only a limited number of specific powers. In any event, even the most complete arbitration agreements, arbitration rules or laws cannot cover every situation that an arbitrator may face in carrying out his or her duties.

5.36. The arbitrator has a general duty to conduct arbitration proceedings fairly, impartially and in accordance with the agreed procedure. This also implies that the tribunal has the power to take steps consonant with such duty. Accordingly, it is generally accepted that an arbitrator has the implied power to give directions for the general conduct of the arbitration on matters such as the exchange of pleadings, the determination of preliminary issues, the use of expert witnesses and the fixing of hearing dates.

5.37. Powers not previously expressly set out and considered implied or inherent are now increasingly provided expressly by law or as part of the rules chosen by the parties. Also, if both the parties' agreement and the relevant rules of law are silent, arbitral tribunals increasingly take this silence not as a prohibition, but rather as authorisation to take the relevant steps. However, the existence of any non-express power should not be inferred lightly, as the arbitral process may be undermined if the arbitral tribunal exercises powers that it does not have or exceeds its powers, and the award may thus be annulled or its enforcement refused if a state court so holds. It is therefore essential that arbitral tribunals understand the scope of their powers to ensure that the use thereof does not undermine the integrity of the arbitral process and the enforceability of the award.

VI. Determination of Tribunal's Substantive Jurisdiction

5.38. Article 16(1) of the Model Law enshrines the doctrine of *kompetenz-kompetenz*. That is, arbitrators have the power to determine whether they have, or do not have jurisdiction to determine all (or part) of the matters referred to arbitration. In other words, arbitrators are competent to determine their own competence.

5.39.   Therefore, a decision about whether a tribunal has jurisdiction will frequently be made by the tribunal itself; the fact that a party has challenged the arbitrators' jurisdiction does not prevent the arbitrators from deciding the merits of that challenge and determining whether they have, or do not have jurisdiction. However, such decision is not and cannot be a source of its jurisdiction, and cannot be a definitive determination of that jurisdiction, because the authority of that decision depends on the final review by the supervisory court. A degree of deference may be given to the tribunal's determination of these questions by national courts, but self-evidently a tribunal may not confer authority on itself. It would not make sense for a tribunal to have the power to decide whether or not the agreement is valid, when the tribunal's decision-making power depends on that agreement being valid. In essence, the doctrine of *kompetenz-kompetenz* gives the tribunal the power to decide whether it has jurisdiction, but it does not prevent the court from conducting a full review of the tribunal's decision.

5.40.   The doctrine of *kompetenz-kompetenz* is recognised in all three countries, with minor differences in each country, as illustrated below.

VI.1. Singapore

5.41.   Singapore recognises the principle of *Kompetenz-Kompetenz*, and arbitrators are given express statutory power to decide on their own jurisdiction, including any objections with respect to the existence or validity of the arbitration agreement. Therefore, if a party wishes to challenge the tribunal's jurisdiction, it can bring that challenge before the tribunal. Such challenge in relation to the jurisdiction of the arbitral tribunal must be raised by no later than the submission of the statement of defence.[15] The tribunal may rule on the issue of jurisdiction either as a preliminary issue or together with the award on the merits.

5.42.   It is noteworthy that under Article 16(3) of the Model Law, only positive rulings on jurisdiction may be challenged in court. Singapore has modified the Model Law to provide the court review of both positive and negative rulings on jurisdiction. As such, the tribunal's ruling on its own jurisdiction, regardless of whether it is a positive or negative ruling, can be appealed to

---

[15]   Arbitration Act Article 21(4); Model Law Article 16(2).

Czech (& Central European) Yearbook of Arbitration®

the High Court within 30 days of the ruling. The High Court's decision on jurisdiction can also be further appealed, provided that the High Court's permission is obtained.[16] While the appeal proceedings in court on the issue of jurisdiction are pending, the tribunal may proceed with the arbitration and issue an award. In practice, however, parties often request, and the tribunal would generally accede to, the suspension of the arbitration. The question of arbitral jurisdiction may further be raised at the enforcement stage of the award.

VI.2. Hong Kong

5.43. Hong Kong has enshrined the principle of *Kompetenz-Kompetenz*, under Section 34 of its Arbitration Ordinance, under which the arbitral tribunal has the power to rule on its own jurisdiction.

5.44. The arbitral tribunal can, from the time at which it is constituted, determine issues of jurisdiction, including whether it has been properly constituted, the existence or validity of the arbitration agreement, and whether matters have been submitted to arbitration pursuant to the arbitration agreement.

5.45. Where a party refutes that the arbitral tribunal has jurisdiction to determine the dispute, that party can raise such a plea no later than when submitting the statement of defence, but the arbitral tribunal can admit a later plea if it considers the delay justified.[17]

5.46. The arbitral tribunal's ruling as a preliminary question that it has jurisdiction is subject to appeal before the local court by any party within 30 days of receiving notice of that ruling. Unlike the position in Singapore, the court's review is binding and not subject to appeal.[18] Moreover, a party refuting that the arbitral tribunal has jurisdiction to determine the dispute can apply to have an award set aside before the Hong Kong courts.[19]

VI.3. Malaysia

5.47. The *Kompetenz-Kompetenz* doctrine is equally applicable in Malaysia. Section 18(1) of the Arbitration Act provides that an arbitral tribunal may rule upon its own jurisdiction, including any objections to the existence or validity of an arbitration

---

[16] International Arbitration Act Section 10; Model Law Article 16(2).
[17] Arbitration Ordinance Section 34(1).
[18] Arbitration Ordinance Section 34(4).
[19] Arbitration Ordinance Sections 13 and 81.

agreement.[20] According to Section 18(3) of the Arbitration Act, a plea that the arbitral tribunal does not have jurisdiction must be raised by no later than the submission of the statement of defence.

5.48. Where the arbitral tribunal rules on such a plea as a preliminary question that it has jurisdiction, any party can appeal to the court within 30 days after having received notice of that ruling.[21] Unlike the position in Singapore, such a decision of the court is non-appealable.[22] The arbitral tribunal is entitled to rule on the issue of jurisdiction either as a preliminary question or in an award on the merits.

5.49. Furthermore, it is stated in the Arbitration Act that a plea that the arbitral tribunal is exceeding the scope of its authority shall be raised as soon as the matter alleged to be beyond the scope of its authority is raised during the arbitral proceedings. Nevertheless, the arbitral tribunal may admit such a plea if it considers the delay justified.

VII. Doctrine of Separability

5.50. The issue often arises as to what should happen to an arbitration clause if the contract in which it was contained was terminated, whether through breach or frustration, or by rescission, or avoided by reason of illegality. The doctrine of separability has evolved to save the application of the arbitration clause. This doctrine is found under the same Article 16(1) of the Model Law, as discussed above. This means that the arbitration agreement is separate from the contract in which it is contained (assuming that the arbitration agreement is comprised of an arbitration clause in a contract).

5.51. Therefore, an arbitration clause in a contract constitutes a self-contained contract collateral or ancillary to the underlying contract. By this doctrine, an arbitration clause being a collateral obligation in a contract survives the termination or avoidance of all the primary obligations assumed under the underlying contract. In other words, a decision by the arbitral tribunal that a contract is null and void does not in and of itself mean that the arbitration clause is invalid.

5.52. This doctrine has been given statutory expression in the arbitration legislation in all three countries: in Section 21 of

---

[20] The arbitral tribunal's powers to decide on its own jurisdiction or competence or the scope of its authority or the existence or validity of the arbitration agreement has been recognised by the Malaysian courts in *Press Metal Sarawak Sdn Bhd* v. *Etiqa Takaful Bhd* [2016], 5 MLJ 417; *TNB Fuel Services Sdn Bhd* v. *China National Coal Group Corp* [2013], 4 MLJ 857.
[21] Arbitration Act Section 18(8).
[22] Arbitration Act Section 18(10).

Czech (& Central European) Yearbook of Arbitration®

Singapore's International Arbitration Act, in Section 34(1) of Hong Kong's Arbitration Ordinance, and in Section 18(2) of Malaysia's Arbitration Act.

VIII. Cases in Relation to Challenges to Tribunal's Jurisdiction

5.53. Article 16(2) of the Model Law provides that jurisdictional objections should be raised by no later than the submission of the statement of defence. Therefore, a respondent must make any jurisdictional objection on a timely basis. Otherwise, it may be deemed to have waived its right to object. The main objective behind this provision is to preclude belated adjudication on questions of jurisdiction and to avoid wasting the time and costs of the parties.

5.54. As discussed above, an arbitrator's ruling on jurisdiction is not definitive. First, the court of the seat may review that ruling:

- under Article 16(3) – if a preliminary ruling on jurisdiction is made prior to rendering an award on the merits; or alternatively;
- under Article 34 – if the decision on jurisdiction is contained in a partial or final award on the merits.

5.55. Aside from that, an enforcement court, whether the court of the seat or otherwise, may consider jurisdictional issues upon an application to enforce the award under Article 36 of the Model Law or Article V of the New York Convention.

5.56. In practice, the courts are generally reluctant to set aside an award on jurisdictional grounds if the disputing party did not raise any objections during the arbitration proceedings. The cases below will shed some light on the approach of the courts in different countries when deliberating issues raised in relation to arbitral jurisdiction.

VIII.1. Singapore

5.57. The case of *Astro Nusantara International BV and others v. PT Aunda Prima Mitra and others* [2012] SGHC 212 illustrates that the court will be reluctant to set aside an award challenged on the grounds that the tribunal lacked jurisdiction at the enforcement stage. The Singapore High Court, in holding so, stated that:

- in relation to a domestic international arbitration award, an unsuccessful party cannot just remain passive and resist recognition and enforcement only when enforcement proceedings are brought, and that a proactive application to set aside the award on a prescribed ground is needed within the correct timescale; and

- in relation to a ruling on jurisdiction heard as a preliminary issue, an unsuccessful party must submit the ruling to the court for review within the statutory time limit, and if it does not do so and continues with the arbitration, it cannot then revive a jurisdictional objection on enforcement.

5.58. In another case of *PT First Media TBK* v. *Astro* **[2013] SCGA 47**, the Singapore High Court decided that the respondent cannot reserve its jurisdictional objection to the setting-aside stage if it has not objected to an arbitrators' preliminary ruling on jurisdiction. The judge stated that, to allow a respondent to reserve its objection to the setting-aside stage (post award) may allow it to "indulge in tactics that result in immense delays and cost".

5.59. However, the Court of Appeal took a different position. Firstly, the Court of Appeal highlighted the existence of "active" and "passive" remedies available to a respondent under the scheme of the Model Law.

5.60. Under this classification:

- Articles 16 and 34 are "active" remedies, in that they provide for the respondent to take a positive step in challenging the jurisdiction of an arbitrator; while
- Article 36 involves a "passive" remedy, in that the respondent can wait until the claimant brings an enforcement application, and challenge the jurisdiction of the arbitral tribunal at that stage.

5.61. Therefore, a party could choose to pursue either an active remedy – by challenging the preliminary award on jurisdiction – or a passive remedy – by challenging enforcement. The fact that the respondent had not applied under Article 16(3) to review a preliminary ruling on jurisdiction did not prevent it from resisting enforcement of the award under Article 36. In other words, the fact that the respondent had not availed itself of an active remedy did not deny it a passive remedy.

5.62. The court went on to opine that the failure by an award debtor to avail itself of the remedy in Article 16 would preclude it from raising a jurisdictional objection at the setting-aside stage under Article 34 (post award).

5.63. This active/passive remedy dichotomy has been criticised for promoting inefficiency in the arbitral process. This would increase the costs and time, particularly if the respondent continues to participate in the arbitration following a ruling on jurisdiction against it.[23]

5.64. Interestingly, the Court of Appeal in the case of *Rakna Arakshaka Lanka Ltd* v. *Avant Garde Maritime Services Pte Ltd* [2019] SGCA 33 allowed a non-participating party to have an arbitral award set aside even though such party did not raise the jurisdiction objection within the time limits prescribed by Article 16(3) of the Model Law. The respondent in the arbitration, Rakna, did not attend or participate in any way, nor did it respond to the Tribunal's directions.

5.65. The Court of Appeal recognized that the objective of Article 16 of the Model Law was to require jurisdictional challenges to be brought out early in the arbitral proceedings, so as to avoid wasting resources and to minimise delays to the proceedings.

5.66. However, the Court of Appeal then held that the law does not compel a respondent to take part in arbitral proceedings by stating that:

> "...if the respondent believes that the arbitration tribunal has no jurisdiction... he is perfectly entitled to sit by and do nothing..." and that "in the absence of a clear duty on the respondent to participate in the arbitration proceedings imposed either by the Model Law or the [International Arbitration Act] we find it difficult to conclude that a non-participating respondent should be bound by the award no matter the validity of his reasons for believing the arbitration was wrongly undertaken."

5.67. In deciding so, the Court of Appeal was careful to distinguish between the position of a non-participating respondent versus a respondent who failed in its jurisdiction objection and then participates in the arbitration. In the latter case, the respondent would have contributed to the wasted costs, and it is fair to say to such a respondent that it cannot then bring a setting aside application after the time limit prescribed in Article 16(3), though it can continue to resist enforcement.

5.68. Importantly, the court cautioned that such move to not participate in the proceedings may be a risky course of action, as the respondent may be mistaken in its belief that the tribunal lacks jurisdiction and ultimately finds itself with a valid award against it.

---

[23] Doug Jones, *What Now for Article 16(3)?*, 2(2) EUROPEAN INTERNATIONAL ARBITRATION REVIEW 243 (2014).

VIII.2. Hong Kong

5.69.   In the case of *Arjowiggins HKK2 Ltd v. X Co* [2016] HKEC 2472, the Hong Kong High Court firmly rejected an application to set aside, and held that parties must raise any objections during the underlying arbitration proceedings, rather than seeking to hold them in reserve or uncover them after the fact. In this case, the respondent had not raised any objection during the proceedings, and had even raised counterclaims against the claimant. The judge reiterated the point that she made in a number of other recent judgments, which is - a party must raise any objection without undue delay, and that failure to do so shall be deemed a waiver of its right to object.

5.70.   In dealing with applications to set aside an arbitral award, or to refuse enforcement of an award, the conduct complained of *"must be serious, even egregious"*,[24] before the court would find that there was an error sufficiently serious as to have undermined due process.

5.71.   This was shown in the case of *AB v. CD, HCCT 27/2020,* where the Court of First Instance set aside an arbitral award due to a lack of arbitral jurisdiction, as the wrong company was named as the respondent in the proceedings. In this case, the respondent had chosen not to participate in the arbitration. To this end, the court agreed with AB Engineering that it had no obligation to participate in an arbitration to which it disputes being a party.

5.72.   Hong Kong courts have always favoured a pro-arbitration stance. That being said, the courts take very seriously the fundamentals of the arbitral process, pertaining to the validity of arbitration agreements and the jurisdiction of the arbitral tribunal. This case confirms the court's recognition of the 'Dallah principle', i.e., a party that disputed jurisdiction was entitled not to participate in arbitration proceedings if it took the view that the proceedings were not valid.

VIII.3. Malaysia

5.73.   *In the case of **Bauer (M) Sdn Bhd v. Daewoo Corp** [1999] 4 MLJ 545*, the court held that a failure to raise a jurisdictional objection did not prevent an objecting party from later challenging the award on the same jurisdictional grounds in setting aside or enforcement proceedings.

5.74.   However, there has been a shift in arbitral jurisprudence in Malaysia since this case, and since the Arbitration Act was amended in 2005, as reflected in the case of ***Sunway Creative***

---

24   *Grand Pacific Holdings Ltd v. Pacific China Holdings Ltd* [2012], 4 HKLRD 1 (CA).

Stones Sdn Bhd v. *Syarikat Pembenaan Yeoh Tiong Lay Sdn Bhd and Anor* [2020] MLJU 658. In this case, the Malaysian High Court refused to set aside an arbitral award, because the applicant had not challenged the arbitrator's jurisdiction and conduct when the issues arose during the arbitral proceedings. It further expressed that the decision in *Bauer (M) Sdn Bhd v. Daewoo* was inconsistent with the intention of Article 16 of the UNCITRAL Model Law and, in turn, Section 18 of the Arbitration Act.

5.75. Section 18(5) of the Arbitration Act, worded similarly to Article 16(2) of the UNCITRAL Model Law, required a party to challenge any excess of jurisdiction as soon as the alleged infraction arose during the arbitral proceedings. Analysing this, the Court held that if a party fails altogether to invoke the right to challenge an arbitrator's jurisdiction whilst arbitration proceedings are ongoing, that party cannot thereafter apply to set aside the award on jurisdictional grounds. It emphasised that such lack of protest can be deemed a waiver of a party's right to set aside an arbitral award on the same grounds at a later date.

5.76. This position is in stark contrast with the Singaporean approach to jurisdictional objections in *Rakna Arakshaka Lanka Ltd v. Avant Garde Maritime Services (Private) Limited* [2019] SGCA 33 (supra), where the Singapore Court of Appeal found that a non-participating respondent was entitled to stand by while the claimant proceeded with the arbitration without losing its right to challenge the arbitral jurisdiction in setting aside proceedings before the supervisory court.

IX. Jurisdiction to Order Interim Measures

5.77. Article 17 of the Model Law provides that a tribunal may, unless agreed otherwise by the parties, order interim relief at the request of a party. There is no prescription of what this relief may encompass, save that it is as the arbitral tribunal may deem necessary in respect of the subject-matter of the dispute. The Model Law does not prescribe the test that a tribunal should apply in determining whether to grant this relief. Consequently, it is open to the tribunal to determine the test that it should apply, subject to any prescription of national law in that jurisdiction.

IX.1. Singapore

5.78. An arbitral tribunal in Singapore is empowered to grant interim relief to the parties before it. Under Section 12(1) of the International Arbitration Act, an arbitral tribunal has the power to give directions for, amongst other things, security for costs, discovery of documents and interrogatories, giving of evidence by affidavit, the preservation, interim custody or sale of any property that is or forms part of the subject-matter of the dispute, securing the amount in dispute, ensuring that any award that may be made in the arbitral proceedings is not rendered ineffectual by the dissipation of assets by a party, or an interim injunction or any other interim measure. An arbitral tribunal also has the power to administer oaths and take the affirmations of parties and witnesses, unless, of course, the parties have agreed otherwise. The powers of the arbitral tribunal under the Arbitration Act are similar.[25]

5.79. Further, Section 12A(3) of the International Arbitration Act states that the High Court of Singapore has the same power as the tribunal for the purpose of and in relation to an action or a matter in court. Significantly, the Court has the power to make such an order irrespective of whether the place of the arbitration is in Singapore. This means that the Singapore Courts have the power to grant interim relief in support of an arbitration seated in another jurisdiction, provided that it is considered an international arbitration within the definition of the International Arbitration Act.

IX.2. Hong Kong

5.80. Under the Arbitration Ordinance, a tribunal generally has the power to grant interim relief similar to that granted by the Hong Kong Courts. For instance, a tribunal has the power to grant Mareva injunctions, or an Anton Piller order. A tribunal can also require a party requesting interim measures to provide security, which is similar to the Hong Kong Court's direction for fortification from a party seeking urgent injunctive relief.

5.81. The tribunal's power is derived from Sections 35 and 56 of the Arbitration Ordinance (adopting Article 17 of the Model Law), which empower the tribunal to order interim measures to:
- maintain or restore the status quo pending the determination of the dispute;
- take action that would prevent, or refrain from taking action that is likely to cause, current or imminent harm or prejudice to the arbitral process itself;
- provide means of preserving assets out of which a subsequent award may be satisfied; and/or

---

[25] Sections 28 and 31 of the Arbitration Act.

- preserve evidence that may be relevant or material to the resolution of the dispute.

5.82. However, the parties can agree to opt out of such provisions in the arbitration agreement. Also similar to Singapore, the Hong Kong Court has broad jurisdiction under Section 21L and Section 21M of the High Court Ordinance to grant interim relief in support of arbitration proceedings in or outside Hong Kong, as long as those proceedings give rise to an award that is ultimately enforceable in Hong Kong.

IX.3. Malaysia

5.83. The Arbitration Act grants Malaysian courts the power to grant interim relief pursuant to Section 11 of the Arbitration Act, which states that a party may, both before and during arbitral proceedings, apply to the High Court for any interim measure listed in Section 11(1)(a)-(h). As the High Court ruled in *Cobrain Holding Sdn Bhd* v. *GDP Special Projects* [2010] 1 LNS 1834, these powers may not be excluded by an agreement of the parties.

5.84. Additionally, Section 19(1) of the Arbitration Act provides that a party may apply for one of the following orders:

- security for costs;
- discovery of documents and interrogatories;
- giving of evidence by affidavit;
- preservation, interim custody or sale of any property that is the subject-matter of the dispute.

5.85. Principally, the arbitral tribunal may grant an interim measure, whether in the form of an award or in another form, at any time prior to the issuance of the final award, to order a party to:

- maintain or restore the status quo, pending the determination of the dispute;
- take action that would prevent or refrain from taking action that is likely to cause current or imminent harm to or prejudice the arbitral process itself;
- provide means to preserve assets out of which a subsequent award may be satisfied;
- preserve evidence that may be relevant or material to the resolution of the dispute; or
- provide security for costs of the dispute.

5.86. Amendments to the Arbitration Act in 2018 slightly revised Section 19(1), bringing it in line with the most recent changes to the Model Law, now also allowing for *ex parte* requests for interim relief, without notice to the other party.

Czech (& Central European) Yearbook of Arbitration®

X. Conclusion

5.87. The lack of jurisdiction of the tribunal is frequently invoked by disgruntled parties to challenge the validity of an arbitral award. They will often argue that the tribunal was not vested with the powers to adjudicate the dispute. However, the pro arbitration stance taken by the courts means that the courts will be slow to set aside an arbitral award on such grounds, save under exceptional circumstances or where there has been a violation of notions of morality and justice. Singapore, Hong Kong and Malaysia have an unequivocal judicial policy of facilitating and promoting arbitration, and have clearly identified the role of the courts as to support, and not to displace, the arbitral process.

5.88. This pro-arbitration landscape in Asian jurisdictions is in place to keep up with the competitive international arbitration scene. Undoubtedly, this contributed to the rise in arbitration in Asia. Being the world's largest economic region, there is still significant room for further economic development, especially in the post-pandemic era, considering their swift recovery from Covid-19. It is certain that the demand for arbitration will continue to rise in Asia. In fact, new arbitration institutions have been established in the region in response to the increasing demand. One recent example is the launch of the Beihai Asia International Arbitration Centre in Singapore in 2019. Furthermore, with China's consistent persuasion of the Belt and Road Initiative across Asia, it is likely that in future we will witness more disputes being adjudicated with the preferred arbitral institutions in Asia, and more governmental efforts in building the essentials to develop their own country as an important arbitration centre.

| | |

Summaries

DEU [*Zuständigkeit der Schiedsgerichte, Kompetenz-Kompetenz und die Abtrennbarkeitsdoktrin in ausgewählten Ländern Südostasiens: aktueller Stand, Entwicklung und eine globale Komparation*]
Unzufriedene Streitparteien berufen sich oft auf Zweifel hinsichtlich der Zuständigkeit der Schiedsgerichte in der Hoffnung, der Schiedsspruch werde aufgehoben werden. Sinn und Zweck des vorliegenden Artikels ist eine Prüfung der Grundsätze, nach denen Schiedsgerichte, deren Gerichtsbarkeit und deren Zuständigkeit

im jeweiligen Rechtsstreit bestimmt werden. Generell bezieht das Schiedsgericht seine Zuständigkeit aus der Schiedsvereinbarung, den Prozessregeln, dem anzuwendenden nationalen Recht und etwaigen implizit verankerten Kompetenzen. Die Kompetenz-Kompetenz-Doktrin, die in dieser Hinsicht zum Alltag geworden ist, erkennt Schiedsrichtern die Befugnis zu, darüber zu entscheiden, ob sie die Kompetenz besitzen, über alle (oder einige) der Angelegenheiten zu entscheiden, die ihnen zur Verhandlung und Entscheidung im Schiedsverfahren vorgelegt wurden, oder eben nicht. Allerdings ist diese Frage einer abschließenden Prüfung durch das zuständige Gericht unterworfen, welches eine Kontrollfunktion betreffend das Schiedsverfahren ausübt. Die Diskussion der Schiedsgerichtsbarkeit in diesem Artikel konzentriert sich auf die drei wichtigsten Sitze des Schiedsverfahrens in Asien: Singapur, Hongkong und Malaysien. Alle diese Länder haben das New Yorker Übereinkommen von 1958 sowie das UNCITRAL-Mustergesetz für internationale Handelsschiedsverfahren angenommen. Diese beiden rechtlichen Rahmenwerke bilden auch weiterhin den wichtigsten Standard, der von den o.g. Ländern angewandt wird, wenn es um die Entscheidung geht, ob das jeweilige Schiedsgericht zuständig ist oder nicht.

CZE **[*Pravomoc rozhodčích soudů, Kompetenz-Kompetenz a doktrína oddělitelnosti ve vybraných zemích jihovýchodní Asie: stav, vývoj a globální srovnání*]**
Pochybností ohledně pravomoci rozhodčích soudů se často dovolávají nespokojené strany v naději, že rozhodčí nález bude zrušen. Smyslem tohoto článku je prozkoumání zásady určení, pravomoci a oprávnění rozhodčího soudu k rozhodování ve sporu. Obecně rozhodčí soud odvozuje svou pravomoc z rozhodčí smlouvy, procesních pravidel, použitelného vnitrostátního práva a případných implicitně zakotvených pravomocí. Zevšednělá doktrína Kompetenz-Kompetenz přiznává rozhodcům oprávnění rozhodnout o tom, zda mají pravomoc rozhodovat ve všech (nebo některých) záležitostech předložených k projednání a rozhodnutí v rozhodčím řízení, nebo nikoliv. Tato otázka však podléhá konečnému přezkumu příslušným soudem vykonávajícím nad rozhodčím řízením kontrolní funkci. V tomto článku se diskuse ohledně pravomoci rozhodčích soudů zaměří na tři hlavní sídla rozhodčího řízení v Asii, a sice Singapur, Hongkong a Malajsii. Všechny tyto země přijaly Newyorskou úmluvu z roku 1958, jakož i Vzorový zákon UNCITRAL pro mezinárodní obchodní arbitráž. Tyto dva rámce jsou i nadále hlavními standardy

aplikovanými výše uvedenými zeměmi při rozhodování o tom, zda rozhodčí soud je nadán pravomocí, či nikoliv.

| | |

POL   [*Kompetencje sądów arbitrażowych, Kompetenz-Kompetenz i klauzule salwatoryjne w wybranych krajach południowowschodniej Azji: stan, rozwój i perspektywa globalna*]
Artykuł został poświęcony prezentacji i analizie najnowszych trendów i przypadków z praktyki arbitrażowej w kwestiach dotyczących kompetencji w krajach azjatyckich common law, czyli w Singapurze, Hongkongu i Malezji. Następnie porównuje ich ramy legislacyjne, w znacznej mierze do siebie zbliżone, bowiem oparte w każdym z tych krajów na systemie common law. Artykuł omawia również znaczenie kompetencji trybunału arbitrażowego i podejmuje polemikę co do tego, w jaki sposób kompetencje są powierzane sądowi arbitrażowemu i kto o jego kompetencjach decyduje.

FRA   [*La compétence des tribunaux arbitraux, la kompetenz-kompetenz et la doctrine de la séparabilité dans des pays choisis de l'Asie du Sud-Est : situation,* évolutions, *comparaison globale*]
Le présent article examine les tendances et les affaires les plus récentes dans la pratique arbitrale concernant les questions de compétence, et ce dans trois pays asiatiques du common law, à savoir Singapour, Hong Kong et la Malaisie. Les auteurs procèdent à une comparaison de leurs cadres législatifs, qui sont largement similaires du fait d'appartenir au système du common law. Enfin, l'article analyse la question de la compétence du tribunal arbitral et s'interroge sur la manière dont cette compétence lui est conférée et qui en décide.

RUS   [*Компетенция арбитражных судов, Kompetenz-Kompetenz и доктрина отделимости в некоторых странах Юго-Восточной Азии: состояние, развитие и глобальное сравнение*]
В данной статье представлены и проанализированы последние тенденции и случаи из арбитражной практики по вопросам компетенции в трех азиатских странах common law – в Сингапуре, Гонконге и Малайзии. Затем следует сравнение их законодательств, которые во многом схожи, поскольку все она основана на системе common law. Кроме того, в статье рассматривается значение компетенции

арбитражного суда, а затем обсуждается, каким способом арбитражный суд наделяется компетенцией и кто принимает решение о его компетенции.

ESP [*Competencia de los tribunales arbitrales, Kompetenz-Kompetenz y la doctrina de la divisibilidad en países del sudeste asiático seleccionados: estado actual, desarrollo y comparación global*]

Este artículo presenta y examina las últimas tendencias en el arbitraje y varios casos recientes relacionados con las cuestiones jurisdiccionales en los tres países asiáticos de derecho consuetudinario: Singapur, Hong Kong y Malasia. A continuación, se comparan sus marcos legislativos que, en gran medida, son similares, ya que todos se basan en el sistema jurídico del common law. Después, se aborda la cuestión de la competencia de los tribunales de arbitraje y se analizan los procedimientos de adjudicación de la competencias y la cuestión de quién decide sobre ella.

| | |

Bibliography:

GARY B. BORN, INTERNATIONAL COMMERCIAL ARBITRATION, The Netherlands: Kluwer Law International (2009).

ZACHARY DOUGLAS, THE INTERNATIONAL LAW OF INVESTMENT CLAIMS, Cambridge: Cambridge University Press (2009).

Ross Grantham, Darryn Jensen, *The Proper Role of Policy in Private Law Adjudication*, UNIVERSITY OF TORONTO LAW JOURNAL 191 (2018).

Doug Jones, *What Now for Article 16(3)?*, 2(2) EUROPEAN INTERNATIONAL ARBITRATION REVIEW 243 (2014).

Czech (& Central European) Yearbook of Arbitration®

Mercedes Romero | Rafael Montejo

Validity and Assessment of Pathological Arbitration Clauses in Relation to Judicial Intervention in its Review

Key words:
Arbitration clause |
Invalidity of the arbitration
agreement | Kompetenz-
kompetenz principle |
Judicial intervention |
Enforcement of arbitral
award | Annulment of an
arbitral award

Abstract | *Submission to arbitration requires a manifest expression of will in the relevant contract in what is often referred to as the arbitration agreement or arbitration clause. Otherwise, the arbitrator (and sometimes national courts) could consider itself to lack jurisdiction to deal with the matter. Sometimes, this problem does not really lie on the absence of an arbitration clause but on a poor drafting of the clause. In these cases, we are referring to a pathological arbitration clause. The arbitration clause can be pathological for different reasons, leading to the following categorization: uncertain clauses, when the lack of clarity is derived from a vague wording of the clause; inoperative clauses, when the clause is impossible to make effective; and hybrid clauses, when the agreement presents a submission to both arbitration and the judicial jurisdiction at the same time. In most of these cases, the solution will consist of determining whether the aim of the parties was to submit to arbitration or not. However, the determination of this will to submit to arbitration can also be problematic in the stage of its judicial interlocutory review. This leads to a debate on whether this review should be an in-depth review or should be restricted to a prima facie analysis of the mere existence of a clause, specially if considering that there are other stages where an in-depth review could be made.; both of which are analysed in the present article.*

Mercedes Romero is the partner in charge of the Litigation and Arbitration practice in the Madrid office of DAC Beachcroft. She has over 16 years of experience advising clients across a range of sectors including construction, engineering, energy, financial, telecom and sports. She has also taken part in complex judicial and arbitral proceedings, as well as insolvency proceedings and international enforcement proceedings. She has been recognized by Chambers Global and Chamber Europe.
E-mail: mromero@dacbeachcroft.com

Rafael Montejo has worked in the Dispute resolution and arbitration department of different international law firms, where he has been involved in various arbitration proceedings, both national and international. He is currently in the Department of litigation and arbitration, DAC Beachcroft, Madrid. He is a published author in a relevant Spanish legal magazine.
E-mail: rmontejo@dacbeachcroft.com

I.   The Pathological Arbitration Clause

6.01.   Submission to arbitration requires explicit written consent from all parties involved in the contract leading to the dispute. The New York Convention describes it as an 'agreement in writing.'[1] This consent may be expressed after the dispute arises, in a separate agreement, but it is a common - and recommended - practice to give this consent in the relevant contract through the dispute resolution clause, in what is referred to as the 'arbitration clause.'

6.02.   Despite the great importance of the arbitration clause, more often than not the parties do not approach their drafting thoroughly. They do not anticipate future conflicts and it is usually the last clause of the agreement to be composed when the parties are the most eager to finish the negotiations and sign the contract. This is why it is commonly called the 'champagne clause' or 'midnight clause.'

6.03.   Consequently, this wish to solve eventual disputes through arbitration is not always expressed as accurately as it should be, leading to situations where it is not clear for the Arbitrators, the Arbitration Court or the national courts whether the arbitration clause is valid and thus if the dispute is to be solved through arbitration. Therefore, we are dealing with a *pathological arbitration clause* when the parties' intention to resort to arbitration, or the conditions in which they want to do it, have not been expressed in clear and unequivocal terms.

6.04.   There are various types of pathological clauses, numerous ways in which an arbitration clause may suffer from this ambiguity.

I.1.   Uncertain Arbitration Clauses

6.05.   Uncertain Arbitration clauses are those in which the lack of clarity is derived from a vague wording of the clause. This uncertainty can be due to an excessively narrow drafting of the clause or a drafting that is too broad, to the point where the parties' intention is not properly defined, or it is even contradictory in its terms.

6.06.   An example of the first case would be the following: 'Arbitration. All disputes are to be solved in an amicable way.' Although it could be argued that the wish to resort to arbitration is somehow expressed, otherwise it would not even be considered, its clarity is questionable and no prevision is included regarding the form

---

[1]   Article 2(2) of the United Nations Convention on the Recognition and Enforcement of Foreign Arbitral Awards (New York, 10 June 1958).

of arbitration to which they are submitting their disputes nor the exclusivity of the submission to arbitration.

6.07. An example of the second form of uncertainty would be the following: 'The doubts emerging from the interpretation of the present Agreement or others related, as well as the existence and amount of a claim derived from its compliance, are to be solved by an arbitrating arbitrator or amicable decider, without the form of a trial, whose decision shall not be contested'. In this case, the notion of an 'arbitrating arbitrator or amicable decider' is confusing regarding the exclusivity and enforceability of arbitration.

I.2.   Inoperative Clauses

6.08. Inoperative clauses are those whose enforcement is not possible, even if their wording is clear. This impossibility may be due to the referral to non-existing Arbitration institutions or rules, or because of overly demanding requirements to appoint the arbitrator. For instance: 'The arbitrator must be an English-speaking Hungarian lawyer, majored in biomedical Engineering and familiar with contracts involving the supply of prosthetics to Germany', or 'The arbitration is to be conducted before Zlín's Chamber of Commerce'. Another example of inoperability in an arbitration clause would be that in which the appointed arbitrator has passed away before the dispute emerges.

6.09. In both cases, it is impossible to comply with the arbitration clause, for it refers to a non-existing (or impossible to find) individual or to a non-existing Arbitration Court. The main issue when determining the validity of these clauses will be to establish whether the agreed upon submission to arbitration was subject to the requirements that make it inoperative or the wish to resort to arbitration prevails regardless of these requirements.

I.3.   Hybrid Clauses

6.10. Hybrid clauses (or mixed clauses) are those in which recourse to other means of dispute resolution is not excluded. A textbook hybrid clause would be that which allows the parties to choose between various means of solving the dispute (i.e., an arbitrator or national courts) once it arises. The problem of these clauses is their axiomatic incompatibility with the submission to arbitration since submission to arbitration excludes the judicial jurisdiction by definition. Therefore, the drafting of these clauses is contradictory.

6.11. Notwithstanding the above, not all hybrid clauses will be pathological, only those where the desire to resort to arbitration as a priority method is not clear.

I.4. Validity and Remedy of the Pathological Clause

6.12. The first question arising in relation to the validity of the pathological clause is the applicable law to its interpretation. The determination of the law applicable is not based on a fixed general criterion. Some argue it is the law applicable to the contract that governs the arbitration clause. Others argue the arbitration clause is a separable and independent agreement and must be governed by the law of the seat of the arbitration. For the sake of this paper, since that is not the topic at hand, we will elaborate on the assumption that the applicable law is the one governing the contract, since it is probably the most common position.[2]

6.13. The second question arising from this topic is who would be competent to interpret the pathological clause, which is key to this study and thus will be assessed later in this paper.[3]

6.14. In the following points we will analyse the criteria for interpretation followed in order to cure (or not) a pathological clause.

I.4.1. Uncertain Arbitration Clauses. Interpretation

6.15. Since the literal wording of the clause does not allow the conclusion of whether parties should submit their disputes to arbitration or not, the clause is to be interpreted in relation to the conduct of the parties and the context of its composition. Other principles that can be applied to the interpretation of such clauses are the 'interpretation against the draftsman' or *contra proferentem* interpretation[4] and the principle of estoppel. This precludes a person from pursuing something contrary to what was implied by a previous action or statement.

6.16. According to the Swiss Federal Tribunal, these clauses should be interpreted pursuant to the general rules of contract

---

[2]   GARY B. BORN, INTERNATIONAL COMMERCIAL ARBITRATION, Alphen aan den Rijn: Kluwer Law International (2nd ed. 2014), et. 476.
[3]   See Chapter II. of this article.
[4]   Judgement of the Superior Court of Justice of Madrid of 12 September 2019.

interpretation and hence are to be understood in accordance with the common intent of the parties. If this common intent could not be established, the principle of good faith would apply.[5]

6.17. In Spain, the Superior Court of Justice of Madrid, dealing with an action of annulment of an award, upheld an arbitration clause by arguing the initial wish of the parties was to submit to arbitration on the grounds of the principle of estoppel.

> [...] The commitment and will of the parties to submit to arbitration are clear, **we agree with the arbitrator's application of the principle** *venire contra factum propium non valet,* **i.e. no one can act against his own actions, since this is contrary to the principle of good faith that must govern contractual relations.**[6] (translated by the author) (emphasis added)

I.4.2. *Inoperative Arbitration Clauses. Interpretation*

6.18. In these clauses, the parties' will to submit to arbitration is not as unclear as in the uncertain clauses but some of the important decisions are wrong or non-existing. Therefore, in these cases, validity can be based in a *pro arbitrio* interpretation, by appealing to the principle of utility of the clause and the fill in the gaps of what is missing. For instance, in case the designated arbitrator was unavailable for whatever reason (inexistence, demise, impossibility, etc.), the Court could appoint the competent arbitrator according to its rules, as allowed by many national legislations as in Section 5 of the Federal Arbitration Act of the United States of America and Article 15(3) of the Spanish Arbitration Act.

6.19. In Hong Kong, regarding a clause that provided for arbitration in an unspecified 'third' country with the rules of procedure of a non-existing organization,[7] it was considered by the Court that said clause sufficiently indicated the parties' will to resort to arbitration. It was argued that the clause's defects did not really render it inoperative, for its enforcement was possible

---

[5]   Swiss Federal Tribunal of 21 November 2003, DFT 130 III 66.
[6]   Judgement of the Superior Court of Justice of Madrid of 18 February 2019.
[7]   Verbatim: '3rd country under the rule of the 3rd country and in accordance with the rules of procedure of the International Commercial Arbitration Association' in *Lucky Goldstar International* v. *Ng Moo Kee Engineering Limited* [1993] 2 HKLR 73.

by performing the arbitration in any country different to the parties' and in a place of arbitration chosen by the plaintiff.

6.20. In Spain, the Provincial Court of Madrid applied the principle of utility to make a *pro arbitrio* interpretation of an inoperative clause when the initial intention of the parties can be inferred (as in uncertain clauses).

> [w]e are dealing with a clause that can be remedied if we take into account the 'pro arbitratio' principle, the principle of utility of the contract and the contract interpretation rules (subsequent conduct of the parties, Article 1,282 of the Civil Code), that would allow us to argue the parties' will to submit to arbitration.[8] (translated by the author) (emphasis added)

I.4.3.   Hybrid Arbitration Clauses. Interpretation

6.21. In 'hybrid clauses', the literal wording of the clause is more important than in previous cases, in view of the priority given to arbitration in contrast to the other forms of dispute resolution.

6.22. In Spain, until 2013, these clauses were deemed ineffective and void for considering that their discretion was incompatible with an exclusive submission to arbitration. Since 2013, a more constructive approach is being taken in the reading of these clauses. However, in 2015, the Superior Court of Justice of Canary Islands, Las Palmas, upheld an action of annulment of the award because the parties were submitting firstly to national courts and secondly to arbitration. The thesis sustained by the Court was that arbitration's exclusive nature is by definition incompatible with a provision of choice or alternative of jurisdiction when arbitration is not the primary one.

> The document by which the parties submit to arbitration cannot be deemed to be unequivocal [...], it firstly submits to national courts and secondly and incomprehensibly to arbitration. There is not an unequivocal will, otherwise they would submit to one dispute resolution formula or the other, but not to both jointly, for they are not complementary, but they are exklusive.[9] (translation by author) (emphasis added)

---

8   Judgement of the Superior Court of Justice of Madrid, 03 February 2009.
9   Judgement of the Superior Court of Justice of Islas Canarias (Las Palmas), 19 June 2015.

II.   Judicial Review of the Pathological Arbitration Clause

II.1.   Pathological Clauses in relation to the *Kompetenz-Kompetenz* Principle, Interlocutory Review of the Arbitration Agreement

6.23. The *Kompetenz-Kompetenz* principle has a twofold effect. Firstly, it allows the arbitrator to decide on its own jurisdiction (the positive effect); secondly, it precludes the national courts from dealing with disputes submitted to arbitration (the negative effect).

6.24. However, once the dispute arises, this principle is breached when one of the parties questions the arbitrator's jurisdiction by bringing his case before national courts. In Spanish Law,[10] as in the New York Convention[11] and in the UNCITRAL Model Law,[12] national courts, despite the *Kompetenz-Kompetenz* principle, do not have to refer the parties to arbitration when they deem the clause to be 'null and void, inoperative or incapable of being performed'. Therefore, since a valid arbitration agreement precludes the national courts from hearing the case, the judge will have to make an interlocutory decision on its jurisdiction based on the validity of the arbitration clause. This gives rise to the debate around which this Chapter will revolve: the extent to which national courts should analyse the validity of pathological clauses brought before them for interlocutory consideration.

6.25. This is not a new debate, the extent to which national courts can examine the arbitration agreement prior to the award is an ever-controversial dichotomy in arbitration all around the globe. In fact, Spanish precedents have created a distinction between two broad positions in relation to this matter, the weak thesis and the strong thesis; depending on whether they allow national courts to make a substantive analysis of the arbitration clause or not, respectively.

---

[10]   Article 11(1) of the Spanish Arbitration Act.

[11]   Article II(3): 'The court of a Contracting State, when seized of an action in a matter in respect of which the parties have made an agreement within the meaning of this article, shall, at the request of one of the parties, refer the parties to arbitration, **unless it finds that the said agreement is null and void, inoperative or incapable of being performed'.**

[12]   Article 8(1): 'A court before which an action is brought in a matter which is the subject of an arbitration agreement shall, if a party so requests not later than when submitting his first statement on the substance of the dispute, refer the parties to arbitration **unless it finds that the agreement is null and void, inoperative or incapable of being performed'.**

II.1.1. The Weak Thesis

6.26. The weak thesis separates just enough from the *Kompetenz-Kompetenz* principle to ·consider that judges are to carry out a substantive analysis of the (pathological) arbitration clause in order to determine its validity when the matter is brought before them by one of the parties.

6.27. In relation to UNCITRAL Model Law, it is believed by many judicial authorities in Model Law states that Article 8(1) requires for said in depth analysis when using the word 'find'.

6.28. Article 8(1) literally states:

'A court before which an action is brought in a matter which is the subject of an arbitration agreement shall, if a party so requests not later than when submitting his first statement on the substance of the dispute, refer the parties to arbitration unless **it finds** that the agreement is null and void, inoperative or incapable of being performed.' (emphasis added)

6.29. In this respect, some commentators[13] argue in favour of a full judicial consideration on the grounds of the will of the drafters of the rule. For instance, the drafters could have otherwise proposed an explicit *prima facie* analysis[14] instead of referring the Courts to look for whether the clause is null and void. Therefore, some argue that UNCITRAL Model Law does not restrict the clause's verification to a *prima facie* review, but instead allows for full consideration.

6.30. In fact, we can find decisions in favour of this position in relevant countries like Germany, where the *Bundesgerichtshof* reviewed the arbitration clause to an extent where not only did it appreciate its inoperative nature but also ruled on the ability of the parties to terminate the arbitration agreement as a consequence of that pathology.[15]

6.31. A mixed position can be found adopted by Canadian courts. In *Dell Computer Corp.* v. *Union des Consommateurs*, the Canadian Supreme Court considered that, where issues of law were involved, an in-depth judicial analysis is required.

---

[13] EMMANUEL GAILLARD, JOHN SAVAGE, FOUCHARD GAILLARD GOLDMAN ON INTERNATIONAL COMMERCIAL ARBITRATION, The Hague: Kluwer Law International (1999), et. 672.
[14] UNCITRAL, *Report of the UNCITRAL on the Work of Its Eighteenth Session, U.N. Doc. A/40/17*, XVI Yearbook UNCITRAL 3, 14-15 (1985).
[15] Judgment of 14 September 2000, III ZR 33/00 (German Bundesgerichtshof).

However, if only issues of fact are concerned, *prima facie* judicial consideration is appropriate.[16]

6.32. Other countries pursuing the weak thesis by virtue of the UNCITRAL Model Law are New Zealand,[17] Australia,[18] England,[19] Austria,[20] Croatia,[21] Mexico,[22] Kenya[23] and Spain. In relation to the latter, the following was established by the Supreme Court of Spain in 2017:

> This Court considers that **there are no reasons to argue the strong thesis of the Kompetenz-Kompetenz principle in our legal system** and to limit the judge's scope of analysis when solving the declinatory plea[24] for submission to arbitration".[25] (translation by the author) (emphasis added)

6.33. In a nutshell, according to the weak thesis national courts would have full jurisdiction to make a substantive analysis of the pathological clause even before the case is brought before the arbitration court and hence before the award is made.

II.1.2. The Strong Thesis

6.34. By virtue of the strong thesis, the judge would only be allowed to make a *prima facie* verification of the validity of the arbitration clause. In other words, his analysis would be restricted to merely checking that there is in fact a clause that somehow refers to arbitration, leaving the substantive assessment of its validity to the arbitrator, in line with the *Kompetenz-Kompetenz* principle.

6.35. As we have seen, many states tend to take an approach to the assessment of the arbitration clause in the line of the weak thesis. However, many countries like Switzerland, Singapore,

---

[16] *Dell Computer Corp.* v. *Union des Consommateurs*, [2007] SCC 34 (Canadian S.Ct.).
[17] *Yawata Ltd* v. *Powell*, [2000] DCR 334 (Wellington Dist. Ct.).
[18] *Electra Air Conditioning BV* v. *Seeley Int'l Pty Ltd*, [2008] FCAFC 169 (Australian Fed. Ct.).
[19] *Dallah Real Estate* v. *Ministry of Religious Affairs, Pakistan* [2010] UKSC 46, ¶104 (U.K. S.Ct.).
[20] Judgment of 01 March 2017, XLII Y.B. Commercial Arbitration 348, 350 (Austrian Oberster Gerichtshof) (2017).
[21] Judgment of 21 May 2007, *Berica* v. *Grupa Gava*, CLOUT Case No. 1070 (Croatian High Comm. Ct.).
[22] Judgment of 11 January 2006, Tesis Jurisprudencial 25/2006, Contradicción de Tesis 51/2005-PS (Mexican Nación Suprema Corte de Justicia).
[23] *Karanja* v. *Ndegwa*, Civil Case No. 908/2006 (Nairobi High Ct. 2007); *Obuga* v. *Kenyatta*, Civil Case No. 1159/2006 (Nairobi High Ct. 2006).
[24] The *declinatory plea*, in Spanish Law, is the statement by which, prior to the defence of the claim, the defendant questions the jurisdiction of the court before which the claim has been brought (Article 63 of the Spanish Litigation Act).
[25] Judgement of the Supreme Court of Spain of 27 June 2017.

Hong Kong, India or Canada are following the strong thesis, probably under the influence of French law.[26]

6.36. Under French criterion, most challenges to the parties' underlying contract, including challenges based upon illegality, fraud and initial invalidity, do not permit the arbitration agreement being resolved by French courts, 'unless the clause is manifestly null and void.'[27] The requirement of a 'manifest' appreciation of nullity excludes a substantive analysis by definition. This doctrine is expressly motivated by the wish to prevent delaying tactics.[28]

6.37. As for Switzerland, various decisions by the Swiss Federal Tribunal in the mid-1990s established that the judicial role pre-award should consist of a *prima facie* assessment of the validity of the arbitration clause, limited to the verification of its mere existence.[29] More recently, the Swiss Federal Tribunal stated that 'the court may accept jurisdiction only when it is obvious that there is no valid arbitration agreement between the parties. Therefore, it is enough for the defendant to prevail if the jurisdiction of the state court appears to be superseded *prima facie* by the arbitration clause,'[30] requiring an 'obvious' appreciation of nullity the same way French courts required a 'manifest' one.

6.38. In the U.S., the Federal Arbitration Act provides less guidance in relation to the *Kompetenz-Kompetenz* principle. However, the results from many of their recent precedents is that they approach this matter from a very contractual position. Special consideration should be given to a decision of the Federal Supreme Court in 2019 stating that '[w]hen the parties' contract delegates the arbitrability question to an arbitrator, **a court may not override the contract**. In those circumstances, **a court possesses no power to decide the arbitrability issue**. That is true **even if the court thinks that the argument that the arbitration agreement applies to a particular dispute is wholly groundless**'[31] (emphasis added).

---

[26]   Pierre Mayer, *Comparative Analysis of Power of Arbitrators to Determine Procedures in Civil and Common Law Systems*, in ALBERT JAN VAN DEN BERG, PLANNING EFFICIENT ARBITRATION PROCEEDINGS: THE LAW APPLICABLE IN INTERNATIONAL ARBITRATION, Netherlands: Kluwer Law International (1996), et. 24 – 38.

[27]   Judgment of 19 December 2018, Pourvoi No. 17-28.951 (French Cour de Cassation Civ. 1).

[28]   Application par la Cour des Principes de Validité de la Clause Compromissoire et de Compétence-Compétence, JCP G 2006, II, 10182.

[29]   Judgment of 29 April 1996, 14 ASA Bull. 527 (Swiss Fed. Trib.) (1996); Judgment of 16 January 1995, Compagnie de Navigation et Transports SA v Mediterranean Shipping Co., XXI Y.B. Comm. Arb. 690, 696 (Swiss Fed. Trib.) (1996).

[30]   Judgment of 06 August 2012, DFT 4A_119/2012, 3.2 (Swiss Fed. Trib.).

[31]   *Henry Schein, Inc. v. Archer and White Sales, Inc.* (8th January 2019, Federal Supreme Court of the United States of America).

Czech (& Central European) Yearbook of Arbitration®

II.2. Ulterior Review of the Pathological Clause

6.39. The abovementioned interlocutory consideration is not the only stage at which national courts could have to review the arbitration clause. In fact, it is often after the arbitral award is made that the arbitration agreement is subject to judicial consideration. In the vast majority of the cases, this review is carried out in a more substantive manner rather than a *prima facie* review.

II.2.1. Recognition and Enforcement of the Award

6.40. The New York Convention refers to the arbitration agreement firstly in Article II, in order to define it and in relation to interlocutory judicial consideration, and later in Articles IV and V(1), all of which are to be interpreted together, as an integrated set of legal rules.[32] The New York Convention establishes that the party against whom recognition is invoked can refuse it if it proves that '**said agreement is not valid** under the law to which the parties have subjected it or, failing any indication thereon, under the law of the country where the award was made' (emphasis added). In other words, had the arbitrators accepted an invalid pathological clause, state courts of the country where the enforcement of the award is being sought could reject it on the basis of said clause's invalidity.

6.41. Furthermore, we find precedents from different national courts establishing that an in depth check of the validity of the clause is to be made before recognition (if requested by the aggrieved party) on the basis of Article II(1). Firstly, it was held by the Higher Regional Court of Vienna that Article II of the New York Convention 'is a substantive norm';[33] also, it was established by the Bavarian Regional Court that '[a]n arbitration agreement that does not meet these requirements [Article II] is no basis for any obligation to enforce [an award] under the Convention.'[34]

6.42. In short, it is well established that revisions of the pathological arbitration clause's validity in the stage of recognition (for enforcement) of the award do not have to be limited to a *prima facie* analysis under the New York Convention but rather refer to a deeper analysis.

---

[32] GARY B. BORN, INTERNATIONAL COMMERCIAL ARBITRATION, Alphen aan den Rijn: Kluwer Law International (3rd ed. 2020), et. 269 - 4098.
[33] Judgment of 21 April 2005, 2006 JBl 731 (Oberlandesgericht Wien).
[34] Judgment of 12 December 2002, XXIX Y.B. Commercial Arbitration 761, 764 (Bayerisches Oberstes Landesgericht) (2004).

II.2.2. Action for Annulment of the Award

6.43. The action for annulment is a procedure by which the parties can challenge the validity and consistency of a definitive arbitral award by requesting its annulment before national courts. The scope to which national courts can review the award is assessed in diverse ways depending on the country, sometimes varying even between the courts of the same national jurisdiction. The absence of an international convention harmonizing the matter is no help either.

6.44. However, said uncertainty does not lie in the analysis of the arbitral clause, but on the scope of the analysis of the whole award. In fact, the action for annulment is considered by many to be expressly designed for situations in which the arbitral agreement is invalid or non-existent.

6.45. UNCITRAL Model Law refers to the action of annulment as the 'application for setting aside' and establishes in Article 34(2a) that it proceeds when 'said [arbitration] agreement is not valid' and when 'the award deals with a dispute not contemplated by or not falling within the terms of the submission to arbitration'. In other words, that an analysis of the scope of the arbitration clause is due when requested by one of the parties in the context of an action for annulment.

6.46. In a similar way, the French Code of Civil procedure establishes that national courts can review '(i) the absence, invalidity or expiry of an arbitration agreement',[35] where only the fact that a differentiation between 'absence' and 'invalidity' is made, points to a substantive revision of the arbitration agreement. The Swiss Federal Statute on Private International Law regulates this under the same approach.[36] In some countries like Finland, the scope is even wider, allowing for a full analysis of the award itself;[37] which is also the way Spanish Courts were performing the review for annulment until the Constitutional Court limited its reach to the validity of the arbitration agreement and other formalities in 2021.[38]

6.47. In a nutshell, what is clear is that it is of uniform international application that the action for annulment of the arbitral award allows for an in-depth review of - at least - in relation to the validity of the arbitration agreement (clause) that goes beyond a *prima facie* review.

---

[35] Article 1504 of the French Code of Civil Procedure (cross-reference to Article 1502).
[36] Article 190(2).
[37] Arbitration Act of Finland (967/1992 including amendments up to 460/1999), s. 40(1).
[38] Judgement of Spanish Constitutional Court of 15th February 2021.

III.   Conclusions

6.48.   There are two main conclusions to be drawn from this paper.

6.49.   Firstly, the need to put effort and consideration into the drafting of the arbitration clause in order to avoid all of the abovementioned problems that can derive from the intervention of national courts in the assessment of a pathological clause.

6.50.   Secondly, that due to the lack of harmonization regarding the scope of the judicial interlocutory review of the arbitration agreement, a (pathological) arbitration clause could be subject to up to three - depending on the national jurisdictions involved - reviews of its validity if requested by the relevant party. This procedural redundancy results in a weakening of arbitration for it ties it too closely to the judicial jurisdiction, hence distorting its nature and making it less appealing as a means of dispute resolution.

6.51.   We believe the interlocutory judicial review of the arbitration clause should be restricted to a *prima facie* consideration, meaning that only its existence should be verified; leaving its substantial review to the national courts involved in the ulterior recognition or annulment of the arbitral award.

6.52.   Be that as it may, we insist, this conundrum will not be such if the arbitration agreement is thoroughly drafted in the first place in order to avoid deficiencies, which will always be easier than trying to harmonize the standards of all national courts.

| | |

Summaries

FRA   [*La validité et l'interprétation des clauses compromissoires pathologiques dans le contexte de leur examen judiciaire*]
La soumission d'une affaire à la procédure arbitrale nécessite une manifestation expresse de volonté, exprimée dans un accord spécial, généralement appelé « convention d'arbitrage », ou « clause compromissoire ». Faute d'un tel accord, l'arbitre (ou, dans certains cas, la juridiction nationale) peut se déclarer incompétent pour connaître de l'affaire.
Outre l'absence de clause compromissoire, le problème peut être également dû aux vices de formulation de cette dernière. Dans ce cas, il s'agit d'une clause compromissoire pathologique. La pathologie de la clause compromissoire peut prendre différentes formes, que l'on peut classifier de la manière suivante : clauses imprécises, dont le défaut de précision découle de leur formulation

vague ; clauses inopérantes, dont l'application est impossible ; et clauses hybrides, qui soumettent l'affaire en question aussi bien à un arbitrage qu'à une procédure judiciaire. Dans la plupart de ces cas, la solution consiste à déterminer si les parties avaient ou non l'intention de soumettre le litige à un tribunal arbitral. La détermination de la volonté de se soumettre à un arbitrage peut s'avérer problématique dès le stade de son examen judiciaire préalable. Ceci ouvre la question de savoir si cet examen doit être détaillé, ou bien se limiter à une analyse prima facie, concernant la simple existence de la clause compromissoire en question, notamment au vu du fait qu'il existe d'autres stades auxquels un examen détaillé peut être effectué. L'article analyse les deux options envisagées.

CZE   [***Platnost a posouzení patologických rozhodčích doložek v souvislosti se zásahem soudu v rámci jím vedeného přezkumu***]

Podřízení věci rozhodčímu řízení vyžaduje výslovný projev vůle vyjádřený v příslušné smlouvě, která se obvykle označuje jako rozhodčí smlouva nebo rozhodčí doložkou. Jinak může mít rozhodce (a někdy vnitrostátní soudy) za to, že nemá pravomoc se věcí zabývat.

Někdy tento problém ve skutečnosti nespočívá v neexistenci rozhodčí doložky, ale v jejím vadném znění. V těchto případech hovoříme o patologické rozhodčí doložce. Rozhodčí doložka může být patologickou z různých důvodů, přičemž jednotlivé alternativy lze rozdělit následujícím způsobem: neurčité doložky, kdy nedostatek určitosti plyne z její vágní formulace; neúčinné doložky, kdy danou doložku nelze realizovat; a hybridní doložky, kdy daná dohoda představuje podřízení dané věci rozhodčímu řízení i řízení soudnímu současně. Ve většině těchto případů řešení spočívá ve zjištění, zda strany měly v úmyslu podřídit rozhodování sporu v dané věci rozhodčímu soudu, či nikoliv.

Určení a zjištění takové vůle podřídit se rozhodčímu řízení může být problematické i ve fázi jejího prozatímního soudního přezkumu. To vede k diskusi o tom, zda by měl být tento přezkum přezkumem detailním, nebo zda by měl být omezen na analýzu prima facie co do pouhé existence dané rozhodčí doložky, a to zejména s přihlédnutím ke skutečnosti, že existují i jiné fáze, kdy je možno podrobný přezkum provést; obě varianty jsou v tomto článku rozebrány.

| | |

POL [*Obowiązywanie i ocena patologicznych klauzul arbitrażowych w związku z ingerencją sądu w ramach prowadzonej przez niego kontroli*]
W artykule omówiono, w jaki sposób podporządkowanie się kompetencji trybunału arbitrażowego na mocy zapisu na sąd polubowny może stać się patologiczne i jak ten brak jego uszczegółowienia można naprawić. Następstwa procesowe owej patologii przeanalizowano również w odniesieniu do potencjalnej ingerencji sądów krajowych w ramach tymczasowych postępowań sądowych rozpatrujących skargę, ze szczególnym uwzględnieniem tego, czy rozpatrywanie w tej sprawie powinno zostać ograniczone do analizy prima facie czy nie, skoro istnieje inna faza, w której można przeprowadzić szczegółowe badanie.

DEU [**Die Gültigkeit und Beurteilung pathologischer Schiedsklauseln im Zusammenhang mit der gerichtlichen Intervention im Rahmen einer vom Gericht vorgenommenen Überprüfung**]
Der Artikel analysiert die verschiedenen Arten, in denen die Unterwerfung unter die Gerichtsbarkeit eines Schiedsgerichts im Wege einer Schiedsklausel pathologisch werden kann, und wie der Mangel an Bestimmtheit der Klausel zu beseitigen ist. Die prozeduralen Konsequenzen dieser Pathologie werden außerdem in Bezug auf eine potenzielle Intervention seitens nationaler Gerichte im Rahmen vorläufiger gerichtlicher Prüfungen erörtert, wobei der Schwerpunkt auf der Diskussion liegt, ob eine derartige gerichtliche Überprüfung auf eine Prima facie-Analyse beschränkt ist oder nicht, angesichts des Umstands, dass eine detaillierte Prüfung auch in anderen Phasen vorgenommen werden kann.

RUS [*Действительность и оценка патологических арбитражных оговорок в связи с вмешательством суда в ходе осуществляемого им пересмотра*]
В данной статье анализируются различные варианты того, как установление компетенции арбитража посредством арбитражной оговорки может стать патологическим и какие существуют варианты устранения этого недостатка, выраженного в неточности оговорки. Кроме того, процессуальные последствия этой патологии рассматриваются в связи с потенциальным вмешательством национальных судов в рамках промежуточных судебных пересмотров, причем поднимается вопрос о том, должен ли этот пересмотр ограничиваться анализом prima facie, поскольку

Czech (& Central European) Yearbook of Arbitration®

существуют и другие этапы, на которых возможен подробный пересмотр.

ESP **[*Validez y revisión de las cláusulas arbitrales patológicas y el contexto de su control judicial*]**
Este artículo analiza distintas situaciones en las que la sumisión a la jurisdicción de un tribunal de arbitraje a través de una cláusula de arbitraje puede resultar patológica; adicionalmente, se proponen medidas para reparar la vaguedad de las cláusulas arbitrales. Además, se discuten las implicaciones procesales de esta patología en relación con la eventual intervención de los tribunales nacionales y los controles judiciales interlocutorios; el texto presta atención a la discusión sobre si el control judicial debe limitarse a un análisis prima facie cuando existen otras etapas en las que se puede llevar a cabo una revisión detallada.

| | |

Bibliography:

GARY B. BORN, INTERN'ATIONAL COMMERCIAL ARBITRATION, Alphen aan den Rijn: Kluwer Law International (2nd ed. 2014).

GARY B. BORN, INTERNATIONAL COMMERCIAL ARBITRATION, Alphen aan den Rijn: Kluwer Law International (3rd ed. 2020).

EMMANUEL GAILLARD, JOHN SAVAGE, FOUCHARD GAILLARD GOLDMAN ON INTERNATIONAL COMMERCIAL ARBITRATION, The Hague: Kluwer Law International (1999).

Pierre Mayer, *Comparative Analysis of Power of Arbitrators to Determine Procedures in Civil and Common Law Systems*, in ALBERT JAN VAN DEN BERG, PLANNING EFFICIENT ARBITRATION PROCEEDINGS: THE LAW APPLICABLE IN INTERNATIONAL ARBITRATION, Netherlands: Kluwer Law International (1996).

UNCITRAL, *Report of the UNCITRAL on the Work of Its Eighteenth Session, U.N. Doc. A/40/17*, XVI Yearbook UNCITRAL 3, 14-15 (1985).

Czech (& Central European) Yearbook of Arbitration®

Anastasia Vezyrtzi

Jurisdiction in Parallel Proceedings: Court Jurisdiction v Arbitration Agreement

Key words:
parallel proceedings |
jurisdiction | Kompetenz-
Kopentenz principle | scope
of judicial review | invalidity
of the arbitration agreement
| lis pendens | forum non
conveniens | res judicata |
seat of arbitration

Abstract | *This paper deals with the complex map of parallel proceedings. More precisely, it focuses on situations of concomitant jurisdiction of a national court and an arbitral tribunal in situations where the existence or validity of an arbitration agreement is challenged and both adjudicatory bodies are equally entitled to independently decide on their own jurisdiction. The paper explores the claim that predictability and stability of the law call for a good coordination between judicial and arbitral proceedings through efficient mechanisms and supra-national provisions that will remedy current uncertainties and ensure not only a coherent regime for parallel proceedings but also an efficient and stable arbitration process.*

| | |

Dr. Anastasia Vezyrtzi is post-doc researcher, Law School, Aristotle University of Thessaloniki. She holds a Ph.D. in Civil Procedural Law from Aristotle University of Thessaloniki and an LL.M. from Columbia Law School (New York). She has practiced as a lawyer since 2005 and is currently a partner at the ALPHA LAW law firm in Thessaloniki. She is also an accredited civil and commercial mediator in Greece and in the UK, a certified negotiator, having mastered her skills through the completion of the Harvard Negotiation Master Class (Harvard Law School, PON), as well as a certified Data Protection Officer (DPO).
E-mail: avezirtzi@hotmail.com

Czech (& Central European) Yearbook of Arbitration®

I. The Problem of Proceedings Pending in Parallel Between a National Court and an Arbitral Tribunal

I.1. Introduction: Jurisdictional Conflicts of Competence and Concomitant Jurisdiction when Validity of an Arbitration Agreement is Challenged

7.01. This article relates to the difficulties that international commercial arbitration encounters under the current legal framework in terms of its interface with national jurisdictions. These are situations of concomitant jurisdiction of a national court and an arbitral tribunal when proceedings on the same subject matter and between the same parties are in progress in parallel. More specifically, this jurisdictional overlap is made possible when one party challenges the existence or validity of an arbitration agreement and, therefore, both adjudicatory bodies are equally empowered to independently decide on their own jurisdiction. On one hand, the arbitral tribunal's inherent power - indeed duty[1] - to determine its own jurisdiction derives from the principle of competence-competence,[2] one of the internationally accepted cornerstones of international arbitration. More specifically, the positive effect of competence - competence, today recognized in a vast majority of countries, allows arbitral tribunals to proceed even if parallel proceedings are pending. On the other hand, according to the provision of Article II(3) of the 1958 New York Convention,[3] the national court can also declare itself competent to hear a dispute in case the arbitration agreement is 'null and void, inoperative or incapable of being performed'.

7.02. The task of coordinating jurisdiction and the need to eliminate jurisdictional conflicts of competence is crucial not only for the development and efficiency of international commercial arbitration but also for the interests of harmonious administration of justice in general. Contradicting decisions jeopardize the consistency and integrity of any legal order.

---

[1] See JAN PAULSSON, GEORGIOS PETROCHILOS, UNCITRAL ARBITRATION, The Netherlands: Kluwer Law International 188-189 (2018). As it is stated, the mandate of the arbitral tribunal to determine objections to its jurisdiction deprives a recalcitrant party of an opportunity to frustrate arbitral proceedings and remove the matter to state courts simply by challenging the foundation of the tribunal's jurisdictional power.

[2] For an analysis of the principle of competence-competence see among others NADJA ERK, PARALLEL PROCEEDINGS IN INTERNATIONAL ARBITRATION. A COMPARATIVE EUROPEAN PERSPECTIVE, The Netherlands: Kluwer Law International 25 ff. (2014).

[3] Convention on the Recognition and Enforcement of Foreign Arbitral Awards, done in New York on 10 June 1958 (New York Convention).

Multi-fora disputes generate undoubtedly substantial concerns due to the high costs of duplicative proceedings and the risk of inconsistent decisions. Therefore, this article will explore the claim that predictability and stability of the law call for a good coordination between judicial and arbitral proceedings through efficient mechanisms and supra-national provisions that will discourage obstructing litigation, but mostly enhance the effectiveness of arbitration awards.

I.2. The Broad Discretion Left to Contracting States under the New York Convention Regarding Referral to Arbitration and the Scope of Review of the Arbitration Agreement's Validity

7.03. Due to the general wording of the exception included in Article II(3) of the New York Convention, broad discretion is left to contracting States to decide whether the court should resolve the validity issue itself or allow it to be decided in arbitration. The issue is delicate as it regards the jurisdictional sovereignty of each State depending at the same time on the national law's general stance on arbitration. Getting started with the fact that the provisions governing jurisdiction regarding parallel proceedings have not yet been harmonized, national jurisdictions - that are at the same time major hubs for arbitration - offer different approaches regarding on one hand referral to arbitration and on the other hand the scope of review of the arbitration agreement's validity to be applied by the national courts. This inevitably causes great uncertainty.

7.04. The scope of review of the national court depends, therefore, on the arbitration law of the forum,[4] with some jurisdictions, such as Germany, supporting a *full review* of the validity of the arbitration agreement and others - more arbitration friendly - such as the United States, adopting a *prima facie* examination. Another approach is followed by the Swiss Federal Supreme Court which introduces a distinction in the scope of review depending on whether the arbitral proceedings take place in Switzerland or abroad. More specifically, when the seat of arbitration is abroad the court can carry out a 'full review' while only a *prima facie* review when the tribunal is seated

---

[4]   See in detail STEPHAN WILSKE, TODD J. FOX, NEW YORK CONVENTION, COMMENTARY, München: Verlag C.H. Beck 183-184 (Reinmar Wolff ed., 2012).

in Switzerland.[5] This bifurcation of the scope of review was strongly criticized though in legal theory.[6]

7.05. Finally, a more progressive approach is that followed by French arbitration law which incorporates the negative effect of competence-competence[7] regardless of whether the seat of arbitration is in France or abroad.[8] Therefore, in case the arbitration has already commenced, a rule of chronological priority in favor of the arbitrators is created. Consequently, as an effort to centralize litigation concerning the existence and validity of the arbitration agreement, the national court is prevented from inquiring about the validity of the arbitration agreement. Arbitrators have priority to decide any challenge on their jurisdiction, premature court intervention is prohibited and review by the courts is allowed only at the end of the arbitral process.

7.06. The modern approach of recognition of a rule of priority of the arbitrators in the determination of their jurisdiction, although gaining increasing acceptance,[9] is still strongly debated.[10] The major concern regarding implementation of the negative effect of competence-competence as a clear-cut principle relates to the fact that it does not offer effective protection of party's right of access to court, especially in view of *bona fide* parties that do not challenge arbitral jurisdiction only as a dilatory tactic. In addition, acceptance and implementation of the negative effect of competence-competence may harbor more potential for avoiding conflicts as it grants a priority rule to the arbitral tribunal, but at the same time a right to review the jurisdiction

---

[5] Swiss Federal Supreme Court Decision 121 III 38 (2b) = XXI Y.B. Com Arb. 690, 694 (1996).

[6] For an analysis of the criticism see NADJA ERK, *supra* note 2, at 42-43: one of the arguments against this bifurcation was that different scopes of review discriminate against parties who have chosen an arbitral seat abroad and is, therefore, not in accordance with the more-favorable-right-provision in Article VII(1) of the New York Convention.

[7] For a detailed analysis of the negative effect of competence-competence see among others Emmanuel Gaillard and Yas Banifatemi, *Negative effect of competence-competence: The rule of priority in favor of the arbitrators*, in ENFORCEMENT OF ARBITRATION AGREEMENTS AND INTERNATIONAL ARBITRAL AWARDS: THE NEW YORK CONVENTION IN PRACTICE, United Kingdom: Cameron May Ltd. 257 ff. (Emmanuel Gaillard and Domenico Di Pietro eds., 2008).

[8] Under Article 1448 of the (revised) French Code of Civil Procedure '[w]hen a dispute subject to an arbitration agreement is brought before a court, such a court shall decline jurisdiction, except if an arbitral tribunal has not yet been seized of the dispute and if the arbitration agreement is manifestly void or manifestly not applicable'. For an analysis of this important provision which codifies the negative effect of Competence-Competence see NADJA ERK, *supra* note 2, at 37-40; Guido Carducci, *The Arbitration Reform in France: Domestic and International Arbitration*, 28(1) ARBITRATION INTERNATIONAL 125, 134, 150 (2012).

[9] See in detail Emmanuel Gaillard, Yas Banifatemi, *supra* note 7, at 261 ff.

[10] For an analysis of the policy considerations in favor of the implementation of the negative effect of competence-competence as well as the concerns regarding the efficiency of such a rule see NADJA ERK, *supra* note 2, at 51-56: The author holds that 'the negative effect of competence-competence may, in terms of efficiency, be interpreted as both a blessing and a curse'.

Czech (& Central European) Yearbook of Arbitration®

of the tribunal still remains at the stage of enforcement of an arbitral award to the detriment of time and expense.

7.07. To sum up, the divergence of the different national jurisdictions as to the implementation of the negative effect of competence-competence coupled with the different scope of court's review to be applied generate ambiguity and inconsistency. In that respect it is worth noting that the UNCITRAL Model Law,[11] which has been adopted by a significant number of States and reflects in a way worldwide consensus on key aspects of international arbitration practice, does not contain any indication regarding either the implementation of such a rule of priority in favor of the arbitrators or the scope of review[12] to be applied by the national courts while examining the agreement to arbitrate.

7.08. From the above analysis it is evident that the map of parallel litigation is truly a rather complex one. The critical issue though is not only to avoid concomitant jurisdiction between national courts and arbitral tribunals, but also to allocate jurisdiction in such a way that renders the whole process of determining jurisdiction more efficient. The mechanisms at hand for coordinating duplicative proceedings and avoiding irreconcilable decisions at the recognition and enforcement stage have proven inadequate and therefore, legislative intervention in a supra-national level is essential in order to remedy current uncertainties and ensure not only a coherent regime for parallel proceedings but also an efficient and stable arbitration process.

II. *Lis Pendens* as a Proposed Mechanism to Address Situations of Parallel Proceedings in International Commercial Arbitration

7.09. The doctrine of *lis pendens* has evolved in national legal systems when faced with concurrent proceedings between two domestic courts or between a domestic court and a foreign court. Arbitration and court proceedings are governed by separate jurisdiction and enforcement conventions. In case a party challenges the existence, validity or applicability of an arbitration agreement then there is an arguable basis for

---

[11] UNICTRAL Model Law on International Commercial Arbitration 1985 (UNICTRAL Model Law): It was adopted by the United Nations Commission on International Trade Law in 1985 and was amended in 2006.

[12] In favor of the approach that the legislative history of Article 8(1) UNICTRAL Model Law seems to suggest a 'full review' see GARY B. BORN, INTERNATIONAL COMMERCIAL ARBITRATION, The Netherlands: Kluwer Law International 882 (1st ed., 2009); *contra* in favor of a *prima facie* review see Frédéric Bachand, *Does Article 8 of the Model Law call for full or prima facie review of the arbitral tribunal's jurisdiction?*, 22(3) ARBITRATION INTERNATIONAL 463, 469 ff. (2006).

applying the *lis pendens* principle in international arbitration as there are two presumptively *prima facie* competent fora capable of resolving the same jurisdictional issue.[13] The question though is whether the *lis pendens* doctrine in relation to jurisdictional issues can provide an efficient mechanism for managing parallel proceedings in the context of international arbitration where the integrity of the arbitral procedure needs to be protected. Furthermore, it should be explored which national solution should or could be transposed into the international arbitration setting.

7.10. It should be noted that the New York Convention and the UNCITRAL Model Law do not contain a *lis pendens* rule.[14] On the contrary Article 8(1) of the UNCITRAL Model Law embraces an exactly opposite approach as it authorizes the parties to initiate parallel arbitral proceedings even where court litigation has already been commenced in the same matter.[15] Only the European Convention on International Commercial Arbitration[16] establishes in Article VI(3) a rule that the national court seized 'after' arbitral proceeding have been initiated shall stay its proceeding to give precedence to the arbitrator's determination of jurisdiction. Moreover, from the perspective of national jurisdictions, the strict 'first-filing' approach of the civil notion of *lis pendens* in a litigation context contradicts with the common law doctrine of *forum non conveniens* where *lis pendens* is one of several factors considered when a court assesses its jurisdiction.[17]

7.11. It is true that in the intensively debated case *Fomento v. Colon*,[18] the Swiss Federal Tribunal not only applied to an international arbitration the rule of *lis pendens* but also adopted the civil notion of a rigid first-to-file rule. Therefore, by accepting that an arbitral tribunal has an *ex officio* duty to suspend its own consideration of jurisdictional issues due to prior-initiated state

---

[13]   GARY B. BORN, INTERNATIONAL COMMERCIAL ARBITRATION, The Netherlands: Kluwer Law International 3795-3796 (2014).

[14]   See NADJA ERK, *supra* note 2, at 110-112.

[15]   See NADJA ERK, *supra* note 2, at 112.

[16]   Adopted on 21 April 1961.

[17]   For an analysis of the notion of *lis pendens* in civil law jurisdictions compared with the notion of the doctrine of *forum non conveniens* in common law jurisdictions see Philip de Ly, Audley Sheppard, *ILA Final Report on Lis Pendens and Arbitration*, 25(1) ARBITRATION INTERNATIONAL 3, 7 ff. (2009).

[18]   *Fomento de Construcciones y Contratas S.A.* v. *Colon Container Terminal S.A.*, Decision of 14 May 2001, (DSFSC) 127 [2001] III 279; For an analysis of the Swiss decision see GARY B. BORN, supra note 13, at 3799 ff.; Christian Oetiker, *The principle of lis pendens in international arbitration: The Swiss decision in Fomento v. Colon*, 18(2) ARBITRATION INTERNATIONAL 137 ff., 254 (2002); Bernardo M. Cremades, Magdalena Ignacio, *Parallel Proceedings in International Arbitration*, 24(4) ARBITRATION INTERNATIONAL 507, 513-514 (2008); Emil Brengesjö, *Parallel proceedings in International Arbitration*, *in* ANTONIA KRZYMOWSKA, CAROLINE NORDKLINT, M ÅRTEN SCHULTZ, STOCKHOLM CENTRE FOR COMMERCIAL LAW ÅRSBOK VI, Stockholm: Stockholm Centre for Commercial Law 21, 32 ff. (2015).

court proceedings, it created a presumption[19] that the rules applicable to the courts are applicable to arbitral tribunals as well. However, the Swiss legislator overturned the *Fomento* ruling in a statute enacted on 06 October 2006 and reaffirmed the arbitral tribunal's jurisdiction to rule on its own jurisdiction by modifying Article 186 of the Federal Statute on Private International Law (PILA).

7.12. The paradigm of the *Fomento* case highlights once again the degree of recognition of the autonomous nature of arbitration. When a contract-based arbitration competes with a national court proceeding and both tribunals may assert jurisdiction, then the rule of competence-competence specifically safeguards the arbitrators' power to rule on their own jurisdiction without premature court intervention. Moreover, as it is pointed out in legal theory, 'in the absence of arbitration rules specifically addressing the litispendence principle, the power to apply the principle can only be grounded in the arbitrator's inherent authority over the conduct of the proceedings'.[20] Any determinations regarding which of the two competing jurisdictions should entertain the case can only be made case by case.[21] Therefore, as also recommended by the ILA Committee[22] in its Final Report on *lis pendens* and arbitration, *lis pendens* in arbitration is largely about case management rather than the application of rigid criteria. The flexible common law approach serves better than a strict chronological priority rule towards that direction. As a result, in the arbitration context the mechanism of *lis pendens* can only be viewed as a potential tool for regulation but not for efficient elimination of parallel proceedings as its application depends on each tribunal's discretion. Finally, it is worth noting that contrary to the European Regulation 1215/2012[23] (Brussels Ia Regulation) where the strict priority rule for resolving cases of *lis pendens* is further supported by an automatic recognition and enforcement system based on the principle of mutual trust

---

[19] See Emmanuel Gaillard, Yas Banifatemi, *supra* note 7, at 271.
[20] Douglas Reichert, *Problems with Parallel and Duplicate Proceedings: The Litispendence Principle and International Arbitration*, 8(3) ARBITRATION INTERNATIONAL 237, 254 (1992).
[21] Douglas Reichert, Ibid., at 255. See also Florian Kremslehner, *Lis pendens and res judicata in International Commercial Arbitration – How to deal with parallel proceedings – How to determine the conclusive and preclusive effects of arbitral awards*, in CHRISTIAN KLAUSEGGER, PETER KLEIN, FLORIAN KREMSLEHNER, ALEXANDER PETSCHE, NIKOLAUS PITKOWITZ, JENNY POWER, IRENE WELSER, GEROLD ZEILER, AUSTRIAN YEARBOOK, Wien: Manzsche Verlags- und Universitätsbuchhandlung 127, 156-157 (2007): As it is pointed out there are many elements that an arbitral tribunal should consider such as the timing of the parallel proceedings, to what extent will a judgment constitute *res judicata* for the arbitration and vice versa, as well as the practical aspects of continuing or staying the arbitration.
[22] Philip de Ly, Audley Sheppard, *supra* note 17, at 32.
[23] Council Regulation (EC) No 1215/2012 of 12 December 2012 on jurisdiction and the recognition and enforcement of judgments in civil and commercial matters [2012] OJ L351/1.

in the administration of justice, there is no such background of automatic recognition of arbitral awards under the New York Convention.

III. The Doctrine of *Res Judicata* as a Proposed Mechanism to Address Situations of Parallel Proceedings in International Commercial Arbitration: A Call for Supra-National Rules on *Res Judicata*

7.13. The allocation of competence between arbitral tribunals and national courts to decide jurisdictional issues is closely related also to the issue of arguable preclusive and conclusive effects that prior decisions have in subsequent proceedings. The analysis is important as, in practice, the pronouncement of an arbitration clause as invalid can be issued a) by the arbitral tribunal itself, on the basis of the principle of *competence*, b) by the court called upon to decide on the merits of the case, examining the validity question as a preliminary issue and c) by a judge, who is allowed by national law, to decide on a direct action for declaratory relief. Depending on the legislative source and the competent procedural and substantive rules, circulation of these judgments differs leading to paradoxical results. The imminent danger of contradicting decisions on validity constitutes a threat to the predictability and enforceability of judicial and/or arbitral decision making. The issue of the precise preclusive effects that a judgment or award with *res judicata* effect has in further proceedings is crucial to be examined.

7.14. The doctrine of *res judicata*, albeit reflected almost universally across national legal systems, varies considerably among jurisdictions,[24] with differences existing regarding its objective and subjective scope not only between common law and civil law countries, but also among countries belonging to the same tradition.[25] Moreover, although international arbitral awards are widely understood to have preclusive effects,[26]

---

[24] For an in-depth analysis of the doctrine of *res judicata* in domestic laws see SILJA SCHAFFSTEIN, THE DOCTRINE OF RES JUDICATA BEFORE INTERNATIONAL COMMERCIAL ARBITRAL TRIBUNALS, Oxford: Oxford University Press 15 ff. (2016); also Charles Poncet, Luisa Mockler, *Res Judicata: A contribution to the debate on claim preclusion in international arbitration*, in LIBER AMICORUM EN L'HONNEUR DE WILLIAM LAURENCE GRAIG, Paris: LexisNexis 309, 311-316 (2016); Philippe Hovaguimian, *The Res-Judicata effects of foreign judgments in post-award proceedings: To bind or not to bind?*, 34(1) JOURNAL OF ARBITRATION INTERNATIONAL 79, 82-84 (2017).

[25] See GARY B. BORN, *supra* note 13, at 3747 ff, 3764 ff.; Nathalie Voser, Julie Raneda, *Recent Developments on the Doctrine of Res Judicata in International Arbitration from a Swiss Perspective: A Call for a Harmonized Solution*, 33(4) ASA BULLETIN 742, 774-775 (2015).

[26] See GARY B. BORN, *supra* note 13, at 3739.

there is no clarity[27] regarding the law governing *res judicata* in international commercial arbitration. Therefore, different approaches[28] have been proposed for its determination among which the transnational approach being strongly supported[29] as more appropriate since it avoids inappropriate analogies between international commercial arbitration and litigation. Domestic litigation rules of *res judicata* can work as a source of inspiration[30] but it is of paramount importance that at the same time the nature and objectives of international arbitration, as well as the parties' legitimate expectations of finality, efficiency and efficacy, are respected. Predictability and certainty can be better served by the formulation of uniform and autonomous transnational *res judicata* principles, specifically tailored for international arbitration and known in advance from the parties. Codified instruments are preferable[31] and essential for the creation of a coherent regime for parallel proceedings, as they will supply both guidance to the arbitral tribunals and predictability to the parties. However, it is argued[32] that their adoption appears premature.

7.15. Particular attention should be given though also to the content[33] of such transnational *res judicata* principles in order to be

---

[27] See Silja Schaffstein, *The law governing res judicata*, 7(1) EUROPEAN INTERNATIONAL ARBITRATION REVIEW 117, 123 ff. (2018); Nathan Yaffe, *Transnational Arbitral Res Judicata*, 34(5) JOURNAL OF INTERNATIONAL ARBITRATION 795, 796-797 (2017).

[28] For an in depth analysis of possible approaches to *res judicata* before international arbitral tribunals see SILJA SCHAFFSTEIN, *supra* note 24, at 175 ff.

[29] The adoption of the transnational approach is widely supported by legal scholars see among others GARY B. BORN, *supra* note 13, at 3768-3771; Pierre Mayer, *Litispendance, connexité et chose jugée dans l' arbitrage international*, in CLAUDE REYMOND, PIERO BERNARDINI, LIBER AMICORUM CLAUDE REYMOND: AUTOR DE L'ARBITRAGE, Paris: Éditions du Juris-classeur 185, 190 ff. (2004); Stavros Brekoulakis, *The effect of an Arbitral Award and Third Parties in International Arbitration: Res Judicata Revisited*, 16(1) AMERICAN REVIEW OF INTERNATIONAL ARBITRATION 177, 205 ff. (2005); SILJA SCHAFFSTEIN, *supra* note 24, at 186 ff.

[30] SILJA SCHAFFSTEIN, *supra* note 24, at 211: As it is noted '[f]ormulating transnational res judicata rules inspired by domestic litigation rules would avoid the application of a foreign, unfamiliar, and possibly unexpected law to res judicata'.

[31] In favor of a multilateral treaty solution see Sigvard Jarvin, *Lis pendens et res judicata dans l' arbitrage international: vers une pratique harmonisée?*, in JAN KLEINEMAN, PETER WESTBERG, STEPHAN CARLSSON, FESTSKRIFT TILL LARS HEUMAN, Stockholm: Jure Förlag 241, 256-259 (2008); Gabrielle Kaufmann-Kohler, *How to handle parallel proceedings: A practical approach to issues such as competence-competence and anti-suit injunctions*, 2(1) DISPUTE RESOLUTION INTERNATIONAL 110, 113 (2008); in favor of a protocol to the New York Convention filling the gaps see Hans van Houte, *Why not include Arbitration in the Brussels Jurisdiction Regulation*, 21(4) ARBITRATION INTERNATIONAL 509, 516-517 (2005).

[32] See Frédéric Bachand, *Parallel proceedings involving objections to arbitral jurisdictions: A closer look at the presumed intention of the parties*, in STAVROS L. BREKOULAKIS, THE EVOLUTION AND FUTURE OF INTERNATIONAL ARBITRATION, The Netherlands: Kluwer Law International B.V. 219, 220 (2016).

[33] One major issue regarding the content of the rules is whether it is better to follow a strict, formalistic approach to the application of the triple identity test (identity of parties, identity of subject matter, identity of cause of action) or a less formalistic, substance-over-form approach. Another issue is whether common law concepts of issue estoppel should be endorsed. Finally, an issue that would also have to be addressed is whether should be adopted a more extensive notion of *res judicata*, which not only covers the dispositive

appropriate in an international setting, as well as to the sources[34] to be taken into account for its determination. Although imposing procedural constraints on international arbitrators, uniform *res judicata* rules will offer guidance, not only avoiding duplicate proceedings, but also preventing approaches and results that vary from one arbitration to another. In the same vein, the fundamental feature of flexibility may be partially restricted if policy considerations of finality, legal certainty and predictability will be better served in practice. However, it is essential that the transnational *res judicata* rules should primarily be developed in light of common international commercial arbitration law and practice and generally accepted principles. These can also be inspired by domestic and transnational litigation rules on *res judicata*.[35] Useful guidance[36] towards the creation of a set of a truly comprehensible set of transnational rules on *res judicata* is finally offered by the ILA Recommendations on Res Judicata and Arbitration.[37] However, while supporting the adoption of the transnational approach and proposing a good compromise of the various trends found in civil and common law jurisdictions, the Recommendations end up following a mixed approach and seem to suffer in terms of their impact from the fact that they leave a number of key-issues unresolved, referring for their determination to the conflict-of laws rules.[38]

7.16. In conclusion the coordination between arbitral awards and national court judgments rendered in identical or related cases is of great importance as it was the party's intention when choosing arbitration, to have their dispute resolved efficiently, by a final, binding and enforceable award. Therefore, having the dispute re-assessed and re-litigated neither serves this legitimate interest nor protects the integrity of the judgment/award. As there are currently no rules in international commercial arbitration law and practice assuring this coordination, transnational principles of *res judicata* should be elaborated in order to provide the

---

part of an award but also the underlying reasoning. For these concerns regarding the scope of *res judicata* see SCHAFFSTEIN, *supra* note 24, at 252 ff., 295; Florian Kremslehner, *supra* note 21, at 134-136; Charles Poncet, Luisa Mockler, *supra* note 24, at 320-323.

[34] For an analysis of the sources of transnational *res judicata* principles see in detail SILJA SCHAFFSTEIN, *supra* note 24, at 208-212.

[35] For an analysis of the sources of transnational *res judicata* principles see in detail SILJA SCHAFFSTEIN, *supra* note 24, at 208-212.

[36] See Nathalie Voser, Julie Raneda, *supra* note 25, at 774-775.

[37] See in detail Filip De Ly, Audley Sheppard, *ILA Final Report on Res Judicata and Arbitration*, 25(1) ARBITRATION INTERNATIONAL 67 ff. (2009). As it is pointed out (see NADJA ERK, *supra* note 2, at 235-236) '[t]he ILA recommendations on res judicata may be consulted as a set of transnational soft law rules by analogy, but do not have a binding character'.

[38] Luca Radicati di Brozolo, *Res Judicata and international arbitral awards*, in PIERRE TERCIER, POST AWARD ISSUES: ASA SPECIAL SERIES NO. 38, New York: JurisNet LLC 127, 146 (2011); Nathalie Voser, Julie Raneda, *supra* note 25, at 774.

Czech (& Central European) Yearbook of Arbitration®

much needed guidance and minimize the risk of contradictory and irreconcilable decisions or awards.

IV. Further Proposed Amendments in Order to Improve the Regime of Parallel Proceedings

7.17. Apart from the development of transnational *res judicata* principles, the problem of concomitant jurisdiction of a national court and an arbitral tribunal should be also addressed at an earlier stage through the adoption of certain rules that will remedy or minimize current ambiguities and uncertainties. First of all, Article II(3) of the New York Convention should be amended in order to stipulate a uniform standard of review for deciding on the validity of the arbitration agreement, with a *prima facie* approach being more preferable[39] as it is more arbitration friendly and in any case it is counterbalanced with the court's power to review the existence and validity of the arbitration agreement at the post-award phase. On one hand, it may be accurate that the advantage of a full review on the validity of the arbitration agreement at the pre-award stage better preserves at an early stage the parties' time and resources as the arbitral award risks to be set aside or declared invalid.[40] On the other hand, as it is pointed out by some scholars,[41] such power of full scrutiny would drain of its substance the fundamental principle of competence-competence as the arbitrators' power to rule on their own jurisdiction would be practically negated.

7.18. Another possible way forward could be to award a preeminent role in performing supervisory functions to the courts of the seat of arbitration. Conferring exclusive jurisdiction on the court of the designated seat of arbitration - connected with a rapid judicial process regarding adjudication on the validity of the arbitration agreement, as well as with uniform conflict of law rules governing such validity - would be a preferable measure

---

[39] See Dorothee Schramm, Elliott Geisinger, Philippe Pinsolle, in HERBERT KRONKE, PATRICIA NACIMIENTO, DIRK OTTO, NICOLA CHRISTINE PORT, RECOGNITION AND ENFORCEMENT OF FOREIGN ARBITRAL AWARDS: A GLOBAL COMMENTARY ON THE NEW YORK CONVENTION, The Netherlands: Kluwer Law International 110 (2010); Doak Bishop, Wade M. Coriell, Marcello Medina-Campos, *The 'Null and Void' Provision of the New York Convention*, in ENFORCEMENT OF ARBITRATION AGREEMENTS AND INTERNATIONAL ARBITRAL AWARDS: THE NEW YORK CONVENTION IN PRACTICE, United Kingdom: Cameron May Ltd. 275, 283-286 (Emmanuel Gaillard and Domenico Di Pietro eds., 2008); STEPHAN WILSKE, TODD J. FOX, *supra* note 4, at 184.
[40] See Peter Schlosser, *The competence of arbitrators and of Courts*, 8(2) ARBITRATION INTERNATIONAL 189, 193 (1992); Emil Brengesjö, *supra* note 18, at 27.
[41] See Emmanuel Gaillard, Yas Banifatemi, *supra* note 7, at 260-261; *contra* see Peter Schlosser, Ibid, at 203-204 according to whose opinion "'No sound reason exists to construe "Kompetenz-Kompetenz" stipulations in a way to disempower courts to rule promptly and conclusively on their jurisdiction should one of the parties have recourse to them prior to its opponent commencing arbitration proceedings'.

for centralization of decision-making regarding validity at the courts of a single, known in advance, jurisdiction rather than scattering supervisory jurisdiction among a plurality of courts of different countries.[42] The advantage of this proposal is that competition between different state courts is excluded and concentrated to the courts of the seat, a solution that provides increased predictability to both arbitration and related litigation.

7.19.   One should also recall that during the legislative initiative for amendment of the European Regulation 44/2001[43] (Brussels I Regulation), special attention was given to the role played by the seat of arbitration both in the Heidelberg Report[44] and the European Commission's proposal,[45] although the present *status quo*[46] after the path chosen by the Recast Brussels Regulation adopts a different approach. Of course, as it is correctly underlined, at the end 'the answer to the issue of parallel proceedings is anchored in the arbitrator's interpretation of the arbitration agreement itself, in accordance with the principle of Kompetenz-Kompetenz'.[47] From another perspective though it is true that the arbitral tribunal would be more willing to stay its proceedings and defer to the courts of the seat which will always have the final saying on the validity of the arbitration

---

[42]   See Frédéric Bachand, *supra* note 32, at 225 ff.

[43]   Council Regulation (EC) No 44/2001 of 22 December 2000 on jurisdiction and the recognition and enforcement of judgments in civil and commercial matters [2001] OJ L12/1.

[44]   Burkhard Hess, Thomas Pfeiffer, Peter Schlosser, *Report on the Application of Regulation Brussels I in the Member States*, Study JLS/C4/2005/03 (Munich 2007) available at: http://courtesa.eu/wp-content/uploads/2019/03/study_application_brussels_1_en.pdf (accessed on 23 June 2021), Art. 134 et. 65: 'Thus, the following provision could be added as a new Article 27 A: "A court of a Member State shall stay the proceedings once the defendant contests the jurisdiction of the court with respect to existence and scope of an arbitration agreement if a court of the Member State that is designated as place of arbitration in the arbitration agreement is seized for declaratory relief in respect to the existence, the validity and/or scope of the arbitration agreement"': Basically, the Heidelberg Report suggested granting exclusive jurisdiction in ancillary proceedings concerned with the support of arbitration, to the courts of the Member State in which the arbitration takes place. – For more details see Guido Carducci, *Arbitration, anti-suit injunctions and Lis Pendens under the European Jurisdiction Regulation and the New York Convention*, 27(2) ARBITRATION INTERNATIONAL 171, 191-192 (2011); Claudio Consolo, *Brussels I Regulation, arbitration and parallel proceedings: A discussion of the Heidelberg Proposal (in the light of West Tankers and Endesa)*, in FERRUCCIO AULETTA, GIAN PAOLO CALIFANO, GIUSEPPE DELLA PIETRA, NICOLA RASCIO, SULL' ARBITRATO STUDI OFFERTI A GIOVANNI VERDE, Napoli: Jovene Editore 245, 250 ff. (2010).

[45]   Commission (EC), *Proposal for a Regulation of the European Parliament and of the Council on jurisdiction and the recognition and enforcement of judgments in civil and commercial matters (recast)*, COM(2010) 748 final, 14 December 2010: The Commission proposed inserting a new *lis pendens* rule in the Regulation giving priority to the court at the seat of arbitration or the arbitral tribunal to rule on the existence or validity of the arbitration agreement. For a presentation of the European Commission's proposal see Burkhard Hess, *Die Reform der Verordnung Brüssel I und die Schiedsgerichtsbarkeit*, in HERBERT KRONKE, KARSTEN THORN, GRENZEN ÜBERWINDEN – PRINZIPIEN BEWAHREN. FESTSCHRIFT FÜR BERND VON HOFFMANN, Bielefeld: Gieseking E.U.W. 648, 650 ff. (2011).

[46]   For the interface between arbitration and Member State court proceedings after the adoption of Regulation 1215/2012 see among others Guido Carducci, *The new EU Regulation 1215/2012 of 12 December 2012 on Jurisdiction and International Arbitration*, 29(3) ARBITRATION INTERNATIONAL 467 ff. (2013); Luise Hauberg Wilhelmsen, *The Recast Brussels I Regulation and Arbitration: Revisited or Revised?*, 30(1) ARBITRATION INTERNATIONAL 169, 181 ff. (2014).

[47]   Bernardo M. Cremades, Magdalena Ignacio, *supra* note 18, at 539.

agreement as allowed by the review of the arbitral award at the end of the arbitral process. Besides, users of international arbitration want, or at least accept, some judicial supervision of the arbitral proceedings as they practically never exclude[48] the possibility of seeking the annulment of arbitral awards despite a growing number of arbitration statutes[49] and institutional rules[50] allowing them to do so.

7.20. Lastly, it has been proposed[51] as a workable rule to delegate to the arbitral tribunal the power to rule, in a final matter, on jurisdictional objections that do not call into question the existence or validity of the agreement, an approach favored by U.S. Federal courts.[52] Therefore, according to the same opinion[53] when the respondent does not claim that it has never been bound by the arbitration agreement but merely raises an issue regarding its scope, termination or waiver, then based on the presumed intention of the parties, such type of issues are part of those that the parties have agreed to arbitrate. Subsequently, any attempt by the responding party to bring such objections to a court would contravene Article II(3) of the New York Convention.

V.   Concluding Remarks

7.21. The improvement of the regime of parallel proceedings, if successful, would ensure a good coordination between judicial and arbitral proceedings, discourage obstructing litigation,

---

[48]   See Frédéric Bachand, *supra* note 32, at 227.

[49]   See CHRISTOPHE SERAGLINI, JÉRÔME ORTSCHEIDT, DROIT DE L'ARBITRAGE INTERNE ET INTERNATIONAL, Paris: Montchrestien 853 (2013) – For an analysis of the issue of waiver clauses see also Catherine Bratic, 'The Parties Hereby Waive All Recourse ... But Not That One.' Why Parties Adopt Exclusion Agreements and Why Courts Hesitate, 12(2) DISPUTE RESOLUTION INTERNATIONAL 105 (2018) – For a recent example see Russian Federal Law No. 382-FZ of 29 December 2015 'On Arbitration (Arbitral Proceedings) in the Russian Federation' Article 40; International Commercial Arbitration Law of the Russian Federation, Article 34(1) ('[...]If an arbitration agreement of the parties provides for administration of a dispute by a permanent arbitration institution, the parties may by their direct agreement stipulate that the award is final. The final award is not subject to setting aside.[...]'): More specifically under Russia's waiver law, which came into effect in September 2016, annulment may be waived in both domestic and international arbitrations, regardless of the domicile of the parties, but only if the arbitration is administered by an approved arbitral institution. Therefore, waiver is prohibited for *ad hoc* arbitrations.

[50]   See e.g., ICC Rules of Arbitration, Article 35(6) (2021) ('Every award shall be binding on the parties. By submitting the dispute to arbitration under the Rules, the parties ... shall be deemed to have waived their right to any form of recourse insofar as such waiver validly can be made.'); ICDR International Arbitration Rules, Article 33(1) (2021) ('The parties ... absent agreement otherwise, waive irrevocably their right to any form of appeal, review, or recourse to any court or other judicial authority, insofar as such waiver can validly be made.'); LCIA Arbitration Rules, Article 26.8 (2020) ('the parties also waive irrevocably their right to any form of appeal, review or recourse to any state court or other legal authority, insofar as such waiver shall not be prohibited under any applicable law.'); HKIAC Administered Arbitration Rules, Article 35.2 (2018) ('The parties and any such person waive their rights to any form of recourse or defense in respect of the setting-aside, enforcement and execution of any award, in so far as such waiver can validly be made').

[51]   Frédéric Bachand, *supra* note 32, at 221-223.

[52]   See GARY B. BORN, *supra* note 12, at 932 ff., 1087-1089.

[53]   Frédéric Bachand, *supra* note 32, at 223.

eliminate multiplication of conflicting decisions, but mostly enhance the effectiveness of arbitration awards in the interest of arbitration itself. The greatest challenge though is the measure of court control and court intervention in relation to arbitrator's jurisdiction which is 'archetypal of the degree of recognition of the autonomy of international arbitration'.[54] Notwithstanding the fact that the principle of competence-competence is at the heart of the self-contained character of international arbitration, in the current state of the international arbitration system the critical question posed is whether international arbitration is a fully autonomous process that should operate in accordance with supra-national and self-contained rules or if it should always be anchored to a particular national legal system.

7.22.   The optimal solution to the problem of parallel proceedings would clearly be one articulated in transnational normative texts. Nevertheless, the proposals[55] for either a multilateral treaty or at least a protocol to the New York Convention filling the gaps and the issues left open by the Convention, could be workable solutions in the future only if there was a pro-arbitration stance from most countries as any proposal, in order to be efficient, needs to be widely agreed-to. The development of international arbitration law has indeed benefited during the last decades exactly due to the vast acceptance of the New York Convention. Nowadays, arbitration continues to be an absolute necessity in international trade and, hence, the national legal systems need to adjust to the increased popularity of this dispute resolution mechanism and give up any parochial distrust emerging from the fact that the authority of the arbitral tribunal does not emanate from a state's sovereignty but from the parties' arbitration agreement. They also need to reassess their individual dynamic as international arbitration venues, avoid any undue interference of courts to the arbitration process but mostly embrace the fact that solutions developed in litigation and on a national level cannot suffice to bring about a coherent, homogenous and efficient regime for handling parallel proceedings related to international commercial disputes.

7.23.   The nature and objectives of international commercial arbitration need to be respected although it is true that one of its most important features, the wide degree of autonomy granted to parties and arbitrators, would inevitably have to be limited for the sake of predictability, certainty and consistency. Therefore, the readiness of arbitral tribunals to adjust to the new

---

[54]   Emmanuel Gaillard, Yas Banifatemi, *supra* note 7, at 273.

[55]   See *supra*, at footnote 31.

legal framework may be a move towards an ultimately more restrictive international legal order. However, as rules or tools available nowadays in international arbitration are insufficient to fully deal with the issue of parallel proceedings and provide coordination, the improvement of the current regime is essential to avoid conflicting dispute settlement outcomes and ensure finality which is fundamental in every legal system.

| | |

Summaries

DEU [*Gerichtsbarkeit in parallel geführten Verfahren: Zuständigkeit der Gerichte versus Schiedsvereinbarung*]
Der Beitrag befasst sich umfassend mit dem Problem von parallel geführten Verfahren – konkret konzentriert er sich auf Situationen, in denen die Zuständigkeit der Gerichte und Schiedsgerichte parallel gegeben ist, der Fall die Anfechtung der Existenz bzw. Gültigkeit einer Schiedsvereinbarung betrifft und die beiden Entscheidungsträger in ihrer unabhängigen Kompetenz betreffend die eigene Gerichtsbarkeit einander gleichgestellt sind. Der Beitrag analysiert die These, dass Vorhersehbarkeit und Stabilität des Rechts eine gute Koordination zwischen dem Gerichtsverfahren und dem Schiedsverfahren erfordert. Diese soll mittels wirksamer Mechanismen und supranationaler Regelungen erzielt werden, mit denen bestehende Unsicherheiten beseitigt werden, was nicht nur die Existenz eines kohärenten Systems für parallel geführte Verfahren gewährleistet, sondern außerdem auch ein effektives und stabiles Schiedsverfahren.

CZE [*Pravomoc v souběžně vedených řízeních: soudní pravomoc v. rozhodčí smlouva*]
Tento příspěvek se zabývá složitou problematikou souběžně vedených řízení. Konkrétně se zaměřuje na situace souběžné pravomoci soudu a rozhodčího soudu v případech, kdy je napadena existence nebo platnost rozhodčí smlouvy a oba rozhodující orgány jsou rovnocenně oprávněny nezávisle rozhodnout o vlastní pravomoci. Příspěvek analyzuje tvrzení, že předvídatelnost a stabilita práva vyžaduje dobrou koordinaci mezi soudním a rozhodčím řízením prostřednictvím účinných mechanismů a nadnárodních úprav, které povedou k odstranění stávajících nejistot a zajistí nejen existenci soudržného režimu

Czech (& Central European) Yearbook of Arbitration®

pro souběžně vedená řízení, ale i efektivní a stabilní rozhodčí řízení.

| | |

POL [*Kompetencje w postępowaniach prowadzonych równolegle: kompetencje sądów a umowa arbitrażowa*]
Artykuł omawia przypadki równoległych kompetencji sądów i trybunałów arbitrażowych tam, gdzie zostaje podważone istnienie lub ważność umowy arbitrażowej, a oba organy rozpatrujące sprawę są kompetentne do niezależnego rozstrzygnięcia w sprawie własnych kompetencji. Ponadto prezentuje analizę tezy, iż przewidywalność i stabilność prawa wymaga skutecznych mechanizmów i przepisów ponadnarodowych, które doprowadzą do usunięcia istniejącej niepewności oraz zagwarantują istnienie spójnego trybu na wypadek postępowań prowadzonych równolegle.

FRA [*La compétence dans les procédures parallèles : compétence judiciaire et convention d'arbitrage*]
Le présent texte analyse les cas de compétences parallèles d'une juridiction et d'un tribunal arbitral dans des situations où l'existence ou la validité de la convention d'arbitrage est contestée et où les deux autorités sont ainsi en droit de statuer indépendamment sur leur propre compétence. L'article examine également l'argument selon lequel la prévisibilité et la stabilité du droit nécessitent des mécanismes efficaces et des règles supranationales qui puissent éliminer les incertitudes existantes et garantir un régime cohérent applicable aux procédures parallèles.

RUS [*Компетенция в параллельных разбирательствах: компетенция суда против арбитражного соглашения*]
В статье рассматриваются случаи параллельной компетенции суда и арбитражного суда в случаях, когда оспаривается существование или действительность арбитражного соглашения, благодаря чему оба вышеуказанных органа имеют право самостоятельно принимать решение о своей компетенции. Далее в статье анализируется утверждение, что предсказуемость и стабильность законодательства требуют наличия эффективных механизмов и транснациональных правил для устранения существующих неопределенностей и

Czech (& Central European) Yearbook of Arbitration®

обеспечения существования согласованного режима параллельных разбирательств.

ESP [*Competencia en procesos concurrentes: competencia y convenio arbitral*]
El artículo aborda los casos de competencia concurrente del tribunal nacional y el tribunal de arbitraje en situaciones en las que se impugna la existencia o la validez de un acuerdo de arbitraje, y ambos organismos, por tanto, están facultados para decidir de forma independiente sobre su propia competencia. Además, el texto analiza el argumento de que la previsibilidad y la estabilidad del derecho requieren mecanismos eficaces y normas supranacionales que eliminen las incertidumbres existentes y garanticen la existencia de un régimen coherente de los procesos paralelos.

| | |

Bibliography:

Frédéric Bachand, *Does Article 8 of the Model Law call for full or prima facie review of the arbitral tribunal's jurisdiction?*, 22(3) ARBITRATION INTERNATIONAL 463 (2006).

Frédéric Bachand, *Parallel proceedings involving objections to arbitral jurisdictions: A closer look at the presumed intention of the parties*, in STAVROS L. BREKOULAKIS, THE EVOLUTION AND FUTURE OF INTERNATIONAL ARBITRATION, The Netherlands: Kluwer Law International B.V. (2016).

Doak Bishop, Wade M. Coriell, Marcello Medina-Campos, *The 'Null and Void' Provision of the New York Convention*, in ENFORCEMENT OF ARBITRATION AGREEMENTS AND INTERNATIONAL ARBITRAL AWARDS: THE NEW YORK CONVENTION IN PRACTICE, United Kingdom: Cameron May Ltd. (Emmanuel Gaillard and Domenico Di Pietro eds., 2008).

GARY B. BORN, INTERNATIONAL COMMERCIAL ARBITRATION, The Netherlands: Kluwer Law International (1st ed., 2009).

GARY B. BORN, INTERNATIONAL COMMERCIAL ARBITRATION, The Netherlands: Kluwer Law International (2nd ed., 2014).

Catherine Bratic, *'The Parties Hereby Waive All Recourse … But Not That One.' Why Parties Adopt Exclusion Agreements and Why Courts Hesitate*, 12(2) DISPUTE RESOLUTION INTERNATIONAL 105 (2018).

Stavros Brekoulakis, *The effect of an Arbitral Award and Third Parties in International Arbitration: Res Judicata Revisited*, 16(1) AMERICAN REVIEW OF INTERNATIONAL ARBITRATION 177 (2005).

Emil Brengesjö, *Parallel proceedings in International Arbitration*, in ANTONIA KRZYMOWSKA, CAROLINE NORDKLINT, M ÅRTEN SCHULTZ, STOCKHOLM CENTRE FOR COMMERCIAL LAW ÅRSBOK VI, Stockholm: Stockholm Centre for commercial law (2015).

Luca Radicati di Brozolo, *Res Judicata and international arbitral awards*, in PIERRE TERCIER, POST AWARD ISSUES: ASA SPECIAL SERIES NO. 38, New York: JurisNet LLC (2011).

Guido Carducci, The Arbitration Reform in France: Domestic and International Arbitration, 28(1) ARBITRATION INTERNATIONAL 125 (2012).

Guido Carducci, *Arbitration, anti-suit injunctions and Lis Pendens under the European Jurisdiction Regulation and the New York Convention*, 27(2) ARBITRATION INTERNATIONAL 171 (2011).

Guido Carducci, *The new EU Regulation 1215/2012 of 12 December 2012 on Jurisdiction and International Arbitration*, 29(3) ARBITRATION INTERNATIONAL 467 (2013).

Claudio Consolo, *Brussels I Regulation, arbitration and parallel proceedings: A discussion of the Heidelberg Proposal (in the light of West Tankers and Endesa)*, in FERRUCCIO AULETTA, GIAN PAOLO CALIFANO, GIUSEPPE DELLA PIETRA, NICOLA RASCIO, SULL' ARBITRATO STUDI OFFERTI A GIOVANNI VERDE, Napoli: Jovene Editore (2010).

Bernardo M. Cremades, Magdalena Ignacio, *Parallel Proceedings in International Arbitration*, 24(4) ARBITRATION INTERNATIONAL 507 (2008).

NADJA ERK, PARALLEL PROCEEDINGS IN INTERNATIONAL ARBITRATION. A COMPARATIVE EUROPEAN PERSPECTIVE, The Netherlands: Kluwer Law International (2014).

Emmanuel Gaillard, Yas Banifatemi, Negative effect of competence-competence: The rule of priority in favor of the arbitrators, in ENFORCEMENT OF ARBITRATION AGREEMENTS AND INTERNATIONAL ARBITRAL AWARDS: THE NEW YORK CONVENTION IN PRACTICE, United Kingdom: Cameron May Ltd. (Emmanuel Gaillard and Domenico Di Pietro eds., 2008).

Luise Hauberg Wilhelmsen, *The Recast Brussels I Regulation and Arbitration: Revisited or Revised?*, 30(1) ARBITRATION INTERNATIONAL 169 (2014).

Burkhard Hess, *Die Reform der Verordnung Brüssel I und die Schiedsgerichtsbarkeit*, in Hans van Houte, *Why not include Arbitration in the Brussels Jurisdiction Regulation?*, 21(4) ARBITRATION INTERNATIONAL 509 (2005).

Philippe Hovaguimian, *The Res-Judicata effects of foreign judgments in post-award proceedings: To bind or not to bind?*, 34(1) JOURNAL OF ARBITRATION INTERNATIONAL 79 (2017).

Sigvard Jarvin, *Lis pendens et res judicata dans l' arbitrage international: vers une pratique harmonisée?*, in JAN KLEINEMAN, PETER WESTBERG, STEPHAN CARLSSON, FESTSKRIFT TILL LARS HEUMAN, Stockholm: Jure Förlag (2008).

Gabrielle Kaufmann-Kohler, *How to handle parallel proceedings: A practical approach to issues such as competence-competence and anti-suit injunctions*, 2(1) DISPUTE RESOLUTION INTERNATIONAL 110 (2008).

Florian Kremslehner, *Lis pendens and res judicata in International Commercial Arbitration – How to deal with parallel proceedings – How to determine the conclusive and preclusive effects of arbitral awards*, in CHRISTIAN KLAUSEGGER, PETER KLEIN, FLORIAN KREMSLEHNER, ALEXANDER PETSCHE, NIKOLAUS PITKOWITZ, JENNY POWER, IRENE WELSER, GEROLD ZEILER, AUSTRIAN YEARBOOK, Wien: Manzsche Verlags- und Universitätsbuchhandlung (2007).

HERBERT KRONKE, KARSTEN THORN, GRENZEN ÜBERWINDEN – PRINZIPIEN BEWAHREN. FESTSCHRIFT FÜR BERND VON HOFFMANN, Bielefeld: Gieseking E.U.W. 648 (2011).

Philip de Ly, Audley Sheppard, *ILA Final Report on Lis Pendens and Arbitration*, 25(1) ARBITRATION INTERNATIONAL 3 (2009).

Filip De Ly, Audley Sheppard, *ILA Final Report on Res Judicata and Arbitration*, 25(1) ARBITRATION INTERNATIONAL 67 (2009).

Pierre Mayer, *Litispendance, connexité et chose jugée dans l' arbitrage international*, in CLAUDE REYMOND, PIERO BERNARDINI, LIBER AMICORUM CLAUDE REYMOND: AUTOR DE L'ARBITRAGE, Paris: Éditions du Juris-classeur 185 (2004).

Christian Oetiker, *The principle of lis pendens in international arbitration: The Swiss decision in Fomento v. Colon*, 18(2) ARBITRATION INTERNATIONAL 137 (2002).

JAN PAULSSON, GEORGIOS PETROCHILOS, UNCITRAL ARBITRATION, The Netherlands: Kluwer Law International (2018).

Charles Poncet, Luisa Mockler, *Res Judicata: A contribution to the debate on claim preclusion in international arbitration,* in LIBER AMICORUM EN L'HONNEUR DE WILLIAM LAURENCE GRAIG, Paris: LexisNexis (2016).

Douglas Reichert, *Problems with Parallel and Duplicate Proceedings: The Litispendence Principle and International Arbitration,* 8(3) ARBITRATION INTERNATIONAL 237 (1992).

CHRISTOPHE SERAGLINI, JÉRÔME ORTSCHEIDT, DROIT DE L'ARBITRAGE INTERNE ET INTERNATIONAL, Paris: Montchrestien (2013).

SILJA SCHAFFSTEIN, THE DOCTRINE OF RES JUDICATA BEFORE INTERNATIONAL COMMERCIAL ARBITRAL TRIBUNALS, Oxford: Oxford University Press (2016).

Silja Schaffstein, *The law governing res judicata,* 7(1) EUROPEAN INTERNATIONAL ARBITRATION REVIEW 117 (2018).

Peter Schlosser, *The competence of arbitrators and of Courts,* 8(2) ARBITRATION INTERNATIONAL 189 (1992).

Dorothee Schramm, Elliott Geisinger, Philippe Pinsolle, in HERBERT KRONKE, PATRICIA NACIMIENTO, DIRK OTTO, NICOLA CHRISTINE PORT, RECOGNITION AND ENFORCEMENT OF FOREIGN ARBITRAL AWARDS: A GLOBAL COMMENTARY ON THE NEW YORK CONVENTION, The Netherlands: Kluwer Law International (2010).

Nathalie Voser, Julie Raneda, *Recent Developments on the Doctrine of Res Judicata in International Arbitration from a Swiss Perspective: A Call for a Harmonized Solution,* 33(4) ASA BULLETIN 742 (2015).

STEPHAN WILSKE, TODD J. FOX, NEW YORK CONVENTION, COMMENTARY, München: Verlag C.H. Beck (Reinmar Wolff ed., 2012).

Nathan Yaffe, *Transnational Arbitral Res Judicata,* 34(5) JOURNAL OF INTERNATIONAL ARBITRATION 795 (2017).

Czech (& Central European) Yearbook of Arbitration®

Czech Republic

Poland

Selected Case Law of Czech Courts Related to Arbitration

Alexander J. Bělohlávek

ORCID iD 0000-0001-5310-5269
https://orcid.org/0000-0001-5310-5269

Czech (& Central European) Yearbook of Arbitration®

I.   Essence of Arbitration and Arbitrability

8.01.   Connected, *inter alia*, to the provisions of Section 1 of Act of the Czech Republic No. 216/1994 Coll., on Arbitration and the Enforcement of Arbitral Awards

ArbAct: Section 1 [Scope of Act; Independence and Impartiality][1]
Current Version of Section 1 of ArbAct:
This Act sets forth rules regulating:
(a) the resolution of disputes by independent and impartial arbitrators,
(b) the resolution of disputes arising from the administration of an association by an arbitration commission of the association in line with the provisions of the Civil Code,[7] and
(c) the enforcement of arbitral awards.
Footnotes Forming Part of Normative Text:
7) Section 265 of the Civil Code.[2]

---

[1]   The titles of the individual Parts and Sections provided in square brackets are not part of the normative text and have been supplemented by the author for better transparency of the contents.

Section 1 of ArbAct in Effect as of 01 April 2012:

This Act sets forth rules regulating the resolution of property disputes by independent and impartial arbitrators and the enforcement of arbitral awards.[3]

Section 1 of ArbAct Prior to Act No. 466/2011 Coll.:[4]

(1) This Act sets forth rules regulating the resolution of property disputes by independent and impartial arbitrators and the enforcement of arbitral awards.

(2) This Act does not apply to the resolution of disputes involving public non-profit institutional healthcare facilities established under special laws.

Legislative Developments Since 01 April 2012:

Section 1 of the ArbAct, as amended by Act No. 245/2006 Coll., Act No. 296/2007 Coll., Act No. 7/2009 Coll., Act No. 466/2011 Coll., Act No. 19/2012 Coll. and Act No. 91/2012 Coll., was newly reformulated by Act No. 303/2013 Coll., Amending Selected Legislation in Connection with the Adopted Recodification of Civil Law, as amended – see Part Seventeen, Article XX of the last mentioned Act which took effect on 01 January 2014.

---

[2] Section 265 of the Civil Code 2012 in effect since 01 January 2014 (cit.): *If an arbitration committee is established, it shall resolve disputes falling within the association's self-governance to the extent determined by the by-laws; unless the by-laws determine the competence of the arbitration committee, it shall resolve disputes between members and the association concerning the payment of membership fees and review decisions to expel a member from the association.* The provision is further elaborated on in Sections 266 to 268 of the same Act. Procedural rules are contained in Sections 40e to 40k of the ArbAct.

[3] The wording of Section 1 of the ArbAct was the subject of legislative interpretation, because the adoption of the ArbAct Amendment in the form of Act No. 19/2012 Coll., in effect since 01 April 2012, suffered from an obvious error. The current (full) text printed in this publication corresponds to the text published, for instance, in the ASPI system, as well as in the ÚZ (full texts) series no. 893, Ostrava: Sagit, 2012 and elsewhere. The author also believes that Section 1 of the ArbAct, valid and effective from 01 April 2012, thus only contained the former first subsection.

[4] Act No. 466/2011 Coll. of 06 December 2011 (promulgated and effective since 30 December 2011) repealed Subsection (2) in its entirety, leaving only the previous Subsection (1); the subsection is no longer identified with any number. However, the ArbAct Amendment 2012, in effect from 01 April 2012 (Act No. 12/2012), adopted on 20 December 2011, effective date: 01 April 2012, added the following words at the end of the former Subsection (2) (cit.): "... or if the proceedings before the financial arbiter have been commenced or if a decision on the merits has been rendered in such proceedings." As the author analyses below in greater detail, this amendment is a manifest legislative error obviously incapable of having the corresponding legislative effect and has thus not become part of valid legislation.

8.02. Resolution of the Supreme Court of the Czech Republic, Case No. 20 Cdo 2487/2010 of 16 August 2012:[5] [nature of arbitration; essence of arbitration; contractual theory; jurisdictional theory; difference from civil litigation; conditional exclusion of court jurisdiction; *lis pendens*; res *judicata*; autonomy; level and scope of protection afforded to the parties in arbitration by courts; finding law in arbitration]: The fundamental difference from civil procedure in court (i.e. litigation) lies in the delimitation of the managing and decision-making authority – a court in civil litigation, an arbitrator or a permanent arbitral institution in arbitration. The arbitrator's[6] power to hear and resolve a dispute is based on the joint will of the parties to the dispute expressed in their arbitration agreement. This procedural agreement of the parties excludes the jurisdiction of courts (only conditionally, in view of Section 106(1) of the Code of Civil Procedure),[7] and establishes the jurisdiction of (an) arbitrator(s). Based on the voluntary acts of the parties, the **arbitrator thus replaces the court** where the latter should otherwise hear and resolve the case. However, the rights of the parties to direct the dispute resolution procedure are even more far-reaching; the parties to the dispute are, for instance, allowed to select the arbitrators, and to determine the applicable procedural rules, the seat of arbitration, the type of proceedings (oral or written), and even the criteria that should be applied to the merits (Section 25(3) of the ArbAct).[8/9]

---

[5]   Preceding decisions in the case: (i) Resolution of the District Court for Pilsen-City [Czech Republic], Case No. 73 Nc 1420/2009 of 05 November 2009; and (ii) Resolution of the Regional Court in Pilsen [Czech Republic], Case No. 12 Co 12/2010-165 of 10 February 2010.

[6]   The shorthand used by the Supreme Court in the reasoning for the decision should be interpreted as including an arbitrator [*ad hoc*], as well as a permanent arbitral institution.

[7]   Code of Civil Procedure [Czech Republic] (approximate translation, cit.): Section 106 – *(1) As soon as the court discovers, on the respondent's objection lodged together with or before the first act of the respondent on the merits, that the agreement of the parties requires that the case be submitted to arbitrators or to an arbitral committee of an association, the court must desist from further examination of the case and discontinue the proceedings; the court, however, hears the case if the parties declare that they waive the agreement or that they do not insist on having the case heard by the arbitral committee of the association. The court also hears the case if the court determines that the matter is not arbitrable under the laws of the Czech Republic, or that the arbitration agreement is invalid or non-existent, or that examining the agreement in arbitration exceeds the scope of jurisdiction vested in the arbitrators by the agreement, or that the arbitral tribunal refused to hear the case. (2) If the court proceedings under Subsection (1) were discontinued and the same case was submitted to arbitrators or to the arbitral committee of the association, the original motion to commence the proceedings retains its legal effects, provided that the motion to commence the proceedings before the arbitrators or the arbitral committee of the association is lodged no later than within 30 days of receipt of the court's resolution discontinuing the proceedings. (3) If the arbitral proceedings were opened before the court proceedings, the court stays the proceedings on the non-existence, invalidity or expiration/termination of the agreement until the arbitrator(s) decide on their jurisdiction over the case or on the merits.*

[8]   The Supreme Court of the Czech Republic has held that the nature of arbitration in terms of *contractual theory* v. *jurisdictional theory* is also a significant question of law. In this regard, the Supreme Court has invoked the landmark judgment of the Constitutional Court, Case No. I. ÚS 3227/07 of 08 March 2011.

[9]   Act on Arbitration and the Enforcement of Arbitral Awards – Act of the Czech Republic No. 216/1994 Coll. (approximate translation, cit.) – Section 25 [Making Arbitral Award and Reasoning]: Current version: *(1) The arbitral award must be adopted by the majority of the arbitrators, must be made*

(2) Arbitration **excludes parallel civil** [court] **proceedings** concerning the same issue. Arbitral awards have the same effects as final court decisions (Section 28(2) of the ArbAct),[10] which means that arbitral awards constitute *res judicata*, barring the parties from litigating the same claim again in courts. (3) In compliance with the principle of autonomy of will, the law honours the freely expressed will of the parties who wish to have their dispute heard and resolved by an arbitrator; courts are therefore not allowed to intervene in arbitration, except in strictly defined situations specified in the ArbAct. On the other hand, this does not mean that the purpose of arbitration is to eliminate or reduce the degree of protection that would otherwise be afforded to the parties in civil litigation; arbitration, just like litigation, aims at the peaceful resolution of the dispute between the parties. It is just that the parties have a special reason (for instance, expeditiousness or the confidentiality of the information discussed in the proceedings) to believe that arbitration is a more suitable solution. From this perspective, the submission of a dispute to arbitration means the transfer of legal protection to a different decision-making and law-finding authority,[11] rather than the waiver thereof; indeed, any other conclusion would render it conceptually unacceptable to consider arbitration as a dispute resolution method representing an alternative to litigation.

---

in writing, and must be signed by at least the majority of the arbitrators. The operative part of the arbitral award must be clear and unambiguous. (2) The arbitral award must contain reasons, unless the parties have agreed to dispense with reasons; this also applies to any arbitral award rendered pursuant to Section 24(2). (3) When making the award, the arbitrators apply the substantive law applicable to the dispute; they may, however, resolve the dispute according to the rules of equity, but only if the parties have explicitly authorized them to do so.

The Act in effect as of 01 April 2012: (1) The arbitral award must be adopted by the majority of the arbitrators, must be made in writing, and must be signed by at least the majority of the arbitrators. The operative part of the arbitral award must be clear and unambiguous. (2) The arbitral award must contain reasons, unless the parties have agreed to dispense with reasons; this also applies to any arbitral award rendered pursuant to Section 24(2). An arbitral award rendered in a dispute arising from a consumer contract must always contain reasons and instructions regarding the right to file a motion with the court to annul the award. (3) When making the award, the arbitrators apply the substantive law applicable to the dispute; they may, however, resolve the dispute according to the rules of equity, but only if the parties have explicitly authorized them to do so. In disputes arising from consumer contracts, the arbitrators shall always abide by consumer protection laws and regulations.

Legislative developments since 01 April 2012: Section 25 of the ArbAct as amended by Act No. 245/2006 Coll., Act No. 296/2007 Coll., Act No. 7/2009 Coll., Act No. 466/2011 Coll., Act No. 19/2012 Coll. and Act No. 91/2012 Coll., was newly reformulated by Act No. 258/2016 Coll., Amending Selected Legislation in Connection with the Consumer Credit Act, which took effect on 01 December 2016. The law has reverted to the version that was in effect before 01 April 2012.

[10] A selection of current case-law concerning the nature and effects of an arbitral award is annotated below.

Section 28 of the ArbAct is quoted below in Part IV of this Czech case-law overview.

[11] An arbitrator (permanent arbitral institution) is also designated as "another authority" by judgment of the Constitutional Court of the Czech Republic, Case No. I. ÚS 3227/07 of 08 March 2011.

8.03. **Resolution of the Supreme Court of the Czech Republic, Case No. 20 Cdo 1156/2013 of 26 November 2013:**[12] [duties of arbitrators and nature of their activities; supervisory duties of the courts; review of procedural errors; provision of legal protection; advantages of arbitration; practical usability of arbitration; purpose of the proceedings for annulment of arbitral award; discontinuation of enforcement proceedings; statutory representative; lack of procedural capacity; lack of substantive-law capacity] Arbitrators are not law-finding authorities in arbitration; arbitrators create the obligations binding on the parties in their relationship on behalf of the parties, and their power is not delegated by the sovereign power of the state, but derived from the private inherent power of the parties to determine their future.

8.04. **Judgment of the Supreme Court of the Czech Republic, Case No. 25 Cdo 2790/2013 of 21 October 2014:**[13] [purpose of arbitration; exclusion of judicial review; application of the law; arbitrator bound by valid and applicable law; arbitrator obliged to apply valid and applicable law; scope of the supervisory powers of the court; protection of the advantages of arbitration and their practical usability; exhaustive list of grounds for annulment of an arbitral award; liability of arbitrator; annulment of an arbitral award; general liability requirements] (1)[14] (a) Considering the nature of arbitration, the purpose of which inheres in the fact that the hearing and resolution of a particular type of dispute is transferred from courts to arbitrators, and with respect to the grounds for which an arbitral award can be annulled, one may conclude that the legislator intended to exclude the judicial review of the material correctness of the arbitral award, i.e. the accuracy of the findings of fact and legal assessment of the case. (1) (b) If the court in proceedings for the annulment of an arbitral award were to review the award on the merits, the legal rules regulating arbitral awards would become pointless. (2) Arbitrators are directly bound by, and obliged to apply, valid and applicable law.[15] However, this does not mean that courts may arbitrarily intervene in arbitration. The scope of the courts'

---

[12] Preceding decisions in the case: (i) Resolution of the District Court in Prostějov [Czech Republic], Case No. 15 Nc 6257/2006-53 of 22 November 2011; and (ii) Resolution of the Regional Court in Brno [Czech Republic], Case No. 12 Co 152/2012-65 of 24 October 2012.

[13] Preceding decisions in the case: (i) Judgment of the District Court for Prague 3 [Czech Republic], Case No. 19 C 6/2010-110 of 08 June 2012; and (ii) Judgment of the Municipal Court in Prague [Czech Republic], Case No. 68 Co 513/2012-175 of 25 February 2013.

[14] To this extent, the Supreme Court of the Czech Republic has adopted the conclusions of the Supreme Court articulated in its decision in Case No. 33 Cdo 2675/2007 of 30 October 2009.

[15] The Supreme Court of the Czech Republic has also based this opinion on the conclusions articulated in judgment of the Constitutional Court of the Czech Republic in Case No. I. ÚS 3227/07 of 8 March 2011.

supervision must be carefully balanced in order to make sure that, on one hand, the rule stipulating that arbitration should guarantee legal protection is not eliminated, but on the other, that the advantages of arbitration and its practical usability (expeditiousness, economy) are not entirely wiped out. The list of grounds for the annulment of an arbitral award is exhaustive and does not include a conflict with substantive law or with public policy. The Constitutional Court has held that permitting the review of arbitral awards by a court for being contrary to substantive law is questionable both from the perspective of interpreting the grounds for the annulment of arbitral awards and from the perspective of the concept.

8.05. **Judgment of the Supreme Court of the Czech Republic, Case No. 29 ICdo 11/2014 of 28 January 2016:**[16] **[marital property (joint property of spouses); settlement of marital property; arbitrability]:** **(1)** Unless the dispute over the settlement of marital property is a dispute arising in connection with enforcement proceedings or an incidental dispute, it can be heard and resolved in arbitration. **(2)** The liquidator, who has acquired the right to dispose of the debtor's estate upon the declaration of bankruptcy of the debtor, and the debtor are both bound (within the limits of Section 159a(4) of the Code of Civil Procedure)[17] by a final judgment in which the court settled the marital property of the debtor (in insolvency) and his or her spouse before the insolvency proceedings were opened. **(3)** The same applies to an arbitral award in which the arbitrator settled the marital property of the debtor (in insolvency) and his or her spouse before the insolvency proceedings were opened and which has the effects of a final court ruling.[18]

8.06. **Resolution of the SC, Case No. 20 Cdo 3324/2017 of 21 March 2018:**[19] **[autonomy; contractual autonomy; standard form contract;** *bonos mores;* **independence and impartiality;**

---

16 The annotation is adopted from: Petr Vojtek, *Výběr rozhodnutí v oblasti civilněprávní*, 23(7-8) SOUDNÍ ROZHLEDY 249 (2017).

17 Code of Civil Procedure [Czech Republic] (approximate translation, cit.): Section 159a – *(1) Unless the Act stipulates otherwise, the operative part of a final judgment is binding solely on the parties to the proceedings. (2) The operative part of a final judgment delivered in matters listed in Section 83(2) is binding on the parties to the proceedings, as well as other persons or entities with a claim against the respondent as concerns identical claims from an identical conduct or status. Special laws set forth the cases in and the extent to which the operative part of a final judgment is binding on persons or entities other than the parties to the proceedings. (3) To the extent that the operative part of a final judgment is binding on the parties to the proceedings and, if applicable, other persons or entities, it is also binding on all authorities. (4) As soon as the case has been resolved with final force and effect, it cannot be reopened to the extent to which the operative part of the judgment is binding on the parties and any other persons or entities, as applicable.*

18 See Section 28(2) of the ArbAct.

19 Preceding decisions in the case: (i) Resolution of the District Court in Karviná – Havířov Office [Czech Republic], Case No. 127 EXE 1563/2016-28 of 10 November 2016; and (ii) Resolution of the Regional Court in Ostrava [Czech Republic], Case No. 9 Co 9/2017-44 of 27 February 2017.

Czech (& Central European) Yearbook of Arbitration®

economic dependence of the arbitrator; enforcement proceedings; prohibition of a review on the merits in enforcement proceedings] **(1)** Arbitration is based on the principle of contractual freedom, meaning that the parties are entirely free to decide whether they enter into an arbitration agreement and thereby exclude the courts' jurisdiction over their property dispute. **(2) Arbitration agreements as "standard form agreements" are not unusual or irregular, but rather used in practice when the parties wish to submit their dispute to arbitration**; such procedure is also not subject to any explicit statutory restrictions, whether in the context of B2C contracts or otherwise, as long as a higher degree of protection afforded to the weaker party is guaranteed; such procedure may even (generally) be found more favourable, because one may expect that consumer protection rules (such as Section 3(3) to (5);[20] Section 4(3),[21] or Section 8 of the ArbAct)[22] will not be ignored by the professional, as opposed to arbitration agreements negotiated "word for word" *ad hoc*.[23] **(3)** The execution itself of the arbitration agreement on a pre-printed standard form that contains the names of the individual *"ad hoc"* arbitrators does not render the arbitration agreement invalid for being *contra bonos mores*. The invalidity of such an agreement would require the

---

[20] Subsections (3) to (5) of Section 3 of the ArbAct applied until 01 December 2016 (for a quotation, see below in Part III of the case-law selection). However, that provision continues to apply to arbitration agreements entered into before 01 December 2016.

[21] Section 4(3) was repealed as of 01 January 2014. The wording invoked by the annotated decision (approximate translation, cit.): *(3) In order to meet the requirement of no criminal record under subsections (1) and (2), the person must have no previous final conviction for a criminal offence, unless the person's criminal record is expunged and the person is deemed never to have been convicted.*

[22] Act on Arbitration and the Enforcement of Arbitral Awards – Act of the Czech Republic No. 216/1994 Coll. (approximate translation, cit.) – Section 8 [Lack of Bias]:
Current version: *(1) The arbitrator is disqualified from hearing and resolving the case if his or her connection to the case, the parties, or their representatives gives rise to doubts about his or her lack of bias. (2) The candidate who is to be selected or appointed arbitrator or who was selected or appointed arbitrator must notify the parties or the court without delay of any and all circumstances that could give rise to legitimate doubts regarding the candidate's lack of bias and which would disqualify the candidate as arbitrator.*
The Act in effect as of 01 April 2012: *(1) The arbitrator is disqualified from hearing and resolving the case if his or her connection to the case, the parties, or their representatives gives rise to doubts about his or her lack of bias. (2) The candidate who is to be selected or appointed arbitrator or who was selected or appointed arbitrator must notify the parties or the court without delay of any and all circumstances that could give rise to legitimate doubts regarding the candidate's lack of bias and which would disqualify the candidate as arbitrator. (3) When resolving disputes from consumer contracts, the arbitrator is obliged to inform the parties before the hearing whether he or she has made or participated in the making of an arbitral award in the past 3 years or whether he or she has been an arbitrator in pending arbitration over a dispute to which any of the parties is or was a party. The time limit under the preceding sentence shall be calculated from the day when the arbitration covered by the reporting obligation terminated to the day of commencement of the arbitration in which the arbitrator is bound by the reporting obligation.*
Legislative Developments Since 01 April 2012: Section 8 of the ArbAct as amended by Act No. 245/2006 Coll., Act No. 296/2007 Coll., Act No. 7/2009 Coll., Act No. 466/2011 Coll., was newly reformulated by Act No. 19/2012 Coll., in effect since 01 April 2012. Further amendments were implemented as of 01 January 2014 and as of 01 December 2016.

[23] The Supreme Court of the Czech Republic has invoked its previous case-law, specifically Resolution Case No. 20 Cdo 4022/2014 of 23 January 2018.

existence of other important circumstances[24] that would suggest or indicate that the negotiation of the arbitration agreement with the consumer and the contents itself of the arbitration agreement are *contra bonos mores,* and consequently, the arbitration agreement can be found invalid.[25] **(4)** The principle of independent and impartial decisions guiding adjudication performed by judges also applies to decision-making performed by arbitrators. An arbitrator can be disqualified from hearing the case and delivering the arbitral award only if it is **obvious** that **the nature or intensity** of his or her connection to the case, the parties or their representatives **is such that the arbitrator will be unable to make independent and impartial decisions despite the statutory obligations.** This typically occurs **if the arbitrator simultaneously supports a party or a witness or, as applicable, if the arbitration or the outcome thereof could affect the arbitrator's rights**; this also applies if the arbitrator is related to the parties or has a **friendly or manifestly hostile relationship toward the parties, or a relationship of economic dependence.**[26] **(5) Economic dependence** is interpreted as an **immediate or direct economic relationship, such as the arbitrator being simultaneously an employee of one of the parties to the arbitration agreement, the party's business partner, or a colleague in an employment or similar relationship; the simple fact that the arbitrator becomes entitled to a fee with respect to each case disposed of by the arbitrator does not constitute economic dependence.** Otherwise, an identical objection could also be raised against permanent arbitral institutions, which, as a matter of fact, can also be repeatedly nominated by the parties to a dispute in their arbitration clauses.[27] **(6)** Deficiencies, if any, of the law-finding process [in arbitration] do not transfer to enforcement proceedings, and the **correctness on the merits of the decision submitted for enforcement cannot be challenged in the enforcement proceedings** in any manner whatsoever (including by means of an objection challenging any alleged deficiencies of the law-finding process). **(7)** The review of the validity of a credit facility agreement from the perspective of its (non)compliance with *bonos mores,* in line with judgments of

---

[24] The Supreme Court of the Czech Republic has invoked its previous case-law, specifically Resolution of the Supreme Court of the Czech Republic Case No. 30 Cdo 2401/2014 of 16 July 2014.
[25] The Supreme Court of the Czech Republic has invoked its previous case-law, specifically Resolution of the Supreme Court of the Czech Republic Case No. 20 Cdo 4022/2014 of 23 January 2018.
[26] The Supreme Court of the Czech Republic has invoked its previous case-law, specifically Judgment of the Supreme Court of the Czech Republic Case No. 23 Cdo 3150/2012 of 30 September 2014.
[27] The Supreme Court of the Czech Republic has invoked its previous case-law, specifically Judgment of the Supreme Court of the Czech Republic Case No. 23 Cdo 3150/2012 of 30 September 2014.

the Constitutional Court, does not constitute a review on the merits of the enforcement order.[28/29] Nevertheless, the ultimate finding of the (in)validity of the credit facility agreement in terms of the quoted judgments of the Constitutional Court (which in turn determines the validity or invalidity of the arbitration agreement and the jurisdiction of the arbitrator or lack thereof) requires an examination of the **particular circumstances attending the entering into of the credit facility agreement**, including a consideration of the criteria set by the case-law of the Supreme Court in relation to contractual penalties, interest, security interest securing the payment of the claim, etc.[30]

II. Arbitrability

8.07. Connected, *inter alia*, to the provisions of Section 2 of Act of the Czech Republic No. 216/1994 Coll., on Arbitration and the Enforcement of Arbitral Awards

---

[28] The Supreme Court of the Czech Republic has invoked the case-law of the Constitutional Court of the Czech Republic, specifically the judgment of the Constitutional Court of the Czech Republic in Case No. I. ÚS 199/11 of 26 January 2012, and the judgment of the Constitutional Court of the Czech Republic in Case No. III. ÚS 4084/12 of 11 December 2014.

[29] See also judgment ÚS 3962/18 of 06 April 2021.

[30] The Supreme Court of the Czech Republic has invoked its previous case-law, specifically the resolution of the Supreme Court of the Czech Republic in Case No. 20 Cdo 1387/2016 of 28 February 2017, as well as the resolution of the Supreme Court of the Czech Republic in Case No. 20 Cdo 4022/2017 of 23 January 2018.

ArbAct: Section 2 [Arbitrability][31]

Current Version of Section 2 of ArbAct:

(1) The parties are free to agree that their property disputes, with the exception of disputes arising from contracts entered into between a consumer and a professional, disputes arising from the enforcement of decisions and incidental disputes, which would otherwise fall within the jurisdiction of the courts, or which are subject to arbitration under special laws, shall be decided by one or more arbitrators or by a permanent arbitral institution (arbitration agreement).

(2) The arbitration agreement will be valid if the law allows the parties to resolve the subject matter of their dispute by settlement.[1)]

(3) The arbitration agreement may apply to:

   (a) an individual dispute that has already arisen (post-dispute arbitration agreement), or

   (b) all disputes that would arise in the future under a defined legal relationship or under a defined category of legal relationships (arbitration clause).
   (4) Unless the arbitration agreement stipulates otherwise, it governs both the rights directly arising from the legal relationships and the issue of the legal validity of these legal relationships, as well as any rights associated with the aforementioned rights.

(5) The arbitration agreement is also binding on the legal successors to the parties, unless explicitly excluded by the parties in their agreement.

Footnotes Forming Part of Normative Text:

1) Section 99 of the Code of Civil Procedure.[32]

Section 2 of ArbAct in Effect as of 01 April 2012:

(1) The parties are free to agree that their property disputes, except disputes arising from the enforcement of decisions and except incidental disputes, which would otherwise fall within the jurisdiction of the courts, or which are subject to arbitration under special laws, shall be decided by one or more arbitrators or by a permanent arbitral institution (arbitration agreement).

No amendments in Subsections (2) through (5).

Legislative Developments Since 01 April 2012:

Section 2 of the ArbAct has only been amended once since the effective date of the ArbAct Amendment implemented by Act No. 19/2012 Coll. (01 April 2012), specifically with respect to the first subsection; the amendment was implemented by Act No. 258/2016 Coll., Amending Selected Legislation in Connection with the Adoption of the Consumer Credit Act – see Part Seven, Article VIII of the said Act, which took effect on 01 December 2016. The said Act prohibited arbitration agreements in disputes from B2C relationships and, apparently with a view to enhancing this imperative, also incorporated the explicit exclusion of objective arbitrability of B2C disputes in Section 2(1) of the ArbAct. Such (B2C) disputes are, nevertheless, still arbitrable if the parties entered into their arbitration agreement prior to 01 December 2016. The number of such disputes is, however, dwindling.

8.08.   **Judgment of the Supreme Court of the Czech Republic, Case No. 29 Cdo 3613/2009 of 30 November 2011:**[33] **[arbitrability; bill of exchange/promissory note; endorsement of a bill of**

---

[31]   The titles of the individual Parts and Sections provided in square brackets are not part of the statutory text and have been supplemented by the author for better transparency of the contents.

[32]   Code of Civil Procedure [Czech Republic] (approximate translation, cit.): Section 99 – (1) *If the nature of the case allows such procedure, the parties to the proceedings can terminate the proceedings by a judicial settlement. The court endeavours to persuade the parties to settle; to this end, the presiding judge primarily discusses the case with the parties, draws their attention to the applicable law and the opinions of the Supreme Court, as well as the decisions published in the Sbírka soudních rozhodnutí a stanovisek [Court Reports] that relate to the case, and, depending on the circumstances of the case, recommends the possibilities for the amicable resolution of the dispute to the parties. If appropriate, in view of the nature of the case, the presiding judge also draws the parties' attention to the possibility of mediation under the Mediation Act, or social consultancy under the Social Services Act. (2) The court shall decide whether it approves the settlement; the court shall not do so if the settlement is contrary to the law. In such case, the court shall continue the proceedings after the resolution becomes final. (3) An approved settlement has the same effects as a final judgment. However, the court may issue a judgment setting aside the resolution on the approval of the settlement if the settlement is invalid under substantive law. The motion can be lodged within three years of the day when the resolution on the approval of the settlement becomes final.*

[33]   Preceding decisions in the case: (i) Judgment of the Municipal Court in Prague [Czech Republic], Case No. 47 Cm 61/2007-28 of 30 March 2007, and (ii) Judgment of the High Court in Prague [Czech Republic], Case No. 9 Cmo 495/2008-242 of 04 March 2009.

exchange/promissory note; legal succession] **(1)** A dispute over the payment of a bill of exchange/promissory note can also be the subject of an arbitration agreement. Claims from bills of exchange/promissory notes are property claims. The second requirement under Section 2(2) of the ArbAct, i.e. that the parties are free to resolve the subject matter of their dispute by settlement, is fulfilled as well.[34] **(2)** As concerns the issue of whether or not the arbitration clause negotiated by the parties to the present proceedings also covers claims from a bill of exchange/promissory note, the court has held – from the perspective of the facts of the case, under circumstances comparable to the present case (the said case also concerned a dispute over the payment of a bill of exchange/promissory note securing another claim where the arbitration clause was incorporated – together with an agreement that the bill of exchange/promissory note shall secure the payment of the claim – in the contract from which the claim secured by the bill of exchange/promissory note was to arise), with reference to the interpretation rules incorporated in Section 35(2) of the Civil Code 1964[35] and Section 266 of the Commercial Code[36] and the principle governing the interpretation of juridical acts,[37] that if the agreement on having the claim secured by the bill of exchange/promissory note, as well as the arbitration clause,

---

[34] Invoking the judgment of the Supreme Court of the Czech Republic in Case No. 29 Cdo 1130/2011 of 31 May 2011, which is annotated separately.

[35] The Civil Code 1964 was replaced by the Civil Code 2012 with effect from 01 January 2014. Civil Code 1964 [Czech Republic] (approximate translation, cit.): Section 35 - *(1) An expression of will can be implemented by act or omission; it can be express or performed in any other manner that gives rise to no doubts about the party's intention. (2) Juridical acts expressed in words must be construed not only according to their linguistic expression, but primarily also according to the will of the party who performed the juridical act, unless the will conflicts with the linguistic expression. (3) Juridical acts expressed in any manner other than words shall be construed in compliance with the usual meaning of the method of their expression. To this end, regard shall be had to the will of the person or entity who performed the juridical act, and the good faith of the intended recipient of the juridical act shall be protected.*

[36] The Commercial Code was replaced by the Civil Code 2012 and by the Business Corporations Act 2012 with effect from 01 January 2014. Commercial Code 1991 [Czech Republic] (approximate translation, cit.): Section 266 - *(1) An expression of will shall be construed according to the intention of the acting party if the intention was known or must have been known to the intended recipient of the expression of will. (2) If the expression of will cannot be construed pursuant to Subsection (1), the expression of will shall be construed in compliance with the meaning that would be normally attributed to the expression of will by a person in the position of the intended recipient of the expression of will. Terms used in commercial transactions shall be construed in compliance with the meaning that is normally attributed to them in such transactions. (3) The interpretation of will pursuant to Subsections (1) and (2) shall have due regard to all circumstances relating to the expression of will, including contract negotiations and the practice established between the parties, as well as the parties' subsequent behaviour, if allowed by the nature of the case. (4) If in doubt, an expression of will that contains a term allowing for varying interpretations must be construed to the disadvantage of the party who was the first to use the term in the negotiations. (5) If the decisive criterion under this Part of the Act is the contracting party's registered office, place of business, place of enterprise or premises, or place of residence, the decisive place is the place specified in the contract until a change thereof is notified to the other party.*

[37] Here invoking the decision of the Supreme Court of the Czech Republic published under No. 35/2001 of Sbírka soudních rozhodnutí a stanovisek [Court Reports], and in the judgment of the Constitutional Court of the Czech Republic in Case No. I. ÚS 625/03 of 14 April 2005.

are both part of the same juridical act (contract), no reasonable doubt arises as to the fact that the words "... the jurisdiction to resolve any and all disputes over claims that directly or otherwise arose from (...) or in connection with this contract..." also cover the dispute over the payment of the bill of exchange/promissory note that secured the payment of the claim arising from the contract. **(3)** The entity to which the bill of exchange/promissory note was endorsed after a protest was made for default on payment or after the time limit for protest expired,[38] is bound by the existing arbitration agreement pursuant to Section 2(5) of the ArbAct as the legal successor to the original creditor.[39]

8.09.   Resolution of the Supreme Court of the Czech Republic, Case No. 32 Cdo 3163/2011 of 9 February 2012:[40] [associated legal relationships; preliminary issue; jurisdiction of arbitrators v. jurisdiction of courts] **(1)** The fact that an assessment of a legal relationship established by a contract that contains an arbitration clause is a preliminary issue vis-à-vis an assessment of a legal relationship established by another juridical act or event does not create any legal connection between the two legal relationships in terms of Section 2(4) of the ArbAct.[41] **(2)** The court is not stripped of the jurisdiction to hear the dispute over restitution (release of a particular asset) in consequence of the fact that the assessment of whether or not the claimant effectively rescinded the purchase contract following the respondent's default on the payment of the purchase price depends on whether or not the claimant's claim arising from the right to receive the purchase price was offset against the respondent's mutual claim from a legal relationship that was established by a contract containing an arbitration clause, hence primarily whether or not the respondent had any mutual claim from such a legal relationship at all (whether the claim existed).

---

[38]   Here concerning the effects of an endorsement implemented only after a protest was made for default on payment or after the time limit for protest expired, cf. Article I Section 20(1) of Act No. 191/1950 Coll. and the case-law of the Supreme Court of the Czech Republic, such as judgment of the Supreme Court of the Czech Republic, Case No. 29 Odo 1636/2005 of 25 April 2007, published in: (151) SOUDNÍ JUDIKATURA (2007).

[39]   Cf. also Pavel Horák, *Objektivní arbitrabilita – možnosti rozhodčího řízení* [title in translation – *Objective Arbitrability – Possibilities of Arbitration*], 9 BULLETIN ADVOKACIE 23 (2018).

[40]   The *ratio decidendi* has been adopted from: Výběr rozhodnutí, *Rozhodčí smlouva, pravomoc soudu a práva související s těmi, kterých se smlouva týká* [title in translation – *Arbitration Agreement, Court Jurisdiction and Rights Associated with Those Covered by the Agreement*], 18(6) SOUDNÍ ROZHLEDY 211-212 (2012). An annotation of the decision is provided in the same place.

[41]   This provision is quoted above in the introduction to Part II of this case-law selection.

8.10. **Resolution of the Supreme Court of the Czech Republic, Case No. 22 Cdo 1643/2012 of 23 July 2012:**[42] **[property dispute; limits of the right to enter into an arbitration clause; possibility of entering into and approving a settlement in court; dispute over restitution (release of an asset); lease agreement; dispute relating to a lease agreement; determination of the number of arbitrators; determination of the manner in which the arbitrators are to be appointed; anticipated component of the arbitration agreement; (in)dispensable component of an arbitration agreement; legal succession]** **(1)** Property disputes are all disputes the subject matter of which is directly reflected in the assets possessed by the parties, and which concern subjective rights of which the parties may dispose.[43] **(2)** The statutory limits to the parties' right to negotiate a valid arbitration clause are based on the same circumstances that limit the right to enter into and approve a settlement in court.[44] **(3)** No arbitration agreement can be validly entered into in matters the nature of which does not allow a settlement.[45] **(4)** A dispute over restitution related to a legal relationship between the parties established by a lease agreement is a dispute in terms of Section 2(4) of the ArbAct. If the "main" contract contains an arbitration clause, the arbitration will cover the dispute from the contract, as well as any related dispute, including a dispute over the release of assets that are being unlawfully withheld on the basis of the (allegedly invalid, as argued by the claimant) contract. **(5)** If the arbitration clause is incorporated in a lease agreement, the former is also binding on the new owner (acquirer) of the real estate as the landlord.[46] **(6)** The determination of the number of arbitrators and their identity, or the determination of the method whereby the number and the identity of the arbitrators shall be determined,

---

[42]   Preceding decisions in the case: (i) Decision of the District Court Pilsen – South [Czech Republic], Case No. 9 C 385/2011, and (ii) Resolution of the Regional Court in Pilsen [Czech Republic], Case No. 15 Co 101/2012-106 of 21 February 2012. The Supreme Court dismissed the cassation appeal. This decision was also invoked by Pavel Horák, *Objektivní arbitrabilita – možnosti rozhodčího* řízení [title in translation – *Objective Arbitrability – Possibilities of Arbitration*], 9 BULLETIN ADVOKACIE 23 (2018); see also the author's reference to the same case-law (see Footnote 14).

[43]   In this regard, the SC also invoked LJUBOMÍR DRÁPAL, JAROSLAV BUREŠ ET AL., OBČANSKÝ SOUDNÍ ŘÁD I. §1 AŽ 200za. KOMENTÁŘ [title in translation – CODE CIVIL OF CIVIL PROCEDURE I. SECTION 1 TO 200ZA. A COMMENTARY], Prague: C. H. Beck (2009), et. 706.

[44]   In this regard, the Supreme Court of the Czech Republic invoked: (i) Resolution of the Supreme Court of the Czech Republic, Case No. 32 Odo 181/2006 of 06 June 2007, and (ii) Resolution of the Supreme Court of the Czech Republic, Case No. 26 Odo 353/2006 of 12 July 2007.

[45]   In this regard, the Supreme Court of the Czech Republic also invoked the resolution of the Supreme Court of the Czech Republic in Case No. 20 Cdo 2312/2000 of 25 October 2000, and an annotation of the decision in: Rozhodnutí soudů z oblasti občanského, obchodního a pracovního práva, 1 SOUDNÍ JUDIKATURA 25 (2001). The case concerned a dispute over eviction from and vacation of a real estate property; the court has held that such a dispute is arbitrable.

[46]   The decision of the Supreme Court of the Czech Republic also invokes Section 680(2) of the Civil Code.

is an anticipated, but not an indispensable, component of the arbitration agreement. If the arbitration agreement lacks the said component, Section 7(2) of the ArbAct[47] in conjunction with Section 9 of the ArbAct[48] provide for the mechanism of an *ex post* selection of an arbitrator. Clearly, this principle must apply not only if the arbitration agreement contains no provision on the method of appointing the arbitrators, but also if such a provision in the arbitration agreement cannot be deemed valid.

8.11. Resolution of the Supreme Court of the Czech Republic, Case No. 32 Cdo 4061/2010 of 25 September 2012:[49] [arbitrability; eviction from a real estate property (vacating a real estate property); property dispute; invalidity of the main contract; invalidity of the arbitration clause; cause of invalidity; separability / separation of the main contract from the arbitration agreement; permanent arbitral institution; agreement on the jurisdiction of a permanent arbitral institution as an acceptance of the Rules thereof] (1) Unless the cause of invalidity applies to the arbitration clause covering the disputes arising from that contract, the invalidity of the contract shall not affect the validity of the arbitration clause.[50] **(2)** An objection of invalidity of the arbitration agreement for its alleged ambiguity is manifestly groundless if the parties have agreed that any existing dispute shall be submitted to a permanent arbitral institution. Unless the parties agreed otherwise in their arbitration clause, they are deemed to have submitted to the Rules specified in Section 13(2) of the ArbAct that were valid and applicable at the commencement of the arbitral proceedings before the permanent arbitral institution. **(3)** If the parties have agreed that their disputes shall

---

[47] Act on Arbitration and the Enforcement of Arbitral Awards – Act of the Czech Republic No. 216/1994 Coll. (approximate translation, cit.) – Section 7 [Selection of Arbitrators]: *(1) The arbitration agreement should, as a rule, determine the number of arbitrators and their identity, or stipulate the method whereby the number and the identity of the arbitrators shall be determined. The arbitrator may also be selected by a person agreed upon by the parties or following a method of appointment specified in the rules on arbitration pursuant to Section 19(4). The final number of arbitrators must always be odd. (2) If the arbitration agreement lacks the determination pursuant to Subsection (1), each party shall appoint one arbitrator and these arbitrators shall elect the chairman of the panel.*

[48] Act on Arbitration and the Enforcement of Arbitral Awards – Act of the Czech Republic No. 216/1994 Coll. (approximate translation, cit.) – Section 9 [Appointment of Arbitrator by Court]: *(1) If the party who is obliged to appoint an arbitrator fails to do so within 30 days of the other party's request or if the appointed arbitrators cannot agree on the chairman of the panel within the same time period, the arbitrator or the chairman of the panel shall be appointed by the court, unless the parties have agreed otherwise. The motion can be lodged with the court by any of the parties or any of the already appointed arbitrators. (2) Unless the parties have agreed otherwise, the court shall appoint a new arbitrator at the request submitted by any of the parties or arbitrators if the appointed arbitrator resigns from office or is incapable of acting as arbitrator.*

[49] Preceding decisions in the case: (i) Resolution of the District Court for Prague-East [Czech Republic], Case No. 3 C 414/2009-31, and (ii) Resolution of the Regional Court in Prague [Czech Republic], Case No. 32 Co 106/2010-61 of 26 May 2010.

[50] Subsequent case-law following this decision of the Supreme Court of the Czech Republic: e.g. Resolution of the Supreme Court of the Czech Republic, Case No. 25 Cdo 4840/2014 of 9 March 2016.

be submitted to arbitration, a decision on the dispute is also the result of dispute resolution. **(3)** A dispute over the obligation to accept an eviction and vacate the real estate is a property dispute in terms of Section 2(1) of the ArbAct.[51] Use of the real estate by the respondent and payment of rent undoubtedly affect the assets of the landlord and of the tenant, just like the eviction from and vacation of the real estate property and the associated expiration of the obligation to pay rent.

8.12. Judgment of the Supreme Court of the Czech Republic, Case No. 23 Cdo 2628/2010 of 22 January 2013: [arbitrability; separability / separation; expiration of the main contract; invalidity of the main contract; invalidity of the arbitration agreement; failure to raise an objection during the arbitral proceedings that the arbitration agreement expired; proceedings for annulment of an arbitral award; validity of the arbitration clause cannot be reviewed if the objection was not raised during the arbitral proceedings] **(1)** The objection that the main contract expired cannot be automatically extended to the expiration of the arbitration agreement. The arbitration agreement is an autonomous provision in the contract. The expiration of the main contract does not automatically cancel the arbitration agreement.[52] **(2)** Unless the objection was raised during the arbitral proceedings that the arbitration clause expired, the court cannot, in the proceedings for the annulment of the arbitral award, with reference to Section 33 of the ArbAct,[53] address the issue of whether or not the arbitration agreement expired.[54]

8.13. Resolution of the Supreme Court of the Czech Republic, Case No. 22 Cdo 1337/2011 of 11 September 2013: [jurisdiction

---

[51] See also the resolution of the Supreme Court of the Czech Republic in Case No. 20 Cdo 2312/2000 of 25 October 2000.

[52] Subsequently see also, *inter alia*, the resolution of the Supreme Court of the Czech Republic in Case No. 25 Cdo 4840/2014 of 9 March 2016.

[53] Act on Arbitration and the Enforcement of Arbitral Awards – Act of the Czech Republic No. 216/1994 Coll. (approximate translation, cit.) – Section 33 [Dismissal of Motion to Annul Arbitral Award]:

Current version: *The court shall dismiss a motion to annul an arbitral award that is based on the grounds specified in Section 31(b) or (c) if the party requesting the annulment failed to raise the corresponding objection in the arbitral proceedings before the party's first act on the merits of the case, despite having an opportunity to do so.*

The Act in effect as of 1 April 2012: *The court shall dismiss a motion to annul an arbitral award that is based on the grounds specified in Section 31(b) or (c) if the party requesting the annulment failed to raise the corresponding objection in the arbitral proceedings before the party's first act on the merits of the case, despite having an opportunity to do so. This does not apply to disputes arising from consumer contracts.*

[54] In this regard, however, the arbitration clause was ultimately reviewed in the proceedings for the annulment of the arbitral award, but only because the relationship was established by a contract between a professional and a consumer; in such a case, the court was obliged to review the issue on its own motion in order to ensure such interpretation of the law that complies with EU law (consumer protection). No arbitration agreements in B2C relationships are allowed after 1 December 2016; consequently, the issue is of marginal importance and the annotation here focuses solely on the general conclusion of the Supreme Court articulated by the court with respect to relationships other than B2C relationships.

of courts; restitution (release of an asset); protection of ownership]: There has never been any doubt that protection of ownership under the Civil Code is covered by the jurisdiction of courts.[55] [*Note:*] The case had no connection to arbitration. The subject matter of the proceedings was a claim for restitution. The decision confirms the broad jurisdiction of courts; hence, there are principally no doubts that arbitral tribunals could make decisions regarding an obligation of restitution if an arbitration agreement existed.

8.14.   **Resolution of the Supreme Court of the Czech Republic, Case No. 29 Cdo 2648/2013 of 19 March 2014:[56] [dispute; non-contentious proceedings; determination of (ownership) title to a share; arbitrability; duty to recognize an arbitration clause under the New York Convention (1958); importance of the nature of the proceedings; nature of a claim/asset; settlement; right to settle; bilateral relationship of the parties]** (1) Proceedings for the determination of (ownership) title to a share in a limited liability company constitute proceedings concerning a "dispute" from a contract for the transfer of a shareholder's share, and such proceedings are "non-contentious". However, this fact itself does not mean that no settlement can be made in such proceedings and, consequently, an arbitration clause negotiated. (2) The assessment of whether or not a settlement can be made in the case is contingent on the nature of the asserted claim, not the general nature of the proceedings as such. (3) The nature of the proceedings, i.e. whether the proceedings are contentious or non-contentious, is not in itself decisive for the conclusion on the arbitrability of the case. (4) A settlement can also be made in proceedings for the determination of whether or not a legal relationship or a right exist, because the decisive factor for the statutory right to make a judicial settlement consists only in the conditions of permissibility thereof, as specifically applicable to the given case.[57] (5)[58] (a) The nature of the case generally allows a

---

[55]   The *ratio decidendi* was, after a minor edit, adopted from: Tomáš Těmín, *Právní názor účastníků: Pravomoc soudu* [Title in translation – *Legal Opinion of the Parties: Court Jurisdiction*], (3) BULLETIN ADVOKACIE 46-48 (2014). The *ratio decidendi* was formulated by the editorial board of Bulletin advokacie.
[56]   Preceding decisions in the case: (i) Resolution of the Municipal Court in Prague, Case No. 72 Cm 41/2012 of 7 August 2012, and (ii) Resolution of the High Court in Prague [Czech Republic], Case No. 7 Cmo 416/2012-124 of 29 April 2013. See also Pavel Horák, *Objektivní arbitrabilita – možnosti rozhodčího řízení* [title in translation – *Objective Arbitrability – Possibilities of Arbitration*], 9 BULLETIN ADVOKACIE 25-26 (2018), as well as 21(7-8) SOUDNÍ ROZHLEDY 280 (2017). See also: SJ 27/23015, C 13570.
[57]   In this regard, the Supreme Court of the Czech Republic invoked the judgment of the Supreme Court of the Czech Republic in Case No. 30 Cdo 641/2005 of 04 January 2006.
[58]   In this regard, the Supreme Court of the Czech Republic invoked (i) the decision of the Supreme Court of the Czech Republic in Case No. 30 Cdo 641/2005 of 04 January 2005, and (ii) the judgment of the Supreme Court of the Czech Republic in Case No. 29 Odo 1222/2005 of 19 December 2007, as well as, *inter*

settlement in those cases in which the parties are in a typical bilateral relationship, as long as the substantive law does not prevent them from regulating their legal relationship by dispositive acts [dispositive juridical acts]. **(5) (b)** The nature of the case excludes the possibility of a settlement primarily in those cases in which the proceedings can be opened on the court's own motion, or in which a person's personal status is adjudicated on, or in which the substantive law does not allow the resolution of the case by the agreement of the parties to the legal relationship. **(6)** A dispute from a contract for the transfer of a shareholder's share is fully eligible for settlement and, consequently, the negotiation of an arbitration clause. The subject matter of the proceedings in this case is a property claim that the parties are entirely free to dispose of under the applicable substantive law (the parties may regulate their mutual legal relationships by dispositive juridical acts, i.e. resolve the case by an agreement, among others), and the proceedings do not fall into the category of proceedings that could be opened on the court's own motion or proceedings in which a person's personal status is adjudicated on (the proceedings do not deal with matters concerning a business company's status). **(7)** The obligation to recognise an arbitration clause also arises from Article II of the New York Convention (1958). [*From the facts of the case*]: The case concerned proceedings for the determination of (ownership) title to shares in a limited liability company. The first-instance court discontinued the proceedings, because the main contract (contract for the transfer of a share) contained an arbitration clause appointing VIAC [AUT]. Conversely, the appellate court referred to Section 9(3)(g) of the Code of Civil Procedure[59] and held that the case was not arbitrable and that the proceedings were non-contentious; as such, the nature of the proceedings prevented the resolution of the case by a judicial settlement and, consequently, disallowed an arbitration agreement. The Supreme Court, however, set aside the appellate court's decision and the case was reverted to the appellate court for a new hearing.

8.15. Judgment of the Supreme Court of the Czech Republic, Case No. 23 Cdo 3958/2013 of 25 March 2014:[60] [guarantee;

---

alia, (iii) LJUBOMÍR DRÁPAL, JAROSLAV BUREŠ ET AL., OBČANSKÝ SOUDNÍ ŘÁD I. §1 AŽ 200za. KOMENTÁŘ [title in translation – CODE CIVIL OF CIVIL PROCEDURE I. SECTION 1 TO 200ZA. A COMMENTARY], Prague: C. H. Beck (2009), et. 643.

[59] At that time, it also fell within the scope of Section 200e of the Code of Civil Procedure (the law has been amended in the meantime).

[60] Preceding decisions in the case: (i) Judgment of the District Court in Třebíč [Czech Republic], Case No. 8 C 46/2012-44 of 05 February 2013, which set aside the arbitral award of 18 May 2012; and (ii) Judgment of the Regional Court in Brno, Jihlava Office [Czech Republic], Case No. 54 Co 348/2013-61 of 02 July 2013.

subjective scope of the arbitration clause; arbitration clause (non)binding on third parties; unjust enrichment; compensation for damage and losses; prohibition of a review on the merits; exclusively procedural scope of the review in proceedings for annulment of an arbitral award] (1) No provision of the ArbAct suggests that the arbitration clause would be binding on persons or entities outside the legal relationship in which the jurisdiction of an arbitrator or a permanent arbitral institution is established by the arbitration clause to render an arbitral award in the case. Where Section 2(4) of the ArbAct[61] refers to "rights associated with the aforementioned rights", it shall be interpreted as meaning the rights that were established between the parties to the arbitration clause in connection with the legal relationship for which the arbitration clause was agreed, i.e. compensation for damage or losses sustained as a result of a breach of contract, unjust enrichment, etc. However, the arbitration clause **does not apply** to legal relationships involving third parties that did not give their consent with arbitration.[62/63] (2) An arbitration clause entered into solely by the debtor and the creditor that is incorporated in a contract that also includes a guarantee statement does not automatically extend to the legal relationship between the creditor and the guarantor.

8.16.   **Judgment of the Supreme Court of the Czech Republic, Case No. 29 Cdo 3309/2015 of 27 October 2015:**[64] [*res judicata*, **jurisdiction**] An identical case concerning the same subject matter of the proceedings and the same parties that was already resolved by an arbitral award rendered by an arbitrator who lacked the jurisdiction to render such an arbitral award does not constitute *res judicata*.

8.17.   **Judgment of the Supreme Court of the Czech Republic, Case No. 29Icdo 11/2014 of 28 January 2016:**[65] [**marital property (joint property of spouses); settlement of marital property; arbitrability; effects of an arbitral award; binding effects of**

---

[61]   This provision is quoted above in the introduction to Part II of this case-law selection.
[62]   The Supreme Court of the Czech Republic has invoked its previous case-law, specifically its judgment in Case No. 23 Cdo 2351/2007 of 31 March 2009, published under No. 2/2010 in Sbírka soudních rozhodnutí a stanovisek [Court Reports].
[63]   The Supreme Court of the Czech Republic has invoked its previous case-law, specifically its judgment in Case No. 23 Cdo 111/2009 of 23 February 2011.
[64]   The *ratio decidendi* has been adopted from: Výběr rozhodnutí, 22(11-12) SOUDNÍ ROZHLEDY 371 (2017).
[65]   The annotation was adopted from: Petr Vojtek, *Výběr rozhodnutí v oblasti civilněprávní*, 23(7-8) SOUDNÍ ROZHLEDY 249 (2017). See also Pavel Horák, *Objektivní arbitrabilita – možnosti rozhodčího řízení* [title in translation – *Objective Arbitrability – Possibilities of Arbitration*], 9 BULLETIN ADVOKACIE 26 (2018), with reference to JAN DVOŘÁK, JIŘÍ SPÁČIL, SPOLEČNÉ JMĚNÍ MANŽELŮ V TEORII A JUDIKATUŘE [title in translation – MARITAL PROPERTY IN THEORY AND CASE-LAW], Prague: Wolters Kluwer (3rd ed. 2011), et. 20.

an arbitral award] **(1)** Unless the dispute over the settlement of marital property is a dispute arising in connection with enforcement proceedings or an incidental dispute, it can be heard and resolved in arbitration. **(2)** The liquidator, who has acquired the right to dispose of the debtor's estate upon the declaration of bankruptcy of the debtor, and the debtor are both bound (within the limits of Section 159a(4) of the Code of Civil Procedure)[66] by a final judgment in which the court settled the marital property of the debtor (in insolvency) and his or her spouse before the insolvency proceedings were opened. **(3) The same applies to an arbitral award in which the arbitrator settled the marital property** of the debtor (in insolvency) and his or her spouse before the insolvency proceedings were opened and which has the effects of a final court judgment.[67]

8.18. **Resolution of the Supreme Court of the Czech Republic, Case No. 25 Cdo 4840/2014 of 9 March 2016:**[68] **[arbitrability; compensation for damage and losses; lease agreement; separability / separation; expiration of the main contract; invalidity of the main contract; invalidity of the arbitration agreement; payment order; appeal; first act on the merits; challenging court jurisdiction; interpretation of the arbitration agreement; application of substantive law in the interpretation of the arbitration agreement] (1) (a)** The objection that the main contract expired cannot automatically be extended to the expiration of the arbitration agreement. The arbitration agreement is an autonomous provision in the contract. The expiration of the main contract does not automatically cancel the arbitration agreement.[69] **(1) (b)** Unless the cause of invalidity applies to the arbitration clause covering the disputes arising from that contract, the invalidity of the contract shall

---

[66] Code of Civil Procedure [Czech Republic] (approximate translation, cit.): Section 159a – *(1) Unless the Act stipulates otherwise, the operative part of a final judgment is binding solely on the parties to the proceedings. (2) The operative part of a final judgment delivered in matters listed in Section 83(2) is binding on the parties to the proceedings, as well as other persons or entities with a claim against the respondent for identical claims from an identical conduct or status. Special laws set forth the cases in and the extent to which the operative part of a final judgment is binding on persons or entities other than the parties to the proceedings. (3) To the extent that the operative part of a final judgment is binding on the parties to the proceedings and, if applicable, other persons or entities, it is also binding on all authorities. (4) As soon as the case has been resolved with final force and effect, it cannot be reopened to the extent to which the operative part of the judgment is binding on the parties and any other persons or entities, as applicable.*

[67] See Section 28(2) of the ArbAct.

[68] Preceding decisions in the case: (i) Judgment of the District Court for Prague 5 [Czech Republic], Case No. 18 C 82/2010-332 of 03 June 2013, and (ii) Resolution of the Municipal Court in Prague [Czech Republic], Case No. 14 Co 148/2014-408 of 13 May 2014. Also quoted in: Pavel Horák, *Objektivní arbitrabilita – možnosti rozhodčího řízení* [title in translation – *Objective Arbitrability – Possibilities of Arbitration*], 9 BULLETIN ADVOKACIE 27 (2018). The judgment also comments on the effects and the binding force of an arbitral award.

[69] In this place, the Supreme Court of the Czech Republic also invoked the judgment of the Supreme Court of the Czech Republic in Case No. 23 Cdo 2628/2010 of 22 January 2013.

not affect the validity of the arbitration clause.[70] **(2)** An appeal against a payment order cannot be deemed the first act of the party on the merits. If an objection against the jurisdiction of courts due to the existence of an arbitration agreement is lodged in such a case as late as in the reply to the lawsuit following the annulment of the payment order, the objection is lodged in time. The reply to the lawsuit is the first act of the party on the merits.[71] **(3)** The contents of the arbitration clause must be interpreted in compliance with the rules contained in the Civil Code.[72] **(5)** The wording of the arbitration agreement (cit.) "[...] *any and all disputes and discrepancies arising from this Agreement or in connection with* [...]", establishes the arbitral tribunal's jurisdiction to resolve disputes between the parties for compensation for damage or losses sustained not only as a direct result of a breach of the obligations from the contract, but also disputes between the parties for compensation for damage or losses sustained in connection with the parties' legal relationship established under the contract. Hence, the powers of the arbitral tribunal in the given case also extend to the resolution of a dispute over compensation for damage and losses sustained as a result of the fact that after the contractual relationship was terminated, the future landlord seized the assets that the future tenant had brought with the former's consent into the would-be leased premises. Indeed, it is clear that the parties willed any and all of their disputes that could arise in connection with the contractual relationship established by the contract on a future lease agreement to be submitted to arbitration without any limitation of the scope of the clause and without the exclusion of any cases. [*From the factual and legal findings*]: An objection was raised in the said case that, *inter alia*, the arbitration agreement expired due to the expiration of the main contract.

---

[70] In this place, the Supreme Court of the Czech Republic invoked (i) the judgment of the Supreme Court of the Czech Republic in Case No. 29 Odo 1222/2005 of 19 December 2017, and (ii) the resolution of the SC in Case No. 32 Cdo 4061/2010 of 25 September 2015.

[71] In this place, the Supreme Court of the Czech Republic invoked (i) the resolution of the Supreme Court of the Czech Republic in Case No. 32 Cdo 34/2010 of 30 August 2011, as well as (ii) the judgment of the SC in Case No. 33 Odo 1455/2006 of 15 December 2006.

[72] The said case referred to the Civil Code 1964 and, *per analogiam*, the Commercial Code (both the Civil Code 1964 and the Commercial Code were replaced by the Civil Code 2012 and the Business Corporations Act 2012 with effect from 01 January 2014). For more details concerning the said issue, see also Alexander J. Bělohlávek, *Procesní smlouvy a kvalifikace rozhodčích a prorogačních smluv: aplikace hmotněprávní úpravy na smlouvy s procesním* účinkem *pro futuro* [Title in translation – *Procedural Agreements and Qualification of Arbitration and Choice-of-Court Agreements: Application of Substantive Law to Agreements with Procedural Effects Pro Futuro*], 151(9) PRÁVNÍK 389–418 (2012); Alexander J. Bělohlávek, *The definition of procedural agreements and the importance to define the contractual nature of the arbitration clause in international arbitration*, in MARIANNE ROTH, MICHAEL GEISTLINGER, YEARBOOK OF INTERNATIONAL ARBITRATION. VOL II, Antwerp / Copenhagen / Zurich / Vienna: Intersentia / Neuer Wissenschaftlicher Verlag (2012), et. 21–50.

8.19. Judgment of the Supreme Court of the Czech Republic, Case No. 23 Cdo 3439/2014 of 30 March 2016:[73] [investment services contract; arbitrability] The parties to a property dispute arising from the provision of investment services are free to agree that their dispute shall be submitted to an arbitrator or a permanent arbitral institution.[74]

8.20. Judgment of the Supreme Court of the Czech Republic, Case No. 23 Cdo 1782/2017 of 11 July 2017:[75] [objective arbitrability; profit share; payment of profits] (1) The distribution of profits and assumption of losses in a partnership can be subject to rules that are incorporated in the Memorandum of Association and depart from the applicable law (Section 82 of the Commercial Code;[76] the law applicable since 01 January 2014 is Section 112 of the Business Corporations Act);[77] consequently, a partner's claim for a profit share against the partnership can be the subject of a settlement. (2) Provided that the remaining criteria of arbitrability are met (a property dispute that does not involve a consumer and that would be subject to court jurisdiction in the absence of an arbitration clause), the partner's claim for a profit share can be the subject of an arbitration clause (Section 2 of the ArbAct).

8.21. Judgment of the Supreme Court of the Czech Republic, Case No. 23 Cdo 3085/2016 of 05 April 2017:[78] [objective arbitrability; rights *in rem*; security interest (lien); acknowledgment of debt; identification of the arbitrator

---

[73] The annotation has been adopted from: Petr Vojtek, *Výběr rozhodnutí v oblasti civilněprávní*, 23(7-8) SOUDNÍ ROZHLEDY 249 (2017).

[74] Adopted from: Jan Hušek, *Rozhodčí doložka – Smlouva o poskytování investičních služeb*, (8) OBCHODNÍ PRÁVO 311 [title in translation - Commercial Law] (2016).

[75] The ratio decidendi has been adopted from: Jan Hušek, *Rozhodčí smlouva (doložka) – Podíl na zisku obchodní společnosti*, (11) OBCHODNÍ PRÁVO 409 [title in translation - Commercial Law] (2017).

[76] Commercial Code 1991 [Czech Republic] (approximate translation, cit.): Section 82 - *(1) Profits shall be distributed among the shareholders equally. Unless the Memorandum of Association stipulates otherwise, the profit share calculated on the basis of the financial statements is due and payable within three months after the financial statements are approved. (2) Any loss identified in the financial statements shall be assumed equally by the shareholders. (3) Subsections 1 and 2 shall apply, unless the Memorandum of Association stipulates otherwise.*

[77] Business Corporations Act 2012 [Czech Republic] (approximate translation, cit.): Section 112 - *(1) Profits and losses shall be distributed among the shareholders equally. (2) A shareholder shall be entitled to a profit share amounting to 25% of the amount paid by him or her to fulfil the contribution obligation. If the company's profit is not sufficient for the payment of such a profit share, it shall be distributed among the shareholders according to the proportion of the amounts paid by them to fulfil their contribution obligation. The remaining profit shall be distributed among the shareholders in compliance with Subsection (1). (3) Where a profit share is granted to a shareholder pursuant to Section 103(2), the provisions of Subsection (2) or (3) shall only apply to the part of the profit that is not distributed in this manner. (4) Where the Memorandum of Association contains a provision that departs from Subsection (1) only for the profit share or only for the share in loss, such provision of the Memorandum of Association shall, in case of doubt, be deemed to apply both to profit share and share in loss.*

[78] The ratio decidendi has been adopted from: Jan Hušek, *Rozhodčí řízení – Arbitrabilita – Zástavní parvo – Uznání závazku – Označení osoby rozhodce*, (9) OBCHODNÍ PRÁVO 319 [title in translation - Commercial Law] (2017).

in the arbitration agreement] **(1)** A dispute concerning a security interest (lien) must also be deemed a property dispute, because it belongs to the category of absolute property rights. The acknowledgement of debt falls into the category of property disputes too, because it affects the parties' assets (Section 2(2) of the ArbAct). **(2)** An arbitration clause also covers disputes concerning the determination of the (non)existence of the right to performance from a security interest (lien) or the acknowledgment of debt or, as applicable, the validity of such relationships (Section 2(4) of the ArbAct).[79] **(3)** If the parties enter into an arbitration agreement in which they agree on a particular arbitrator as an individual identified by his or her name, surname, registered office or place of business, and other identification data (occupation of the individual), the identification is flawless. **(4)** If the person to be appointed as arbitrator resolving the dispute must meet certain qualification criteria (such as being an attorney), the parties' will to that extent must be expressed in a clear and unambiguous manner in the arbitration clause; this requirement is not met if the designation of "attorney" is simply another piece of information identifying the arbitrator.

8.22. **Judgment of the Supreme Court of the Czech Republic, Case No. 23 Cdo 4576/2016 of 11 April 2017:**[80] **[invalidity of the arbitration clause; reference to Rules; legal entity other than a permanent arbitral institution; selection of arbitrator; *res judicata*; objections and challenges must be made in the course of the arbitral proceedings] (1)** If the arbitration clause lacks any direct identification of an ad *hoc* arbitrator and only refers to "Rules on Arbitration" issued by a legal entity other than a permanent arbitral institution established under the law,[81] the arbitration clause (as a whole) is null and void pursuant to Section 39 of the Civil Code 1964[82] for being contrary to the law.[83] **(3)** The Arbitration Act (ArbAct) does not prevent the

---

79   This provision is quoted above in the introduction to Part II of this case-law selection.
80   Preceding decisions in the case: (i) Judgment of the District Court in Liberec [Czech Republic], Case No. 22 C 148/2011-64 of 24 January 2014; and (ii) Judgment of the Regional Court in Ústí nad Labem, Liberec Office [Czech Republic], Case No. 36 Co 145/2014-92 of 28 March 2014.
81   See Section 13 of the ArbAct.
82   Civil Code 1964 [Czech Republic] (approximate translation, cit.): Section 39 – *A juridical act is invalid if the content or the purpose thereof violates or evades the law or is* contra bonos mores.
83   The Supreme Court of the Czech Republic invoked its previous case-law, specifically the decision of the Grand Chamber in Case No. 31 Cdo 1945/2010 of 11 May 2011. However, it is necessary to make reference to subsequent case-law, which tends to favour partial invalidity. This decision rather attests to a transitional phase in which the case-law shifted from fully liberal autonomy to principal restrictions on pain of nullity of the arbitration agreement (this phase is typical for the second decade of the current century), and reverted to the autonomous concept in terms of the respect for partial invalidity.

issue of the arbitrator's jurisdiction (or lack thereof) from being examined in enforcement proceedings as well.[84]

8.23. **Judgment of the Supreme Court of the Czech Republic, Case No. 23 Cdo 2741/2016 of 05 April 2017:**[85] [objective arbitrability; security interest (lien); rights *in rem*; acknowledgment of debt; property value; property relationship; hire purchase; invalidity; contestability; acknowledgment of debt] **(1)** The category of property disputes primarily includes disputes from a (private-law) property relationship on the basis of which a right *in rem*, a right from a contract or any other right or property value has been or is to be transferred for consideration, as well as disputes from a property relationship the subject matter of which is the purchase of a hired asset, used rights or other property values. It also includes a property relationship established in connection with any of the above-mentioned legal relationships in consequence of their modification or expiration, or with respect to their invalidity or contestability. Hence, a property right within the meaning of a "property dispute", or "dispute over property rights" under the Arbitration Act (ArbAct) must be interpreted very broadly; it can include any and all disputes reflected in the assets of the parties to the legal relationship, i.e. disputes the subject matter of which can be expressed in property values, provided that they can be appraised in money and their value can be calculated. **(2)** A dispute concerning a security interest (lien) and a dispute concerning the acknowledgment of debt must also be deemed property disputes in terms of Section 2(1) of the ArbAct.[86]

8.24. **Judgment of the High Court in Prague [Czech Republic], Case No. 5 Cmo 103/2018 of 22 May 2018:**[87] [finding of invalidity of an arbitration agreement; legal interest] There can be no legal interest in a court's finding that the relevant arbitration agreement is invalid once the arbitration is opened.

8.25. **Resolution of the Supreme Court of the Czech Republic, Case No. 29 Cdo 4089/2016 of 30 August 2018:**[88] [causal

---

[84] The Supreme Court of the Czech Republic has invoked the case-law of the Constitutional Court of the Czech Republic, specifically (i) the judgment in Case No. II. ÚS 3406/10 of 14 March 2013, as well as (ii) the judgment in Case No. IV. ÚS 2078/12 of 26 February 2014.

[85] The *ratio decidendi* has been adopted from: Výběr rozhodnutí, 25(1) SOUDNÍ ROZHLEDY 20 (2019). The decision was also published in: 100/2018, C 16490). See also Pavel Horák, *Objektivní arbitrabilita – možnosti rozhodčího řízení* [title in translation – *Objective Arbitrability – Possibilities of Arbitration*], 9 BULLETIN ADVOKACIE 27 (2018).

[86] This provision is quoted above in the introduction to Part II of this case-law selection.

[87] The *ratio decidendi* has been adopted from: Výběr rozhodnutí, (7-8) SOUDNÍ ROZHLEDY 235 (2017). No further information concerning the case is available, although it would undoubtedly be important.

[88] The *ratio decidendi* (excerpt from the decision adjusted for publication purposes) has been adopted from: Jan Hušek, *Rozhočí doložka – Kauzální pohledávka – Zajišťovací směnka – Pravomoc rozhodce*, 28(9) OBCHODNÍ PRÁVO 35 [title in translation - Commercial Law] (2019).

claim; bill of exchange/promissory note as a security instrument; arbitration clause] If the agreed arbitration clause is incorporated in a juridical act (contract) different from the parties' agreement on having their causal claims secured by a bill of exchange/promissory note, and if the contract is silent in this respect on the bill of exchange/promissory note as a security instrument, the only disputes or claims that can be submitted to arbitration are disputes or claims arising from the said juridical act/contract, and the arbitration clause does not cover any claims arising from the bill of exchange/promissory note used as a security instrument, and such disputes are not subject to the arbitrator's jurisdiction.

III. Form, terms, execution and validity of an arbitration agreement

8.26. Connected, *inter alia*, to the provisions of Section 3 of Act of the Czech Republic No. 216/1994 Coll., on Arbitration and the Enforcement of Arbitral Awards

ArbAct: Section 3 [Form, terms and execution of an arbitration agreement][89]

Current Version of Section 3 of ArbAct:

(1) The arbitration agreement must be executed (entered into) in writing; otherwise, it is invalid. The arbitration agreement is also considered executed in writing if it is negotiated by telegraph, fax or any electronic means that would provide a record of the terms of the agreement and the identification of the individuals or entities who concluded the arbitration agreement.

(2) However, if the arbitration clause is incorporated in the terms and conditions governing the main contract to which the arbitration clause applies, the arbitration clause is also considered validly negotiated if a written offer of the main contract with the arbitration clause was accepted by the other party in any manner clearly indicating the latter party's consent with the terms of the arbitration agreement.

Article IX of Act No. 258/2016 Coll., Amending Selected Legislation in Connection with Consumer Credit Act:

1. The validity of an arbitration agreement shall be governed by Act No. 216/1994 Coll., as applicable at the moment at which the arbitration agreement is entered into.

2. Arbitrations commenced on the basis of arbitration agreements entered into before the effective date of this Act shall be conducted and resolved pursuant to the former laws and regulations.

3. Arbitrators entered on the list of arbitrators as of the day preceding the effective date of Act No. 216/1994 Coll. shall be subject to the wording of Sections 40a to 40d of this Act applicable before the effective date of this Act.

Section 3 of ArbAct in Effect as of 01 April 2012 (until 1 December 2016):

(1) The arbitration agreement must be executed (entered into) in writing; otherwise, it is invalid. The arbitration agreement is also considered executed in writing if it is negotiated by telegraph, fax or any electronic means that would provide a record of the terms of the agreement and the identification of the individuals or entities who concluded the arbitration agreement.

(2) However, if the arbitration clause is incorporated in the terms and conditions governing the main contract to which the arbitration clause applies, the arbitration clause is also considered validly negotiated if a written offer of the main contract with the arbitration clause was accepted by the other party in any manner clearly indicating the latter party's consent with the terms of the arbitration agreement.

(3) An arbitration agreement for the resolution of disputes arising from consumer contracts must be negotiated separately, not integrated in the terms and conditions governing the main contract; otherwise, the arbitration agreement is invalid.

(4) The professional shall provide the consumer with a proper explanation reasonably preceding the execution of the arbitration clause, so that the consumer can assess the potential consequences of entering into the arbitration clause for the consumer. Proper explanation shall be interpreted as meaning the explication of all consequences of the arbitration clause.

(5) The arbitration clause concluded pursuant to Subsection (3) must also contain truthful, accurate and complete information on:
(a)   the arbitrator or the fact that the arbitral award will be delivered by a permanent arbitral institution,
(b)   the manner in which arbitration is to be commenced and conducted,
(c)   the fee paid to the arbitrator and the anticipated types of costs the consumer may incur in arbitration, and the rules for successfully claiming compensation for such costs,
(d)   the place of arbitration,
(e)   the method of service of the arbitral award on the consumer, and
(f)   the fact that a final arbitral award is enforceable.

(6) If the arbitration clause vests the jurisdiction to resolve the dispute in a permanent arbitral institution, the requirement under Subsection (5) is also fulfilled by reference to the statutes and rules of permanent arbitral institutions issued under Section 13.[90]

Legislative Developments Since 01 April 2012:

Section 3 of the ArbAct, as amended by Act No. 245/2006 Coll., Act No. 296/2007 Coll., Act No. 7/2009 Coll., Act No. 466/2011 Coll., Act No. 19/2012 Coll. and Act No. 91/2012 Coll., was newly reformulated by Act No. 258/2016 Coll., Amending Selected Legislation in Connection with the Consumer Credit Act – see Part Seven, Article VIII of the said Act, which took effect on 01 December 2016. In view of the fact that no arbitration clauses can be entered into in consumer contracts since 01 December 2016, Subsections (3) to (6) in Section 3 of the ArbAct were also repealed with effect as of the said date. However, arbitration agreements entered into before 01 December 2016 shall be subject to the version of the ArbAct in effect as of the day on which the arbitration agreement was entered into. Hence, arbitration agreements entered into from 01 April 2012 to 30 November 2016 shall be subject to Section 3 of the ArbAct in effect during the said period.[91]

8.27.   **Judgment of the Supreme Court of the Czech Republic, Case No. 29 Cdo 3309/2015 of 27 October 2015:**[92] **[endorsement of a bill of exchange/promissory note, new creditor, jurisdiction over a motion for annulment of an arbitral award]** As the legal successor to the original creditor, the claimant to whom the bill of exchange/promissory note was endorsed after a protest was made for default on payment or after the time limit for protest expired, is bound by the existing arbitration agreement entered into by the creditor.

---

[89]   The titles of the individual Parts and Sections provided in square brackets in this publication are not part of the normative text and have been supplemented by the author for better transparency of the contents.

[90]   Act on Arbitration and the Enforcement of Arbitral Awards – Act of the Czech Republic No. 216/1994 Coll. (approximate translation, cit.) – Section 13 [Permanent arbitral institutions]: *(1) Permanent arbitral institutions may only be established by another law or only if another law expressly allows their establishment. (2) Permanent arbitral institutions can issue their own statutes and rules, which must be published in the Business Journal; these statutes and rules may determine the method of appointment and the number of arbitrators, and may stipulate that the arbitrators shall be selected from a list administered by the permanent arbitral institution. The statutes and rules may also determine how the arbitrators shall conduct the proceedings and render their decisions, as well as resolve other issues connected with the activities of the permanent arbitral institution and the arbitrators, including rules regulating the costs of proceedings and fees for the arbitrators. (3) If the parties agreed on the jurisdiction of a particular permanent arbitral institution and failed to agree otherwise in the arbitration agreement, they shall be deemed to have submitted to the regulations specified in Subsection (2), as applicable on the day of commencement of the proceedings in the permanent arbitral institution. (4) No entity may carry out its activities using a name that evokes a misleading impression that the entity is a permanent arbitral institution under this law, unless a different law or regulation or an international agreement integrated in the legal system authorizes the entity to use the name.*

[91]   See Article IX of Act No. 258/2016 Coll., quoted above.

[92]   The *ratio decidendi* has been adopted from: Výběr rozhodnutí, 22(11-12) SOUDNÍ ROZHLEDY 370-371 (2017).

Czech (& Central European) Yearbook of Arbitration®

8.28. **Judgment of the Supreme Court of the Czech Republic, Case No. 23 Cdo 4093/2015 of 03 May 2016:**[93] **[telefax; form of juridical act; written form]** A juridical act performed by telefax meets the requirement of the written form if the document transmitted by telefax is signed by the person who performs the juridical act.

8.29. **Resolution of the Supreme Court of the Czech Republic, Case No. 20 Cdo 1095/2016 of 12 August 2016:**[94] **[dismissal of an application for enforcement; discontinuation of the enforcement proceedings; prohibition of enforcement; jurisdiction; nullity of the arbitration agreement; settlement; agreement on the approval of settlement; unambiguous arbitration agreement; doubts about the validity of the arbitration agreement; arbitration agreement replaced by a new one]** **(1)** Unless the agreement entered into by and between the obligor and the obligee and approved by the competent court pursuant to Section 99(1) and (2) of the Code of Civil Procedure clearly indicated which arbitration clause (incorporated in a clearly identified agency agreement) was to be replaced by it, the agreement cannot be deemed capable of establishing the jurisdiction of an arbitrator to resolve a particular dispute. **(2)** If there are any doubts about the validity of the arbitration clause or, as applicable, a lack of jurisdiction of the arbitrator, the parties are free to make another agreement on such jurisdiction, even if the original arbitration clause is obviously invalid. **(3)** However, the new agreement on the choice of arbitrator must be sufficiently unambiguous to specifically express the will to resolve disputes in arbitration and thereby prevent any doubts about the existence of the particular arbitrator's jurisdiction to resolve a particular dispute.

8.30. **Judgment of the Constitutional Court of the Czech Republic, Case No. III. ÚS 1336/18 of 08 January 2019:**[95] **[partial invalidity of the arbitration agreement; excessive formalism; autonomy of the parties; selection of arbitrator]** If the courts dismiss the application for enforcement against the debtor on grounds of an arbitration clause that the courts consider null and void as a whole because a part of the clause fulfilled the requirements of transparency (specified a particular

---

[93]　The *ratio decidendi* has been adopted from: Petr Vojtek, *Výběr rozhodnutí v oblasti civilněprávní*, (9) SOUDNÍ ROZHLEDY 293 (2017). Also published in: SJ 55/2017, C 15808. The case did not concern arbitration (arbitration agreement), but the conclusions made by the Supreme Court can be generalised. The case was subsequently submitted to the Constitutional Court, but the constitutional complaint was ultimately rejected by Decision Case No. IV. ÚS 2654/2016.

[94]　Preceding decisions in the case: (i) Resolution of the District Court in Pardubice [Czech Republic], Case No. 34 EXE 3182/2013-97 of 31 March 2015; and (ii) Resolution of the Regional Court in Hradec Králové – Pardubice Office [Czech Republic], Case No. 18 Co 404/2015-161 of 30 July 2015.

[95]　This decision is also annotated in connection with objective arbitrability in: Výběr rozhodnutí, 25(1) SOUDNÍ ROZHLEDY 20 (2019). The decision was also published in: Sbírka rozhodnutí, 100/2018, C 16490.

arbitrator who was supposed to resolve the dispute), whereas another part thereof did not (because the choice of arbitrator was at the discretion of one of the parties), despite the fact that the respective dispute was indeed ultimately resolved by an arbitrator who was determined properly in the arbitration clause from the perspective of the requirements posed on the transparency of arbitration clauses, the courts' procedure must be qualified as overly formalistic and ultimately interfering with the parties' autonomy of will.[96]

8.31. Resolution of the Supreme Court of the Czech Republic, Case No. 20 Cdo 4022/2017 of 23 January 2018:[97] [standard form contracts; discontinuation of the enforcement proceedings; repeated appointment as arbitrator; discontinuation of the enforcement proceedings as an exceptional protective measure] (1) The fact alone that the arbitration agreement entered into with a consumer pursuant to the ArbAct was executed as a standard form contract cannot justify the finding of the invalidity of the arbitration agreement for being allegedly *contra bonos mores* pursuant to Section 580 of the Civil Code,[98] nor does it justify the discontinuation of the enforcement proceedings. **(2)** An arbitrator cannot be disqualified from the hearing and resolution of a case merely on the basis of an allegation that the arbitrator has been repeatedly and on a long-term basis nominated to serve as arbitrator by one of the parties to the arbitration agreement. **(3)** The ArbAct and the protection it affords in any envisaged civil litigation cannot be circumvented with the hope of finding such protection in any subsequent enforcement proceedings; if any protection is to be proffered in, and as late as, the enforcement proceedings, then

---

[96] The Constitutional Court of the Czech Republic distinguished the case from the opinions articulated, *inter alia*, in the following rulings of the SC:
» Resolution of the Grand Chamber of the Civil and Commercial Division of the Supreme Court of the Czech Republic, Case No. 31 Cdo 1945/2010, also published in Sbírka, 2011, No. 11, et. 409,
» Judgment of the Supreme Court of the Czech Republic, Case No. 23 Cdo 1112/2013 of 28 November 2013,
» Judgment of the Supreme Court of the Czech Republic, Case No. 33 Cdo 2504/2014 of 29 September 2014,
» Resolution of the Supreme Court of the Czech Republic, Case No. 21 Cdo 4529/2014 of 16 December 2014
to the effect that the partial invalidity of the agreement on the selection of arbitrators would destabilise the legal relationships of the parties to arbitration to such an extent that the arbitration clause would have to be declared invalid as a whole in consequence thereof. The Constitutional Court has argued that, conversely, the principles of contractual freedom necessitate an approach according to which the will of the parties shall be protected to the maximum possible extent. Also adopted from an annotation published in Výběr rozhodnutí, (4) SOUDNÍ ROZHLEDY 117 (2019).
[97] The *rationes decidendi* have been adopted from: Petr Vojtek, *Přehled rozhodnutí NS neschválených v roce 2018 do sbírky soudních rozhodnutí a stanovisek*, (2) SOUDNÍ ROZHLEDY 39-40 (2019).
[98] Civil Code 2012 [Czech Republic] (approximate translation, cit.): Section 580 – *(1) A juridical act is also invalid if it is* contra bonos mores *or contrary to a statute, if so required by the sense and purpose of such statute. (2) A juridical act is invalid if something impossible is to be performed thereunder.*

the only justification for such procedure can be the necessity of intervention justified by exceptionally persuasive arguments (primarily invoking constitutional law), i.e. only if the contents of the arbitral award, the enforcement of which is sought, conflicts with the fundamental principles of a democratic legal system.

8.32. **Judgment of the High Court in Prague [Czech Republic], Case No. 5 Cmo 103/2018 of 22 May 2018:**[99] **[finding of invalidity of an arbitration agreement; legal interest]** There can be no legal interest in a court's finding that the relevant arbitration agreement is invalid once the arbitration is opened.

8.33. **Resolution of the Supreme Court of the Czech Republic, Case No. 23 Cdo 3439/2018 of 16 May 2019:**[100] **[form of arbitration agreement; electronic communication, e-mail; New York Convention (1958); European Convention on International Commercial Arbitration;** *lex specialis***; qualified electronic signature]** **(1)** As concerns the issue of the validity of an arbitration agreement entered into by and between entities from different States in international commerce by an exchange of e-mails without a qualified electronic signature, it is appropriate to apply the New York Convention on the Recognition and Enforcement of Foreign Arbitral Awards (New York Convention 1958) as a *lex specialis* vis-à-vis the European Convention on International Commercial Arbitration. **(2)** The requirement that the arbitration agreement must be contained in an "exchange of letters or telegrams" must be interpreted as including an exchange of communication by e-mail. If no qualified electronic signature on the arbitration agreement contained in an exchange of e-mails is *stricto sensu* required, the persons or entities from different States are free to execute a valid arbitration agreement in international commerce by an exchange of e-mails without a qualified electronic signature.[101]

8.34. **Judgment of the Constitutional Court of the Czech Republic, Case No. I ÚS 3962/18 of 06 April 2021: [invalidity of the arbitration agreement; mandatory review of the arbitration agreement; separability of the main contract / agreement from the arbitration agreement]** Courts of general jurisdiction may[102] examine in the enforcement proceedings whether

---

[99] The *ratio decidendi* has been adopted from: Výběr rozhodnutí, (7-8) SOUDNÍ ROZHLEDY 235 (2017).
[100] The *rationes decidendi* adopted from: Judikatura, 27(19) PRÁVNÍ ROZHLEDY 679–681 (2019).
[101] Also annotated in: Výběr rozhodnutí, 26(11-12) SOUDNÍ ROZHLEDY 377 (2020). Published with the following *ratio decidendi* (cit.): *Individuals or entities from different States may enter into a valid arbitration agreement in terms of Article II of the New York Convention (1958) by an exchange of e-mails that do not contain a qualified electronic signature.*
[102] The entire *ratio decidendi* has been adopted from: Výběr rozhodnutí, 21(6) SOUDNÍ ROZHLEDY 198-199 (2017). However, the quoted source has somewhat distorted the text of the decision, because the published version uses the term "must" whereas the judgment explicitly states "may". It is a major qualitative difference.

a proper arbitration agreement was entered into, be it an arbitration clause or a post-dispute arbitration agreement, and whether the arbitrators had jurisdiction to deliver the arbitral award at all. Principal defects discovered in the enforcement order may result in a discontinuation of the enforcement proceedings pursuant to Section 268(1)(h) of the Code of Civil Procedure.[103] Findings concerning the invalidity of the main contract / agreement may, depending on the circumstances, also concern the invalidity of the arbitration agreement.[104]

[*Reasoning*]: The case essentially reacts to obviously extreme *contra bonos mores* situations, etc. But it is interesting to note the concept of invalidity in connection with the principle of the separability of the arbitration agreement from the main contract/ agreement, as reflected by the court of general jurisdiction and by the Constitutional Court of the Czech Republic. Indeed, the court of first instance based its decision in the case, whereby the court granted the applicant's motion for the discontinuation of the enforcement proceedings, on the opinion that if a credit facility agreement is *contra bonos mores* and therefore clearly invalid, the arbitration agreement – negotiated for the purpose of resolving disputes arising from the former – is invalid as well, which in turn means that the arbitrator does not have jurisdiction. However, the appellate court based its resolution on the prohibition of a review on the merits of the decision, the enforcement of which is sought, which – according to the appellate court – follows from the principle of the separability of the arbitration agreement from the main contract/agreement. The appellate court held that the arbitration agreement was not invalid in such case, and that the court of first instance should only have addressed the formal and material enforceability of the enforcement order. However, the Constitutional Court has repeatedly held that the courts of general jurisdiction conducting enforcement proceedings should examine whether a proper arbitration agreement was entered into, be it an arbitration clause or a post-dispute arbitration agreement, and whether the arbitrators had jurisdiction to deliver the arbitral award at all. The opinion of the Constitutional Court of the Czech Republic, already articulated in the judgment of the Constitutional Court

---

[103] The *ratio decidendi* has been adopted from: Výběr rozhodnutí, 21(6) SOUDNÍ ROZHLEDY 198-199 (2017).
[104] The *ratio decidendi* was published in: Výběr rozhodnutí, 21(6) SOUDNÍ ROZHLEDY 198-199 (2017) and contained the following summary (cit.): *The opinion of the Constitutional Court that the invalidity of the credit facility agreement renders the arbitration clause invalid also applies in the case of a separate arbitration agreement, the contents and purpose of which suggest that it could be deemed an arbitration clause.* But this summary is incorrect and could essentially suggest that the principle of separability was denied by the Constitutional Court of the Czech Republic, which, however, is not the case.

186 |

in Case No. III. ÚS 4084/12, that the invalidity of a credit facility agreement results in the invalidity of the arbitration clause, also applies, as the Constitutional Court has held in the present case, in the case of a separate arbitration agreement, the contents and purpose of which allow it to be considered an arbitration clause. Hence, as the Constitutional Court has ruled, if the appellate court put forward the principle of separability of the arbitration agreement from the main contract/agreement, it is necessary to have regard to the applicant's allegation that the main contract/agreement and the arbitration agreement form **one business construct** in the present case: the arbitration agreement was signed on the same day as the proposal to enter into the revolving credit facility agreement and, consequently, the agreements were clearly intertwined, as neither could exist without the other, which testifies to the nature of the arbitration agreement as an arbitration clause. Consequently, the fact alone that the arbitration agreement was agreed in a separate document can under no circumstances justify, from the perspective of constitutional law, the waiver of the review (and assessment in light of *bonos mores*) of the entire process of contract formation, including the negotiation of the arbitration agreement. The approach of the appellate court in the said case was, according to the Constitutional Court, a manifestation of an excessive legal formalism, which should have no place in a democratic country honouring the principle of the rule of law, especially in similar cases in which one of the parties is in a manifestly weaker position. [*Author's Notes*]: The Constitutional Court's ruling might *prima facie* suggest that its legal conclusions negate the principle of the separability of the arbitration agreement from the main contract. The opposite is true, though. The Constitutional Court has simply held that, in view of the circumstances of the case, the grounds for the invalidity of the main contract (agreement) must be extended to cover the arbitration agreement as well, because the entire concept of the main contract (contractual terms and conditions) and of the arbitration agreement are principally *communicating vessels* (*connected construct*).

IV. Nature and Enforceability of Arbitral Award

8.35. Connected, *inter alia*, to the provisions of **Section 28 of Act of the Czech Republic No. 216/1994 Coll., on Arbitration and the Enforcement of Arbitral Awards**

Czech (& Central European) Yearbook of Arbitration®

ArbAct: Section 28 [Legal Force and Effect, Enforceability][105]

Current Version of Section 28 of ArbAct:

(1) The arbitral award executed in writing must be served on the parties and, having been duly served, stamped with the confirmation of legal force and effect.

(2) If the arbitral award cannot be subject to review pursuant to Section 27 or if the time limit for filing the motion for review pursuant to Section 27 has expired without the motion having been lodged, the award has the effects of a final and conclusive court judgment and is enforceable by courts upon receipt.

Section 28 of ArbAct in Effect as of 1 April 2012:

Identical

Legislative Developments Since 1 April 2012:

No amendments adopted in the relevant period

8.36.   **Resolution of the Supreme Court of the Czech Republic, Case No. 29 NSČR 29/2009 –A-108 KSOS 31 INS 3370/2008 of 17 February 2011:**[106] **[insolvency proceedings; nature of the arbitral award in the course of the proceedings for annulment of the arbitral award; formal finality; effects of legal force and effect; formal effects; material effects; binding force of the operative part of the arbitral award; suspension of enforceability; creditor's claim in insolvency proceedings]** (1) The suspension of enforceability of a judicial decision is without prejudice to the effects of the legal force and effect of the decision, manifested (i) by the fact that it cannot be challenged by an appeal as a regular remedy (formal finality) and (ii) by the binding effects and irreversibility of the operative part of the decision (material finality). **(2)** An insolvency petitioner's claim awarded by a final arbitral award that has the effects of a final court decision cannot be classified as contested

---

[105]   The titles of the individual Parts and Sections provided in square brackets are not part of the statutory text and have been supplemented by the author for better transparency of the contents.

[106]   The *rationes decidendi* have been adopted from the database of the Supreme Court of the Czech Republic. The Supreme Court has essentially clearly agreed that claims relying on a final arbitral award are enforcement orders. It is all the more surprising, then, to come across decisions such as the decision of the Regional Court in Prague [Czech Republic], Case No. 37 ICm 1216/2011-53 of 06 March 2012, issued in insolvency proceedings conducted in the said court under Case No. KSPH 37 INS 14063/2010, available at: http://kraken.slv.cz/37ICm1216/2011 (accessed on 15 February 2022).

(unsupported in terms of Section 105 of the Insolvency Act)[107] based on the fact alone that the proceedings for the annulment of the arbitral award are pending in which the court allowed a suspension of the enforceability of the arbitral award.

8.37. Resolution of the Regional Court in Pilsen [Czech Republic], Case No. 18 Co 25/2012 of 19 January 2012:[108] **[service of documents to the obligor's registered address; when the dropping of documents in the mailbox is prohibited; proper service; expiration of the period for collecting the document]** If the arbitrator orders the service of the arbitral award to the obligor's registered address, but prohibits the possibility of simply dropping it in the mailbox in case the arbitral award is to be served on the basis of the expiration of the period for collecting the award pursuant to Section 49(4) of the CCP,[109] the enforcement order is not properly served and the court shall dismiss the motion for enforcement. The reason is that the service of a document by the expiration of the period for collecting it is contingent on the requirement that the service shall comprise the implementation of any and all procedural

---

[107] Insolvency Act – Act [of the Czech Republic] No. 182/2006 Coll. (approximate translation, cit.): Section 105 – *If the insolvency petition is filed by a creditor, the creditor is obliged to prove an outstanding claim against the debtor and enclose an application for registration of the claim with the creditor's petition; if the claim belongs to the category of claims that otherwise do not require registration, the claim is deemed registered pursuant to Section 203 after the decision on insolvency is issued.*

[108] The *ratio decidendi* has been adopted from: Karel Svoboda, *K problému doručování rozhodčích nálezů podle § 49 odst. 4 občanského soudního řádu, vyloučí-li rozhodce jejich vhození do schránky I.* [title in translation – *Service of Arbitral Awards pursuant to Section 49(4) of Code of Civil Procedure in Case Arbitrator Prohibits Dropping Arbitral Award in Mailbox I*], 18(6) SOUDNÍ ROZHLEDY 212 (2012). An annotation of the decision is provided in the same place.

[109] Code of Civil Procedure [Czech Republic] (approximate translation, cit.): Section 49 – *Service of Documents to Addressee Personally* – (1) Documents shall be served to the addressee personally if such service is required by law or ordered by the court. (2) If the delivering authority did not reach the addressee, the document shall be kept with the relevant authority and a written notice shall be left for the addressee in an appropriate manner, requesting that the addressee collect the document. If the notice cannot be left in the place where the document was to be served, the delivering authority shall return the document to the court-sender and make a note of the day on which the addressee was not reached. The court-sender shall put up a notice on the official board requesting the addressee to collect the document at the court. (3) The document is deposited (a) on the premises of the postal offices provider, if the document is being served by the provider, (b) at the court to which the document was returned because no notice could be left at the place of delivery, (c) at the district court with territorial jurisdiction over the place of delivery, if Paragraphs (a) and (b) do not apply. (4) If the addressee fails to collect the document within 10 days from the day on which the document was ready for collecting, the document is deemed served on the last day of this period whether or not the addressee was aware that the document was so deposited. The delivering authority shall drop the document in the addressee's home mailbox or any other mailbox used by the addressee after the said period expires without the document being collected, unless the court prohibits such procedure, whether at the request of a party or on its own motion. If no such mailbox exists, the document shall be returned to the court-sender and a notice thereof shall be put up on the court's official board. (5) Service pursuant to Subsection (4) is prohibited with respect to a document if such a prohibition is stipulated by law or ordered by the presiding judge. In such case, the delivering authority shall return the document to the court-sender after the expiration of the 10-day period following the day on which the document was ready for being collected. (6) Service of a document via the public data network is deemed service of the document to the addressee personally. (7) If the delivering authority discovers that the addressee passed away, the document shall be returned with a report to the court-sender.

acts that secure the most likely placing of the document at the addressee's disposal.

8.38. Resolution of the High Court in Olomouc, Case No. 36 ICm 2130/2010, 12 VSOL 35/201-69 (KSOS 36 INS 11470/2010), of 02 February 2012:[110] **[insolvency proceedings, evidencing a claim, document]** Although a final arbitral award is not a decision of a public authority, it has analogous effects as a judicial decision. Consequently, a claim evidenced in insolvency proceedings by a final arbitral award is proven in compliance with Section 177 of the Insolvency Act.[111]

8.39. Resolution of the Supreme Court of the Czech Republic, Case No. 20 Cdo 2487/2010 of 16 August 2012:[112] **[nature of arbitration; essence of arbitration; contractual theory; jurisdictional theory; difference from civil litigation; conditional exclusion of court jurisdiction; *lis pendens*; *res judicata*; autonomy; level and scope of protection afforded to the parties in arbitration by courts; finding law in arbitration]** The fundamental difference from civil procedure in court (i.e. litigation) lies in the definition of the managing and decision-making authority – a court in civil litigation, an arbitrator or a permanent arbitral institution in arbitration. The arbitrator's[113] power to hear and resolve a dispute is based on the joint will of the parties to the dispute expressed in their arbitration agreement. This procedural agreement of the parties excludes the jurisdiction of the courts (only conditionally, in view of Section 106(1) of the Code of Civil Procedure)[114] and establishes the jurisdiction of (an) arbitrator(s). Based on the

---

[110] Adopted from: ONDŘEJ RICHTER, VĚŘITELÉ A UPLATŇOVÁNÍ POHLEDÁVEK V INSOLVENČNÍM ŘÍZENÍ. KOMENTÁŘ. [title in translation – CREDITORS AND REGISTRATION OF CLAIMS IN INSOLVENCY PROCEEDINGS. A COMMENTARY.], Prague: C. H. Beck (2014), et. 115.

[111] Insolvency Act – Act [of the Czech Republic] No. 182/2006 Coll. (approximate translation, cit.): Section 177 – *Applications whereby claims are to be registered must be lodged together with the documents referred to in the application. Enforceability of a claim shall be proven by a public deed.*

[112] Preceding decisions in the case: (i) Resolution of the District Court for Pilsen-City [Czech Republic], Case No. 73 Nc 1420/2009 of 5 November 2009; and (ii) Resolution of the Regional Court in Pilsen [Czech Republic], Case No. 12 Co 12/2010-165 of 10 February 2010.

[113] The shorthand used by the Supreme Court of the Czech Republic in the reasons for the decision should be interpreted as an arbitrator [*ad hoc*], as well as a [permanent] arbitral institution.

[114] Code of Civil Procedure [Czech Republic] (approximate translation, cit.): Section 106 – *(1) As soon as the court discovers, upon the respondent's objection lodged together with or before the first act of the respondent on the merits, that the agreement of the parties requires the case to be submitted to arbitrators or to an arbitral committee of an association, the court must desist from further examination of the case and discontinue the proceedings; the court, however, hears the case if the parties declare that they waive the agreement or that they do not insist on having the case heard by the arbitral committee of the association. The court also hears the case if the court determines that the matter is not arbitrable under the laws of the Czech Republic, or that the arbitration agreement is invalid or non-existent, or that examining the agreement in arbitration exceeds the scope of jurisdiction vested in the arbitrators by the agreement, or that the arbitral tribunal refused to hear the case. (2) If the court proceedings under Subsection (1) were discontinued and the same case was submitted to arbitrators or to the arbitral committee of the association, the original motion to commence the proceedings retains its legal effects, provided that the motion to commence the proceedings before the arbitrators or the arbitral committee of the association is lodged no later than within 30 days of*

voluntary acts of the parties, **the arbitrator thus replaces the court** where the latter should otherwise hear and resolve the case. However, the rights of the parties to direct the dispute resolution procedure are even more far-reaching; the parties to the dispute are, for instance, allowed to select the arbitrators, and to determine the applicable procedural rules, the seat of arbitration, the type of proceedings (oral or written), and even the criteria that should be applied to the merits (Section 25(3) of the ArbAct).[115][116] **(2)** Arbitration **excludes parallel civil** [court] **proceedings** concerning the same issue. Arbitral awards have the same effects as final court decisions (Section 28(2) of the ArbAct),[117] which means that arbitral awards constitute *res judicata*, barring the parties from litigating the same claim again in the courts. **(3)** In compliance with the principle of the autonomy of will, the law honours the freely expressed will of the parties who wish to have their dispute heard and resolved by an arbitrator; courts are therefore not allowed to intervene in arbitration, except in strictly defined situations specified in the Arbitration Act. On the other hand, this does not mean that the purpose of arbitration is to eliminate or reduce the

---

receipt of the court's resolution discontinuing the proceedings. (3) If the arbitral proceedings were opened before the court proceedings, the court stays the proceedings on the non-existence, invalidity or expiration/termination of the agreement until the arbitrator(s) decide on their jurisdiction over the case or on the merits.

[115] The Supreme Court of the Czech Republic has held that the nature of arbitration in terms of *contractual theory* v. *jurisdictional theory* is also a significant question of law. In this regard, the Supreme Court of the Czech Republic invoked the landmark judgment of the Constitutional Court of the Czech Republic in Case No. I. ÚS 3227/07 of 08 March 2011, which favoured the jurisdictional essence of arbitration.

[116] Act on Arbitration and the Enforcement of Arbitral Awards – Act of the Czech Republic No. 216/1994 Coll. (approximate translation, cit.) – Section 25 [Making Arbitral Award and Reasoning]: Current version: *(1) The arbitral award must be adopted by the majority of the arbitrators, must be made in writing, and must be signed by at least the majority of the arbitrators. The operative part of the arbitral award must be clear and unambiguous. (2) The arbitral award must contain reasons, unless the parties have agreed to dispense with reasons; this also applies to any arbitral award rendered pursuant to Section 24(2). (3) When making the award, the arbitrators apply the substantive law applicable to the dispute; they may, however, resolve the dispute according to the rules of equity, but only if the parties have explicitly authorized them to do so.*

The Act in effect as of 1 April 2012: *(1) The arbitral award must be adopted by the majority of the arbitrators, must be made in writing, and must be signed by at least the majority of the arbitrators. The operative part of the arbitral award must be clear and unambiguous. (2) The arbitral award must contain reasons, unless the parties have agreed to dispense with reasons; this also applies to any arbitral award rendered pursuant to Section 24(2). An arbitral award rendered in a dispute arising from a consumer contract must always contain reasons and instructions regarding the right to file a motion with the court to annul the award. (3) When making the award, the arbitrators apply the substantive law applicable to the dispute; they may, however, resolve the dispute according to the rules of equity, but only if the parties have explicitly authorized them to do so. In disputes arising from consumer contracts, the arbitrators shall always abide by consumer protection laws and regulations.*

Legislative developments since 01 April 2012: Section 25 of the ArbAct, as amended by Act No. 245/2006 Coll., Act No. 296/2007 Coll., Act No. 7/2009 Coll., Act No. 466/2011 Coll., Act No. 19/2012 Coll. and Act No. 91/2012 Coll., was newly reformulated by Act No. 258/2016 Coll., Amending Selected Legislation in Connection with the Consumer Credit Act, which took effect on 1 December 2016. The law has reverted to the version that was in effect before 01 April 2012.

[117] An approximate translation of the provision is quoted in the introduction to this Part IV of selected case-law.

degree of protection that would otherwise be afforded to the parties in civil litigation; arbitration, just like litigation, aims at the peaceful resolution of the dispute between the parties. It is just that the parties have a special reason (for instance, expeditiousness or the confidentiality of the information discussed in the proceedings) to believe that arbitration is a more suitable solution. The submission of a dispute to arbitration means the transfer of legal protection to a different decision-making and law-finding authority,[118] rather than the waiver thereof; indeed, any other conclusion would render it conceptually unacceptable to consider arbitration as a dispute resolution method representing an alternative to litigation.

8.40. **Resolution of the Supreme Court of the Czech Republic, Case No. 29 Cdo 2254/2011 of 27 June 2013:**[119] [*res judicata*; effects of a final arbitral award] A final arbitral award has the effects of a final court decision and constitutes *res judicata*[120] in relation to identical cases.[121]

8.41. **Resolution of the Supreme Court of the Czech Republic, Case No. 29 Cdo 392/2011 of 31 July 2013:**[122] [incidental dispute; insolvency proceedings; decision making according to the principles of equity] (1) "Another authority" in terms of Section 199(2) of the Insolvency Act[123] also means an arbitrator or a [permanent] arbitral institution.[124] The regime applicable to the review of an enforceable claim awarded by a final decision of a "competent authority" also covers an enforceable claim

---

[118]   An arbitrator (permanent arbitral institution) is also designated as "another authority" by judgment of the Constitutional Court of the Czech Republic, Case No. I. ÚS 3227/07 of 08 March 2011.
[119]   Preceding decisions in the case: (i) resolution of the Regional Court in Hradec Králové [Czech Republic], Case No. 34 Cm 146/2009 of 23 April 2010, and (ii) resolution of the High Court in Prague [Czech Republic], Case No. 4 Cmo 146/2010-47 of 25 February 2011.
[120]   In this regard, the Supreme Court of the Czech Republic also invoked resolution of the Supreme Court of the Czech Republic, Case No. 29 NSČR 29/2009 of 17 February 2011, published as no. 108/2011 in Sbírka soudních rozhodnutí a stanovisek [Court Reports].
[121]   As to the issue of *the same case*, the Supreme Court of the Czech Republic summarizes the postulates inferred from the current case-law and invokes, *inter alia*, (i) resolution of the Supreme Court of the Czech Republic, Case No. 20 Cdo 463/99 of 31 January 2001, (ii) judgment of the Supreme Court of the Czech Republic, Case No. 20 Cdo 2481/99 of 28 November 2001, or (iii) resolution of the Supreme Court of the Czech Republic, Case No. 20 Cdo 2931/99 of 12 December 2001.
[122]   One of the preceding decisions was judgment of the High Court in Prague [Czech Republic], Case No. 15 Cmo 250/2009-100 of 18 February 2010.
[123]   Insolvency Act – Act [of the Czech Republic] No. 182/2006 Coll. (approximate translation, cit.): Section 199 – *(1) The liquidator who rebutted an enforceable claim shall file a lawsuit with the insolvency court within 30 days of the review hearing whereby the rebuttal will be claimed against the creditor who had registered the enforceable claim. The time period shall not expire if the lawsuit is received by the court on or before the last day of the time period. (2) The grounds for rebutting the existence or the amount of an enforceable claim awarded by a final decision of the competent authority may only consist in the facts which were not asserted by the debtor in the proceedings preceding the issue of the decision; however, the rebuttal may not be based on a different legal assessment of the case. (3) In his or her lawsuit under subsection (1), the claimant may only invoke such circumstances against the rebutted claim for which the claim was rebutted by the claimant.*
[124]   Cf. also judgment of the Constitutional Court of the Czech Republic, Case No. I. ÚS 3227/07 of 8 March 2011.

awarded by a final arbitral award delivered by an arbitrator or a [permanent] arbitral institution. If the arbitral award takes the effects of a final judicial decision, it is logically, as such, reviewable in insolvency proceedings in the same way as a final judicial decision. **(2)** The possibility of rebutting an enforceable claim awarded by a final arbitral award is not prevented by the fact that the parties explicitly authorised the arbitrator to resolve the dispute in compliance with the principles of equity (Section 25(3) of the ArbAct).[125]

8.42. **Resolution of the Supreme Court of the Czech Republic, Case No. 30 Cdo 3678/2013 of 21 May 2014:**[126] [service of documents; agreement of the parties on service of documents; service of documents to a data mailbox] **(1)** The ArbAct regime following the ArbAct Amendment allows the parties to agree on the means whereby the arbitral award will be served. **(2)** As concerns the service of the arbitral award in arbitration, whether the parties agreed on the means of such service is always to be determined. In the absence of the parties' agreement, it is necessary to apply the provisions of the CCP that provide for the service of documents. **(3)** The service of documents through the public data network to data mailboxes is provided for in the Electronic Acts Act, which enables documents to be served sent by individuals, individuals doing business and legal entities (other than public authorities). **(4)**

---

[125] Act on Arbitration and the Enforcement of Arbitral Awards – Act of the Czech Republic No. 216/1994 Coll. (approximate translation, cit.) – Section 25 [Making the arbitral award and reasons]:
Current version: *(1) The arbitral award must be adopted by the majority of the arbitrators, must be made in writing, and must be signed by at least the majority of the arbitrators. The operative part of the arbitral award must be clear and unambiguous. (2) The arbitral award must contain reasons, unless the parties have agreed to dispense with reasons; this also applies to any arbitral award rendered pursuant to Section 24(2). 2. (3) When making the award, the arbitrators apply the substantive law applicable to the dispute; they may, however, resolve the dispute according to the rules of equity, but only if the parties have explicitly authorized them to do so.*
The Act in effect as of 01 April 2012: *(1) The arbitral award must be adopted by the majority of the arbitrators, must be made in writing, and must be signed by at least the majority of the arbitrators. The operative part of the arbitral award must be clear and unambiguous. (2) The arbitral award must contain reasons, unless the parties have agreed to dispense with reasons; this also applies to any arbitral award rendered pursuant to Section 24(2). 2. An arbitral award rendered in a dispute arising from a consumer contract must always contain reasons and instructions regarding the right to file a motion with the court to annul the award. (3) When making the award, the arbitrators apply the substantive law applicable to the dispute; they may, however, resolve the dispute according to the rules of equity, but only if the parties have explicitly authorized them to do so. In disputes arising from consumer contracts, the arbitrators shall always abide by consumer protection laws and regulations.*
Legislative developments since 01 April 2012: Section 25 of the ArbAct, as amended by Act No. 245/2006 Coll., Act No. 296/2007 Coll., Act No. 7/2009 Coll., Act No. 466/2011 Coll., Act No. 19/2012 Coll. and Act No. 91/2012 Coll., was newly reformulated by Act No. 258/2016 Coll., Amending Selected Legislation in Connection with the Consumer Credit Act, which took effect on 1 December 2016. The law has reverted to the version that was in effect before 01 April 2012.
[126] One of the preceding decisions was the resolution of the Municipal Court in Prague [Czech Republic] in Case No. 23 Co 241/2013-10 of 06 June 2013.

However, Section 18a of the EAA[127] stipulates that service of documents from the data mailboxes of such persons or entities to their data mailboxes is only allowed if they made the relevant request at the Ministry of Interior (see Section 2(2) of the EAA[128] and Section 18a(1) of the EAA).[129] [*Author's Note*]: This decision was made in enforcement proceedings and concerns arbitration in which the arbitral award was rendered on 18 October 2012. Hence, the resolution does not factor in Section 19a of the ArbAct.

8.43.   Resolution of the Supreme Court of the Czech Republic, Case No. 23 Cdo 168/2014 of 25 November 2014:[130] [arbitral award

---

[127]   Act of the Czech Republic No. 300/2008 Coll. on Electronic Acts and Authorized Conversion of Documents (approximate translation, cit.): Section 18a – *Delivery of documents of natural persons, self-employed natural persons (entrepreneurs) or legal entities – (1) The information system of data mailboxes allows delivery of documents from the data mailbox of a natural person, a self-employed natural person (entrepreneur) or a legal entity to an activated data mailbox of another person or entity. The data mailbox of a natural person can be blocked by the holder thereof with respect to the delivery of documents from the data mailbox of a natural person, a self-employed natural person (entrepreneur) or a legal entity. (2) A document delivered pursuant to the first sentence of Subsection (1) is delivered at the moment the person who has access to the document in view of the scope of his/her authorisation logs into the data mailbox. (3) Unless the person under Subsection (2) logs into the data mailbox within 10 days after the day on which the document was delivered to the data mailbox, the document is deemed delivered on the last day of this time limit. (4) The delivery of the document pursuant to the first sentence of Subsection (1) is subject to a fee payable to the data mailbox information system operator; the fee shall be calculated by the price-setting authority according to the applicable price regulations⁵⁾. The fee shall be paid by the natural person, self-employed natural person (entrepreneur) or legal entity from whose data mailbox the document was sent. The said person/entity may also declare that he/she will pay for the delivery of a reply to the document delivered pursuant to the preceding sentence. On behalf of and with the consent of the natural person, self-employed natural person (entrepreneur) or legal entity from whose mailbox the document was dispatched, the fee under the first sentence may also be paid by another natural person, self-employed natural person (entrepreneur) or legal entity.*

[128]   Act of the Czech Republic No. 300/2008 Coll. on Electronic Acts and Authorized Conversion of Documents (approximate translation, cit.): Section 2 – *Data mailbox - (1) A data mailbox is an electronic repository intended for (a) service of documents by public authorities, (b) performance of acts vis-à-vis public authorities, (c) service of documents by natural persons, self-employed natural persons (entrepreneurs) and legal entities. (2) Data mailboxes are created and administrated by the Ministry of Interior (the "Ministry").*

[129]   Act of the Czech Republic No. 300/2008 Coll. on Electronic Acts and Authorized Conversion of Documents (approximate translation, cit.): Section 18a – *Delivery of documents of natural persons, self-employed natural persons (entrepreneurs) or legal entities – (1) The information system of data mailboxes allows delivery of documents from the data mailbox of a natural person, a self-employed natural person (entrepreneur) or a legal entity to an activated data mailbox of another person or entity. The data mailbox of a natural person can be blocked by the holder thereof with respect to the delivery of documents from the data mailbox of a natural person, a self-employed natural person (entrepreneur) or a legal entity. (2) A document delivered pursuant to the first sentence of Subsection (1) is delivered at the moment the person, who has access to the document in view of the scope of his/her authorisation, logs into the data mailbox. (3) Unless the person under Subsection (2) logs into the data mailbox within 10 days after the day on which the document was delivered to the data mailbox, the document is deemed delivered on the last day of this time limit. (4) The delivery of the document pursuant to the first sentence of Subsection (1) is subject to a fee payable to the data mailbox information system operator; the fee shall be calculated by the price-setting authority according to the applicable price regulations⁵⁾. The fee shall be paid by the natural person, self-employed natural person (entrepreneur) or legal entity from whose data mailbox the document was sent. The said person/entity may also declare that he/she will pay for the delivery of a reply to the document delivered pursuant to the preceding sentence. On behalf of and with the consent of the natural person, self-employed natural person (entrepreneur) or legal entity from whose mailbox the document was dispatched, the fee under the first sentence may also be paid by another natural person, self-employed natural person (entrepreneur) or legal entity.*

[130]   Preceding decisions in the case: (i) Resolution of the District Court for Prague 1 [Czech Republic], Case No. 65 C 58/2013-20 of 13 February 2013; and (ii) Resolution of the Municipal Court in Prague [Czech Republic], Case No. 55 Co 193/2013-69 of 25 April 2013.

imposing an expression of will; suspension of enforceability; consequences of enforcing an arbitral award; imminent serious harm] An arbitral award imposing an expression of will must be viewed as a judicial decision as concerns the possibility of suspending its enforceability. Hence, such assessment of the suspension of enforceability shall be governed by the case-law concerning judicial decisions imposing an expression of will. If the enforceability cannot be suspended of the part of an judicial decision that imposes an expression of will, the enforceability of an arbitral award imposing an expression of will pursuant to Section 32(2) of the ArbAct cannot be suspended to the said extent either.

8.44. Resolution of the Regional Court in Hradec Králové [Czech Republic], Case No. 23 Co 188/2014:[131] **[contractual penalty, material enforceability, review; enforcement proceedings]** (1) An arbitral award is materially enforceable if the operative part thereof imposes an obligation to pay a contractual penalty calculated as a percentage of a stipulated amount from a particular date to the moment at which the principal is paid. (2) Even if the arbitral award contains an operative part that should not be taken over from a lawsuit and used in a decision made in court proceedings, this deficiency can no longer be remedied at the stage of enforcement. If the review of an award is only allowed exceptionally in cases stipulated by the law, it would be nonsensical to transfer the review on the merits to the enforcement proceedings; the nature of the latter dictates that such proceedings ought to be more formal.[132]

8.45. Judgment of the Supreme Court of the Czech Republic, Case No. 29 ICdo 11/2014 of 28 January 2016:[133] **[arbitrability; dispute over the settlement of marital property (joint property of spouses); property dispute; binding effect of the operative part of an arbitral award;** *res judicata***; effects relating to finality (legal force and effect)]** The operative part of a final judgment is binding on the parties; to the extent to which the operative part of a final judgment is binding on the

---

[131] The annotation has been adopted from: Výběr rozhodnutí, 21(7-8) SOUDNÍ ROZHLEDY 276 (2017).

[132] The issue has also been analysed by Igor Pařízek, *K dalšímu posunu judikatury u rozhodčích doložek* [title in translation – *Developments in Case-Law Concerning Arbitration Clauses*], (2) PRÁVNÍ ROZHLEDY 61 et seq. (2015). The decision was discussed together with the resolution of the SC in Case No. 20 Cdo 4656/2008 of 26 November 2010, in which the Supreme Court has adopted a contrary view, and which is the only decision of the cassation court that deals with a comparable issue; however, the tribunal embraced the conclusion reached in the decision of the Regional Court in Hradec Králové [Czech Republic], annotated in this publication.

[133] Preceding decisions in the case: (i) Judgment of the Municipal Court in Prague [Czech Republic], Case No. 88 ICm 2057/2011-53 of 12 July 2012; and (ii) Judgment of the High Court in Prague [Czech Republic], Case No. 88 ICm 2057/2011, 103 VSPH 291/2012-119 (MSPH 88 INS 8429/2010) of 02 October 2013. The decision also deals with the arbitrability of disputes over the settlement of marital property.

parties, it is also binding on all authorities. The case cannot be retried to the extent of such binding effects of the operative part of the judgment. That said, the effects are connected with the finality (legal force and effect) of the judicial decision, not the enforceability thereof. The same applies, within the limits of the arbitrator's jurisdiction, to an arbitral award rendered by an arbitrator that cannot be subject to review pursuant to Section 27 of the ArbAct or an award with respect to which the time limit for filing the motion for review pursuant to Section 27 of the ArbAct has expired without the motion having been lodged and which, consequently, acquires the effects of a final judicial decision and is enforceable by courts at the moment at which it has been served.

8.46.   **Judgment of the Constitutional Court of the Czech Republic, Case No. I ÚS 1274/16 of 03 March 2016:**[134] **[arbitrator; appointment of the arbitral tribunal; transparency; arbitral award; jurisdiction of arbitrator; enforcement order]** If the arbitral award was not rendered by an arbitrator who was appointed (selected) according to transparent rules, and if the outcome of such decision-making cannot be accepted either, the arbitral award is not an eligible enforcement order. It is also necessary to have regard to the resolution of the Supreme Court of the Czech Republic in Case No. 31 Cdo 1945/2010 of 11 May 2011, which indicates that the Court has unified the approach to the invalidity of arbitration clauses; it also represents the relevant moment at which the courts must be deemed to have adopted the unified approach to the invalidity of arbitration clauses. Subsequent decisions merely elaborate on the impacts that the preceding conclusions have on the enforcement proceedings. Hence, since 11 May 2011, the courts must have been aware that contested arbitration clauses are invalid and, consequently, cannot establish the jurisdiction of an arbitrator to issue a decision eligible as an enforcement order.

8.47.   **Judgment of the Supreme Court of the Czech Republic, Case No. 23 Cdo 3376/2016 of 12 July 2016:**[135] **[service of an arbitral award; agreement on procedure]** (1) After the amendment of Section 23 [ArbAct] by Act No. 19/2012 Coll., the parties to arbitration have been allowed to agree on the procedure whereby the arbitral award will be served (Section 19 of the ArbAct, and since 1 January 2014 see also Section 19a of the ArbAct); consequently, there is no need for the service to comply with Section 45 et seq. of the CCP. (2) The agreement

---

[134]   The *ratio decidendi* has been adopted from: Výběr rozhodnutí, (9) SOUDNÍ ROZHLEDY 283 (2017).
[135]   The *ratio decidendi* have been adopted from the website of the Supreme Court of the Czech Republic.

on the method of conducting the arbitration, including an agreement on a mailing address different from the provisions of the Statute or Rules of the arbitral tribunal, must be contained in the arbitration agreement, i.e. in the arbitration clause, if applicable (Section 13(3) of the ArbAct). **(2)** If the agreement on the mailing address was not incorporated in the arbitration clause and the mailing address was provided only in the purchase order, it does not constitute a special arrangement regarding the means of service in arbitration, but merely an agreement of the parties on the means of communication between the parties, for instance, in connection with the delivery of purchase orders, invoices, etc. **(3)** If the claimant fails to inform the arbitral tribunal of the address for mailing documents and if the tribunal is unable to serve documents to the claimant's data mailbox, the claimant must be served at an address known to the arbitral tribunal, including service implemented by a public data network to the claimant's electronic address (Section 10(1) and (4) of the Rules of the Arbitration Court attached to the Economic Chamber of the Czech Republic and Agricultural Chamber of the Czech Republic); this, however, does not apply to documents that must be served personally (Section 10(3) of the Rules of the Arbitration Court attached to the Economic Chamber of the Czech Republic and Agricultural Chamber of the Czech Republic). **(4)** If the arbitral tribunal does not succeed in delivering documents that must be served personally to the address (registered address) of the claimant entered in the Commercial Register or, as applicable, the Trade Licensing Register and mentioned in the purchase order, the arbitral tribunal applies Section 10(9) of the Rules of the Arbitration Court attached to the Economic Chamber of the Czech Republic and Agricultural Chamber of the Czech Republic and proceeds to the appointment of a person authorised to receive documents.

8.48. **Judgment of the Supreme Court of the Czech Republic, Case No. 23 Cdo 4576/2016 of 11 April 2017:**[136] **[invalidity of the arbitration clause; reference to Rules; legal entity other than a permanent arbitral institution; selection of arbitrator; *res judicata*; objections must be raised in the course of arbitration] (1)** If the arbitrator was appointed by reference to "Rules on Arbitration" issued by a legal entity other than a permanent arbitral institution established by law (statute),[137] the

---

[136] Preceding decisions in the case: (i) Judgment of the Regional Court in Ústí nad Labem, Liberec Office [Czech Republic], Case No. 36 Co 145/2014-92 of 28 March 2014.
[137] See Section 13 of the ArbAct.

arbitral award is not an eligible enforcement order in terms of Section 40(1)(c) of the Enforcement Code,[138] which could be the basis for the opening of enforcement proceedings; the reason is that the arbitrator appointed under an invalid arbitration clause (Section 39 of the Civil Code 1964[139]) lacked jurisdiction to render the arbitral award under the ArbAct. If, despite the above said, the enforcement proceedings were nonetheless opened in such case and if the lack of jurisdiction on the part of the authority that rendered the enforcement order is (*ex post facto*) established by court, the enforcement proceedings must be discontinued at each and every stage for inadmissibility under Section 268(1)(h) of the CCP.[140] **(2)** An identical case concerning the same subject matter of the proceedings and the same parties that was already resolved by an arbitral award rendered by an arbitrator who lacked the jurisdiction to render such an arbitral award does not constitute *res judicata*.[141]

8.49. **Judgment of the Supreme Court of the Czech Republic, Case No. 29 ICdo 93/2016 of 20 September 2018:**[142] **[prohibition of a review on the merits; statement of fact; insolvency proceedings; contesting the existence of a claim; contesting the amount of a claim; error; factual assessment; legal assessment]** The fact that the arbitral tribunal erred in holding a fact claimed by the debtor in the arbitration preceding the final arbitral award immaterial at the level of law or fact, and erred as to the contents of the statements of fact made by the debtor

---

[138] Enforcement Code – Act [of the Czech Republic] No. 120/2001 Coll., on Court Enforcement Officers and Enforcement (approximate translation, cit.): Section 40 – *(1) An enforcement order is (a) an enforceable decision of a court or an enforcement officer that awards a right, establishes an obligation or seizes property, (b) an enforceable decision of a court or another law enforcement authority in criminal proceedings that awards a right or seizes property, (c) an enforceable arbitral award, (d) a notarial record with a consent to enforcement, prepared under special legislation, (e) an enforceable decision or another enforcement order of a public authority, (f) other enforceable decisions and approved settlements and documents, the enforcement of which is allowed by law. (2) Unless the enforcement order stipulates a deadline for the performance of the obligation, the presumption is that the obligations imposed by the enforcement order are to be fulfilled within 3 days, or if the decision orders eviction from a dwelling, 15 days after the decision becomes final. (3) If the enforcement order specified in Paragraphs (a), (b) or (c) of Subsection (1) orders that the obligation is to be fulfilled by two or more obligors and the performance is divisible, all obligors are bound to perform the obligations in equal shares, unless the enforcement order stipulates otherwise. (4) A court decision on the sale of collateral can be enforced if the decision identifies the obligee and the obligor, the collateral and the amount of the secured claim and any interest and associated dues.*

[139] Civil Code 1964 [Czech Republic] (approximate translation, cit.): Section 39 – *A juridical act is invalid if the content or the purpose thereof violates or evades the law or is* contra bonos mores.

[140] The Supreme Court of the Czech Republic invoked its previous case-law, specifically its decision in Case No. 31 Cdo 958/2012 of 10 July 2013, published under No. 92/2013 in Sbírka soudních rozhodnutí a stanovisek [Court Reports].

[141] The Supreme Court of the Czech Republic invoked its previous case-law, specifically its resolution in Case No. 23 Cdo 4460/2014 of 30 September 2015.

[142] The *ratio decidendi* has been adopted from: Petr Vojtek, *Výběr rozhodnutí v oblasti civilněprávní*, (3) SOUDNÍ ROZHLEDY 90 (2020). Also published under No. Rc 104/2019. *Per analogiam*, see also: Jan Hušek, *Rozhodčí řízení – Doručování – Dohoda o doručovací adrese – Ustanovení osoby pověřené k přijímání písemností*, (10) OBCHODNÍ PRÁVO 361 [title in translation - Commercial Law] (2017).

therein, does not give the liquidator or the creditor the right to claim the same fact as grounds for contesting the existence or amount of the enforceable claim (rebuttal) awarded by the final arbitral award; the fact still constitutes a fact claimed by the debtor in arbitration in terms of Section 199(2) of the Insolvency Act[143] and Section 200(6) of the Insolvency Act.[144/145]

V. Bibliography

Alexander J. Bělohlávek, *Procesní smlouvy a kvalifikace rozhodčích a prorogačních smluv: aplikace hmotněprávní* úpravy *na smlouvy* s *procesním* účinkem *pro futuro* [Title in translation – *Procedural Agreements and Qualification of Arbitration and Choice-of-Court Agreements: Application of Substantive Law to Agreements with Procedural Effects Pro Futuro*], 151(9) PRÁVNÍK 389–418 (2012).

Alexander J. Bělohlávek, *The definition of procedural agreements and the importance to define the contractual*

---

[143] Insolvency Act – Act [of the Czech Republic] No. 182/2006 Coll. (approximate translation, cit.): Section 199 – *(1) The liquidator who rebutted an enforceable claim shall file a lawsuit with the insolvency court within 30 days of the review hearing whereby the rebuttal will be claimed against the creditor who had registered the enforceable claim. The time period shall not expire if the lawsuit is received by the court on or before the last day of the time period. (2) The grounds for rebutting the existence or the amount of an enforceable claim awarded by a final decision of the competent authority may only consist in the facts that were not asserted by the debtor in the proceedings preceding the issue of the decision; however, the rebuttal may not be based on a different legal assessment of the case. (3) In his or her lawsuit under Subsection (1), the claimant may only invoke such circumstances against the rebutted claim for which the claim was rebutted by the claimant.*

[144] Insolvency Act – Act [of the Czech Republic] No. 262/2006 Coll. (approximate translation, cit.): Section 200 – *Rebutting Claim by Registered Creditor – (1) Creditors have the right to rebut in writing claims lodged by other creditors. The rebuttal must contain the same requisite information as a lawsuit under the Code of Civil Procedure and must clearly indicate whether the rebuttal contests the existence, amount or rank of the claim. The rebuttal can only be lodged via a form, the requisites of which are prescribed by implementing legislation. The template of the form shall be announced by the Ministry by means enabling remote access; this service must be provided free of charge. (2) Regard to the registered creditor's rebuttal shall only be had if it contains any and all requisite information and if it is delivered to the insolvency court no later than 3 business days before the day of the review hearing concerning the contested claim; Section 43 of the Code of Civil Procedure shall not apply. After the deadline expires, the asserted grounds for the rebuttal can no longer be changed. If the rebuttal is lodged in such form that requires, at the time of the review hearing concerning the contested claim, the supply of additional information in writing, the submission of an original of the rebuttal or, as applicable, the submission of a written pleading with identical contents, the rebuttal shall be disregarded. (3) If the insolvency court concludes that the registered creditor's rebuttal shall be disregarded, the court shall reject the rebuttal by a decision that can only be made before the end of the review hearing concerning the contested claim. (4) The decision under Subsection (3) shall be served separately on the creditor who contested the claim, the creditor to whom the contested claim belongs, the debtor and the liquidator. The decision can be appealed only by the creditor who contested the claim (lodged the rebuttal). (5) Unless the insolvency court rejects the rebuttal, it shall be deemed, after the decision is made on the method of resolving the insolvency, but no earlier than 10 days after the end of the review hearing, to constitute a lawsuit whereby the creditor lodged his or her rebuttal at the insolvency court vis-à-vis the creditor who had registered the claim. (6) The grounds for rebutting the existence or the amount of an enforceable claim awarded by a final decision of the competent authority may only consist in the facts that were not asserted by the debtor in the proceedings preceding the issue of the decision; however, the rebuttal may not be based on a different legal assessment of the case.*

[145] The case continued with a constitutional complaint, which was rejected as being obviously unsubstantiated. See the resolution of the Constitutional Court of the Czech Republic in Case No. I ÚS 4058/18 of 02 April 2019.

nature of the arbitration clause in international arbitration, in MARIANNE ROTH, MICHAEL GEISTLINGER, YEARBOOK OF INTERNATIONAL ARBITRATION. VOL II, Antwerp / Copenhagen / Zurich / Vienna: Intersentia / Neuer Wissenschaftlicher Verlag (2012), et. 21–50.

LJUBOMÍR DRÁPAL, JAROSLAV BUREŠ ET AL., OBČANSKÝ SOUDNÍ ŘÁD I. §1 AŽ 200za. KOMENTÁŘ [title in translation – CODE CIVIL OF CIVIL PROCEDURE I. SECTION 1 TO 200ZA. A COMMENTARY], Prague: C. H. Beck (2009), et. 706.

JAN DVOŘÁK, JIŘÍ SPÁČIL, SPOLEČNÉ JMĚNÍ MANŽELŮ V TEORII A JUDIKATUŘE [title in translation – MARITAL PROPERTY IN THEORY AND CASE-LAW], Prague: Wolters Kluwer (3rd ed. 2011), et. 20.

Pavel Horák, *Objektivní arbitrabilita – možnosti rozhodčího řízení* [title in translation – *Objective Arbitrability – Possibilities of Arbitration*], 9 BULLETIN ADVOKACIE 23 (2018), as well as 21(7-8) SOUDNÍ ROZHLEDY 280 (2017).

Jan Hušek, *Rozhodčí doložka – Smlouva o poskytování investičních služeb*, (8) OBCHODNÍ PRÁVO 311 [title in translation - Commercial Law] (2016).

Jan Hušek, *Rozhodčí řízení – Arbitrabilita – Zástavní parvo – Uznání závazku – Označení osoby rozhodce*, (9) OBCHODNÍ PRÁVO 319 [title in translation - Commercial Law] (2017).

Jan Hušek, *Rozhodčí řízení – Doručování – Dohoda o doručovací adrese – Ustanovení osoby pověřené k přijímání písemností*, (10) OBCHODNÍ PRÁVO 361 [title in translation - Commercial Law] (2017).

Jan Hušek, *Rozhodčí smlouva (doložka) – Podíl na zisku obchodní společnosti*, (11) OBCHODNÍ PRÁVO 409 [title in translation - Commercial Law] (2017).

Jan Hušek, *Rozhočí doložka – Kauzální pohledávka – Zajišťovací směnka – Pravomoc rozhodce*, 28(9) OBCHODNÍ PRÁVO 35 [title in translation - Commercial Law] (2019).

Judikatura, 27(19) PRÁVNÍ ROZHLEDY 679–681 (2019).

Igor Pařízek, *K dalšímu posunu judikatury u rozhodčích doložek* [title in translation – *Developments in Case-Law Concerning Arbitration Clauses*], (2) PRÁVNÍ ROZHLEDY 61 (2015).

ONDŘEJ RICHTER, VĚŘITELÉ A UPLATŇOVÁNÍ POHLEDÁVEK V INSOLVENČNÍM ŘÍZENÍ. KOMENTÁŘ. [title in translation – CREDITORS AND REGISTRATION

OF CLAIMS IN INSOLVENCY PROCEEDINGS. A COMMENTARY.], Prague: C. H. Beck (2014), et. 115.

Rozhodnutí soudů z oblasti občanského, obchodního a pracovního práva, 1 SOUDNÍ JUDIKATURA 35 (2001).

Karel Svoboda, *K problému doručování rozhodčích nálezů podle § 49 odst. 4 občanského soudního řádu, vyloučí-li rozhodce jejich vhození do schránky I.* [title in translation – *Service of Arbitral Awards pursuant to Section 49(4) of Code of Civil Procedure in Case Arbitrator Prohibits Dropping Arbitral Award in Mailbox I*], 18(6) SOUDNÍ ROZHLEDY 212 (2012).

Tomáš Těmín, *Právní názor účastníků: Pravomoc soudu* [Title in translation – *Legal Opinion of the Parties: Court Jurisdiction*], (3) BULLETIN ADVOKACIE 46-48 (2014). The *ratio decidendi* was formulated by the editorial board of Bulletin advokacie.

Petr Vojtek, *Přehled rozhodnutí NS neschválených v roce 2018 do sbírky soudních rozhodnutí a stanovisek*, (2) SOUDNÍ ROZHLEDY 39-40 (2019).

Petr Vojtek, *Výběr rozhodnutí v oblasti civilněprávní*, (9) SOUDNÍ ROZHLEDY 293 (2017).

Petr Vojtek, *Výběr rozhodnutí v oblasti civilněprávní*, 23(7-8) SOUDNÍ ROZHLEDY 249 (2017).

Petr Vojtek, *Výběr rozhodnutí v oblasti civilněprávní*, (3) SOUDNÍ ROZHLEDY 90 (2020).

Výběr rozhodnutí. *Rozhodčí smlouva, pravomoc soudu a práva související s těmi, kterých se smlouva týká* [title in translation – *Arbitration Agreement, Court Jurisdiction and Rights Associated with Those Covered by the Agreement*], 18(6) SOUDNÍ ROZHLEDY 211-212 (2012).

Výběr rozhodnutí, (7-8) SOUDNÍ ROZHLEDY 235 (2017).

Výběr rozhodnutí, 21(6) SOUDNÍ ROZHLEDY 198-199 (2017).

Výběr rozhodnutí, 21(7-8) SOUDNÍ ROZHLEDY 276 (2017).

Výběr rozhodnutí, (9) SOUDNÍ ROZHLEDY 283 (2017).

Výběr rozhodnutí, 22(11-12) SOUDNÍ ROZHLEDY 371 (2017).

Výběr rozhodnutí, (4) SOUDNÍ ROZHLEDY 117 (2019).

Výběr rozhodnutí, 25(1) SOUDNÍ ROZHLEDY 20 (2019).

Výběr rozhodnutí, 26(11-12) SOUDNÍ ROZHLEDY 377 (2020).

Poland

Czech (& Central European) Yearbook of Arbitration®

Arbitration Case Law 2021

Kamil Zawicki, attorney at law, co-managing partner, Kubas Kos Gałkowski, Bartłomiej Pobożniak, associate, Kubas Kos Gałkowski, Angelika Ziarko, associate, Kubas Kos Gałkowski

Key words:

invalidity of an arbitration clause | signing the arbitration clause on behalf of the company by an unauthorised person | Polish arbitration law

States involved:

[**POL**] – [Poland]

Decision of the Supreme Court of Poland of 10 March 2021, file ref. no V CSKP 64/21

Laws Taken into Account in This Ruling:

Kodeks postępowania cywilnego z dnia 17 listopada 1964 r. [Code of Civil Procedure of 17 November 1964] [k.p.c.] [POL], published in: Dziennik Ustaw [Journal of Laws] 1964, No. 43, item 296, as amended; Articles: 1165(1),[1] 1165(2),[2] 1180(1).[3]

Kodeks cywilny z dnia 23 kwietnia 1964 [The Civil Code of 23 April 1964] [k.c.] [POL], published in: Dziennik Ustaw [Journal of Laws] 1964, No. 16, item 93, as amended; Article 58(1).[4]

Ustawa o Krajowym Rejestrze Sądowym z dnia 20 sierpnia

---

[1]   If an action concerning a dispute covered by an arbitration clause is brought before a court, the court shall dismiss the claim or the motion for non-litigious proceedings if the defendant or a party to the non-litigious proceedings raised a charge of the arbitration clause before entering into a dispute on the merits.
[2]   The provision of paragraph 1 shall not apply where the arbitration clause is invalid, ineffective, unenforceable or no longer in force, or where the arbitral tribunal has decreed its lack of competence.
[3]   The arbitral tribunal may determine its own competence, including the existence, validity, or effectiveness of an arbitration clause. The invalidity or expiry of the underlying contract containing the arbitration clause shall not of itself render the arbitration clause invalid or extinct.
[4]   An act in law that is contrary to the statute or intended to circumvent the statute shall be invalid unless the relevant provision provides for a different effect, in particular that the invalid provisions of the act are replaced by the relevant provisions of the statute.

Czech (& Central European) Yearbook of Arbitration®

1997 r. [National Court Register Act] [u.k.r.s.] [POL], published in: Dziennik Ustaw [Journal of Laws] 1997, No. 121, item 769, as amended; Article 14,[5] Article 17(1).[6]

[Rationes Decidendi]:

9.01. If a contract that includes an arbitration clause in its content is signed by a person who is not and has never been entitled to represent the company, the contract's invalidity shall also extend to the arbitration clause. Therefore, a state court and not an arbitration tribunal is competent to resolve a dispute arising from such a contract. The fact that the person signing the contract was entered in the National Court Register as a member of the company's management board is irrelevant if the entry in the Register was made as a result of unlawful actions.

[Description of the facts and legal issues]:

9.02. In 2004 and 2006, the claimant and the defendant company entered into two share purchase agreements containing arbitration clauses. Any disputes arising from the agreements were to be referred to an arbitral tribunal in Cyprus. The claimant company was represented by N. J. However, N. J. had never been a member of the management board of the claimant company and therefore had no right to represent it. Court in other proceedings established that the resolution of the supervisory board based on which N. J. was appointed to the management board was invalid. However, when the agreements were concluded, N. J. was disclosed in the National Court Register as a member of the management board of the claimant company.

9.03. Under Article 17(1) of the National Court Register Act, it is presumed that the data entered in the National Court Register are accurate. In turn, under Article 14 of the u.k.r.s., an entity obligated to apply for entry in the Register may not invoke in relation to third parties acting in good faith to data that have not been entered in or have been deleted from the Register. Thus, the main legal issue in the case pertained to whether the abovementioned provisions provide a sufficient legal basis to find that concluded agreements and the arbitration clauses contained therein should be considered valid in relations between the parties.

9.04. The claimant company brought an action before the Regional Court. The defendant invoked the arbitration agreement.

---

[5] An entity obligated to apply for entry in the Register may not invoke data which have not been entered in the Register or which have been deleted from it against third parties acting in good faith.

[6] Data entered in the Register shall be presumed to be accurate.

Consequently, the Regional Court rejected the statement of claims under Article 1165(1) CCP by recognising the arbitration clause's effectiveness and the arbitration court's competence to hear the case.

9.05. The claimant and the prosecutor participating in the proceedings filed complaints against the above-indicated decision with the Court of Appeals. The applicants demanded that the Regional Court hear the action.

[Decision of the Court of Appeals]:

9.06. The Court of Appeals shared the opinion of the Regional Court that both the concluded agreements and the arbitration clauses contained therein should be deemed valid between the parties. The Court of Appeals noted that under the law then in force, a legal transaction made by a person who was not authorised to represent the company was, as a rule, invalid and did not produce legal effects.[7] However, the court pointed out that this is not an absolute rule, as the provisions of law, including the u.k.r.s., provide for several regulations aimed at protecting third parties acting in good faith against the effects of invalidity of a legal transaction.

9.07. In the opinion of the Court of Appeals, the provisions of Article 14 and Article 17(1) of the National Court Register Act constituted such grounds in the case under consideration. If the defendant was in good faith, i.e., did not know that N. J. was not a member of the claimant's management board or could not easily obtain this information. Under the National Court Register Act, the claimant could not invoke this circumstance against the defendant. Consequently, in the Court of Appeals' view, in the relationship between the claimant and the respondent, the agreements concluded, and the arbitration clauses contained therein should be deemed valid and effective. Thus, if the defendant invoked arbitration clause, the statement of claims brought before the state court should have been rejected under Article 1165(1) CCP.

[Decision of the Supreme Court]:

9.08. The Supreme Court agreed with the prosecutor's allegations, reversed the appealed decision, and remitted the case to the Court of Appeals for re-examination. In the opinion of the Supreme Court, the application of the provisions of the National

---

[7] The current legal status provides for the possibility of confirmation of such an act [in law] by the company, which results in „repairing" the action. In the absence of confirmation, however, the act remains invalid.

Court Register Act as done by the lower courts was too far-reaching.

9.09. The Supreme Court pointed out that, admittedly, following the case law, a third party may not effectively raise a charge of invalidity of an agreement concluded by a company in a situation where the member of the management board who signed the agreement had been already dismissed (was no longer a member of the management board) but was still listed in the National Court Register. However, according to the Supreme Court, such a situation should be distinguished from the facts of the case in question. N. J. had never been an effectively appointed member of the management board of the claimant company. The entry of N.J. in the National Court Register as a member of the claimant's management board was based on unlawful actions. The provisions of the u.k.r.s. do not extend the protection of good faith to such situations. In the opinion of the Supreme Court, in such circumstances, there are no reasons to protect the effectiveness of an act in law performed by an unauthorised person. The concluded share sale agreements, and the arbitration clauses contained therein, were invalid under Article 58(1) of the Civil Code.

9.10. The Supreme Court noted that the principle of autonomy of the arbitration clause does not speak against the declaration of invalidity of the arbitration clause either. Under the provision of Article 1180(1) CCP, the invalidity or loss of effect of the underlying agreement in which an arbitration clause is included does not by itself mean the invalidity or the clause's loss of effect. However, this provision refers to situations where the reasons for the invalidity or expiration of the agreement are specific to the agreement itself and do not concern the arbitration clause. In the case at hand, the reasons for invalidity of the agreement and the arbitration clause were the same, i.e., an unauthorised person signed the agreements (and arbitration clauses).

9.11. Given the circumstances above, in the opinion of the Supreme Court, there were no grounds to reject the statement of claims in the case. Under Article 1165(2) CCP, a statement of claims is not rejected if the arbitration clause is invalid, ineffective, unenforceable, or expired.

Czech (& Central European) Yearbook of Arbitration®

Key words:
setting aside the award | jurisdiction | right of defence | Polish arbitration law

States involved:
[**POL**] – [Poland]

Judgement of the Supreme Court of 10 May 2021, file ref. no I CSKP 64/21

Laws Taken into Account in this Ruling:
Kodeks postępowania cywilnego z dnia 17 listopada 1964 r. [Code of Civil Procedure of 17 November 1964] [k.p.c.] [CCP], published in: Dziennik Ustaw [Journal of Laws] 1964, No. 43, item 296, as amended; Articles 365(1),[8] 1180(3),[9] 1206(1)(3),[10] Article 1213(1).[11]

[Rationes Decidendi]:

9.12. If the arbitral tribunal dismisses the party's objection to the tribunal's jurisdiction, then the jurisdiction of the arbitral tribunal can be evaluated by the state court in the proceedings initiated by either party under Article 1180(3) CCP. The state court analyzes the effectiveness and the validity, and existence of the arbitration agreement at hand. If the state court renders a final decision as to the jurisdiction of the arbitral tribunal, such a decision is binding during the setting aside proceedings (Article 365(1) CCP). As a result, the party is also precluded

---

[8] A final judgment is binding not only on the parties and the court that issued it, but also on other courts and other state bodies and public administration bodies, and in cases provided for by statute, also on other persons.

[9] The objection referred to in paragraph 2 may be decided upon by the arbitral tribunal in a separate decision. If the arbitral tribunal dismisses the objection in such a decision, either party may, within two weeks after the date of service of the decision to that party, apply to the state court for a decision. The commencement of proceedings before the state court shall not stay the consideration of the case by the arbitral tribunal. The provisions of Article 1207 shall apply to the proceedings before the state court accordingly. The decision of the court may be appealed against.

[10] A party may by way of an application demand that the award of the arbitral tribunal be set aside if:
1) there was no arbitration agreement, the arbitration agreement is invalid, ineffective or has lost its force according to the law applicable to it, (...)
3) the award of the arbitral tribunal relates to a dispute not covered by the arbitration agreement or exceeds the scope of such agreement; however, if the decision on matters covered by the arbitration agreement is separable from the decision on matters not covered by the agreement or exceeding its scope, the award may be set aside only with respect to matters not covered by the agreement or exceeding its scope; exceeding the scope of the arbitration agreement may not constitute grounds for setting aside the award if the party that participated in the proceedings did not raise objections to the determination of claims outside the scope of the clause (...).

[11] The court decides on recognition or enforcement of the arbitral award of the arbitral tribunal or the settlement concluded before the arbitral tribunal at the request of a party. The party is required to attach to the request the original or a copy certified by the arbitral tribunal of the award or settlement concluded before it, as well as the original arbitration agreement or an officially certified copy thereof. If the award of the arbitral tribunal or the settlement concluded before it or the arbitration agreement are not drafted in Polish, the party is obliged to attach a certified translation thereof into Polish.

from raising arguments as to the jurisdiction of the arbitral tribunal in their application on the setting aside of an arbitral award if it fails to do so during arbitral proceedings.

[Description of the Facts and Legal Issues]:

9.13. As to the facts of the case, in 2010, A (seller) and C (buyer) entered into a share purchase agreement. The purchase price was to be paid in four instalments. The sales agreement also contained an arbitration agreement.

9.14. Additionally, in the same year, F and C entered into a surety agreement under which F guaranteed that if C did not pay A the purchase price specified in the sales agreement in part or in full, it would do so. F and C implemented an arbitration agreement therein.

9.15. C did not pay A the fourth instalment of the purchase price. A pursued its claim for payment against C before an arbitral tribunal. In 2011 the arbitral tribunal awarded A its claim. A state court declared the award enforceable against C based on Article 1213(1) CCP.

9.16. In 2013 the state court dismissed C's claim for removing the enforceability clause from the above-mentioned arbitral award. C argued that A is barred from enforcing the arbitral award against it, as A's claim ceased to exist due to the set-off made by C. The courts of two instances did not share C's position and ultimately dismissed its claim.

9.17. Meanwhile, in 2011 A brought a claim against F (a guarantor) before an arbitral tribunal. F objected as to the arbitral tribunal's jurisdiction because there was no arbitration agreement between A and F. The arbitral tribunal dismissed F's objection and declared itself competent to hear the case. The arbitral tribunal found that the arbitration agreement concluded between A and C in the sales agreement. Still, the arbitration agreement also came to effect between A and F.

9.18. F initiated the proceedings before a state court under Article 1180(3) CCP (based on Article 16(3) of UNCITRAL Model Law) and requested that the court resolve the issue of the arbitral tribunal's jurisdiction. In 2014 the court dismissed F's application and decided that the arbitral tribunal had jurisdiction to hear the case. The court of the second instance dismissed F's complaint.

9.19. In 2015 the arbitral tribunal awarded A's claim against F in full. In particular, the arbitral tribunal found that F's set off, which was based on C's claims against A, was unsuccessful. The arbitral tribunal also stated that it was not necessary to take evidence on the circumstances regarding the set-off, because they were irrelevant to the case and also the findings made by state courts in the proceedings between A and C, in which the courts found that the set-off was unsuccessful, were binding onto the arbitral tribunal. Moreover, the arbitral tribunal found that A and F effectively concluded a surety agreement and thus also entered into an arbitration agreement, an element of the surety relationship.

[Decision of the Regional Court]:

9.20.   The Regional Court dismissed F's application for the setting aside of the arbitral award.

9.21.   First, the Regional Court found that the ruling regarding the arbitral tribunal's jurisdiction also implicitly encompasses a ruling on the existence of the arbitration agreement in question. That was because Article 1180(3) CCP assumed that a judgment of a state court confirming the jurisdiction of an arbitral tribunal was the only logical consequence of the existence, validity, and effectiveness of an arbitration agreement. The Regional Court noted that the court, while ruling upon the arbitral tribunal's jurisdiction under Article 1180(3) CCP thoroughly analysed the effectiveness and the existence and validity of the arbitration agreement between A and F.

9.22.   Second, the Regional Court stated that in any case based on Article 365(1) CCP, it was bound by the previous ruling on the arbitral jurisdiction rendered by the state court under Article 1180(3) CCP. Thus, F was precluded from raising objections regarding the jurisdiction of the arbitral tribunal, as this issue was already decided in a final manner. Therefore, the Regional Court dismissed F's arguments as to the lack of jurisdiction of the arbitral tribunal.

9.23.   Third, the Regional Court found that F was not unable to present his case. The Regional Court noted that not taking evidence and dismissing the party's request for evidence did not constitute a deprivation of an opportunity for a party to defend its rights if, as in this case, the arbitral tribunal duly motivated its procedural decision under the accepted procedural rules.

[Decision of the Court of Appeals]:

9.24.   The Court of Appeals dismissed F's appeal and shared the position of the Regional Court.

9.25.   The Court of Appeals adopted the findings of the Regional Court regarding the jurisdiction of the arbitral tribunal as its own. The Court of Appeals also agreed that the court had already determined the issue of the arbitral tribunal's jurisdiction during the proceedings based on Article 1180(3) CCP.

9.26.   The Court of Appeals additionally noted that the arbitral tribunal correctly conducted the evidentiary proceedings. The Court of Appeals found that it was proven by the contents of the arbitral award that the factual circumstances of the case were thoroughly analysed. In particular, the reasoning of the arbitral award proved that the arbitral tribunal also examined the circumstances of F's set-off.

[Decision of the Supreme Court]:

9.27.   In the final judgement of 10 May 2021, file ref. no I CSKP 64/21, the Supreme Court dismissed F's cassation complaint regarding the setting aside application. The Supreme Court shared the views previously presented by the courts in the case.

9.28.   First, the Supreme Court underlined that it was of paramount importance to the resolution of the case to determine whether the courts while examining the application of setting aside of the arbitral award, were indeed bound by the previous court decision in this regard rendered based on Article 1180(3) CCP.

9.29.   The Supreme Court noted that if the arbitral tribunal dismissed the objection raised by a party that the tribunal lacked jurisdiction, a state court might review the legitimacy of this position only in the proceedings initiated based on Article 1180(3) CCP. The purpose of this procedure is to prevent the issue of the arbitral tribunal's jurisdiction from being resolved in a binding manner only after the conclusion of the arbitral proceedings. Therefore, this review mode precludes the possibility of successfully invoking such objection as to the jurisdiction in the party's application for setting aside an arbitral award on the grounds outlined in Article 1206(1)(1) and (3) CCP. That is since the previous ruling binds the court reviewing such an application based on Article 365(1) CCP.

9.30.   The Supreme Court emphasised that the binding ruling on the jurisdiction of the arbitral court based on Article 1180(3) CCP made it impossible (in the absence of new factual circumstances that occurred after the award was issued) – by force of Article 365(1) CCP – to set aside an arbitral award under Article 1205 et seq. CCP. It also made it impossible to set aside an arbitral award due to the absence of an arbitration agreement (Article 1206(1)(1) CCP) as the possibility of invoking this objection was previously exhausted by initiating the proceedings based on Article 1180(3) CCP.

9.31.   Second, the Supreme Court found that irrespective of whether the dismissal of evidentiary requests made by F by the arbitral tribunal could be qualified at all as tantamount to depriving the party of the possibility to defend its rights, still the arbitral tribunal's position on the effectiveness of the set-off was adopted after a thorough analysis and did not justify setting it aside on this basis. The arbitral tribunal based its findings on the set-off not only because F had not proven that the set-off was effective but also on the analysis and interpretation of the agreement between A and C. In the cassation appeal, F had not formulated any new objections that would make it possible to assess and undermine this view. This, in turn, meant that F's argument in this regard was unsubstantiated.

News & Reports

Czech (& Central European) Yearbook of Arbitration®

News & Reports

New Russian Law Allows Russian Companies and Businessmen to Disregard Arbitration Clauses and Jurisdiction Agreements Providing for Consideration of Their Disputes Outside Russia

I. Introduction

The Law of the Russian Federation No 171-FZ dated 08 June 2020 with the long title 'On Introduction to the *Arbitrazh* Procedural Code of the Russian Federation of Amendments In Order to Protect Rights of Physical Persons and Legal Entities with Regard to Restrictive Measures Introduced by a Foreign State, Alliance and (or) Union of States and (or) a State (Interstate) Office of a Foreign State or Alliance and (or) Union of States' (Law No 171-FZ) so far has attracted little attention from the international legal community. Some alerts were published prior to its entry into effect or shortly after.[1] The *Arbitrazh* Procedural Code of the Russian Federation (the APC, which Code was amended by Law No 171-FZ) regulates the procedure of consideration of disputes by Russian commercial courts. Although these are called in Russian, the *arbitrazh* courts, this title does not mean, that those courts may be construed as arbitral tribunals. In theory, any and all amendments to the APC may not have any connection with non-Russian litigation and arbitration proceedings, which proceedings, by definition, are regulated by foreign laws and rules, rather than by the Russian APC. However, in practice this set of amendments to the APC will affect the realities of contemporary litigation and arbitration practice involving Russian citizens and legal entities all over the world.

This article was written with a task to attract the attention of colleagues to Law No 171-FZ, specifically (i) norms of Law No 171-FZ; (ii) litigation and arbitration proceedings which may be affected by the introduction of Law No 171-FZ; and (iii) judicial practice of Russian courts following the introduction of Law No 171-FZ and also recent case law from the UK which considers matters connected with disputes involving sanctioned companies or individuals.

---

[1]   For example: https://info.dechert.com/10/14235/june-2020/russia-has-introduced-a-law-seeking-to-protect-the-rights-of-sanctioned-russians.asp?sid=d3893003-cac0-489f-8047-32a45ced64a9 (accessed on 14 November 2021); https://hsfnotes.com/litigation/2020/06/16/russian-courts-to-have-exclusive-jurisdiction-over-sanctioned-persons/ (accessed on 14 November 2021).

II.   Norms of Law No 171-FZ

Law No 171-FZ introduces to the APC (and Russian legislation in general) the entirely new notion of a person against which there were taken some restrictive measures introduced by a foreign State, alliance and (or) union of States and (or) a State (interstate) office of a foreign State or alliance and (or) union of States. That persons could be (i) Russian citizens (natural persons); (ii) Russian legal entities; or (iii) foreign legal entities which were subjected to some restrictive measures due to their connection with Russian citizens or juridical entities (collectively – "the Affected Persons").

Law No 171-FZ inserts into the APC the new Article 248.1, under which article the State *arbitrazh* courts of the Russian Federation are now granted *the exclusive jurisdiction* to consider any and all disputes involving the Affected Persons and even disputes involving any other persons (including both natural persons and legal entities) to the extent such disputes or their participants are connected with some restrictive measures taken against the Affected Persons. Russian lawmakers send a clear signal to foreign authorities: once you restrict any Russian or its local affiliate, be sure, that all disputes involving that person (even indirectly) shall be decided only by Russian State *arbitrazh* courts, no matter what was written in foreign laws, arbitration rules and even contracts signed by the Affected Person.

Law No 171-FZ also introduces to the APC the new Article 248.2 which allows Russian *arbitrazh* courts to issue *anti-suit injunctions* prohibiting already pending litigation or arbitration abroad or prohibiting the filing of corresponding claims against the Affected Persons with foreign courts or arbitral tribunals. An injunction may be rendered on the motion of the interested Affected Person. The reasons for granting such injunctions are twofold: it could be either the mere fact that the applicant to the Russian *arbitrazh* court qualifies as the Affected Person; or that person's plea of incapability of performance of existing jurisdiction agreement or arbitration clause as a result of the application of some foreign restrictive measures to that Affected Person.

Accordingly, under Law No 171-FZ the Affected Persons are allowed to (i) move their existing disputes which should be submitted to foreign courts and arbitral tribunals to Russian *arbitrazh* courts if the corresponding claim has not been already submitted for consideration of a foreign court or arbitral tribunal; or (ii) seek an anti-suit injunction which prohibits the filing of the corresponding claims abroad or orders termination of ongoing proceedings against the Affected Person. So, the interested Russian counter-party to arbitration or litigation (or a foreign company somehow connected with Russian Affected Persons) may seek the assistance of Russian *arbitrazh* courts and move the ongoing disputes

Czech (& Central European) Yearbook of Arbitration®

just due to the mere fact of issuance of some restrictive measures against it. It is not required to prove that the result of the application of those measures precludes it from the protection of its legal rights in the foreign court or arbitral tribunal.

Of course, that development of Russian law comes at odds with existing standards of international procedural law. One could ask a reasonable question: how could the Russian lawmakers interfere in the jurisdiction of foreign courts, arbitral tribunals and laws?[2] Law No 171-FZ does not provide any answer to that simple question. After the bill was submitted to the Parliament, certain Russian legal experts dared to say that passing of such bill would 'contradict the basic principles of international law'[3] or criticized it at the final stages of its adoption.[4] But the voice of those experts was ignored by the lawmakers and the President of the Russian Federation signed the bill just six days after it was voted on by the Russian Parliament. This would indicate that the Parliament was confident that all foreign judges and arbitrators would obey its laws.

One may also ask, what was the reason to include into this law the norm about the incapability of performance of a jurisdiction agreement or arbitration clause if the mere fact of issuance of restrictive measures is sufficient for protection under Law No 171-FZ? There is no answer to that simple question either. Also there appears to be no restrictive measures introduced by foreign States or organizations which preclude the Affected Person from seeking and obtaining legal advice in civil proceedings. For example, Mr Oleg Deripaska, appearing on the list of Specially Designated Nationals (SDN-list) of the US Government, is still very active in US and British courts and arbitral institutions.[5] One may also recall a recent action of Mr Arkady Rotenberg, another sanctioned person, against certain European banks.[6] There is no doubt, pleading such cases requires sophisticated legal representation, and those sanctioned persons have full access to it, and Russian lawmakers knew that when they adopted Law No 171-FZ.

[2] Russia is not a party to the Lugano Conventions of 1988 and 2007, on Jurisdiction and The Enforcement of Judgments in Civil and Commercial Matters or to the Regulation (EU) No 1215/2012 of the European Parliament and of the Council of 12 December 2012 on jurisdiction and the recognition and enforcement of judgments in civil and commercial matters. It does not have any international treaties with Western countries providing for an equivalent of mechanism of *lis pendens* established by Section 9 of the Regulation (EU) No 1215/2012.
[3] Conclusion of the Committee on legislation of the State Duma of the Russian Federation of 24 June 2019, available at: https://sozd.duma.gov.ru/bill/754380-7 (accessed on 14 November 2021).
[4] The Central Bank Detected a Collission with the Constitution in Amendments providing for the Move of Judicial Disputes to Russia, Interfax, 19 August 2019, available at: https://www.interfax.ru/business/673168 (accessed on 14 November 2021); The Antisanction-Oriented Localization of Justice, Interfax 26 May 2020, available at: www.interfax.ru/russia/710419 (accessed on 14 November 2021).
[5] For example: https://www.usnews.com/news/world/articles/2021-06-14/us-judge-dismisses-russian-tycoon-deripaskas-lawsuit-against-us-filing (accessed on 14 November 2021).
[6] For example: https://www.reuters.com/article/us-finland-russia-sanctions-idUSKBN1ZC19L (accessed on 14 November 2021).

It is noticeable that the norm of the first sentence of paragraph 1 of Article 248.1 of the APC concerning the exclusive jurisdiction of Russian judiciary is formulated in a conditional mode: the *arbitrazh* courts of the Russian Federation are granted the exclusive jurisdiction to consider any and all disputes involving the Affected Persons 'unless it is provided otherwise by an international treaty of the Russian Federation or agreement of the parties providing for consideration of disputes with their participation by foreign courts or international commercial arbitrations located outside the territory of the Russian Federation'. This 'conditional' *unless* wording deserves a commentary. It looks like the exclusive jurisdiction of the *arbitrazh* courts of the Russian Federation does not appear to be in place in case (i) there exists some international treaty of the Russian Federation which confirms the jurisdiction of some foreign court or arbitration; or (ii) there exists some jurisdiction agreement or arbitration clause providing for the jurisdiction of some foreign court or arbitral tribunal. Both grounds for application of that *unless* condition shall be considered.

Russia does not have any international treaty with non-CIS States providing for recognition of the jurisdiction of the foreign courts in commercial matters. That does not prevent a Russian physical person and companies from signing the jurisdiction agreements providing for settlement of certain disputes by non-Russian courts. Those jurisdiction agreements however shall not be based on any international treaty of Russia for the purposes of the 'conditional' wording of Article 248.1 of the APC.

However, Russia participates in the 1958 New York Convention On the Recognition and Enforcement of Foreign Arbitral Awards and the 1961 European Convention On International Commercial Arbitration. Those Conventions seem to be the only international treaties of Russia concluded with non-CIS States providing for recognition of the jurisdiction of foreign arbitral tribunals. Does that mean that this new norm of Article 248.1 of the APC should not be applied in cases in which the Affected Person signed an arbitration clause in accordance with any of those Conventions? *In theory*, the wording of Article 248.1 of the APC would allow an affirmative answer this question. If there exists an arbitration clause which is consistent with the norms of those Conventions, it looks like the *arbitrazh* courts of the Russian Federation are not granted the exclusive jurisdiction to settle disputes involving the Affected Persons. The same should also be the case if there exists an arbitration clause or choice-of-court agreement providing for jurisdiction of a foreign court or arbitration binding the Affected Person – according to the second ground of the *unless* conditional wording of Article 248.1 of the APC.

The positive answer must be qualified with the consideration that Law No 171-FZ allows the Affected Person to seek to move the case to Russia or rendition of an anti-suit injunction in case it believes that the foreign restrictive measures resulted in its existing arbitration clause (or jurisdiction agreement) becoming *incapable of being performed* or created some 'obstacles to access to justice' (paragraph 4 of Article 248.1 of the APC). Accordingly, that conditional *unless* wording of paragraph 1 of Article 248.1 of the APC appears to be useless: paragraph 4 of Article 248.1 of the APC does not use any conditional mechanisms. Unfortunately, the present judicial practice of the *arbitrazh* courts in Russia does not allow to expect that this controversy between two paragraphs of Article 248.1 of the APC shall be interpreted in favour of the validity and support of the corresponding arbitration clause or choice-of-court agreement. Even prior to the enactment of Law No 171-FZ, Russian State *arbitrazh* courts were eager to question the validity of arbitration clauses providing for arbitration abroad. Even standard ICC arbitration agreements at some point in time were construed as incapable of being performed.[7]

Accordingly, the controversial wording of Law No 171-FZ allows the Affected Person to move the dispute to Russia or to obtain an anti-suit injunction from a Russian *arbitrazh* court just because the Affected Person alleges in Russian *arbitrazh* court some difficulties with the defence of its rights abroad. The Law No 171-FZ does not provide for any guidance as to why that person believes that the imposed restrictions compromise its ability to defend its case in a foreign court or tribunal. It is possible that Russian *arbitrazh* courts sometimes being extremely hostile to foreign arbitrations,[8] would not require any proof of incapability of performance of the corresponding arbitration clauses (or jurisdiction agreements) – a simple contention may be enough. There is no doubt, that considering the cases 'moved' to their 'exclusive jurisdiction' under Law No 171-FZ, Russian *arbitrazh* courts shall disregard norms of foreign law about exclusive jurisdiction over those matters by foreign courts. Russian law simply does not provide for any rules for resolving a collision of two simultaneous 'exclusive jurisdictions' in such case.

Moreover, Law No 171-FZ does not set forth any criteria for eligibility of its protection: the description of Affected Person appears to be so broad, that not only persons immediately appearing on the list of

---

[7]   The problem of validity of references to the ICC Arbitration Rules most recently returned in the matter of *Dredging and Maritime Management SA v. Inzhtransstroy* (case No A40-176466/2017), in which *arbitrazh* court judges in 2018 concluded that the standard ICC arbitration clause was incapable of being performed; this was lower *arbitrazh* court judgment was left intact by the Supreme Court of the Russian Federation, although later on in other disputes those standard ICC arbitration clauses were nevertheless considered to be valid. It is important to explain that there exists no case law system in Russia, only selected judgments and mandatory guidance of the Supreme Court are mandatory for the lower courts considering similar matters.
[8]   BOSEMAN LISE (ed.), ICCA INTERNATIONAL HANDBOOK ON COMMERCIAL ARBITRATION, Supplement 116, National Report on the Russian Federation, Kluwer Law International (2021), et. 77.

Specially Designated Nationals (SDN-list) of the US Government (under the CAATSA)[9] or being subjected to Unexplained Wealth Orders issued in the UK[10] – basically anybody who was faced with a routine check of origin of its assets in the West may claim the status of the Affected Person under that law. This is not another problem of legal technique. Setting up those protective measures, the Russian lawmakers were not inclined to limit the number of persons who could seek that protection.

Interestingly enough, the Affected Person is under *no duty* to seek the protection offered to it under Law No 171-FZ. It enjoys the full liberty to proceed with litigation or arbitration abroad and seek enforcement of the corresponding judgment or arbitral award rendered in its favour (Article 248.1(5) of the APC). This is probably the only national law that grants the courts the exclusive jurisdiction to consider certain categories of disputes basing solely on the *discretionary volition* of a private party participating in that dispute.

But what is even more interesting, is that although under Law No 171-FZ Russian *arbitrazh* court may assume exclusive jurisdiction over a foreign dispute *only if* the corresponding claim has not been already submitted for settlement by a foreign court or arbitral tribunal (Article 248.1(3)(1) of the APC), it may *at any time* render an anti-suit injunction which orders termination of ongoing foreign proceedings against the Affected Person. The question remaining is what happens to the claim already submitted to a foreign court or arbitral tribunal prior to such injunction? The Law No 171-FZ is silent on that. Logically, that claim may be moved to the Russian *arbitrazh* court – but Article 248.1(3)(1) of the APC mentioned above clearly and unconditionally forbids consideration of claims being similar to claims which were already submitted for consideration to a foreign court or arbitral tribunal. The similarity of claims wording of Article 248.1(3)(1) of the APC follows the international standard of 'triple-identity' (the same subject matter of relief, the same legal grounds and the same parties).[11] The consequences of the use of an anti-suit injunction under this law is the forbidding of the foreign legal proceedings, while the Russian *arbitrazh* courts are formally proscribed from considering the corresponding claim.

It shall be logical to assume that by issuing an anti-suit injunction prohibiting arbitration or litigation abroad, the Russian *arbitrazh* court hence displays its readiness to have the matter resolved in Russia. That

---

[9]   Countering America's Adversaries Through Sanctions Act (CAATSA) from 02 August 2017 (Public Law 115-44).
[10]   James Collins, Yuri Botiuk, Ben Wells, *Fresh Unexplained Wealth Orders granted following new Court of Appeal ruling*, CIS ARBITRATION FORUM (14 April 2020), available at: http://www.cisarbitration.com/2020/04/14/fresh-unexplained-wealth-orders-granted-following-new-court-of-appeal-ruling/ (accessed on 14 November 2021).
[11]   International Law Association, International Commercial Arbitration Committee, Interim Report on *Res Judicata* and Arbitration (2005), et. 2.

logic was recently confirmed in the English Court of Appeal decision in *Enka* v. *Chubb*[12] explaining that English courts are competent to grant anti-suit injunctions in support of arbitrations seated in London. However, doing so the Court of Appeal presumed that the parties in that matter had impliedly chosen the governing law of the arbitration agreement to be the law of the seat, which was the English law. Although that approach of the English Court of Appeal was later revisited by the Supreme Court,[13] which concluded that unless the parties displayed their intention to submit arbitration to the law which differs from the law governing the contract in general, the arbitration law must coincide with *lex contractus*, no matter which place was selected as the seat of arbitration, English courts clearly displayed their desire to respect non-English jurisdiction of foreign courts and arbitrations. Of course, that constitutes a big contrast to future decisions of Russian *arbitrazh* courts to be based on Law No 171-FZ, allowing Russian judges to assume exclusive jurisdiction over a matter in which the only connection with Russian courts would be a discretional motion of some Affected Person or its affiliate under Article 248.1 of the APC.

Finally, Law No 171-FZ allows the Russian *arbitrazh* court which rendered the anti-suit injunction to award to the Affected Party 'an amount which equals the size of the claim' which was filed abroad against the Affected Person plus the legal costs, in case the foreign opponents disobey Russian court's anti-suit injunction (Article 248.2(10) of the APC). The wording of the law concerning 'an amount which equals the size of the claim' does not help to answer any reasonable questions stemming from that norm: (i) should this amount (which should be construed as a type of a fine) be awarded simultaneously with the anti-suit injunction, or sometime later if the other party to the dispute nevertheless proceeds with foreign litigation or arbitration? (ii) what is the reason to connect the 'amount' of the fine against the foreign party to some non-Russian proceeding for disobeying the anti-suit injunction issued by Russian *arbitrazh* court with the amount of claim filed by that party against the Affected Person with the foreign court or tribunal? (iii) what are the chances to enforce the judgment of the Russian *arbitrazh* court awarding that fine?

The law also does not clarify which Affected Persons are eligible for protection under Law No 171-FZ as a matter of its entry into effect. Does it apply to those, against which the restrictive measures are taken after 19 June 2020 (the date of entry into effect of that law), or just anybody, who believes to be affected by restrictions which were imposed before that date? It is equally unclear, whether Law No 171-FZ concerns legal proceedings in the foreign jurisdictions which take place after 19 June

---

[12]   [2020] EWCA Civ 574, 29 April 2020.
[13]   [2020] UKSC 38, 09 October 2020.

2020, or also cases which were submitted for litigation or arbitration before that date.

III. Litigation and Arbitration Practice Which May Be Affected by the Introduction of Law No 171-FZ

Russian courts, in general, have a very low rating of trust. According to the confidential survey of the Federal Service of Defence (a secret service responsible for the protection of the Russian President and top bureaucrats) among Russian legal experts and businessmen, 66.9 per cent of participants of that survey believe Russian courts to be biased and manipulated.[14] This was solely the opinions of Russian experts and businessmen, and did not include people from the street or foreigners. The problems of the Russian judicial system were even reported at the level of the UN.[15]

Even less is the trust in the Russian judicial system of foreign business owners. For example, in May 2019, the Moscow Times published the article *"Global Automakers Accuse Russian Courts of Graft"* reporting concerns in a complaint by Hyundai, Kia, Mercedes and Jaguar Land Rover that allege that judges in some courts in Krasnodar were using consumer protection claims to scam them out of 200 million roubles (over USD 3 million) in 2016-2018.[16] Most people are aware of the story of Mr Michael Calvey[17] and his colleagues, who invested in Russia for decades and were abruptly jailed after attempting to resolve a dispute with their business counterparty in LCIA.[18] They spent years under arrest in Moscow and were sentenced to criminal punishment although some allege that there was no proof of any harm caused by their actions. Their commercial dispute was moved to the Russian *arbitrazh* courts and promptly decided in favour of Mr Calvey's opponents. The Ruling in *Finvision Holdings* v. *Evision Holdings Limited*[19] was rendered prior to enactment of Law No 171-FZ and may serve as a good example of the justice for foreigners which may be found in Russia.

---

[14]   RBC Magazine, *A closed poll of the FSO showed a record business distrust of the security forces Why entrepreneurs do not believe in the fight against corruption and ask to change the Criminal Code*, RBC Magazine (28 May 2019), available at: https://www.rbc.ru/society/28/05/2019/5cebe7939a794754023bf449 (accessed on 14 November 2021).

[15]   The Report of the Special Rapporteur on Russia on the independence of judges and lawyers, prepared under the auspices of the UN General Assembly in 2014, available at: https://www.refworld.org/docid/5398136a4.html (accessed on 14 November 2021).

[16]   Available at: https://www.themoscowtimes.com/2019/05/29/global-automakers-accuse-russian-courts-of-graft-a65785 (accessed on 14 November 2021).

[17]   Available at: https://www.dw.com/en/russia-us-investor-michael-calvey-receives-suspended-sentence/a-58788389 (accessed on 14 November 2021).

[18]   For example Pierre Briançon, *Ordeal of U.S. investor in Moscow may end — but that wouldn't mean Russia has turned business-friendly*, MARKETWATCH (2020), available at: https://www.marketwatch.com/story/ordeal-of-us-investor-in-moscow-may-end-it-wouldnt-mean-russia-has-turned-business-friendly-2020-02-17 (accessed on 14 November 2021).

[19]   The *Arbitrazh* Court of the Amur District in case No A04-1784/2019, 24 May 2019.

The growing hostility of Russian *arbitrazh* courts to foreign judgments and arbitral awards[20] was even brought to the attention of English courts. For example, in *Tatneft* v. *Bogolyubov & Ors.*[21] Mr Justice Butcher observed that in 2015 Russian *arbitrazh* courts allowed recognition and enforcement in Russia of 7 of 9 of English judgments and awards which were moved for exequatur in that country, in 2016 of 6 of 12, and in 2018 only 2 of 5 (paragraph 22(b)).

There is no doubt that Russian *arbitrazh* courts may be very happy to apply the Law No 171-FZ in the broadest possible manner, not requiring the applicants to prove that they were really restricted in their operations outside Russia, or that their ability to present their cases in foreign proceedings (described as 'obstacles to access to justice' according to the wording of paragraph 4 of Article 248.1 of the APC) was somehow compromised by the restrictive measures taken against them. Even the wording of Article 248.1(3)(1) of the APC that the Russian *arbitrazh* court may assume the exclusive jurisdiction over the foreign dispute *only if* the corresponding claim has not been already submitted for settlement by a foreign court or arbitral tribunal, most likely, will be ignored. In the author's opinion, the task of Law No 171-FZ seems to be to move all cases involving the Affected Persons to Russia, and with that in mind the legal hurdle of an existing, submitted case in all probability, will be ignored or overcome.

Russian *arbitrazh* courts are also known to construe norms of the APC providing exclusive jurisdiction to those courts as a hurdle to international arbitration of those disputes. These problems already occurred to arbitral proceedings in Russia involving arbitration of leases of immovable property and corporate disputes.[22] There is no doubt, that now, based on exclusive jurisdiction provided to Russian *arbitrazh* courts under Article 248.1 of the APC, Russian *arbitrazh* judges may disregard any and all jurisdiction agreements and arbitration clauses referring to consideration of disputes outside Russia.

It is most likely that foreign courts and arbitrators will not be ready to obey the anti-suit injunctions issued by Russian *arbitrazh* courts under Article 248.2 of the APC. It is probable that they will proceed with hearing the merits and rendering the corresponding judgments or awards. But the chances of enforceing those judgments or awards in Russia is very low. According to statistics from 2018, of the seventy-three foreign awards applied in Russia for enforcement in 2018, only thirty-three have been recognized and enforced; in 26 cases, recognition and

---

[20] See, ODA HIROSHI, RUSSIAN ARBITRATION LAW AND PRACTICE, Oxford: Oxford University Press (2020), et. 172.

[21] [2019] EWHC 1400 (Comm.).

[22] Pettibone Peter, *The Nonarbitrability of Corporate Disputes in Russia*, 2(29) ARBITRATION INTERNATIONAL (2013), 263, 264; Konovalova, N. V., Agaltsova, M. V., *Arbitrability of Disputes Arising out of Shareholders' Agreements*, 4 ZAKON 112, 118 (2014) (in Russian).

enforcement was denied; in six cases, the applications were returned for administrative reasons; and eight cases were terminated. Accordingly, of the fifty-nine cases pleaded, recognition and enforcement was granted only in thirty-three, which equals some fifty-five per cent.[23] According to the author's research, the statistics for 2019 and 2020 are no better. Those general figures, in fact, do not reflect that in most serious cases the enforcement of foreign awards in Russia was declined, while smaller ones had a greater chance to succeed. Those statistics, already quite pessimistic, were based on Russian judicial practice before the arrival of Law No 171-FZ which granted Russian *arbitrazh* courts new grounds for exclusive jurisdiction concerning the disputes involving the Affected Persons.

It is important to observe that the situation in which a foreign court or arbitral tribunal proceeds with an already submitted claim despite the anti-suit injunction rendered by a Russian *arbitrazh* court is not the only scenario of legal proceedings possible after the arrival of Law No 171-FZ. Three other scenarios are possible: (i) the claim is submitted to some of the Russian *arbitrazh* courts prior to commencement of proceedings in the foreign jurisdiction and heard by it on the merits; (ii) the anti-suit injunction is issued by a Russian *arbitrazh* court prior to commencement of proceedings in the foreign jurisdiction; and (iii) the claim is submitted to an *arbitrazh* court in Russia after the anti-suit injunction was issued by an *arbitrazh* court. The later scenario is basically contrary to the wording of Article 248.1(3)(1) of the APC mentioned above. That wording forbids to hear the case on the merits in an *arbitrazh* court in Russia if the particular claim is similar to a claim already submitted for consideration to a foreign court or arbitral tribunal. However it sounds unrealistic that a Russian *arbitrazh* court would decline to hear a matter within its exclusive jurisdiction basing on that purely technical inconsistency of the wording of Law No 171-FZ. All four of those scenarios could be extremely unfortunate for the non-Russian counter-parties of the Affected Persons – of course, unless those counter-parties can fully trust the independence and professionalism of Russian judges. Most likely, the Affected Persons who succeed in the move of their cases to Russia would obtain judgments in their favour, no matter, what happens with parallel proceedings in the foreign jurisdiction.

In fact, even prior to the enactment of Law No 171-FZ Russian *arbitrazh* courts already welcomed claims of Russian oligarchs against foreign based companies. For example, in September 2019 it was reported that Mr Oleg Deripaska sued the *Telegraph*, the *Time* and the *Nation* for their allegedly defamatory *foreign* publications in the *Arbitrazh* Court of the Krasnodar Region. On 25 October 2019 that *arbitrazh* court granted in

---

[23] *ICCA International Handbook supra* note 9, at 82.

full Mr Deripaska's claim against the foreign media despite their having no property, no business and no representation in Russia in general or in the Krasnodar Region in particular. The study of that Ruling in that *Deripaska* v. *the Telegraph and ors*[24] reveals that this *arbitrazh* court obviously (i) did not have jurisdiction to consider that claim; and (ii) mixed up incompatible remedies of Russian law concerning rebuttal of defamatory statements and tort. It appears to have just 'rubber-stamped' Mr Deripaska's claim against defendants over whom the court had no jurisdiction under Russian law. Now, after enactment of Law No 171-FZ, the number of judgments rendered by Russian courts against foreign defendants and being similar in their content to this one, has many reasons to multiply. Jurisdiction of Russian *arbitrazh* courts over this type of claims shall be based on the norms of that new law, rather than on the questionable reasoning submitted by Mr Deripaska's lawyers in the *Arbitrazh* Court of the Krasnodar Region.

IV.   Recent Judicial Practice

The first dispute to be considered is the matter *Instar Logistics* v. *Nabor Drilling International Limited*. From the study of judgments rendered by Russian *arbitrazh* courts of fourt instances, the history of the dispute can be summarized as follows. In 2012, the parties concluded a General Contract under which the Russian company *Instar Logistics* undertook to render certain services in Russia to *Nabor Drilling* (one of the world's largest drilling companies). The General Contract was governed by English law and provided for the resolution of disputes under the ICC Arbitration Rules (Russian courts did not specify the seat of the arbitration). Later on, in 2018, *Instar Logistics* was entered on the OFAC's (the U.S. Department of the Treasury's Office of Foreign Assets Control) list of Specially Designated Nationals, and, probably for that reason, *Nabor Drilling* did not pay for *Instar's* services for the amount of some USD 40,000. Using that symbolic debt as a cause, *Instar Logistics* filed a claim with the Russian *Arbitrazh* court of the city of Moscow seeking amendment of the order forms concluded by it with *Nabor Drilling*, and also seeking replacement of applicable English law and ICC arbitration clause with Russian law and Russian *arbitrazh* courts jurisdiction.

Russian *arbitrazh* courts of all three instances granted the claim(s) as far as it concerned the change of applicable law and forum – it is unclear, what happened with the claim of the arrears, maybe it was settled somehow, since no pecuniary relief was awarded. It is interesting, that the first two instances of Russian *arbitrazh* courts granted the claim for the change of applicable law and forum *before* Law No 171-FZ entered into force. The Russian judges did not appear to need it in order to go

---

[24]   The *Arbitrazh* Court of the Krasnodar Region of 25 October 2019, no. A32-43312/2019.

along with with the claimant that after the claimant was entlisted in the list of Specially Designated Nationals, only Russia was a safe place of forum and only Russian law as the applicable law could provide to *Instar Logistics* rights equal to those of *Nabor Drilling*. Only the judgment of the third instance[25] has a reference to Law No 171-FZ which had been entered into force. That was a reference to the claimant's pleading which probably did not affect any conclusions of the court, leaving intact judgments of the two lower instances.

The general conclusion is that these decisions constitute a 'political' case in which the foreign defendant, although vigorously defending, had no chance. Study of all the judgments in *Instar Logistics* v. *Nabor* reflect the judges' support of the dubious position of *Instar Logistics* that it has no ability to defend its case in the course of a foreign arbitration. Further there was no description of any legal arguments of the defendant. This is often the casewhen Russian judges are not at all concerned about their reputation such as in the case of *Deripaska* v. *the Telegraph and ors* in which the foreign defendants decided not to participate. However, not all matters in Russian courts connected with Law No 171-FZ may be construed as 'political'.

Surprisingly enough, other matters connected with application of Law No 171-FZ reveal a different picture. In the case of *Russia Today* v. *Barclays Bank Plc*, Russian *Arbitrazh* courts declined to consider a claim of the Russian State-controlled propaganda agency against an English bank. The reason for that claim was the freezing of the claimant's account in England because the head of the claimant, Mr Dmitry Kiselev, became entlisted in the list of sanctioned persons of the European Union.[26] *Arbitrazh* courts of two lower instances declined to hear the case because of the lack of jurisdiction – also this took place prior to entry into force of the Law No 171-FZ. When the matter reached the third instance of the *arbitrazh* courts (the court of cassation) that law was already in force, but even references to it did not compel that instance to set aside lower courts' judgments.[27]

In a different matter, *Sylovye Mashiny* v. *Vostokenergo*, the Russian company *Sylovye Mashiny* claimed contractual payments from the Ukrainian company *Vostokenergo* for delivery and installation of power equipment in Ukraine. The claim was based on several contracts, all of them governed by the Ukrainian law. Some of the contracts provided for resolution of disputes at the arbitration court of the Chamber of Trade and Commerce of the country of origin of the respondent, other

---

[25] Judgment of the *Arbitrazh* Court of the Moscow Circuit rendered on 06 July 2020, no. A40-149566/2019.
[26] Council Regulation (EU) No 269/2014 of 17 March 2014 concerning restrictive measures in respect of actions undermining or threatening the territorial integrity, sovereignty and independence of Ukraine, available at: https://eur-lex.europa.eu/legal-content/EN/TXT/?uri=CELEX%3A32014R0269 (accessed on 14 November 2021).
[27] Judgment of the *Arbitrazh* Court of the Moscow Circuit rendered on 31 July 2020, no. A40-107039/19.

contracts provided for arbitration based on SCC rules with Russian as the language of the proceeding. The contracts date back to 2013, and in 2014 *Sylovye Mashiny* was entered on US and Ukrainian lists of sanctioned persons. That was the reason for the Ukrainian company to seize payments referring to the event of *force majeur*. Moreover, according to evidence of the claimant, it failed to commence an SCC arbitration because all banks to which it applied in 2019 and 2020 failed to pay the registration fee in favour of SCC, which resulted in termination of the proceedings without to hear the case(s).

A month after the Law No 171-FZ entered into force, *Sylovye Mashiny* submitted its claim to the *Arbitrazh* Court of the city of St. Petersburg. That court heard the claim on its merits, applied particular provisions of the Ukrainian substantive law and granted the claim in full, awarding the respondent to pay some USD 3.6 million; the jurisdiction was based exclusively on the provisions of Law No 171-FZ.[28] By contrast to the matter of *Instar Logistics* v. *Nabor*, in this case, all arguments against the jurisdiction brought by the defendant have been reflected in that judgment and the the issue of jurisdiction has been considered on the merits. Russian judges agreed that on the face of the evidence provided by *Sylovye Mashiny* the claimant had no chance to commence a foreign arbitration.

In *Sovfracht* v. *Mohiddin Daud and Sri Shah* another Russian company appearing on the list of sanctioned persons,[29] called *Sovfracht*, tried to claim damages amounting to over USD 10 million from some nationals of India, seeking the sale of their immovable property in Mumbai. The underlying contract was concluded back in 2004, and it remains unclear, why *Sovfracht* submitted its claim only in 2020 and what was the law applicable to the merits and what was the dispute resolution clause of that contract (if any). Despite the claimant's reference to Law No 171-FZ as a ground for the jurisdiction of the Russian *arbitrazh* courts to hear that claim, the *arbitrazh* courts of two lower instances in Moscow did not find themselves competent to hear a claim against immovable property in India and for that reason they dismissed the claims without hearing them in the merits. But the cassation *arbitrazh* court of the Moscow Circuit reversed those judgments and ordered the first instance to commence a substantive hearing on the merits.[30] By the moment of completion this article, the outcome of the case remains unknown.

Finally, there is the most important case decided under the Law No 171-FZ so far, *Uraltransmash* v. *Pojazdy Szynowe PESA Bydgoszcz Spylka*

---

[28] Ruling of 29 April 2021, no. A56-57238/2020.
[29] OFAC, *Treasury Targets Sanctions Evasion Scheme Facilitating Jet Fuel Shipments to Russian Military Forces in Syria* (26 September 2019), available at: https://home.treasury.gov/news/press-releases/sm785 (accessed on 14 November 2021).
[30] Judgment of the *Arbitrazh* Court of the Moscow Circuit rendered on 25 January 2021, no. A40-201344/2020.

Akcyjna (PESA). The Russian *Arbitrazh* courts of all three regular instances declined to order a stay of the ongoing SCC arbitrations, as such stay was sought by the Russian respondent - the Russian company *Uraltransmash*. The parties entered into a contract for delivery of city tram carriages back in 2013. In 2015 the Polish counter-party *PESA* commenced SCC arbitration. *Uraltransmash* participated in the Stockholm seated proceedings, appointed an arbitrator, submitted arguments based on the legal opinion of Polish law experts, but only in 2018 the *Uraltransmash* applied to the *Arbitrazh* Court of the Sverdlovsk Region of Russia seeking invalidity of the SCC arbitration agreement. In 2020, after entry into force of Law No 171-FZ, *Uraltransmash* submitted a motion to the same *arbitrazh* court seeking an anti-suit injunction by termination of the SCC arbitration under the provisions in particular of Law No 171-FZ. The reason for both actions was the fact that *Uraltransmash* is affiliated with *Uralvagonzavod*, a Russian state-controlled company entlisted in the lists of sanctioned persons of the EU and USA.[31]

The outcome of both applications filed by the against *Uraltransmash* was the dismissal of them. The motion for an anti-suit injunction was declined because the Polish opponent produced evidence displaying that *Uraltransmash* was not at all limited in access to justice in Sweden and it did not experience any difficulties in payment of legal fees to foreign experts (although it declined to pay the arbitration fee to SCC and the fee was paid by the Polish claimant in full). The Russian *arbitrazh* court of the first instance also referred to a letter issued by the SCC explaining that although *Uraltransmash* is affiliated with the sanctioned company *Uralvagonzavod*, there are no legal obstacles in payment of whatever arbitration fees and other legal fees in Sweden.[32] That decision was supported by all three regular instances of the *arbitrazh* courts. Following that outcome of the anti-suit injunction proceedings, *Uraltransmash* withdrew later on its claim for invalidity of the SCC arbitration clause.[33] But later on, on 21 September 2021, the Deputy Chairperson of Supreme Court of the Russian Federation Justice Podnosova suddenly decided to reopen the file and revisit the lower courts' judgments in that matter, despite the Supreme Court already declined to do so on 28 May 2021.[34]

It is important, that information from the SCC about the availability of its services to the sanctioned persons contained in judgment of 24 November 2020 (as cited above) seems to be at odds with the facts described in the *Sylovye Mashiny* v. *Vostokenergo* judgments considered above. Maybe PESA's arbitration commenced in Stockholm in 2015 did

Czech (& Central European)® Yearbook of Arbitration

---

[31]   Council Regulation (EU) no. 833/2014 of 31 July 2014 concerning restrictive measures in view of Russia's actions destabilising the situation in Ukraine.
[32]   Ruling of the *Arbitrazh* Court of the Sverdlovsk Region of 24 November 2020, case no. A60-36897/2020.
[33]   Judgment of the 17th *arbitrazh* Court of Appeal, 17 March 2021, case no. A60-62910/2018.
[34]   Ruling no. 309-ЭС21-6955.

not experience the same problems which allegedly took place in 2019 and 2020 when Sylovye Mashiny wished to file their request for arbitration with SCC. Might it be, Sylovye Mashiny simply did not manage to find a bank encouraged enough to transfer the arbitration fee to the SCC, since the sole reason for Sylovye Mashiny's failure to file its Request for Arbitration with SCC (according to Russian judgments rendered in that matter) was its inability to wire the corresponding funds to Stockholm? The future Supreme Court's judgment in the *Uraltransmash* v. *PESA* may become the first explatation of Law No 171-FZ from the Russia's top judicial instance.

None of those judgments constitutes a source of case law in Russia, but even from this assorted collection of judgments, we can see that if the matter is not considered as a 'political' case (like *Instar Logistics* v. *Nabor*), in ignorance of all arguments of the foreign counter-party, Russian *Arbitrazh* courts, are not always prepared to interfere with the performance of foreign contracts subjected to a foreign arbitration (*Uraltransmash* v. *PESA*) unless there is produced some compelling evidence that the Russian counter-party is unable to pay the arbitration fee due to sanctions imposed on it (*Sylovye Mashiny* v. *Vostokenergo*). Of course, practice in Russian courts may change at any moment, and decisions could vary in this new area of law.

This assorted collection of Russian *arbitrazh* courts' judgments has to be supplemented with two recent English cases connected with the unchartered waters of dealings with sanctioned persons.

The Court of Appeal's decision in *Lamesa Investments Limited v. Cynergy Bank Limited*[35] allowed the English bank *Cynergy* to suspend interest payments to *Lamesa*, a company bysed in Cyprus and owned by Mr VictorVekselberg, a Russian businessman entered on OFAC's list of sanctioned persons.[36] The key issue of that case was the interpretation of one specific clause of the Facility Agreement concluded between the parties which provided that *Cynergy* was not required to make any payment if there is an excuse that 'such sums were not paid in order to comply with any mandatory provision of law'. The Court of Appeal – as its decision is cited above - concluded that 'The drafters knew that the Blocking Regulation regarded US secondary sanctions legislation as imposing a "requirement or prohibition" with which EU parties were otherwise required to "comply"' (paragraph 44). This contractual provision allowed the defendant to win the case (although it promised to keep the money owed to *Lamesa* available for future payment).

The second case is *Banco San Juan Internacional, Inc* v. *Petróleos De Venezuela, S.A.,*[37] in which the court has granted summary judgment in

---

35   [2020] EWCA Civ 821 dated 30 June 2020.
36   OFAC's notice of 06 April 2018.
37   [2020] EWHC 2937 (Comm) dated 04 November 2020.

Czech (& Central European) Yearbook of Arbitration®

favour of a bank seeking to recover payments under Credit Agreements entered into with the Venezuelan state-owned oil and gas company, *Petroleos De Venezuela SA* (PDVSA).The court found that the defaulting borrower had no real prospect of successfully defending the claims on the basis of certain US Sanctions[38] imposed on Venezuela which post-dated the execution of the Credit Agreements. Even if the US sanctions *prima facie* rendered the performance of PDVSA's payment obligations possibly illegal, the High Court of Justice found that PDVSA had an obligation under the Credit Agreements to apply for a licence from the OFAC in order to make the payments, which obligation it had failed to discharge. As an important general ovservation, the court stated that (absent any contractual provision to the contrary or a statutory reversal), the legal burden to obtain the necessary licence to effect the repayments was on PDVSA (as the debtor and the party bound to perform). This case sounds different to *Lamesa* v. *Cynergy*, although probably the Credit Agreement of Banko San Juan did not contain the wording of the *Lamesa's* Facility Agreement ('such sums were not paid in order to comply with any mandatory provision of law') which was laid in the foundation of the earlier case.

For this article, it is important to emphasise that both sanctioned persons appearing in those English cases were perfectly capable of obtaining first-class legal services in England, Mr Vekselberg's *Lamesa* was represented even by two recognized English QCs. It is clear, that according to the account of those two cases (and also the Russian judgments in *Uraltransmash* v. *PESA* considered above – prior to interference of the Supreme Court of Russia) entry to sanctions lists does not prevent the sanctioned person from the possibility of presenting its case before the competent foreign court or arbitral tribunal. The very idea of the impossibility of legal representation was erroneously laid in the foundation of the discussed Law No 171-FZ.

V.   Conclusion

One has to observe that while Russian courts are often hostile to foreign judgments and awards, courts and arbitral tribunals of Europe are still open to Russian litigants, even those entered on some sanctions lists. Moreover, English courts are still welcoming recognition of quite dubious Russian courts' judgments, which was confirmed in *Maximov v. OJSC Novolipetsky Metallurgichesky Kombinat.*[39,40] Western judges

---

[38]   OFAC Executive Order 13850 of 28 January 2019, available at: https://home.treasury.gov/news/press-releases/sm594 (accessed on 14 November 2021).

[39]   [2017] EWHC 1911 (Comm) on 27 July 2017.

[40]   Jonathan Kelly, Adam Grant, Marina Zarubin, *English Court Denies Application to Enforce Russian Arbitral Award Set Aside by Russian Courts*, KLUWER ARBITRATION BLOG (2017), available at: http://arbitrationblog.kluwerarbitration.com/2017/10/09/english-court-denies-application-enforce-russian-arbitral-award-set-aside-russian-courts/ (accessed 14 November 2021).

Czech (& Central European) Yearbook of Arbitration®

feel deep respect for their foreign colleagues. That creates the ideal environment for future judgments of Russian *arbitrazh* courts against foreign parties to be rendered on the basis of Law No 171-FZ and also constitutes additional risks for foreign partners of Russian companies.

[Boris R. Karabelnikov]

is an independent arbitrator and law expert, a former Professor of Law, Moscow School of Social and Economic Sciences, a member of the Court of LCIA (2008 to 2013), a member of the drafting subcommittee of the 2014 LCIA Rules, and a former Judge of the Administrative Tribunal of the European Bank for Reconstruction and Development (2007 to 2018). He is also an Arbitrator of the International Commercial Arbitration Court at the Chamber of Commerce and Industry of the Russian Federation since 2006. Presently he resides in Latvia.[41]

E-mail: bkarabelnikov@mail.ru

---

[41]   The article was written with the use of ConsultantPlus and Garant, leading Russian online legislation databases.

News & Reports

Czech (& Central European) Yearbook of Arbitration®

On Rise of On-Line Arbitration Means in Czech Republic

Arbitration in the Czech Republic has a long history, with the first institutional arbitration centre dating back to 1949. The main aim of arbitration is to provide an efficient alternative for resolving (mostly) commercial disputes. In recent years, the efficiency of arbitration (in fact, the efficiency of all provided services) has gone through a major test with the Coronavirus pandemic. This short report presents the challenges of modern arbitration, as well as a few means that are suitable for the resolution of said challenges.

The main focus of this report is therefore aimed at the Arbitration Court attached to the Czech Chamber of Commerce and the Agricultural Chamber of the Czech Republic (hereafter the "Czech Arbitration Court" or "CAC"). The CAC is the Czech arbitration institution with the longest history of institutional arbitration in the Czech Republic (the predecessors of the CAC date back to 1949, when the Arbitration Court attached to the Czechoslovak Chamber of Commerce was established).

Both domestic and international arbitration have faced the biggest issues in respect of the pandemic – discontinued oral hearings, the closing of offices due to travel restrictions and so on. All of the mentioned problems caused the prolongation of proceedings. International arbitration was in even greater danger than domestic, when arbitral tribunals were composed of members from all around the world. Certainly, practices that have been developed in such long-distance international arbitration had a major influence on the modernisation and electronisation of arbitration proceedings.

Arbitration provides an alternative to common court proceedings for several reasons, but certainly the length of the proceedings is one of the biggest advantages that arbitration may provide. Arbitration is deemed quicker and more efficient than the usual common court proceedings, and is also less formal – which is why modern electronic means of communication are a great fit for arbitration. It is nevertheless true that even such modernisation comes with pitfalls with respect to the security of communication, problems arising from non-personal hearings (for example, the examination of a witness) or a lack of technical means of the parties.

The Czech Arbitration Court introduced its first Rules for on-line arbitration back in 2004. The Additional procedures for on-line arbitration[1] (hereafter "on-line rules") present an alternative to the

---

[1]   Available at: https://en.soud.cz/rules (accessed on 09 September 2021).

"standard" type of arbitration, where the whole procedure is conducted, and the dispute is resolved via the Internet. The CAC delivers approximately 30 awards in on-line arbitration each year. On-line arbitration carries many advantages, such as lower fees for arbitration and costs of representation (due to its simplified process), time efficiency and flexibility.

On-line arbitration is nevertheless not well suited to all commercial disputes. It is aimed at straightforward cases where the arbitrator is able to reach a decision based only on the written submissions of the parties, as well as written evidence. It is not possible to hold an oral hearing (even an electronic one) under the on-line rules. If the case does not fall within the scope of on-line arbitration (either the parties are not able to communicate on-line or the merits of the proceedings require further and more thorough discussion), the arbitrator may, at their discretion, revert the proceedings back to classical arbitration under the Rules of The Arbitration Court Attached to the Czech Chamber of Commerce and the Agricultural Chamber of the Czech Republic[2] (hereafter the "Rules").

The entire dispute under on-line rules is conducted via an on-line platform for arbitration, where submissions and evidence are filed. Any required communication between the parties and the administrative centre of the CAC takes place via email. The CAC operates such on-line systems both for on-line arbitration and for alternative domain name dispute resolution. The alternative resolution of domain name disputes enjoys great popularity worldwide, and serves as the prototype for on-line dispute resolution in straightforward cases. The CAC is a provider of Uniform Domain Name Dispute Resolution concerning generic domain names (such as .com, .net, .org, .info), as well as .EU and .CZ alternative dispute resolution.[3]

The CAC addressed the situation concerning the pandemic in an Annex to the on-line rules effective since April 20, 2020 (Supplement to the Rules for Online Arbitration).[4] The change in the tariff of the on-line rules arises from issues connected with the national lockdown of commercial shops and service providers. All such facilities were forced to close their business areas, but were still required to pay rent and service charges. Disputes arising out of such contracts were submitted for discount in on-line arbitration. The CAC believes that this change might facilitate the disputes connected with Covid-related business rent problems in future.

---

[2]   Available at: https://en.soud.cz/rules/rules-consolidated-text-1st-december-2020 (consolidated Rules currently in effect) (accessed on 09 September 2021).

[3]   More information available at: https://adr.eu/ (accessed on 09 September 2021).

[4]   Available at: https://en.soud.cz/rules/tariff-of-arbitration-costs-for-on-line-disputes-2020 (accessed on 09 September 2021).

Arbitral proceedings under the on-line rules remain only a small part of the CAC's case load. That is why the pandemic influenced most of the proceedings before the CAC. In spring 2020, all oral hearings were discontinued due to the lockdown in the Czech Republic. Even though the Czech Arbitration Court maintained the operation of its administrative centre, all proceedings were postponed until national pandemic restrictions would allow gatherings of people.

In this regard, the Czech Arbitration Court had to adjust its Rules with an additional section allowing online oral hearings (until this change, some of the hearings – for example, preparatory hearings – were held on-line). The Rules therefore include Section 28a, which enables a remote oral hearing for arbitration:

(1) The arbitral tribunal may invite the parties to state, within a period that shall not be less than 10 days from the delivery of the summons, whether they agree that the oral hearing in the case according to Section 28 would be replaced by an oral hearing held remotely by technical means (hereinafter a "remote oral hearing"). Should a party fail to express its position within the stipulated period of time, it is assumed that the party agrees to the remote oral hearing.

(2) A remote oral hearing cannot be held if either party expressly disagrees with the remote oral hearing. This is without prejudice to the possibility of inviting the parties under the procedure according to Paragraph (1) to agree to the remote oral hearing repeatedly in the further course of the proceedings.

(3) Details on the holding of remote oral hearings are set out in the Additional Procedures for Holding the Remote Oral Hearings.

(4) The provisions of these Rules regulating oral hearings changed to remote oral hearings shall apply adequately, unless provided otherwise in the Additional Procedures for Holding the Remote Oral Hearing.

Paragraph 1 - The Czech Arbitration Court chooses the opt-out method for the remote oral hearing. The main reason is the right of the parties to choose their preferred form of proceedings. Nevertheless, the failure to respond to the invitation regarding the remote oral hearing from the arbitral panel is deemed to be the consent of the party.

In this regard, the CAC chooses a more conservative approach in ordering a remote hearing. For example, the Austrian practice (confirmed by a common court judgement) allows a remote hearing to be held even when a party refuses such an option.[5] Behind the CAC's approach, there

---

5   Maxi Scherer, Franz Schwarz, Helmut Ortner, J. Ole Jensen, *'First' Worldwide, Austrian Supreme Court Confirms Arbitral Tribunal's Power to Hold Remote Hearings Over One Party's Objection and Rejects Due Process Concerns*, KLUWER ARBITRATION BLOG (24 October 2020), available at: http://arbitrationblog. kluwerarbitration.com/2020/10/24/in-a-first-worldwide-austrian-supreme-court-confirms-arbitral-tribunals-power-to-hold-remote-hearings-over-one-partys-objection-and-rejects-due-process-concerns/ (accessed on 09 September 2021).

is the belief that in case of strong reasons of the parties, the arbitral tribunal shall hear them personally.

Paragraph 2 - Even if the party refused the remote oral hearing, there is a possibility (upon an additional invitation of the arbitral tribunal) for reconsideration of the party. This provision provides the ability to react to the changed circumstances in the proceedings. The arbitral tribunal, however, may never overrule an express refusal of the party to the arbitral proceedings.

Paragraph 3 - Additional Procedures for Holding a Remote Oral Hearing[6] (hereafter "Additional Procedures") implement special principles connected to the specifics of a remote oral hearing. The procedure for the arbitral panel's invitation for the parties' consent to hold a remote oral hearing is presented in detail in Section 2 of the Additional Procedures. These rules also set out the types of remote oral hearing as follows:

a) All parties to the proceedings and the arbitral tribunal are only present at the same time by technical means;

b) The arbitral tribunal is present in person and all parties are only present at the same time by technical means; and

c) Only one of the parties or only one of the members of the arbitration tribunal are present in person, while the remaining parties are only present by technical means (this situation requires another express consent of all parties).

The Additional Procedures also outline basic provisions for the summons to the remote oral hearing and for the technical requirements and support provided by the CAC. The collection of evidence during an on-line hearing is primarily the responsibility of the arbitral tribunal. The Additional procedures require documentary evidence to be submitted correctly to the case file, and allow the questioning of a witness, expert or another person based on the decision of the arbitral tribunal. Section 7 establishes the specifics for the minutes of remote oral hearings.

Paragraph 4 - The main aim of the on-line (or remote) oral hearing is to enable arbitration to proceed even when there are objective obstacles to holding an in-person oral hearing. The on-line hearing is founded on the same principles and therefore requires adherence to the same provisions as in-person oral hearings.

It is possible (especially in international arbitration) that the remote form of oral hearing will become the preferred method for conducting proceedings. Even if this type of electronisation of arbitration may in future be proven valid, there are certain practical issues to be overcome in this area:

6 Available at: https://en.soud.cz/rules (accessed on 09 September 2021).

Proper identification of the parties to the proceedings – online arbitration to some extent requires fairness of the parties. The CAC's Additional Procedures require a video transmission to be available at all times during the remote oral hearing. The guidelines for the arbitrator for holding a remote oral hearing require the proper identification of the parties. The video conference shall only be available once the party signs in.

The **requirement of fairness** is valid as well for the witnesses and experts that are heard before the arbitral tribunal. There should be no other person present in the room with the witness, and the video and audio transmission shall be available throughout the entire process. The **examination of a witness** is a challenging aspect of arbitration, even in standard in-person oral hearings. A fraction of arbitrators therefore refuses to examine witnesses remotely due to the specifics of arbitration.

Arbitration in the Czech Republic is also protected by strict **confidentiality** and by the private nature thereof. No video or audio recordings shall be made without the express consent of the arbitral tribunal. Even the CAC does not record oral hearings, unless specified otherwise by the arbitral tribunal (and with the consent of the parties).

Of course, **security and technical issues** remain big challenges for the modernisation and electronisation of arbitration.

So where does the future of arbitration lie? Will it be an on-line process with remote oral hearings, or will it be the traditional form of arbitration that was mostly known before the coronavirus pandemic? Although the situation in the Czech Republic is still quite dynamic regarding the epidemiologic situation, arbitration has returned to its traditional form for the most part. Recent events have nevertheless changed the way we conduct arbitration, and I believe that other changes are due. Therefore, traditional arbitration is slowly incorporating new procedures and technologies leading to an era of modernisation. Arbitration needs to be prepared for whatever the future may hold, and partial electronisation is certainly a step in the right direction.

[*Lenka Náhlovská*]

secretary of the Arbitration Court attached to the Czech Chamber of Commerce and the Agricultural Chamber of the Czech Republic.

E-mail: nahlovskalenka@soud.cz

News & Reports

The 2021 Rules Revision of the Vienna International Arbitral Centre

At the Vienna International Arbitral Centre (VIAC), 2021 has been a year full of changes. VIAC revised its rules and entered new fields of arbitration.

On 01 July 2021, the new stand-alone Vienna Investment Arbitration Rules (VRI) and the Vienna Investment Mediation Rules 2021 (VMRI) came into force. Furthermore, the VIAC has taken the opportunity to update the Vienna Rules (VR) and the Vienna Mediation Rules (VMR) for commercial disputes to address a number of points arising from international arbitration practice over the past few years and to open up a new field of business, namely disputes relating to succession. Both sets of rules apply to all proceedings commenced after 30 June 2021.

The last reform of the VIAC Rules dates to 2018. The 2018 Vienna Rules have been well received in practice and have proven their worth. The new rules for investment disputes, largely follow the well-tried concept of the standard rules for commercial disputes. However, to address the special features of investment arbitration proceedings, including the involvement of sovereign parties and the implication of public interest and public policy issues, the investment rules entail several modifications and innovations.

Working groups, which consisted of members of the Secretariat, the VIAC Board, the VIAC Advisory Boards and other relevant stakeholders were set up in mid-2020 to draft and revise the VIAC Rules. The working groups have met regularly over the course of 2020-2021 to discuss how to codify existing practices, streamline procedures, and respond to users' demands. On 02 June 2021, the Extended Presiding Committee of the Austrian Federal Economic Chamber approved the amended version of the rules effective from 01 July 2021. The latest version of the commercial rules and the investment rules are available on the VIAC website.[1]

This article comments on the changes of the Vienna Rules and highlights the key features of the Vienna Investment Arbitration Rules.

Czech (& Central European) Yearbook of Arbitration®

---

[1] Available at: https://www.viac.eu/en (accessed on 27 October 2021).

I. VIAC Rules of Arbitration and Mediation 2021

The revised Vienna Rules for commercial disputes were designed to improve the efficiency of the proceedings and are in line with the latest trends in international arbitration.

The Working Group for the Vienna Rules consisted of members of the VIAC Board and the Secretariat (in alphabetical order: Claudia Annacker, Alice Fremuth-Wolf, Günther Horvath, Johanna Kathan-Spath, Paul Oberhammer, Patrizia Netal, Nikolaus Pitkowitz, Dietmar Prager, Lucia Raimanova, Stefan Riegler, Franz Schwarz, Irene Welser). In addition, another Working Group had been set up to develop an Annex 6 for disputes relating to succession, which consisted of members of the Secretariat (Stephan Karall, Alice-Fremuth-Wolf) and members of the VIAC National and International Advisory Boards, representatives of notary publics and other important stakeholders in this field (Elisabeth Kahler, Werner Jahnel, Christian Koller, Michael Nueber, Martin Schauer, Elke Willi, Brigitta Zöchling-Jud).

The changes in the commercial rules are described below. All article references in this Section I are to these rules.

I.1. Article 1

Article 1 now expressly authorizes VIAC to administer commercial proceedings, investment proceedings; to act as appointing authority or administering authority in *ad hoc* proceedings; to administer proceedings based on unilaterally foreseen arbitration agreements (including disputes relating to succession following the newly added Annex 6).

I.2. Electronic Services

The VIAC administers all new proceedings through an electronic case management system (the VIAC Database). In addition, since March 2021, the VIAC Portal is available to parties and arbitrators for the secure exchange of case-related documents. The VR provide for the submission of the statement of claim (in addition to a hard-copy version) and the transmission of documents in electronic form (Articles 7, 12, and 36 paragraph 5 VR and VRI, and Article 3 of the respective mediation rules). Furthermore, Article 30 paragraph 1 VR and VRI and Article 9 paragraph 3 VMR and VMRI clarify that hearings/sessions may be conducted in person 'and by other means' (e.g., remotely via videoconferencing technology, to which the 'Vienna Protocol – A Practical Checklist for Remote Hearings'[2] may be of helpful guidance).

I.3. Third-Party Funding

The new rules contain a separate provision on third-party funding (TPF) – which is limited to disclosure requirements. Thus, Article 6 in paragraph 1.9 now includes a definition of the term according to which TPF:

> refers to any agreement entered into with a natural or legal person who is not a party to the proceedings or a party representative (Article 13), to fund or provide any other material support to a party, directly or indirectly financing part or all of the costs of the proceedings either through a donation or a grant, or in exchange for remuneration or reimbursement that is wholly or partially dependent upon the outcome of the proceedings or in return for any premium payment.

Article 13a paragraph 1 requires parties to disclose both the existence of TPF and the funder's identity in the statement of claim, in the answer to the statement of claim, or immediately upon concluding a third-party funding agreement. Paragraph 2 of Article 13a stipulates that if a party discloses TPF prior to the constitution of the arbitral tribunal, any arbitrator (nominated/appointed) shall be informed of such disclosure to complete the arbitrator's declaration. The above requirements for TPF to be disclosed early are to ensure the independence and impartiality of arbitrators.

I.4.   Encouragement of Settlement

In order to enable and encourage a settlement in arbitration proceedings, it is now clarified in Article 28 paragraph 3 that the arbitral tribunal is entitled to assist the parties in their endeavors to reach a settlement at any time during the proceedings.

I.5.   Time Limit for Rendering the Award

A further amendment to increase the efficiency of the proceedings has been included in Article 32 paragraph 2, which now foresees an explicit time limit for the rendering of the award. According to the new rule, the award shall be rendered no later than three months after the last hearing or the filing of the last authorized submission. The Secretary General

---

[2]   Available at the VIAC website: https://www.viac.eu/en/investment-arbitration/measures-re-covid-19 (accessed on 27 October 2021).

may extend this period upon reasoned request or on its initiative. Exceeding the time limit for the award will not render the arbitration agreement invalid or deprive the arbitral tribunal of its jurisdiction.

I.6. Disclaimer

There has been a minor amendment to the disclaimer provision in Article 46 paragraph 1. The previously applicable limitation of liability of the arbitrator, the tribunal secretary, the Secretary General, the Deputy Secretary General, the Board and its members, as well as the Austrian Federal Economic Chamber and its employees, has been replaced with 'unless such act or omission constitutes willful misconduct or gross negligence' (before: 'to the extent legally permissible'. The same change was made in the VMR for mediators and is mirrored in the investment rules (VRI and VMRI).

I.7. Costs

The cost-related provisions (Articles 38, 42, and 44) have been amended to allow for more flexibility. First, the arbitral tribunal may now, at any stage of the arbitral proceedings, at the request of a party, make a decision on costs pursuant to Article 44 paragraph 1.2 and 1.3 (i.e., all costs except for the administrative and arbitrator's fees) and need not wait for the final award in this respect (Article 38 paragraph 3). Secondly, in determining the advance on costs as well as the arbitrator's fees, the VIAC Secretary General now has greater flexibility to address the high complexity of proceedings, especially in multiparty scenarios.

The schedule of fees in Annex 3 was also slightly adjusted. While the registration fee and the administrative fees for lower amounts in dispute remained unchanged, the administrative fees for amounts in dispute above EUR 100,000 and the arbitrators' fees for amounts in dispute above EUR 200,000 have been raised. The increase reflects the often higher complexity of proceedings with a higher value as well as the extended electronic services of VIAC (new file sharing platform, electronic case management database, etc.). Nonetheless, VIAC remains very attractive for parties in terms of costs compared with other institutions while at the same time ensuring that arbitrators are remunerated fairly.

I.8. VIAC as Appointing and/or Administering Authority

Arbitration proceedings that do not benefit from institutional support (ad hoc proceedings) are often conducted under the UNCITRAL Arbitration Rules. VIAC offers its services as appointing authority (under

Annex 4 to the VR) or as administering authority (under Annex 5 to the VR) in *ad hoc* proceedings and assists the parties in a quick and cost-efficient resolution of their dispute, e.g., by helping in the organization of hearings or the appointment of arbitrators. The new Annexes are also included in the investment rules and provide a detailed but precise framework for such requests, including fees.

I.9. Annex 6

A new Annex 6 contains supplementary rules for disputes relating to succession, which consider the unique characteristics of arbitration proceedings foreseen in a disposition of property upon death. A special model clause was added to the set of model clauses in Annex 1.

II. VIAC Rules for Investment Arbitration and Mediation 2021

VIAC already had some prior engagement with investment disputes by administering contract-based disputes involving state entities and assisting *ad hoc* tribunals in investment disputes. This was possible and permissible under Article 1 paragraph 1.3 VR 2018 and the old Annex 4. Since VIAC was already well-recognized as a neutral forum in the CEE/SEE region, developing stand-alone investment rules was a natural further step for VIAC; in particular, to address demands for an institution administering investment disputes with expertise in that very region. The VRI, in tackling two of the major concerns of users of investment arbitration – duration and costs – sought to plug a gap in the market by providing an affordable and efficient alternative, particularly for resolving small and medium-sized disputes. The VRI may well be adopted in investment treaties or statutes as well as contracts between investors and States, State-owned entities, or intergovernmental organizations (against the backdrop of *Achmea*, particularly where one or both parties are from outside the EU).

VIAC Board member Claudia Annacker chaired the Working Group for the Vienna Investment Arbitration Rules. It consisted of representatives of the VIAC Board and the Secretariat (in alphabetical order: Alice Fremuth-Wolf, Günther Horvath, Johanna Kathan-Spath, Dietmar Prager, Lucia Raimanova, Franz Schwarz, Nathalie Voser).

The key aspects of the investment rules are described below. All article references in this Section II are to these rules.

II.1. Scope of Application and Administration by VIAC

The VRI apply to disputes involving a State, a State-controlled entity or an intergovernmental organization that arise under a contract, treaty, statute or other instrument (Article 1 paragraph 1) where the agreement to submit a dispute to arbitration in accordance with the VRI was expressed (or an offer contained therein that is later accepted by the other party). Unlike with ICSID arbitration, under the VRI there are no objective jurisdictional requirements regarding the parties and the nature of the dispute; parties are entirely free to decide for themselves whether a dispute is an investment dispute that they wish to resolve under these rules. Article 1 paragraph 1 attempts to reduce the time and resources often expended on jurisdictional battles in investment disputes.

The preamble to the investment rules also specifies that

> [w]here the parties to a dispute have previously consented, or a party has previously offered to consent, to arbitration in accordance with rules of arbitration other than the Vienna Investment Arbitration Rules [for example, ICSID Arbitration Rules], a dispute may be submitted instead to arbitration in accordance with the Vienna Investment Arbitration Rules if the parties subsequently expressed their agreement to submit their dispute to arbitration in accordance with the Vienna Investment Arbitration Rules.

While an agreement to apply the VRI implies that the parties agree to the administration by VIAC (Article 1 paragraph 2), the VIAC Board may refuse to administer the proceedings if the arbitration agreement deviates fundamentally from and is incompatible with the VRI (Article 2).

II.2. Waiver of Immunity

Article 4 provides for a waiver of immunity from jurisdiction in respect of proceedings relating to the arbitration to which a State-related party might otherwise be entitled. The provision further clarifies, reflecting the position in most jurisdictions, that this waiver does not include a waiver of immunity from enforcement of an arbitral award, which 'must be expressed separately'.

II.3. Third-Party Funding

For the definition of TPF in Article 6 paragraph 1.11 and comments on Article 13a paragraph 1 and 2, which are identical to the provisions in the commercial rules, see point I.3. above.

The investment rules expressly foresee the tribunal's discretion to order the disclosure of 'specific details of the third-party funding arrangement and/or the third-party funder's interest in the outcome' as well as whether the funder has undertaken to cover any adverse costs liability (Article 13a paragraph 3). The tribunal's power to order the disclosure of 'specific details' of the funding arrangement (and not the whole agreement) is meant to tackle potential implications for security for costs and allocation of costs. However, the mere existence of a TPF arrangement does not automatically justify granting security for costs.

II.4. Joinder, *Amicus Curiae* and Consolidation

For contractual investment arbitration proceedings, the investment rules provide for the possibility of a third party joining the arbitration proceedings, just like in commercial arbitration (Article 14). The VRI do not lay down any particular conditions for or limitations on joinder but leave it to the tribunal to decide, upon hearing all parties (including the third party to be joined) and considering all relevant circumstances, whether a joinder is warranted in a given case.

For treaty and statute-based arbitrations, Article 14a paragraph 1 includes a provision allowing the tribunal to decide whether *amicus curiae* submissions on factual or legal issues by non-disputing parties should be accepted. Article 14a paragraph 2 grants non-disputing treaty parties a right to make written submissions on the interpretation of the applicable treaty. The tribunal may also invite such submissions on its own initiative.

Under Article 15, the VIAC Board may consolidate two or more proceedings pending before VIAC – irrespective of whether they arise under a contract, treaty, statute or other instrument and whether they involve the same parties, the same legal relationship or the same arbitration agreement – if the place of arbitration is the same and the parties agree to consolidation or the same arbitrator(s) was/were nominated or appointed.

The VRI's provisions on joinder, *amicus curiae* and consolidation thus give tribunals and the VIAC the flexibility and discretion needed to resolve complex, multi-party investment disputes in a fair and (cost-) efficient manner.

II.5. Constitution of the Arbitral Tribunal

Unless otherwise agreed by the parties, the investment arbitral tribunal shall consist of three arbitrators, provided that the amount in dispute exceeds EUR 10 million. Where the amount in dispute is less than EUR 10 million, the proceedings shall be conducted by a sole arbitrator, again with the possibility for the VIAC Board to deviate if the complexity of the case or other circumstances do so require (Article 17 paragraph 2). There is also a special feature for the appointment of the chairperson by the Board. In this case, the Secretary General shall transmit a list of candidates for appointment as chairperson to the parties and allow them to strike one name from the list and rank the remaining candidates in order of preference. The Board shall appoint the candidate with the best ranking. If two or more candidates share the best ranking, the Board shall select one of them (Article 17 paragraph 6).

Article 17 paragraph 8 expressly provides that all arbitrators must have nationalities different from those of the parties unless otherwise agreed. Furthermore, a party may request in the statement of claim or in the answer to the statement of claim that the VIAC Board (instead of the co-arbitrators) select the chairperson (Article 17 paragraph 5).

II.6. Duration of Proceedings, Early Dismissal and Time Limit for Rendering the Award

Managing the length of investment arbitrations was specifically highlighted as one of the guiding principles underpinning the drafting of the investment rules. The investment rules contain several provisions that aim to encourage the efficient and speedy resolution of the dispute. According to Article 32 paragraph 2, tribunals must render awards no later than six months after the last hearing or the filing of the last authorized submission. A provision on early dismissal (Article 24a) allows the arbitrator to expeditiously dismiss claims, counterclaims, and defenses, if they are manifestly outside the tribunal's jurisdiction, manifestly inadmissible or manifestly without legal merit. Jurisdictional objections must be raised no later than the first pleading on the merits following the constitution of the tribunal (Article 24 paragraph 1). Furthermore, under Article 45, parties may opt-in for the expedited proceedings also in investment disputes.

II.7. Limited Transparency

Unless the parties have agreed otherwise, arbitration proceedings remain confidential. However, as public interests are at stake in investment proceedings, a certain degree of transparency and inclusion of third parties may be required. Therefore, the VRI expressly provides for joinder and *amicus curiae* (see point II.4.), as well as the publication of limited procedural details and anonymized excerpts of awards. Indeed, the parties may also agree to opt-in for the UNCITRAL Rules on Transparency in Treaty-Based Investor-State Arbitration. VIAC would then refer the parties to the UNCITRAL Transparency Registry.

II.8. Costs

One of the most appealing features of VIAC Investment Arbitration is its comparatively low costs. There is no separate fee schedule for investment proceedings, i.e., the same rates apply as in commercial proceedings. The amount of the registration fee, and the administrative and arbitrators' fees depend on the amount in dispute (see Annex 3, containing the schedule of fees). It is noteworthy that the registration fee is significantly lower than the registration fees charged by other investment arbitration institutions. The overall costs of VIAC investment arbitration can be estimated using the online cost calculator on the VIAC website.[3]

In addition, as in the commercial rules, the VRI also explicitly affirm the power of the tribunal to order security for costs under Article 33. A tribunal sitting under the VRI will only require showing cause that the 'recoverability of a potential claim for costs is, with a sufficient degree of probability, at risk'. TPF is not in itself sufficient for a security for costs order under the VRI – see point II.3. above.

II.9. Vienna Investment Mediation Rules

As with the Vienna Rules for commercial disputes, the investment rules have been complemented by mediation rules (Part II), which may be applied independently of or in conjunction with investment arbitration proceedings. In the previous and still pending discussions of the UNCITRAL Working Group III on Investor-State Dispute Settlement Reform, increasing interest is being placed on investor-state mediation. Therefore, and to meet possible demands for hybrid proceedings such as Arb-Med-Arb in investment disputes, it was decided to add mediation rules also to the VRI and provide for a special model clause.

II.10. VIAC as Appointing and/or Administering Authority

Also, in investment disputes, VIAC may be called upon to act as appointing authority (under Annex 4 to the VRI) or as administering authority (under Annex 5 to the VRI) in *ad hoc* proceedings (see point I.8. above).

Overall, the updates to the Vienna Rules aim to improve the efficiency of the proceedings and are in line with the latest trends in international arbitration while maintaining the well-known and approved structure of the rules. VIAC is one of the first arbitral institutions to publish a separate, dedicated set of procedural rules governing investment

---

[3] Available at: https://www.viac.eu/en/investment-arbitration/cost-calculator (accessed on 27 October 2021).

Czech (& Central European) Yearbook of Arbitration®

arbitration. The 2021 Rules Revision has the potential to foster VIAC's position as a leading institution for the CEE/SEE region, offering its services in resolving international commercial and now also investment disputes.

[Johanna Kathan-Spath]

was a Legal Counsel at the Vienna International Arbitral Centre (VIAC) from October 2019 to November 2021.

E-mail: johanna.kathan@mac.com

News & Reports

International Arbitration Court of the Czech Commodity Exchange in Prague: Current Information on Activities

The International Arbitration Court of the Czech Commodity Exchange, with its seat in Prague, is a permanent arbitration court in the Czech Republic established pursuant to Act No. 229/1992 Coll., on commodity exchanges, in accordance with Act No. 216/1994 Coll., on arbitration and the enforcement of arbitral awards. Following the newly elected presidency of the court, this arbitration institution has undergone a number of fundamental changes since 2017, which aim to bring arbitration proceedings held in the Czech Republic to the level customary in international commercial practice at the most prominent arbitration centres in the world. The standard of the International Arbitration Court of the Czech Commodity Exchange is high-quality, fast and efficient resolution of commercial disputes with a guarantee of maximum transparency. This permanent arbitration court currently arbitrates disputes related to any commodity traded on the commodity exchange, such as electricity, gas, minerals, and timber, as well as disputes related to emission permits and medical materials. For this reason, it is a highly erudite tribunal with international expertise in disputes arising from commodity trading.

At first glance, the most obvious change was the acceptance and use of the abbreviated name PRIAC (*Prague International Arbitration Court*). The reason for this was a certain degree of impracticality in using the formal name, especially in the international environment. Although the formal name of the institution has remained unchanged (i.e. the International Arbitration Court of the Czech Commodity Exchange), the arbitration court will in future be referred to by the abbreviated name PRIAC.[1] This is the common and worldwide practice of major arbitration centres.

The List of Arbitrators has also undergone fundamental changes. This List includes the leading arbitrators and experts in the field. Only a person qualified under the Arbitration Act who demonstrates sufficient knowledge and experience in the law of arbitration may become a PRIAC arbitrator. For this reason, each candidate is individually approved by the Board of the Court, and there is no legal entitlement to be included on the List of Arbitrators. In order to ensure the quality of dispute adjudication, a candidate for being listed must undergo training and an

---

[1]   Available at: www.priac.eu (accessed on 06 January 2022).

interview, and must sufficiently evidence a working knowledge of at least one world language. Also, in line with international practice, the PRIAC transparently publishes the professional CVs of arbitrators on the List, including information on the arbitrator's expertise and language skills, including the indicative number of disputes handled, so that parties are able to obtain as much verified information as possible with respect to their choice of arbitrator. The PRIAC Board has consistently insisted not only on professional, but also moral qualities for the arbitrators on the roster. Thus, a high degree of moral integrity of each candidate is also a prerequisite for the inclusion of an arbitrator on the List.

In the second half of 2018, the PRIAC Mediation Rules were approved as a key instrument for ADR proceedings, making the PRIAC the first permanent arbitration court in the Czech Republic to become an independent body for settling disputes outside arbitration. The current version of the Mediation Rules is published on the PRIAC website.

The most significant change, however, was made to the Rules of the Court of Arbitration. The PRIAC Board completed work on the new Rules of Arbitration (PRIAC Rules) and approved them in a completely revised form. The PRIAC Rules were created with an emphasis on guaranteeing the most efficient, high quality and speedy resolution of disputes, while respecting the rules and accepted international practices. These new PRIAC Rules, compared to the previously valid Rules, completely re-conceive and regulate a number of interesting procedural conventions, which will be highlighted in greater detail below. From the perspective of comparison with other arbitral institutions, these are often quite exceptional conventions, which have no parallel in the Czech Republic, although they do occur in international arbitration practice. The PRIAC and its new arbitration rules could make the Czech Republic more attractive as a "*seat of arbitration*". Some of the newly adopted procedures will be outlined below.

For the resolution of disputes with an international element, it is essential that the Rules have been issued in Czech and English versions, which are equally valid and binding (PRIAC Rules, Article 1(11)). Therefore, the parties do not have to provide their own legal translations of the Czech version of the Regulations in the future, and the PRIAC guarantees the possibility of the direct application of the official English version.

In order to maximize the transparency of the proceedings and to guarantee the appointment of a truly independent arbitrator in the dispute, the PRIAC is the only arbitration centre in the Czech Republic that prohibits a member of the Board from being appointed by the President of the Arbitral Tribunal as a sole arbitrator, a member of the Arbitral Tribunal or its Chairman in a particular dispute decided in the proceedings before the PRIAC for the duration of his/her office

(PRIAC Rules, Article 4(2)). A member of the Board may only serve as an arbitrator if appointed directly by a party or in the case of the election of arbitrators appointed by the parties. An exception is made if they have already participated in the Board's decision on the same case, e.g. an objection of a lack of jurisdiction (PRIAC Rules, Article 4(3)). In any case, however, such a member of the Board is always excluded from decisions of the Board on matters relating to arbitration proceedings in which they act as a party or as a representative of a party or as an arbitrator (PRIAC Rules, Article 4(4)). As logical and transparent as such a provision may seem, the PRIAC is the only arbitration institution in the Czech Republic that applies and explicitly regulates this procedure.

In terms of measures against arbitrator inactivity, the PRIAC Rules have introduced relatively strict requirements for an arbitrator when accepting their position. The arbitrator is obliged *verbis expressis*, before accepting office, to consider carefully whether they have sufficient space to perform their function in a particular dispute so that the proceedings are conducted as efficiently as possible and without any delay (PRIAC Rules, Article 5(3)). The arbitrator is thus subjected to the highest possible level of efficiency in the proceedings (see the expression "*as efficiently as possible*"), and no delays are allowed. Arbitrators are obliged to ensure that the proceedings are conducted in accordance with the principles of procedural economy and maximum efficiency (PRIAC Rules, Article 11(2)).

Any party to a dispute may propose that an arbitrator be removed from office if there are impediments of a non-transitory nature that prevent them from properly performing their duties, or if the arbitrator otherwise fails to perform or violates their duties, which, in addition to manifest violations of binding procedural procedures, is expressly understood to include undue delays in the proceedings (PRIAC Rules, Article 8(3)). Before exercising this option, however, such party must raise its concerns directly in the proceedings before making a corresponding motion, and only after a reasonable period of time has elapsed to seek redress may it move to discharge the arbitrator. Unless this condition is met, the Board shall not consider such a proposal and shall refer it to the arbitrator or the arbitration panel for processing as an objection by a party to a procedural measure without further delay. If no remedy is found even after such objection has been referred to the arbitrator/arbitral tribunal, the party entitled shall have the right to make a renewed request for the discharge of the arbitrator (PRIAC Rules, Article 8(4)). Such a procedure prevents the abuse of this procedural mechanism of the disqualification and arbitrary replacement of a member of the arbitral tribunal without due and obvious reasons. At the same time, it gives arbitrators the opportunity to respond to specific objections by the parties and to seek redress in the proceedings, thereby avoiding the negative consequences of being dismissed by the Presidency of this permanent court.

An arbitrator may be dismissed from office even without a motion by the parties for objective or subjective inactivity. If the Board finds, in the exercise of its powers, that there are impediments to the arbitrator's proper performance of their duties that are not of a temporary nature (in the case of so-called objective inactivity), or if the arbitrator fails to perform or breaches their duties, which means unreasonable delays in the proceedings or a failure to conduct the proceedings with maximum efficiency (in the case of so-called subjective inactivity), the Board shall discuss the discharge of the arbitrator. Before discharging an inactive arbitrator, the Board shall first inform the parties and the remaining arbitrators of the facts, together with an invitation to remedy the situation, after which the Board may proceed to consider the discharge of the arbitrator (PRIAC Rules, Article 8(5)). In the course of the deliberations on the removal of an arbitrator, the Board shall give the parties and all arbitrators the opportunity to comment, and all comments shall be forwarded to all parties and arbitrators. The Board shall have the right to decide that the parties shall not have access to any arbitrator's statement of case and/or part thereof containing internal information on the arbitration panel's activities relating to the hearing and to the factual and legal assessment of the case (PRIAC Rules, Article 8(6)). For the appointment of a new arbitrator, the same rules shall apply by analogy as in the case of the termination of an arbitrator's office during the proceedings, with the new arbitrator always entering the proceedings with the status as of the date of acceptance of the arbitrator's office. The reason for this is to prevent the dispute from being re-heard and causing further delays in the proceedings. If necessary, the arbitral tribunal may (upon or without a motion of the parties) rehear the case even to the extent that it was already heard before the arbitrator was replaced (PRIAC Rules, Article 6(9)).

The dismissal of the arbitrator is also a last resort for this permanent arbitral institution and constitutes interference with the fundamental right of the parties to choose the arbitrator. For this reason, the Board is empowered to take any other appropriate measure to ensure the orderly conduct of the proceedings in the event that the impediments to the performance of the arbitrator's duties and/or their misconduct do not reach such a level of intensity as to justify their removal from office (PRIAC Rules, Article 8(8)).

The language in which the arbitration shall be conducted shall primarily be decided by the parties to the dispute within the framework of their agreement. In the absence of such an agreement, the arbitrators shall decide on the language of the proceedings. In making their decision, they must take into account all of the circumstances of the dispute, including the language of the contract or the language in which the parties have previously communicated (PRIAC Rules, Article 13(1)). The Slovak language is explicitly identified as equivalent due to its similarity to the Czech language (PRIAC Rules, Article 13(6)). All other decisions shall be issued in the language of the proceedings, and oral proceedings shall be held in that language, and all submissions of the parties shall be made in that language. The PRIAC Rules give the arbitrators the explicit authority to disregard any submissions of the parties which, despite their invitation, are not submitted in the language of the proceedings (PRIAC Rules, Article 13(3)). Documentary evidence shall, of course, be submitted in the language in which it is produced and in that language shall be taken into account or otherwise considered in the arbitration. However, if it is in a language other than the language of the proceedings, a translation of such document into the language of the proceedings shall be provided upon request of the opposing party or the decision of the arbitrators. In order to avoid abuse of this mechanism and causing unjustified delays in the proceedings, the arbitrators may refuse a party's request for a translation of documentary evidence where the request is manifestly unfounded and the course of the proceedings shows that the party requesting the translation has dealt with the documents in question in their original form in the context of the legal relationship between the parties (PRIAC Rules, Article 13(5)). Regardless of the language of the proceedings, all communication between the Secretariat of the arbitral tribunal and the parties shall be conducted in Czech or English.

Article 21 of the PRIAC Rules permits the application of the institution of *Amicus Curiae*, except where such a procedure would be expressly prohibited by the *lex arbitri* rules or the procedural principles of the proceedings. The admission of a third party as *Amicus Curiae* is a matter at the sole discretion of the arbitrators, who may request the parties' submissions before making their decision, but are not bound by it. They shall take appropriate measures to preserve the confidentiality of the proceedings on the part of that third party. An *Amicus Curiae* shall have a similar status to that of a party to the proceedings, except that, unlike an intervener, they need not be identified with the submissions of any party to the proceedings. In particular, *an amicus curiae* makes submissions on the merits of the parties' submissions and on procedural issues, so that the arbitrators may ultimately take such submissions into account in an appropriate manner. The PRIAC Order establishes a rebuttable legal presumption that an *Amicus Curiae* defends an independent opinion primarily pursuing professional purposes, interests in promoting the principle of fair adjudication, etc., without regard to the procedural posture or submissions of any of the disputing parties. An application for admission of a third party as an *Amicus Curiae* may be made both by a party to the dispute and by a person interested in acting in that capacity. Such an application must be duly reasoned and should set out the interest of the proposed party in the outcome of the dispute and the facts that the party appearing as *Amicus Curiae* intends to present in the event of its admission. Based on these submissions, the arbitrators will thus consider the admission of such a person, particularly with a view to ensuring that the facts are not already pleaded by any of the parties to the dispute, while at the same time considering whether they can contribute to clarifying the case for the award. The *Amicus Curiae* shall inform the arbitrator of any links to the parties to the dispute or their counsel and shall provide any contact information relating to the preparation and content of the application for the appointment of *the Amicus Curiae* and the funding thereof. The arbitrators shall be empowered to lay down the conditions for the exercise of the functions of *Amicus Curiae in* respect of, inter alia, the length and number of submissions to be made to them and the time limits for their submission. Such decisions of the arbitrators shall be final and may not be challenged.

The newly introduced procedure of security for the costs of the proceedings is an unusual, but very useful tool, and not only in the Czech legal system against abuse of law in arbitration proceedings before the PRIAC. Article 35 of the PRIAC Rules allows arbitrators, on their own initiative or at the request of the defendant, to impose an order on the claimant to provide security for costs if there is a sufficient degree of probability that the enforceability of the defendant's potential claim for costs may be jeopardised in the future. In deciding whether to impose an order for security for costs, arbitrators shall take into account all of the circumstances of the case and, in particular, shall ensure that access to the arbitrators and the right to a hearing are not denied. At the same time, however, arbitrators must ensure that the defendant is not forced to defend a manifestly unfounded claim at the real risk of being unable to recover costs in the event of its success in the case (PRIAC Rules, Article 35(2)). Arbitration before the PRIAC thus protects the defendant in the future from frequent mischief where a plaintiff who is uncertain of their success, before filing a lawsuit, assigns the claim to another (even foreign) company, which in practical terms is either unavailable to the defendant (a foreign company) or has no means to pay the costs of the proceedings in case of their failure, and the defendant would thus be forced to bear the full costs of their legal representation in real terms even when they prevail in the case. At the same time, the PRIAC is aware that requiring security for costs may, if improperly applied, limit the access of one of the parties, usually the claimant, to the arbitration. For this reason, either party may, within 10 days of the receipt of the arbitrators' order for security, request that the PRIAC Board review it (PRIAC Rules, Article 35(3)). The decision of the Board shall be final. The time limit for the payment of the security for costs shall be no less than 14 days, and the action shall not be heard until it has been paid (PRIAC Rules, Article 35(5)).

In order to ensure the maximum efficiency and speed of the proceedings, the arbitrators may decide that no oral hearing will be held, and the dispute will be decided on the basis of the written documents submitted in the event that one of the parties remains completely passive throughout the preparation of the hearing, makes no comments on the case, and makes no other procedural motions (PRIAC Rules, Article 37(7)). At the same time, the parties have the possibility to agree in writing that the dispute will be decided without an oral hearing on the basis of documents only in a so-called simplified procedure. However, this agreement does not bind the arbitrator if the documents submitted prove insufficient for a decision (PRIAC Rules, Article 39(1)). In arbitration practice, a common and quite frequently used procedure is the possibility to invite the parties to express their consent to the case being decided without an oral hearing based on the documents alone within a period of no less than 10 days from the delivery of the invitation. If a party fails to respond to such a request, the arbitrators may assume that the parties agree to the dispute being decided without a hearing. However, the parties to the dispute must be expressly advised of this consequence in the invitation (PRIAC Rules, Article 39(5)).

The PRIAC Rules do not explicitly contain a specific provision for the conduct of online proceedings, and it can be assumed that in the future the conduct of online proceedings will be comprehensively regulated by a specific supplement to the PRIAC Rules. However, the PRIAC Rules allow *verbis expressis* for oral hearings to be held by videoconference. Either both parties or only one party or another person involved in the proceedings may participate in the oral hearing by videoconference. It is also possible to question witnesses, experts or other persons by videoconference, possibly to provide interpretation, etc. Exceptionally, participation by telephone conference is also admissible. However, it shall always be understood that participation by such means of remote transmission shall be deemed to be personal participation in the oral hearing. The use of videoconferencing or telephone conferencing is at the sole discretion of the arbitrators (PRIAC Rules, Article 37(8)).

The parties may agree directly in the arbitration agreement on the possibility of summary proceedings, which means proceedings with the issuance of an arbitral award or an order to discontinue the proceedings within two months from the moment the file is submitted to the arbitrators. All time limits set out in the PRIAC Rules shall be reduced by one-third in summary proceedings, except for the time limit for filing the statement of defence (which shall, however, be reduced to 10 days). However, such proceedings may only be held if the parties have expressly agreed to this possibility. In the absence of such an agreement, either party may file a request for expedited proceedings, but in such a case the time limit for the issuance of the arbitral award or the order for termination of the proceedings is extended to four months. In this case too, all time limits set out in the PRIAC Rules are reduced by half, and the time limit for filing a statement of defence is also reduced to 10 days. The time-limit for requesting an adjournment of the oral hearing remains unchanged (PRIAC Rules, Article 40(1)).

The new PRIAC Rules also introduce new procedures with respect to the issue of evidence that aim to prevent obstruction of the proceedings by a procedurally passive party. In particular, it explicitly allows parties to submit documentary evidence in the original or in copies, introducing a rebuttable legal presumption that the copies correspond to the original. Arbitrators are entitled either on their own initiative or upon the application of any party to order the production of the original version of such document. However, unless either party raises doubts as to the authenticity or completeness of documents submitted by the other parties in copies or electronic form, the irrebuttable presumption of authenticity of such documents shall apply (PRIAC Rules, Article 42(3)). This provision places the activity and responsibility for the authenticity of the documents submitted always on the parties to the dispute, who are presumed to have factual knowledge of these documents, and who would be presumed to make an appropriate procedural objection in the event of the submission of an untrue or altered document. At the same time, it is provided that any document submitted by a party during the proceedings that is not publicly available will be treated as confidential by the parties (PRIAC Rules, Article 42(4)). To avoid unnecessary questioning of witnesses and other persons, the PRIAC Rules expressly provide that the parties are obliged to specify, together with the proposal to conduct such questioning, the purpose of proving the facts that are to be raised in questioning. Should the arbitrators consider that proposals for the examination of witnesses constitute the obstruction and abuse of a party's right to present evidence, they may limit the number of persons whom a party is entitled to propose to examine (PRIAC Rules, Article 43(2)).

The proceedings before the PRIAC provide for the issuance of an order terminating the hearing and closing the case before the conclusion of the proceedings. However, pending the issuance of the award or the order closing the proceedings, the evidence may be reopened by order, or a new oral hearing may be ordered, if necessary to clarify the matter (PRIAC Rules, Article 47). It is also expressly permitted to issue partial and interim awards, to which the procedural provisions relating to the ordinary final award shall apply *mutatis mutandis* (PRIAC Rules, Article 48(6)).

In order to guarantee the highest quality and standard of arbitration, any arbitral award shall be submitted to the Secretariat of the arbitral tribunal in the form of a draft before it is signed, and the President of the arbitral tribunal shall carry out a formal check. As part of this check, the draft award may be returned by the chairman of the PRIAC to the arbitrators with suggested modifications concerning the form of the award, the possible inconsistency thereof, a lack of clarity, as well as with a warning as to any doubts regarding the procedural practices, etc. The chairman of the arbitral tribunal is always obliged to respect the arbitrators' right to freely hear and consider the case (PRIAC Rules, Article 51), and the proposals thereof for modifications of the award may therefore be of a formal nature only. The PRIAC shall not issue any award until the submissions and notices received by the arbitrators have been dealt with and the President or the Board of the arbitral tribunal has given their approval as to its form (PRIAC Rules, Article 51).

The aim of this paper was to inform the professional public about the recent changes in PRIAC proceedings that have been adopted in recent years. With regard to the new PRIAC Rules, this is not a complete list of all changes, but a selection of new procedures, many of which are completely new and unique in the Czech Republic. Thus, with its modern Rules, PRIAC can rank among the leading arbitration institutions and guarantee independent, fast and high-quality dispute resolution by quality arbitrators with high moral credit.

[*JUDr. David Řezníček, LL.M., Ph.D.*]

Attorney-at-Law, České Budějovice, Czech Republic. Member of the Board of the International Arbitration Court of the Czech Commodity Exchange (PRIAC).

E-mail: reznicek@reznicek.com

Bibliography, Current Events, Important Web Sites

Alexander J. Bělohlávek

I.   SELECTED BIBLIOGRAPHY FOR 2021

Opening Remarks:
This overview lists only works published in 2021. The individual chapters into which this overview is divided always cover both substantive and procedural issues.

Titles in translations are indicative.

I.1.   [CZE] – [CZECH REPUBLIC] – Titles published within the Czech Republic

I.1.1.   Monographs

MAGDALENA PFEIFFER; JAN BRODEC; PETR BŘÍZA; MARTA ZAVADILOVÁ, LIBER AMICORUM MONIKA PAUKNEROVÁ, Praha: Wolters Kluwer ČR (2021), ISBN: 978-80-7676-186-5 (paperback); ISBN: 978-80-7676-187-2 (e-Publication).

*   Alexander J. Bělohlávek, *Conflicting Interpretations of International Treaties*, p. 37-46.
*   Jan Brodec, *Vliv lex loci arbitri na průběh mezinárodní obchodní arbitráže* [title in translation – *The Impact of Lex Loci Arbitri on International Commercial Arbitration*], p. 65-74.
*   Giuditta Cordero-Moss, *Private International Law in Arbitration*, p. 93-102.
*   Catherine Kessedjian, *Mediation for Disputes in Investment Matters*, p. 223-230.
*   Květoslav Růžička, *Náklady stran v rozhodčím řízení* [title in translation – *Party Costs in Arbitration Proceedings*], p. 413-420.

NADĚŽDA ROZEHNALOVÁ; JIŘÍ VALDHANS; TEREZA KYSELOVSKÁ, PRÁVO MEZINÁRODNÍHO OBCHODU. VČETNĚ PROBLEMATIKY MEZINÁRODNÍHO ROZHODČÍHO ŘÍZENÍ [title in translation – LAW OF INTERNAIONAL COMMERCE. INCLUDING INTERNATIONAL ARBITRATION ISSUES], Prague: Wolters Kluwer (4th ed. 2021), p. 524, ISBN: 978-80-7676-046-2.

Czech (& Central European) Yearbook of Arbitration®

I.1.2. Periodicals, Collections and Conference Proceedings

Soudní rozhledy [*Court Review*]**, Prague: C. H. Beck, 2021, Vol. 27, ISSN: 1210-6410**[1]

Karel Svoboda, *Kolegium NS nesouhlasí s "moderováním" nemravných exekučních titulů. Co s tím?* [title in translation – *The Supreme Court Chamber Disagrees with the 'Mitigation' of Enforcement Orders Which Are Contra Bonos Mores. Looking for a Solution*], No. 3, p. 78-80.

Soukromé právo [**Title in translation** – *Private Law*]**, Prague: Wolers Kluwer ČR, a.s., 2021, Vol. IX, ISSN: 2533-4239**[2]

Alexander J. Bělohlávek, *Rozsah, účel a charakter speciální úpravy o doručování v zákoně o rozhodčím řízení. Část I* [title in translation – *Extent, Purpose and Nature of Special Rules on Service in the Arbitration Act. Part I*], No. 5, p. 2-9.

Alexander J. Bělohlávek, *Rozsah, účel a charakter speciální úpravy o doručování v zákoně o rozhodčím řízení. Část II* [title in translation – *Extent, Purpose and Nature of Special Rules on Service in the Arbitration Act. Part II*], No. 6, p. 2-9.

Eliška Fischerová, *Appointing authority v rozhodčím řízení* [title in translation – *Appointing Authority in Arbitration*], No. 9, p. 26-32.

Other publications

Bára Bečvářová, *Virtual arbitration hearings in times of Covid-19 (and beyond)*, in RADOVAN MALACHTA; PATRIK PROVAZNÍK, COFOLA INTERNATIONAL 2021. INTERNATIONAL AND NATIONAL ARBITRATION – CHALLENGES AND TRENDS OF THE PRESENT AND FUTURE, Brno: Masaryk University Press (2021).

Petr Bříza, *Czech perspective on validity of international arbitration clauses contained in an exchange of emails under the New York Convention*, 4 ACTA UNIVERSITATIS CAROLINAE IURIDICA (2020), p. 143.

I.2. [SVK] – [SLOVAK REPUBLIC]

Bulletin slovenskej advokácie [*Review of Slovak Bar*] **Bratislava [Slovak Republic]: Slovenská advokátska komora** [*Slovak Bar Association*]**, 2021, Vol. 27, ISSN: 1335-1079, Reg. No of the Ministry of Cultural Affairs of the Slovak Republic: 4161/10**[3]

---

[1] Papers published in Czech.
[2] Papers published in Czech.
[3] Available also on www.sak.sk. Papers published in Slovak langauges. Summaries in Slovak, English and German.

Miriam Galandová, *Procesné nástrahy pri podávaní námietky voči rozhodcovi v rozhodcovskom konaní* [title in translation – *Procedural Pitfalls of Arbitrator Challenge in Arbitration*], No. 9, p. 29-33.

Juraj Gyárfáš, *Súdna ingerencia do rozhodcovského konania. Opatrné budovanie novej dôvery* [title in translation – *Judicial Intervention in Arbitration. Cautiously Building New Trust*], No. 9, p. 8-13.

Michal Hrušovský; Pavel Lacko, *Nezávislosť a nestrannosť rozhodcu v rozhodcovskom konaní v SR* [title in translation – *Independence and Impartiality of Arbitrators in Arbitration in the Slovak Republic*], No. 9, p. 14-19.

Peter Kotvan, *Výhody inštitútu adjudikácie s rozhodcovským konaním* [title in translation – *Benefits of Adjudication with Arbitration*], No. 9, p. 46-49.

Andrea Moravčíková, *Aktuálna judikatúra v oblasti prieskumu rozhodcovského konania všeobecnými súdmi* [title in translation – *Current Case-Law Concerning Review of Arbitration by Courts*], No. 9, p. 20-28.

Robert Němec, *Zásahy soudů do rozhodčích řízení v České republice* [title in translation – *Judicial Intervention in Arbitration in the Czech Republic*], No. 9, p. 42-45.

Peter Plachý; Lucia Raimanová; Matej Košalko, *Efektívnosť dokazovania v medzinárodnej obchodnej arbitráži a pred slovenskými súdmi* [title in translation – *Effectiveness of the Taking of Evidence in International Commercial Arbitration and before Slovak Courts*], No. 9, p. 34-41.

Justičná revue [*Judicial Revue*], Bratislava: Ministry of Justice Slovak Republic, 2021, Vol. 73, ISSN: 1335-6461[4]

Peter Matuška, *Post Achmea: súboj o investičné arbitráže medzi právom EÚ a medzinárodným právom* [title in translation – *Post Achmea: Conflict between EU Law and International Law over Investment Arbitration*], No. 5, p. 597-616.

Czech (& Central European) Yearbook of Arbitration®

---

[4]   Papers published in Czech. Abstracts in English.

I.3. [POL] – [POLAND]⁵

I.3.1. Monographs (incl. chapters in monographs) Collections and Proceedings

Aneta Arkuszewska, *Informatyzacja pozasądowych form rozwiązywania sporów* [title in translation - *Computerisation of alternative forms of dispute resolution*], in KINGA FLAGA-GIERUSZYŃSKA; JACEK GOŁACZYŃSKI, PRAWO NOWYCH TECHNOLOGII [title in translation – LAW OF NEW TECHNOLOGIES], Warsaw: Wolters Kluwer Polska (2021), ISBN: 978-83-8223-513-5.

Paweł Banul, *Rola sądu państwowego w stosunku do sądu polubownego w sprawach cywilnych* [title in translation - *Role of the state court in relation to arbitral tribunal in civil matters*], in MARCIN BIAŁECKI; SŁAWOMIRA KOTAS-TUROBOYSKA; FILIP MANIKOWSKI; ELŻBIETA SZCZEPANOWSKA, NOWELIZACJA POSTEPOWANIA CYWILNEGO. WPŁYW ZMIAN NA PRAKTYKE SADOWA [title in translation – AMENDMENT OF CIVIL PROCEDURE. THE IMPACT OF CHANGES ON COURT PRACTICE], Warsaw: Wolters Kluwer Polska (2021), ISBN: 978-83-8223-407-7.

Marcin Dziurda, *W sądzie jak w arbitrażu – czy to się może udać?* [title in translation - *In court as in arbitral tribunal – can it work?*], in MARCIN DZIURDA; TADEUSZ ZEMBRZUSKI, PRAKTYKA WOBEC NOWELIZACJI POSTEPOWANIA CYWILNEGO. KONSEKWENCJE ZMIAN [title in translation – PRACTICE IN THE FACE OF AMENDMENTS TO CIVIL PRODURE. CONSEQUENCES OF THE CHANGES], Warsaw: Wolters Kluwer Polska (2021), ISBN: 978-83-8246-124-4.

Andrzej Krasuski, *Rozwiązywanie sporów o nazwy domen internetowych* [title in translation - *Resolving disputes over Internet domain names*], in ANDRZEJ KRASUSKI; ANNA WOLSKA-BAGIŃSKA; OLGA ZINKIEWICZ-BEDŹMIROWSKA, DZIAŁANIA NARUSZAJACE PRAWA DO DOMEN INTERNETOWYCH [title in translation – DOMAIN NAME INFRINGEMENT ACTIVITIES], Warsaw: Wolters Kluwer Polska (2021), ISBN: 978-83-8246-276-0.

KAMILA LICHOŃ, OCHRONA KONSUMENTA W POSTEPOWANIU MEDIACYJNYM I ARBITRAŻOWYM [title in

---

⁵ Polish bibliography concerning arbitration and ADR for 2021 compiled with the kind support of Kubas Kos Gałkowski - Adwokaci, Law firm (www.kkg.pl). Kubas Kos Gałkowski specialize (among others) in arbitration and ADR, in particular under the support of Ernestyna Niemiec (associate), Marek Truszkiewicz (associate) and and Kamil Zawick (attorney-at-law and co-managing partner) as editor and chair of the team.

translation – CONSUMER PROTECTION IN MEDIATION AND ARBITRATION PROCEEDINGS], Warsaw: C.H. Beck (2021), ISBN: 978-83-8198-808-7.

Andrzej Olaś, *Zarzut potrącenia a zapis na sąd polubowny* [title in translation - *Set-off defense versus arbitration agreement*], in ANDRZEJ OLAŚ, ZARZUT POTRACENIA W PROCESIE CYWILNYM [title in translation – SET-OFF DEFENSE IN CIVIL PROCEEDINGS], Warsaw: C.H. Beck (2021), ISBN: 978-83-8198-848-3.

ALEKSANDRA ORZEŁ-JAKUBOWSKA, SADOWNICTWO POLUBOWNE W ŚWIETLE STANDARDÓW KONSTYTUCYJNYCH [title in translation – ARBITRATION IN THE LIGHT OF CONSTITUTIONAL STANDARDS], Warsaw: Wolters Kluwer Polska (2021), ISBN: 978-83-8246-233-3.

Zbigniew Pinkalski, *Polubowne rozwiązywanie sporów w sprawach własności intelektualnej* [title in translation - *Amicable dispute resolution in intellectual property matters*], in KATARZYNA JASIŃSKA, METODYKA PRACY PEŁNOMOCNIKA W SPRAWACH CYWILNYCH Z ZAKRESU PRAWA WŁASNOŚCI INTELEKTUALNEJ [title in translation – METHODOLOGY OF ATTORNEY'S WORK IN CIVIL CASES CONCERNING INTELLECTUAL PROPERTY LAW], Warsaw: Wolters Kluwer Polska (2021), ISBN: 978-83-8246-350-7.

CEZARY ROGULA, AGNIESZKA ZEMKE-GÓRECKA, MEDIACJA W PRAKTYCE MEDIATORA I PEŁNOMOCNIKA [title in translation – MEDIATION IN THE PRACTICE OF MEDIATOR AND ATTORNEY], Warsaw: Wolters Kluwer Polska (2021), ISBN: 978-83-8223-809-9.

Magdalena Rzewuska, *Rozstrzygnięcia w związku z postępowaniem przed sądem polubownym* [title in translation - *Decisions in connection with arbitration proceedings*], in MACIEJ RZEWUSKI, ROZSTRZYGNIECIA SADOWE W POSTEPOWANIU CYWILNYM [title in translation – JUDICIAL DECISIONS IN CIVIL PROCEEDINGS], Warsaw: Wolters Kluwer Polska (2021), ISBN: 978-83-8223-651-4.

Karol Ryszkowski, *Ochrona konsumenta w arbitrażu handlowym a nowe technologie* [title in translation - *Consumer protection in commercial arbitration versus new technologies*], in KINGA FLAGA-GIERUSZYŃSKA; RADOSŁAW FLEJSZAR; ELWIRA MARSZAŁKOWSKA-KRZEŚ, DOSTEP DO OCHRONY PRAWNEJ W POSTEPOWANIU CYWILNYM [title in translation – ACCESS TO LEGAL PROTECTION IN CIVIL PROCEEDINGS], Warsaw: C.H. Beck (2021), ISBN: 978-83-8235-843-8.

Karol Ryszkowski, *Arbitraż w sprawach konsumenckich a nowe technologie* [title in translation - *Consumer arbitration versus new technologies*], in ZBIGNIEW DŁUGOSZ; KRZYSZTOF PODGÓTSKI; ELŻBIETA SŁUGOCKA-KRUPA, REKLAMACJE MEFIACJE I INNE POSTEPOWANIA W SPRAWACH KONSUMENCKICH [title in translation – COMPLAINTS, MEDIATION AND OTHER CONSUMER PROCEDURES], Warsaw: C.H. Beck (2021), ISBN: 978-83-8235-546-8.

I.3.2. Periodicals, Collections and Conference Proceedings

ADR ARBITRAŻ I MEDIACJA [title in translation - ADR ARBITRATION AND MEDIATION], Warsaw: C. H. Beck 2021, ISSN: 1898-942X.[6]

- Joanna Botiuk, *ADR, czyli polubowne rozwiązywanie sporów jako nowy instrument w zamówieniach publicznych* [title in translation - *ADR i.e. amicable dispute resolution as a new instrument in public procurement*].

- Łukasz Chyla, *Uwagi odnośnie sytuacji arbitrażu wewnątrzkorporacyjnego w Polsce dwa lata po reformie* [title in translation - *Observations on the situation of corporate arbitration in Poland two years after the reform*].

- Maciej Durbas, *Zapis na sąd polubowny w statucie fundacji rodzinnej – uwagi de lege ferenda* [title in translation - *Arbitration agreement in the family foundation statute - de lege ferenda comments*].

- Olga Ferenc-Pierzyńska, *Mediacja w postępowaniu administracyjnym to nadal „nowa" instytucja* [title in translation - *Mediation in administrative proceedings is still a "new" institution*].

- Jan Gąsiorowski, *Zakres zastosowania zasady równości stron w postępowaniu arbitrażowym. Postulaty de lege ferenda w aspekcie Kodeksu postępowania cywilnego (głos w dyskusji)* [title in translation - *Scope of application of the principle of equality of parties in arbitration proceedings. Postulates de lege ferenda in the aspect of the code of civil procedure (voice in debate)*].

- Radosław Giętkowski, *Mediacja w sprawach dyscyplinarnych studentów* [title in translation - *Mediation in student disciplinary cases*].

---

[6] Quarterly. Papers published in Polish, summaries in English.

• Małgorzata Gosztyła, *Mediacja szkolna – forma kształtowania komunikacji interpersonalnej na poziomie szkoły (w kontekście sprawiedliwości naprawczej i edukacji prawnej młodego pokolenia)* [title in translation - *School mediation - a form of shaping interpersonal communication at school level (in the context of restorative justice and legal education of the young generation)*].

• Barbara Guzik, *Zdatność arbitrażowa sporów dotyczących zaskarżania uchwał zgromadzenia wspólników i walnego zgromadzenia po 8.9.2019 r.* [title in translation - *Arbitrability of disputes concerning challenges to resolutions of shareholders' meetings and general meetings after 8.9.2019*].

• Barbara Jelonek, *Mediacja w Japonii realizowana w ramach Konwencji haskiej dotyczącej cywilnych aspektów uprowadzenia dziecka za granicę* [title in translation - *Mediation in Japan under the Hague Convention on the Civil Aspects of International Child Abduction*].

• Marcin Kwiecień, *Piłkarski Sąd Polubowny – część I* [title in translation - *Football arbitration court – part I*].

• Marcin Kwiecień, *Piłkarski Sąd Polubowny – część II* [title in translation - *Football arbitration court – part II*].

• Krystian Mularczyk, *Ośrodek Mediacji przy Okręgowej Izbie Radców Prawnych we Wrocławiu – podstawy funkcjonowania* [title in translation - *Mediation Centre at the District Chamber of Legal Counsels in Wrocław – basis of operation*].

• Krystian Mularczyk, *Wkład Sądu Arbitrażowego przy Nowotomyskiej Izbie Gospodarczej w promocję międzynarodowego arbitrażu i mediacji* [title in translation - *Contribution of the Court of Arbitration of the Nowy Tomyśl Chamber of Commerce to the promotion of international arbitration and mediation*].

• Piotr Sławicki, *Doręczenia tytułów wykonawczych powstałych w postępowaniu mediacyjnym i arbitrażowym* [title in translation - *Service of enforcement clauses arising out of mediation and arbitration proceedings*].

• Anne-Marie Weber; Magdalena Milejska, *Udział kobiet w powołaniach na arbitrów – różnorodność płciowa w arbitrażu na tle Raportu ICCA* [title in translation - *Participation of* women in arbitral appointments – gender diversity in arbitration against the background of the ICCA Report].

• Małgorzata Wojciechowicz, *Mediacja przed rozwodem. Reforma prawa rodzinnego* [title in translation - *Mediation before divorce. Family law reform*].

• Małgorzata Wojciechowicz, *Status prawny zawodu mediatora sądowego w sprawach cywilnych i rodzinnych* [title in translation - *Legal status of the profession of mediator in civil and family matters*].

BIULETYN ARBITRAŻOWY [ARBITRATION BULLETIN], Warsaw: Sąd Arbitrażowy przy Krajowej Izbie Gospodarczej w Warszawie (2021).[7]

• Katarzyna Bilewska, *Kilka uwag o wprowadzeniu zapisu na sąd polubowny do umowy (statutu) spółki kapitałowej (na tle prawa włoskiego)* [title in translation - *Some remarks on the implementation of arbitration agreements in the statute (articles of association) of a company (against the background of Italian law)*].

• Christopher Chinn, *Some Reflections on Arbitration Hearings in the COVID-19 Era.*[8]

• Monika Diehl; Dominika Jędrzejczyk, *Ugoda w postępowaniu arbitrażowym – praktyczne aspekty* [title in translation - *Settlement agreement in arbitration proceedings – practical aspects*].

• Beata Gessel Kalinowska vel Kalisz, *Interes prawny w powództwie o ustalenie w postępowaniu przed sądem polubownym – glosa do wyroku SA KIG 193/05* [title in translation - *Legal interest in action for declaratory relief in proceedings before an arbitration tribunal – glossary to the judgement SA KIG 193/05*].

• Zuzanna Cieplińska, *Dissenting opinions in arbitral awards – issues of recognition and enforcement in different jurisdictions with special focus on the issue of secrecy of deliberations.*[9]

• Roman Rewald, *Klauzula równoczesnej mediacji-arbitrażu CMA* [title in translation - *Concurrent mediation-arbitration clause of the Center of Arbitration and Mediation*].

---

[7] Published online.
[8] Paper published in English.
[9] Paper published in English.

- Andrzej Szlęzak; Anna Tujakowska, *Związanie sądu polubownego wyrokiem innego sądu polubownego – w świetle orzecznictwa sądu najwyższego, doktryny i w perspektywie prawnoporównawczej* [title in translation - *Binding effect on arbitral award by the award of another arbitration court – In the light of the Supreme Court's jurisprudence, doctrine and comparative legal perspective*].

- Agata Zwolankiewicz, *Better safe than sorry? Lessons ISDS can learn from dispute.*[10]

GLOSA [GLOSSARY], Warsaw: Wolters Kluwer Polska (2021), ISSN: 1233-4634.[11]

- Rafał Kos, *Związanie następcy singularnego zapisem na sąd polubowny oparte na procesowej kwalifikacji zapisu. Glosa do postanowienia SN z dnia 7 listopada 2013 r., V CSK 545/12* [title in translation - *Binding effect of an arbitration agreement on the singular successor due to the agreement's procedural character. commentary on Supreme Court decision of 7 November 2013, V CSK 545/12*].

INTERNETOWY KWARTALNIK ANTYMONOPOLOWY I REGULACYJNY [INTERNET ANTITRUST AND REGULATORY QUARTERLY], Warsaw: Center for Antitrust and Regulatory Studies (2021), ISSN: 2299-5749.[12]

- Małgorzata Kożuch, *Konwencja singapurska a rozwiązywanie sporów inwestycyjnych* [title in translation - *The Singapore Convention versus the resolution of investment disputes*].

IUS NOVUM, Warsaw: Wydział Prawa i Administracji Uczelni Łazarskiego w Warszawie (2021), ISSN: 1897-5577.[13]

- Joseph N. Mbadugha, *Enforceability of arbitration agreements – the interplay between sections 4 and 5 of Nigeria's Arbitration and Conciliation Act, 2004.*[14]

MONITOR PRAWA BANKOWEGO [BANKING LAW MONITOR],

10 Paper published in English.
11 Quarterly. Papers published in Polish, summaries in English.
12 Quarterly. Published online. Papers published in Polish.
13 Quarterly. Papers published in Polish, summaries in English.
14 Paper published in English.

Radzymin: Instytut Szkoleń Prawa Bankowego (2021), ISSN: 2081-9021.[15]

- Taddeo Ferraro, *Klauzula arbitrażowa i notarialne oświadczenie dłużnika o poddaniu się egzekucji w finansowaniu bankowym* [title in translation - *Arbitration clause and notarized statement of debtor's submission to enforcement in bank financing*].

OPENLEX, Warsaw: System Informacji Prawnej LEX (2021).[16]

- Radosław Maruszkin, *Umowy BIT: Polska nie zapłaci ponad 600 mln zł. Omówienie wyroku TS z dnia 26 października 2021 r., C-109/20 (PL Holdings)* [title in translation - *BIT treaties: Poland will not pay more than PLN 600 million. Discussion of the judgment of the CJEU of 26 October 2021, C-109/20 (PL Holdings)*].

PAŃSTWO I PRAWO [STATE AND LAW], Warsaw: Komitet Nauk Prawnych PAN (2021), ISSN: 0031-0980.[17]

- Anna Kalisz, Adam Zienkiewicz, *Kompetencje mediacyjne sędziego w zakresie polubownego rozwiązywania spraw cywilnych (uwagi na tle nowelizacji k.p.c.)* [title in translation - *Mediation competences of a judge in the field of amicable dispute resolution of civil cases (comments on the amendment of the Code of Civil Procedure)*].

- Krzysztof Marek Kolasiński, *Bezstronność i niezależność sportowych sądów polubownych* [title in translation - *Impartiality and independence of sports arbitration courts*].

PERSONEL PLUS [PERSONNEL PLUS], Warsaw: Wolters Kluwer Polska (2021), ISSN: 1899-2412.[18]

---

[15] Monthly. Papers published in Polish.
[16] Online database of legal texts.
[17] Monthly. Papers published in Polish, summaries in English.
[18] Monthly. Papers published in Polish.

Czech (& Central European) Yearbook of Arbitration®

• Agnieszka Siedlecka-Andrychowicz, *Arbitraż w indywidualnych sporach ze stosunku pracy* [title in translation - *Arbitration in individual disputes in employment law*].

PRACA I ZABEZPIECZENIE SPOŁECZNE [EMPLOYMENT AND SOCIAL SECURITY], Warsaw: Polskie Wydawnictwo Ekonomiczne (2021), ISSN: 0032-6186.[19]

• Katarzyna Jurewicz-Bakun, *Mediacja jako jedna z form rozwiązywania sporów indywidualnych w prawie pracy* [title in translation - *Mediation as one of the forms of resolving individual disputes in employment law*].

PRAWO W DZIAŁANIU [LAW IN ACTION], Warsaw: Instytut Wymiaru Sprawiedliwości (2021), ISSN: 2084-1906.[20]

• Konrad Czech, *Wyzwania w zakresie adjudykacyjnego rozstrzygania sporów międzynarodowych dotyczących zmian klimatu – w kierunku zacierania się granic prawa publicznego i prywatnego?* [title in translation - *Challenges to adjudicative resolution of international climate change disputes – towards a blurring of public and private law boundaries?*].

PRZEGLĄD PRAWA HANDLOWEGO [COMMERCIAL LAW REVIEW], Warsaw: Wolters Kluwer Polska (2021), ISSN: 1230-2996.[21]

• Małgorzata Żukrowska, *Spory uchwałowe w postępowaniu arbitrażowym w świetle nowelizacji art. 1157 i 1163 k.p.c. oraz Regulaminów SA KIG i SA Lewiatan, cz. 1* [title in translation - *Resolution Disputes in Arbitration Proceedings in Light of the Amendment of Articles 1157 and 1163 of the Civil Procedure Code and the Rules of the Polish Chamber of Commerce and Lewiatan, Part 1*].

• Małgorzata Żukrowska, *Spory uchwałowe w postępowaniu arbitrażowym w świetle nowelizacji art. 1157 i 1163 k.p.c. oraz*

---

[19] Monthly. Papers published in Polish.
[20] Quarterly. Papers published in Polish, summaries in English.
[21] Monthly. Papers published in Polish, summaries in English.

Regulaminów SA KIG i SA Lewiatan, cz. 2 [title in translation - Resolution Disputes in Arbitration Proceedings in Light of the Amendment of Articles 1157 and 1163 of the Civil Procedure Code and the Rules of the Polish Chamber of Commerce and Lewiatan, Part 2].

PRZEGLĄD PRAWA PUBLICZNEGO [PUBLIC LAW REVIEW], Warsaw: Wolters Kluwer Polska (2021), ISSN: 1896-8996.[22]

- Janusz Gajda, *W odpowiedzi na artykuł Michała Wojewody pt.: „O nieporozumieniach dotyczących klauzuli porządku publicznego uregulowanej w art. 103 Prawa o aktach stanu cywilnego"* [title in translation - In reply to Michał Wojewoda's article „On the misunderstandings concerning the public order clause regulated in Article 103 of the Law on Civil Status Records"].

PRZEGLĄD PRAWNO-EKONOMICZNY [REVIEW OF LAW, BUSINESS AND ECONOMICS], Lublin: Katolicki Uniwersytet Lubelski Jana Pawła II (2021), ISSN: 1898-2166.[23]

- Jarosław Pączek, *Halliburton v. Chubb. An Arbitrator's Duty of Disclosure – Is it a Matter of the Best Practice or a Matter of Law?*[24]

PRZEGLĄD SĄDOWY [COURT REVIEW], Warsaw: Wolters Kluwer Polska (2021), ISSN: 0867-7255.[25]

- Andrzej Olaś, *W stronę modelowego Europejskiego Kodeksu Postępowania Cywilnego: od Projektu Storme do Modelowych Europejskich Reguł Postępowania Cywilnego* [title in translation - Towards a Model European Civil Procedures Code: from the Storme Project to the Model European Rules of Civil Procedure].

PRZEGLĄD USTAWODAWSTWA GOSPODARCZEGO [BUSINESS LAW JOURNAL], Warsaw: Polskie Wydawnictwo Ekonomiczne (2021),

---

[22] Monthly. Papers published in Polish, summaries in English.
[23] Quarterly. Published online. Papers published in Polish.
[24] Paper published in English.
[25] Monthly. Papers published in Polish, summaries in English.

ISSN: 0137-5490.[26]

♦ Maria Cudowska, *Remarks on the arbitrability of corporate disputes in Poland*.[27]

STUDIA PRAWNOUSTROJOWE [LEGAL STUDIES], Olsztyn: Wydział Prawa i Administracji Uniwersytetu Warmińsko-Mazurskiego w Olsztynie, ISSN: 1644-0412.[28]

♦ Anna Franusz, *Arbitraż sporów rodzinnych* [title in translation - *Arbitration of family disputes*].

I.4.   [ROU] – [ROMANIA][29]

Revista Română de Arbitraj [titel in translation – *Romanian Arbitration Journal*], Bucharest : Arbitration Court attached to the Chamber of Commerce and Industry of Romania / Wolters Kluwer Romania, 2021, Vol. 15, Romanian register of publications C.N.C.S.I.S., Code 138, reg. No. 9059/5.11.2008, ISSN: 1842-6859[30]

Cristina Alexe; Andrea Annamaria Chiş; Liviu Zidaru, *Procedura etatică şi procedura arbitrală - Polenizare încrucişată. Câteva propuneri de lege ferenda. National Court Procedures and Arbitral Proceedings – Cross Pollination* [title in translation - *Certain de lege ferenda Proposals*], No. 4, p. 15-46.

Irina M. Coman, *The Role of „Consent Awards" in International Arbitration*, No. 1, p. 91-112.

Cremona Ana Maria Cotoveea, *DAB/DAAB – A comparative view beween FIDIC 1999/2017 editions. Part 1 – Constitution*, No. 1, p. 80-90.

Cristina Ioana Florescu, *Receptive and Rapid Adaptation of Arbitration*

---

[26] Monthly. Papers published in Polish.
[27] Paper published in English.
[28] Quarterly. Papers published in Polish, summaries in English.
[29] For further articles on arbitration in Romania see also *Revista Română de Arbitraj* issued by the International Commercial Arbitration attached to The Chamber Of Commerce And Industry Of Romania (see http://arbitration.ccir.ro/engleza/index.htm). The Romanian bibliography prepared also with a kind support of dr. Alina Cobuz, Managing Partner of Cobuz si Asociatii, the Bucharest based law firm.
[30] Papers published in English, sometime in French and exceptionally in Romanian. Abstracts in English. Table of Content in English, French and Romanian. Published quarterly.

to Pandemic Conditions: Virtual Hearings, No. 3, p. 67-91.

Martina Magnarelli, *More Fox or Hedgehog? Arbiral trbunal´s Decisions on Document Production*, No. 1, p. 41-53.

Reluca Maria Petrescu; Alexandru San, *The 2021 ICC Arbitration Rules New Commitments to Achieving Better Arbitration*, No. 1, p. 15-41.

Reza Shahrokhi; Aidin Kazemi, *Complications and Liability of Arbitral Institutions in Compliance with Sanctions´Regimes*, No. 3, p. 92-108.

Vasuda Sinha; Gabriel Fusea, *Counterclaims in Invesment Arbitration: Key Threshold Issues for Claimantts, Respondents and tribunals*, No. 1, p. 54-79.

Cornelia Tăbirţă, *Câteva date statistice privind starea arbitrajului comercial în România* [title in translation - *Selected Statistics Regarding the State of Commercial Arbitration in Romania*], No. 4, p. 47-66.

II.   CURRENT EVENTS

We sincerely apologize to our readers for omitting this traditional section from this CYArb® edition due to the exceptional circumstances attending the COVID-19 pandemic in 2021 that have resulted in the cancellation of principally all conferences and similar events (at least those where personal attendance is anticipated) since March 2020. CYArb® editors have concluded that it would be difficult to keep account of virtual events, both due to the lack of any clear details concerning these events and due to the absence of references and response. We firmly believe, though, that this section will be renewed and presented to our readers in the next CYArb® edition.

III. IMPORTANT WEB SITES

http://www.czechyearbook.org; http://www.lexlata.pro

Czech (& Central European) Yearbook of Arbitration®

Czech Yearbook of International Law® and Czech (& Central European) Yearbook of Arbitration®
The website is currently available in sixteen languages: English, Bulgarian, Czech, Chinese, Japanese, Korean, Hungarian, German, Polish, Romanian, Russian, Portuguese, Slovenian, Spanish, Ukrainian, Vietnamese. This website allows access to the annotations of all core articles and to information about the authors of these articles as well as to the entire remaining contents (except core articles) of both yearbooks (CYIL and CYArb®).

III.1. [CZE] – [CZECH REPUBLIC]

- http://www.cnb.cz. Česká národní banka (Czech National Bank as the Central bank of the Czech Republic).[1]

- http://www.compet.cz. Office for the protection of competition.[2]

- http://www.concourt.cz. The Constitutional Court of the Czech Republic.[3]

- http://www.csesp.cz. Czech Society for European and Comparative Law.[4]

- http://www.csmp-csil.org. The Czech Society Of International Law.[5]

- http://www.czech.cz. Portal „Hello Czech Republic". Basic information about the Czech Republic and news interesting for foreigners. Rather a promotional portal.[6]

- http://www.czso.cz. Czech Statistical Office.[7]

---

[1] Website available in English and Czech.
[2] Website available in English and Czech. Basic laws and regulations on the protection of competition in the Czech Republic are also available at the website, both in Czech and in English (unofficial translation).
[3] Website available in English and Czech. Part of the (significant) case law also available in English.
[4] Website available in English and Czech.
[5] Website available in Czech. In English only a brief summary of the webpages.
[6] Website available in English, Czech, French, German, Russian and Spanish.
[7] Website available in English and Czech.

• http://dtjvcnsp.org. Česko-německý spolek právníků. [Czech-German Lawyers Association]. Deutsch-Tschechische Juristenvereinigung e.V.[8]

• http://ekf.vsb.cz. Faculty of Economics, VŠB Technical University of Ostrava.[9]

• http://ftp.pse.cz/Info.bas/Cz/Predpisy/brs_statut2.pdf. Statute of Burzovní rozhodčí soud při Burze cenných papírů Praha, a.s. [Exchange Court of Arbitration at the Prague Stock Exchange].[10]

• http://www.hrad.cz.[11] Website of the Office of the President of the Czech Republic.

• http://www.icc-cr.cz. ICC National Committee Czech Republic.

• http://www.iir.cz. Institute Of International Relations Prague.[12]

• http://www.ilaw.cas.cz. Ústav státu a práva Akademie věd ČR, v.v.i. [Institute of State and Law of the Academy of Sciences of the Czech Republic].[13]

• http://www.jednotaceskychpravniku.cz. Jednota českých právníků [Czech Lawyers Union].

• http://www.icc-cr.cz. ICC National Committee Czech Republic.

• http://justice.cz. Czech justice portal including both courts and the Ministry of Justice, prosecution departments, Judicial Academy, Institute of Criminology and Social. Prevention, as well as the Probation and Mediation Service and the Prison Service.[14]

• http://www.law.muni.cz. Faculty of Law, Masaryk University, Brno.[15]

---

[8] Website available in German.
[9] Website available in English and Czech. Some information (regarding post-graduate studies) also available in German. Department of Law see http://en.ekf.vsb.cz/information-about/departments/structure/departments/dept-119 (in English).
[10] The Statute is available in Czech. One of the three permanent arbitration courts established in the Czech Republic by law (statute), in compliance with Section 13 of Act No. 216/1994 Coll., on Arbitration and Enforcement of Arbitral Awards, as subsequently amended.
[11] Website available in English and Czech. This website also allows access to the personal webpage of the President of the Czech Republic.
[12] Website available in English and Czech. This Institute was founded by the Ministry of Foreign Affairs of the Czech Republic.
[13] Website available in English and Czech.
[14] Website available in Czech. The individual websites of the institutions covered by this portal also contain pages or summary information in English.
[15] Website available in English and Czech.

- http://www.mzv.cz. Ministry of Foreign Affairs of the Czech Republic.[16]

- http://www.nsoud.cz. The Supreme Court of the Czech Republic.[17]

- http://www.nssoud.cz. The Supreme Administrative Court of the Czech Republic.[18]

- http://www.ochrance.cz. Public Defender of Rights (Ombudsman).[19]

- http://www.ok.cz/iksp/en/aboutus.html. Institute of Criminology and Social Prevention.[20]

- http://portal.gov.cz. Portal of the Public Administration.[21] This website allows access to the websites of most supreme public administration authorities (including ministries).

- http://www.prf.cuni.cz. Faculty of Law, Charles University in Prague.[22]

- http://www.psp.cz. Parliament of the Czech Republic. Chamber of Deputies.[23]

- http://www.rozhodcisoud.cz. International Arbitration Court of the Czech Commodity Exchange.[24]

- http://www.senat.cz. Parliament of the Czech Republic. Senate.[25]

- http://www.society.cz/wordpress/#awp. Common Law Society.[26]

---

[16] Website available in Czech. Important information from this portal also available in English.
[17] Website available in Czech. Some basic information also in English and French.
[18] Website available in English and Czech.
[19] Website available in English and Czech.
[20] Website available in English and Czech.
[21] Website available in English and Czech.
[22] Website available in Czech. Basic information available in English.
[23] Website available in English and Czech.
[24] Website available in English and Czech. Website of one of the three permanent arbitration courts established in the Czech Republic by law (statute), in compliance with Section 13 of Act No. 216/1994 Coll., on Arbitration and Enforcement of Arbitral Awards, as subsequently amended. This arbitration court was established by Act No. 229/1992 Coll., on Commodity Exchanges, as subsequently amended.
[25] Website available in English and Czech.
[26] Website available in Czech.

- http://www.soud.cz. Arbitration Court attached to the Economic Chamber of the Czech Republic and Agricultural Chamber of the Czech Republic.[27]

- http://www.umpod.cz. Office for International Legal Protection of Children.[28]

- http://www.upol.cz/fakulty/pf/. Faculty of Law. Palacký University, Olomouc.

- http://www.vse.cz. The University of Economics, Prague.[29]

- http://www.zcu.cz/fpr/. Faculty of Law, Western Bohemia University in Pilsen.[30]

III.2. [SVK] – [SLOVAK REPUBLIC]

- http://www.concourt.sk. Constitutional Court of the Slovak Republic.[31]

- http://www.flaw.uniba.sk. Faculty of Law, Comenius University in Bratislava (SVK).[32]

- http://iuridica.truni.sk. Faculty of Law. Trnava University in Trnava (SVK).[33]

- http://www.justice.gov.sk. Ministry of Justice of the Slovak Republic.[34]

- http://www.nbs.sk. Národná banka Slovenska (National Bank of Slovakia as the Central bank of Slovak Republic).[35]

---

[27] Website available in English, Czech, German and Russian. Website of one of the three permanent arbitration courts established in the Czech Republic by law (statute), in compliance with Section 13 of Act No. 216/1994 Coll., on Arbitration and Enforcement of Arbitral Awards, as subsequently amended. This arbitration court was established by Section 19 of Act No. 301/1992 Coll., on the Economic Chamber of the Czech Republic and the Agricultural Chamber of the Czech Republic, as subsequently amended.

[28] The Office is the Central authority responsible for protection of children in civil matters having cross-border implications. Website available in English and Czech.

[29] Website available in English and Czech.

[30] Website available in Czech.

[31] Website available in English and Slovak.

[32] Website available in English and Slovak.

[33] Website available in English and Slovak.

[34] Website available in English and Slovak. This website also allows access to the following portals: Courts, Slovak Agent before the European Court for Human Rights, Slovak Agent before the Court of Justice of the European Union, The Judicial Academy.

[35] Website available in English and Slovak.

- http://www.nrsr.sk. National Council of the Slovak Republic (*Slovak Parliament*).[36]

- http://www.prf.umb.sk. Faculty of Law. Matej Bel University, Banská Bystrica (SVK).

- http://www.prezident.sk. President of the Slovak Republic and Office of the President (SVK).[37]

- http://www.test.sopk.sk. The Court of Arbitration of the Slovak Chamber of Commerce and Industry in Bratislava.[38]

- http://www.uninova.sk/pf_bvsp/src_angl/index.php. Faculty of Law, Pan European University (SVK).[39]

- http://www.upjs.sk/pravnicka-fakulta. Faculty of Law, Pavol Jozef Šafárik University in Košice (SVK).[40]

- http://www.usap.sav.sk. Institute of State and Law, Slovak Academy of Science.[41]

III.3. [AUT] – [AUSTRIA]

- http://www.arbitration-austria.at. Österreichische Vereinigung für Schiedsgerichtsbarkeit. Austrian Arbitration Association (ArbAut).[42]

- http://www.internationales-schiedsgericht.at/. And http://viac.eu. Wiener Internationalen Schiedsgerichts (VIAC). Vienna International Arbitral Centre (VIAC).[43]

III.4. [BLR] – [BELARUS]

- http://www.cci.by/ArbitrCourt/AboutCourt_en.aspx. International Arbitration Court attached to the Belarusian Chamber of Commerce and Industry.[44]

---

[36] Website available in English, French, German and Slovak.
[37] Website available in English and Slovak.
[38] Website available in Slovak. Some basic information available in English.
[39] Website available in English, German and Slovak.
[40] Website available in English and Slovak.
[41] Website available in Slovak.
[42] Website available in English and German.
[43] Website available in English, Czech, German and Russian.
[44] Website available in English and Russian.

III.5.   [BGR] – [BULGARIA]

- http://www.bcci.bg/arbitration/index.html. Arbitration Court at the Bulgarian Chamber of Commerce and Industry.
- http://www.lex.bg. Information server on Bulgarian law.

III.6.   [EST] – [ESTONIA]

- http://www.koda.ee. Arbitration Court attached to the Estonian Chamber of Commerce and Industry.[45]

III.7.   [HRV] – [CROATIA]

- http://www2.hgk.hr/en/about_cce.asp?izbor=pac.   The Permanent Arbitration Court at the Croatian Chamber of Commerce.[46]

III.8.   [HUN] – [HUNGARY]

- http://www.mkik.hu/index.php?id=1406. Court of Arbitration attached to the Hungarian Chamber of Commerce and Industry.[47]
- http://www.mkik.hu/index.php?id=1409&print=1.   Act LXXI [Hungary] of 1994 On arbitration. Nonofficial English translation published on the portal of the Hungarian Chamber of Commerce. [**Law on arbitration**].

III.9.   [LVA] - [LATVIA]

- http://www.chamber.lv. The Arbitration Court of the Latvian Chamber of Commerce and Industry LCCI.[48]

III.10. [LTU] – [LITHUANIA]

- http://www3.lrs.lt/pls/inter3/dokpaieska.showdoc_l?p_id=56461. Law on Commercial Arbitration of The Republic of

---

[45]   Website available in English, Estonian and Russian.
[46]   Website available in Croatian. Basic information available in English. See the English presentation of the arbitration court at the website.
[47]   Website available in Hungarian. Basic information available in English.
282 | [48]   Website available in English, Latvian and Russian.

Lithuania No I-1274 as of 2 April 1996.[49] Official translation by Lietuvos Respulikos Seimas (on the portal of the Parliament of the Republic of Lithuania).

• http://www.arbitrazas.lt. Vilniaus komercinio arbitražo teismas. Vilnius Court of Commercial Arbitration.[50]

III.11. [MKD] – [MACEDONIA]

• http://www.mchamber.org.mk/%28S%28crtmab45gz nlucyny5lvrven%29%29/default.aspx?lId=2&mId=50&s mId=0.[51] The Permanent Court of Arbitration attached to the Economic Chamber of Macedonia *[Стопанската комора на Македонија]*.

III.12. [MDA] – [MOLDOVA]

• http://www.arbitraj.chamber.md/index.php?id=93. Curtea de Arbitraj Comercial International pe linga Camera de Comert si Industrie a Republicii Moldova. The International Commercial Arbitration Court of the Chamber of Commerce and Industry of the Republic of Moldova.[52]

III.13. [POL] – [POLAND][53]

• http://www.sakig.pl/. Sąd Arbitrażowy przy Krajowej Izbie Gospodarczej w Warszawie.[54] Court of Arbitration at the Polish Chamber of Commerce in Warsaw.

• http://www.iccpolska.pl/ Polski Komitet Narodowy Międzynarodowej Izby Handlowej. Polish ICC National Committee.

• http://oirp.bydgoszcz.pl/index.php?page=statut-2. Sądu Polubowny przy Okręgowej Izbie Radców Prawnych w

---

49 Published in: Parliamentary record, 1998-04-01, Nr. 4 (*Teisės aktą priėmė - Lietuvos Respublikos Seimas*).
50 Website available in English, Lithuanian and Polish.
51 Website available in English and Macedonian.
52 Website available in English, Moldovan and Russian.
53 Operation and accessibility of all websites were last checked on 17 November 2010.
54 Website available in English, German, French, Polish and Russian.

Bydgoszczy. Court of Arbitration attached to the Regional Chamber of Legal Advisors in Bydgoscz.[55]

• http://www.gca.org.pl/x.php/1,392/Arbitraz.html. Sąd Arbitrażowy przy Izbie Bawełny w Gdyni. Arbitration Court attached to the Gdynia Cotton Association.[56]

• http://oirp.gda.pl/portal-dla-przedsiebiorcow/sad-polubowny. Stały Sąd Arbitrażowy przy Okręgowej Izbie Radców Prawnych w Gdańsku. Permanent Court of Arbitration attached to the Regional Chamber of Legal Advisers in Gdańsk.[57]

• http://www.igg.pl/1/node/39. Sąd Arbitrażowy przy Izbie Gospodarczej Gazownictwa. Court of Arbitration attached to The Chamber of the Natural Gas Industry.[58]

• http://www.ihk.pl/index.html?id=1635. Sąd Arbitrażowy przy Polsko-Niemieckiej Izbie Przemysłowo-Handlowej. Court of Arbitration attached to the Polish – German Chamber of Commerce and Industry.[59]

• http://www.iph.krakow.pl/?a=page&id=31. Sąd Polubowny przy Izbie Przemysłowo-Handlowej w Krakowie. Court of Arbitration attached to the Chamber of Industry and Trade in Krakow.[60]

• http://www.iph.torun.pl/index.php?aid=113837484143da 38b99fb66. Sąd Polubowny przy Izbie Przemysłowo-Handlowej w Toruniu. Court of Arbitration attached to the Chamber of Industry and Trade in Torun.[61]

• http://isap.sejm.gov.pl. Legal information (laws and regulations) system on the portal of the Sejm [Parliament] of the Republic of Poland.[62]

---

[55] Website available in Polish.
[56] Website available in English and Polish.
[57] Website available in English and Polish.
[58] Website available in Polish. Some basic information, especially about the Chamber, also available in English and German.
[59] Website available in German and Polish.
[60] Website available in Polish.
[61] Website available in Polish.
[62] Website available in Polish. See also http://sejm.gov.pl.

• http://www.kigm.pl/index.php?option=com_content&ta
sk=view&id=60&Itemid=65&lang=p.   Międzynarodowy
Sąd Arbitrażowy przy Krajowej Izbie Gospodarki Morskiej.
International Court of Arbitration attached to the Polish
Chamber of Maritime Commerce in Gdynia.[63]

• http://www.knf.gov.pl/regulacje/Sad_Polubowny/index.html.
Sąd Polubowny przy Komisji Nadzoru Finansowego. Court
of Arbitration attached to the Polish Financial Supervision
Authority.[64]

• http://www.liph.com.pl/index.php?body=7.   Polubowny   Sąd
Łódzkiej Izby Przemysłowo-Handlowej. Court of Arbitration
attached to the Chamber of Industry and Trade in Łódz.[65]

• http://www.nig.org.pl/sa/pl1.html.   Sąd   Arbitrażowy   przy
Nowotomyskiej Izbie Gospodarczej w Nowym Tomyślu. Court
of Arbitration attached to the Chamber of Economy in Nowym
Tomyśl.[66]

• http://www.nsa.gov.pl/. Supreme Administrative Court.[67]

• http://oirp.olsztyn.pl/content/blogsection/23/73/.   Stały   Sąd
Arbitrażowy przy Okręgowej Izbie Radców Prawnych w
Olsztynie. Permanent Court of Arbitration attached to the
Regional Chamber of Legal Advisors in Olsztyn.[68]

• http://www.piit.org.pl/piit2/index.jsp?layout=1&news_
cat_id=62&place=Menu01.   Sąd   Polubowny   ds.   Domen
Internetowych przy Polskiej Izbie Informatyki i Telekomunikacji
w Warszawie. Arbitration Court for Internet Domains attached
to The Polish Chamber of Information Technology and
Telecommunications.[69]

• http://www.polubowny.org/index.html. Centrum Mediacyjne
oraz Stały Sąd Polubowny przy Fundacji Adwokatury Polskiej
i Ośrodku Badawczym Adwokatury im. adw. W. Bayera.

---

[63]   Website available in Polish. Some basic information available in English.
[64]   Website available in English and Polish.
[65]   Website available in Polish.
[66]   Website available in Polish.
[67]   Website available in Polish.
[68]   Website available in Polish.
[69]   Website available in English and Polish.

Mediation Center and Permanent Court of Arbitration attached to the Donation of Polish Bar and Center for Bar Research of W. Bayer.[70]

- http://www.pssp.org.pl/index.htm. Polskie Stowarzyszenie Sądownictva Polubownego – Polish Arbitration Association.

- http://www.riph.com.pl/index.php/Company/sub32. Sąd Arbitrażowy przy Regionalnej Izbie Przemysłowo-Handlowej w Gliwicach. The Permanent Court of Arbitration at the Regional Chamber of Commerce & Industry in Gliwice.[71]

- http://www.sadarbitrazowy.org.pl/. Sąd Arbitrażowy przy Polskiej Konfederacji Pracodawców Prywatnych Lewiatan. Court of Arbitration at the Polish Confederation of Private Employers Lewiatan.[72]

- http://www.oirpwarszawa.pl/kategoria/pokaz/idk/612/ ida/520/strona/. Stały Sąd Polubowny przy Okręgowej Izbie Radców Prawnych w Warszawie. Permanent Court of Arbitration Attached to the Regional Chamber of Legal Advisers in Warszawa.[73]

- http://www.rig.katowice.pl/default.aspx?docId=30. Sąd Arbitrażowy przy Regionalnej Izbie Gospodarczej w Katowicach. Court of Arbitration attached to the Chamber of Economy in Katowice.[74]

- http://www.sa.dig.wroc.pl/sa/index.php?option=com_ content&task=view&id=69&Itemid=28. Sąd Arbitrażowy przy Dolnośląskiej Izbie Gospodarczej we Wrocławiu. Court of Arbitration attached to the Lower Silesia Chamber of Economy in Wrocław.[75]

- http://www.sejm.gov.pl. Sejm Rzeczypospolitej Polskiej. Sejm [Parliament] of the Republic of Poland.[76/77]

---

[70] Website available in Polish.
[71] Website available in Polish. Some basic information also available in English and German.
[72] Website available in English and Polish.
[73] Website available in Polish.
[74] Website available in Polish.
[75] Website available in Polish. Applicable Rules of proceedings available in English and German.
[76] Website available in English and Polish.
[77] See also http://isap.sejm.gov.pl – legal information system available through the portal of Sejm.

- http://www.senat.gov.pl. Senat Rzeczypospolitej polskiej. The Senate of the Republic of Poland.[78]

- http://www.sn.pl/. Supreme Court of the Republic of Poland.[79]

- http://www.ssp.piph.pl/. Stały Sąd Polubowny przy Pomorskiej Izbie Przemysłowo-Handlowej w Gdańsku. Permanent Court of Arbitration attached to the See [Maritime] Chamber of Industry and Trade in Gdańsk.[80]

- http://www.trybunal.gov.pl. Constitutional Court.[81]

- http://www.wib.com.pl/index.php?idkat=11. Sąd Arbitrażowy przy Wielkopolskiej Izbie Budownictwa. Court of Arbitration attached to The Wielkopolska Chamber of Construction.[82]

- http://www.wiph.pl/content/view/69/53/. Sąd Arbitrażowy Izb i Organizacji Gospodarczych Wielkopolski. Arbitration Court attached to the All Polish Chamber of Industry and Trade.[83]

- http://www.zbp.pl/site.php?s=MGM0YzkzYWY1MTc3Nw. Sąd Polubowny przy Związku Banków Polskich. Court of Arbitration attached to the Polish Bank Association (ZBP).[84]

- http://www.ziph.pl/strona,19,polubowny-sad-gospodarczy. Polubowny Sąd Gospodarczy przy Zachodniej Izbie Przemysłowo-Handlowej w Gorzowie Wielkopolskim. Court of Arbitration attached to The Western Chamber of Industry and Commerce in Gorzow Wielkopolski.[85]

---

[78] Website available in English, French, German, Polish and Russian.
[79] Website available in English and Polish.
[80] Website available in Polish.
[81] Website available in English and Polish.
[82] Website available in Polish. Basic information, especially about the Chamber, available in English.
[83] Website available in Polish.
[84] Website available in English and Polish.
[85] Website available in Polish. Basic information and information about the Chamber also available in English, French, German and Russian.

III.14. [ROM] – [ROMANIA]

◆ http://arbitration.ccir.ro. The Court of International Commercial Arbitration attached to The Chamber of Commerce and Industry of Romania.[86]

III.15. [RUS] – [RUSSIAN FEDERATION]

◆ http://www.arbitrations.ru. Russian Arbitration Association.[87]

◆ http://www.iccwbo.ru. ICC National Committee Russian Federation.

◆ http://www.spbcci.ru/engarbitaltribunal. The Arbitration tribunal at Saint-Petersburg Chamber of Commerce and Industry.[88]

III.16. [SVN] – [SLOVENIA]

◆ http://www.sloarbitration.org. The Permanent Court of Arbitration, although attached to the Chamber of Commerce and Industry of Slovenia [CCIS].[89]

◆ http://www.sloarbitration.org/english/introduction/ organization.html. Nonofficial English translations of Slovenian law on or related to arbitration published on the portal of the Permanent Court of Arbitration, although attached to the Chamber of Commerce and Industry of Slovenia. (i) Code of Civil Procedure of Slovenia.[90] (ii) Private International Law And Procedure Act.[91] [Law on arbitration].

---

[86] Website available in English and Romanian.
[87] Website available in English and Russian.
[88] Website available in English and Russian.
[89] Website available in English and Slovenian.
[90] Published in the: Official Gazette of the Republic of Slovenia, No. 26/99.
[91] Published in the: Official Gazette of the Republic of Slovenia, No. 56/99.

Index

Czech (& Central European) Yearbook of Arbitration®

- international   2/1, 3, 4, 6, 8, 9, 10, 12, 14, 15, 16, 17; 5/15, 22

investor
- foreign   2/1, 4, 10

impartiality 5/36; 8/6

issue
-   preliminary   - *see preliminary issue*

J

jurisdiction 1/2, 3, 7, 9, 10, 11, 12, 13, 21, 31, 34, 35, 36, 37, 39, 45, 53, 54; 2/1, 2, 10, 11, 13, 14, 15, 16, 17; 3/5, 6, 8, 15, 17, 19, 21, 22, 24, 25, 26, 27, 28, 29, 35, 37, 38, 41, 42; 4/1, 4, 5, 15, 16, 17, 18, 19, 21, 22, 23, 26, 27, 28, 29, 32, 33, 34, 35, 36, 38, 39, 40, 41, 42, 43, 44, 49, 53, 54, 65, 66, 69, 70, 71, 72, 73, 74; 5/5, 15, 16, 17, 21, 31, 38, 39, 41, 42, 43, 44, 45, 46, 47, 48, 53, 54, 55, 56, 57, 58, 60, 61, 62, 63, 64, 65, 66, 67, 68, 71, 72, 73, 74, 75, 76, 77, 79, 82, 87, 88; 6/10, 22, 23, 24, 33, 37, 43, 50; 7/1, 2, 3, 4, 5, 6, 7, 8, 9, 10, 11, 12, 13, 14, 15, 17, 18, 19, 20, 21; 8/2, 6, 8, 9, 11, 13, 15, 16, 18, 20, 22, 25, 27, 29, 34, 37, 39, 45, 46,

48; 9/1, 6, 7, 10, 11, 14, 18, 19

- arbitral   1/2, 3, 7, 9, 10, 11, 12, 13, 21, 31, 34, 35, 36, 37, 39, 45, 53; 2/1, 2, 10, 11, 13, 14, 15, 16, 17; 3/5, 6, 8, 15, 17, 19, 21, 22, 24, 25, 26, 27, 28, 29, 35, 37, 38, 41, 42; 4/1, 4, 5, 15, 16, 17, 18, 19, 21, 23, 26, 27, 28, 29, 32, 33, 34, 35, 36, 38, 39, 40, 41, 42, 43, 49, 53, 54, 65, 66, 69, 70, 71, 72, 73, 74; 5/5, 15, 16, 17, 21, 31, 38, 39, 41, 42, 43, 44, 45, 46, 47, 48, 54, 56, 57, 58, 60, 63, 64, 65, 66, 67, 71, 72, 74, 75, 76, 77, 79, 82, 87, 88; 6/10, 22, 23, 24, 33, 37, 43, 50; 7/1, 2, 3, 4, 5, 6, 7, 8, 9, 10, 11, 12, 13, 14, 15, 17, 18, 19, 20, 21; 8/2, 6, 8, 9, 11, 13, 15, 16, 18, 20, 22, 25, 27, 29, 34, 37, 39, 45, 46, 48; 9/1, 6, 7, 10, 11, 14, 18, 19

- of arbitral tribunal 1/2, 3, 21, 31, 35, 39, 45, 53; 2/1, 2, 10, 11, 13, 14, 15, 16, 17; 3/5, 15, 17, 19, 21, 22, 27, 28, 29, 35, 38, 41; 4/1, 4, 5, 17, 19, 26, 27, 28, 29, 32, 34, 35, 43, 54, 70; 5/5, 15, 17, 21, 31, 39,

65; **5**/6, 7, 9, 12, 14, 21, 55; **6**/1, 24, 40, 41, 42; **7**/1, 3, 4, 5, 10, 12, 14, 17, 19, 20, 22; **8**/14, 33

O

objection
- raised in the course of arbitration   **8**/22, 48

P

payment   **3**/4, 22; **8**/6, 8, 9, 11, 18, 20, 27; **9**/4
- of profits   **8**/20
penalty
- contractual   **8**/6, 44
preliminary issue   **1**/21; **2**/14; **4**/2; **5**/36, 41, 48, 57; **7**/13; **8**/9
principles of equity   **8**/2, 39, 41
proceedings **1**/2, 21, 26, 35, 41, 46, 54; **2**/1, 3, 9, 14, 17; **3**/1, 3, 4, 6, 13, 15, 16, 27, 28, 31, 34, 38, 40, 41; **4**/2, 3, 5, 6, 7, 8, 9, 10, 11, 12, 13, 14, 15, 16, 17, 18, 19, 20, 21, 23, 24, 25, 26, 28, 29, 30, 31, 32, 33, 34, 35, 36, 37, 38, 39, 40, 41, 43, 44, 45, 46, 47, 48, 49, 50, 51, 52, 53, 54, 55, 56, 59, 60, 61, 62, 63, 65, 66, 67, 68, 70, 71, 72, 73, 74, 75; **5**/5, 6, 7, 13, 22, 33, 34, 36,

42, 49, 56, 57, 65, 66, 68, 69, 71, 72, 73, 74, 75, 76, 78, 82, 83; **6**/35, 45; **7**/1, 2, 3, 4, 8, 9, 10, 11, 12, 13, 14, 15, 17, 19, 21, 22, 23; **8**/2, 3, 4, 5, 6, 8, 11, 12, 13, 14, 15, 16, 17, 22, 29, 31, 34, 36, 38, 39, 41, 42, 44, 46, 47, 48, 49; **9**/1, 2, 5, 7, 8, 14, 15, 18, 19
- arbitral   **1**/2, 21, 26, 35, 41, 46; **2**/1, 3, 9, 14, 17; **3**/1, 3, 4, 6, 13, 15, 16, 27, 28, 31, 34, 38, 40, 41; **4**/2, 3, 5, 6, 7, 8, 9, 10, 11, 12, 13, 14, 15, 16, 17, 18, 19, 20, 21, 23, 24, 25, 26, 28, 29, 30, 31, 32, 33, 34, 35, 36, 37, 38, 39, 40, 41, 43, 45, 46, 47, 48, 49, 50, 51, 52, 53, 54, 55, 56, 59, 60, 61, 62, 63, 65, 66, 67, 68, 70, 71, 72, 73, 74, 75; **5**/5, 6, 7, 13, 22, 33, 34, 36, 42, 49, 56, 57, 65, 66, 69, 71, 72, 74, 75, 76, 78, 82, 83; **6**/35, 45; **7**/1, 2, 3, 4, 8, 9, 10, 11, 12, 13, 14, 15, 17, 19, 21, 22, 23; **8**/2, 3, 4, 5, 6, 8, 11, 12, 13, 14, 15, 16, 17, 22, 29, 31, 34, 36, 38, 39, 41, 42, 44, 46, 47, 48, 49; **9**/1, 2, 7, 8, 14, 15, 18, 19

CALL FOR PAPERS FOR VOLUMES 2023/2024

Did you find the articles in the twelfth volume of CYArb® interesting?

Would you like to react to a current article
or contribute to future volumes?

We are seeking authors for both
the Czech Yearbook on International Law® and the
Czech (& Central European) Yearbook of Arbitration®.

The general topics for the 2023/2024 volumes are following:

CYIL 2023

*Limits to Enforcement of National
Interests*

CYArb® 2023

Public Interest in Arbitration

CYIL 2024

*Force Majeure, Restrictions and
Sanctions*

CYArb® 2024

Abuse of Arbitration

More general and contact information available at:

www.czechyearbook.org
www.lexlata.pro

CYIL – Czech Yearbook of International Law®, 2023
Limits to Enforcement of National Interests

The increasing tendencies of nations to promote their country's own interests may be the reverse side of and a form of defence against globalisation, and in many regards such tendencies naturally also manifest themselves in law. This phenomenon represents a very broad category that includes, for instance, security issues, protection of a nation's own territory or territorial interests, etc. National tendencies in private law include, inter alia, the advancement of a country's own law (national law / law of national origin) as the properly determined applicable law, the application of the public policy exception, or the application of overriding mandatory provisions. Procedural aspects also represent a specific and, naturally, a most welcome topic for our yearbook, with such aspects typically including the jurisdiction of national judicial authorities, as well as the promotion of national interests in supranational judicial authorities, the recognition and enforcement of or, conversely, the refusal to recognise and enforce foreign decisions. We will especially welcome any articles dealing with specific cross-border manifestations of the effort to promote national interests and with their (non)compliance with international law and private international law, and the rules and principles thereof.

CYArb® – Czech (& Central European) Yearbook of Arbitration®, 2023
Public Interest in Arbitration

Various forms of public-law elements and public interest have been increasingly encroaching upon arbitration, whether this involves the status of the parties, factoring in acts that could be prosecuted as anti-money laundering, corruption and many other violations, or the result of the nature of the disputes submitted to arbitration. This corroborates the fact that arbitration has become a widely-used and universal instrument for resolving both domestic and cross-border disputes, even including truly supranational and global disputes. Increasingly rigorous transparency requirements being measured against the traditional privacy and confidentiality of arbitration, the inalienable right of the parties to choose and to appoint the arbitrator being in conflict with the requirements of the maximum independence and impartiality of arbitrators that sometimes restrict the parties' right, and many other intensely discussed issues reveal the fact that arbitration has long ceased to be the exclusive domain of the individual relationship between the parties to the dispute, and that the autonomy of the parties, and indeed of the arbitrators themselves, is gradually being restricted, if not in fact in law. At the same time, however, arbitration is a process that has been measured more and more frequently against civil proceedings in courts, and has gradually become a full-fledged alternative to litigation. It appears as though, unless in entirely exceptional cases, the theory of the anational and autonomous supranational nature of arbitration has given way to the domiciliation of arbitration in a given national environment, determined according to the place (seat) of arbitration in particular states, and to the importance of this place. That said, the influence of specific national procedural standards on arbitration is currently an indisputable fact. This also entails increasing demands for the application of fundamental national procedural rules and their principles in arbitration. This and many other related topics will represent the key subject of the XIIIth edition of CYArb® scheduled for 2023.

CYIL – Czech Yearbook of International Law®, 2024
Force Majeure, Restrictions and Sanctions

Looking at modern history, it is probably impossible to find a time period in which one of these three terms and institutions, *force majeure*, *restrictions* and *sanctions*, would not be applied and discussed by the legal community. Especially recently, we are more often confronted with specific restrictions, or rather with situations in which it is not easy to determine which of the particular institutions and mechanisms we are really dealing with, and which consequences they carry.

The topic aims to focus on these three concepts in order to qualify them as legal institutes and to analyse the manifestations and common signs thereof, as well as to identify their differences, their application and the settlement of disputes arising out of situations brought by force majeure and the application of restrictions and/or sanctions.

CYArb® – Czech (& Central European) Yearbook of Arbitration®, 2024
Abuse of Arbitration

The popularity of arbitration is on the rise in the modern world. Although there is an effort to expand the practicability and reach thereof, it is necessary to keep in mind that it has certain limits. However, due to the latency of the "boundaries" limiting the scope of arbitration, there is a growing effort to abuse arbitration so as to exploit it, or at least use it in such a way and in such situations for which arbitration was not intended. In the same way, however, certain elements of arbitral proceedings are being abused as well, where it is not just a question of pushing these "imaginary boundaries", but rather the abuse of arbitration itself.

In order to ensure and define basic rules (including ethical rules) to prevent the above-mentioned practices, the aim of the chosen topic is to focus on possible cases of abuse of arbitration, both at the substantive and procedural level, in order to identify and clarify them.